Understanding
GLOBAL POLITICS

CHANCHAL KUMAR
LUNGHTHUIYANG RIAMEI
SANJU GUPTA

KW
KNOWLEDGE WORLD
KW Publishers Pvt Ltd
New Delhi

ISBN 978-93-86288-37-0   Paperback
ISBN 978-93-86288-38-7   ebook

Published in India by Kalpana Shukla

KW
KNOWLEDGE WORLD

KW Publishers Pvt Ltd
4676/21, First Floor, Ansari Road
Daryaganj, New Delhi 110002
Phone: +91 11 23263498/43528107
Marketing: kw@kwpub.com
Editorial: jose@kwpub.com
Website: www.kwpub.com

2011 F|P B|A BEST PUBLISHERS AWARD (ENGLISH)

Printed and Bound by Sarat Book House

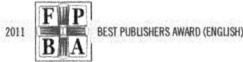

Contents

Global Shifts: Power, Governance and Processes

Acronyms

APEC	Asia Pacific Economic Cooperation
ASEAN	Association of South East Asian Nations
ANC	African National Congress
ABM	Anti-Ballistic Missile
ATS	Antarctic Treaty Systems
BREXIT	Britain Exit
BRICS	Brazil, Russia, India, China, South Africa
BWC	Biological Weapons Convention
BTWC	Biological and Toxin Weapons Convention
CER	Certified Emission Reductions
CWC	Chemical Weapons Convention
CTBT	Comprehensive Test-Ban Treaty
GCM	General Circulation Model
GHGs	Greenhouse Gases
EU	European Union
EURATOM	European Atomic Energy Community
HCFCs	Hydro Chlorofluorocarbon
GATT	General Agreement on Trade and Tariff
IPCC	Intergovernmental Panel on Climate Change
IHL	International Humanitarian Law
ICL	International Criminal Law
ICC	International Criminal Court
ICT	Information Communication and Technology
ICRC	International Committee of the Red Cross
IFRC	International Federation of Red Cross
IPPNW	International Physicians for the Prevention of Nuclear War

ISIS	Islamic State of Iraq and Syria
IMF	International Monetary Fund
IBRD	International Bank for Reconstruction and Development
LIC	Low Income Countries
MAD	Mutually Assured Destruction
MFN	Most Favoured Nation
MTCR	Missile Technology Control Regime
MIRV	Multiple Independently Targeted Re-entry Vehicles
NDB	New Development Bank
NTS	Non-Traditional Security
NNWS	Non-Nuclear Weapon States
New START	New Strategic Arms Reduction Treaty
NTBT	Nuclear Test Ban Treaty
NPT	Nuclear Non-proliferation Treaty
NWS	Nuclear Weapon States
NPT	Nuclear Proliferation Treaty
NSG	Nuclear Suppliers Group
NAFTA	North American Free Trade Agreement
NATO	North Atlantic Treaty Organisation
OAU	Organisation of African Unity
OPCW	Organisation for the Prohibition of Chemical Weapons
ODS	Ozone Depleting Substances
PTBT	Partial Test Ban Treaty
R2P	Responsibility to Protect
SALT-I	Strategic Arms Limitation Talks-I
START	Strategic Arms Reduction Treaty
SORT	Strategic Offensive Reductions Treaty
SLBM	Submarine Launched Ballistic Missile
TTP	Tehrik-i-Taliban Pakistan
TTP	Tehrik-i-Taliban
TNC	Transnational Corporations
UNCHE	United Nations Conference on the Human Environment
UNEP	United Nations Environment Programme
UNFCCC	United Nations Framework Convention on Climate Change

UNCLOS	United Nations Convention on the Law of the Sea
USSR	Union of Soviet Socialist Republics
UNICEF	United Nations International Children's Fund
UNHCR	United Nations High Commissioner for Refugees
UN	United Nations Organisation
UNSC	United Nations Security Council
WTO	World Trade Organisation
WSF	World Social Forum
WFP	World Food Programme
WHO	World Health Organisation

Preface

Global politics is a discipline that widely covers the political and economic dimensions of the accelerating world. In the age of globalisation, the analysis of new ideas become imperative since the old theories and perspective are becoming increasingly more and more irrelevant. In the 21st century, change and continuity is the hallmark of global politics. There is widespread debate on the declining role of Westphalian state system as new Information Communication and Technology (ICT), international economic markets and cultural identities are acquiring prominence. The declining capacity of states in protecting or catering to the needs of their citizen, has also led to the emergence of a plethora of new global actors. The first unit of this book deals with these aspects of globalisation, different conceptions and various perspectives. Though the process of globalisation is not new to international politics, it has resurfaced with new vigour in the later part of the 20th century, especially after the end of the Cold War. Globalisation is a complex phenomenon having multiple dimensions. It is generally taken as a process that knits people, thereby producing worldwide interdependence and featuring the rapid and large scale movement of persons, materials and ideas across the states. The significance of the international political economy in global politics has intensified with the liberalisation process. The global political economy involves thinking reflectively about the changing dimensions of globalisation. The formation of Bretton Woods system or Washington Consensus in 1944, established the salience of new institutionalism. The pace of globalisation also gave birth to global resistance movements. The intensification of globalisation and liberalisation process has also brought divisions among the global community, the concept of "haves and have nots". The World Social Forum calls the international community to have a just and peaceful world order. The forum offers a self-conscious urge to develop an alternative future through the championing of a counter-hegemonic view of globalisation. It emphasises and wants to build a sustainable and inclusive world, wherein every person has a place and where his or her voice is heard. In this process it becomes imperative for the United Nations, being the representative organisation of sovereign nations to decide how to respond to the major challenges facing the fast changing world order in the best possible manner, while also serving the cause of peace and security.

The book analyses the most pressing issues of today: climate change, migration, nuclear non-proliferation treaties, terrorism, and also the feminist theory. Controlling the proliferation of nuclear weapons—and ultimately abolishing them—must be a major global priority. Intergovernmental bodies, such as the United Nations, the International Atomic Energy Agency, and the International Court of Justice (World Court), are constantly directing their energies towards this objective. The book, while highlighting efforts made towards a weapons-free world, also deals with the ecological issues and environmental challenges, and describe how the environmental treaties, laws, legislations and ethics play their respective roles in protecting the environment. Today, this debate has become the central focus in all international environmental regimes. The debate has, however, also given birth to a number of grass-root movements world-wide urging to provide ecological protection. International terrorism is a post-cold war phenomenon when forces driven by religious sentiments and factional sub-nationalism emerged in the aftermath of bi-polarity. Since September 11, 2001 terrorism has shown its face like never before. After September 11 attack, the world realised the gravity and seriousness of the problem of terrorism. Britain, Russia, India, Iran, China, NATO, the UN all have pledged support to the United States in their campaign against terrorists. Migration has been a major feature of the 20th and early 21st centuries. Around the world, people have been forced to flee their homes as a result of political persecution, conflict, and natural and manmade disasters. Most notably, people have been displaced across international borders, to avoid political persecution by fleeing to neighbouring states or travelling long distances to states in other continents in search of international protection. Whether there is crossing of international borders or not, migrations and problem of refugees is at the heart of global politics. Feminist theory is a conflict theory that studies gender, patriarchy, and the oppression of women. It examines women's social roles, experience, interests, and feminist politics in a variety of fields, such as anthropology and sociology, communication, psychoanalysis, economics, literary, education, philosophy, and even linguistics. In recent years, there has been a move towards understanding gender as both an aspect of personal identity and an integral part of social institutions and practices.

The last unit of this book deliberate on the global shifts, power and governance issues in a fast changing world order. The world order is witnessing a phase of greatest transitions. The geo-political realities of today point out to (i) a US whose power seems to be challenged on various fronts, (ii) the ascendancy of new power Centres like China and India, (iii) the salience of regional and economic groupings like the BRICS and the EU, and (iv) the changing role of the international organisations in addressing pressing questions of violent conflict and humanitarian crisis. That the world is increasingly moving towards multipolarity is an emerging fact. The challenging question is not whether the world will be multipolar or not, what is more perplexing is the dilemma, as to what form this multipolarity will take. Global governance is being tested by non-traditional causes of conflict, violence networks involving both governmental and non-governmental actors and the far reaching effects of armed engagement on civilians. Under such a scenario, the notion of security is visualised, understood and debated as a concept detached from mere militaristic explanations, and becoming more 'comprehensive and human'. Non-traditional aspects of security therefore, present an analytical framework keeping the individuals at the centre, and hence is being labelled as human security. Ethnic clashes, refugee problems, religious intolerance, war for resources, economic instability, global warming all are important challenges confronting humanity today. Hence each requires effective multilateralism.

This book presents an opportunity to engage in Applied Global Politics and explore how the core concepts of this discipline can be systematically studied in an empirical context. It will allow students to develop an understanding of the local, national, and global dimensions of various issues and challenges associated with contemporary Global Politics and will facilitate better comprehension of various approaches and schools of thought within the discipline.

Acknowledgement

We would like to express our deepest gratitude to KW Publishers, especially Kalpana Shukla for constantly encouraging us and believing in us, and to Jose Mathew, for his patience and support. Our thanks to the library and staff of the Nehru Memorial as well as the Institute of Defence Studies and Analysis for their cooperation. We would especially like to thank our dearest students, for motivating us to undertake such research ventures.

Chanchal Kumar, Lungthuiyang Riamei and **Sanju Gupta**

Globalisation: Conceptions and Perspectives

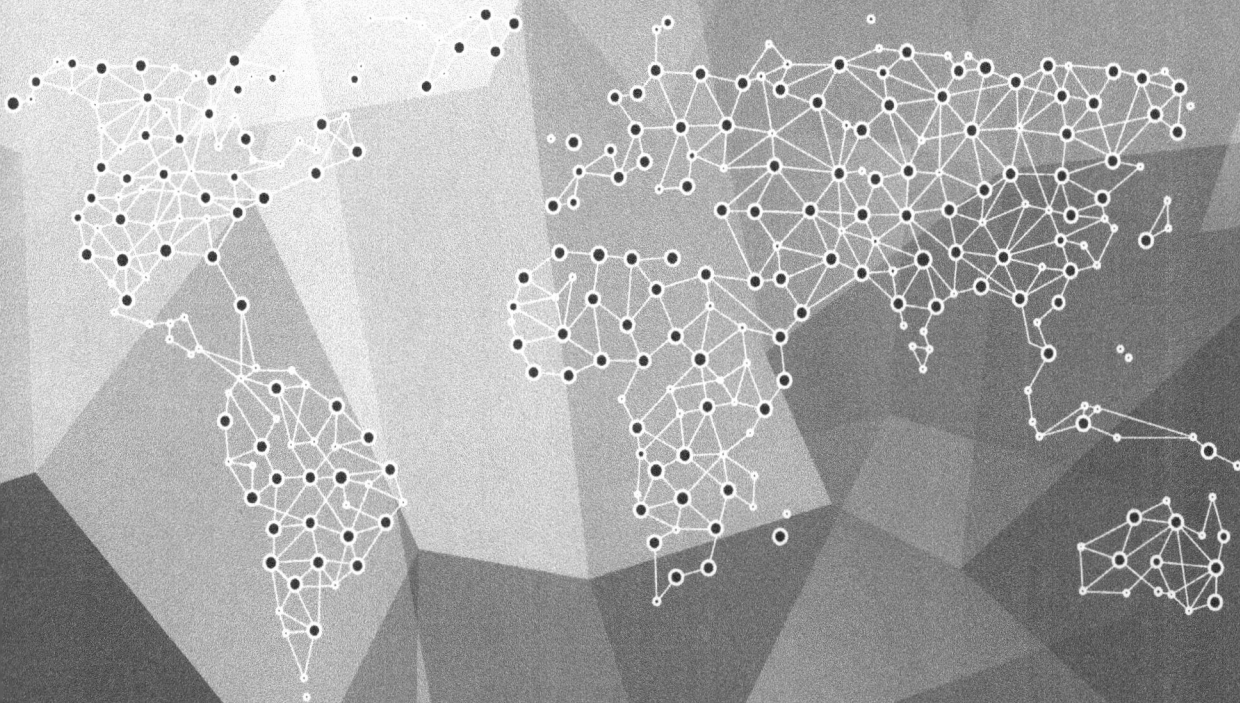

CHAPTER 1

Understanding Globalisation and Its Alternative Perspectives

Globalisation is a term that we are all familiar with today. Humans have travelled and interacted over long distances for thousands of years. Global movement of people, goods, and ideas expanded significantly even in the earlier centuries. It was first made use of in ancient civilisations and then throughout during various periods in the history. The great civilisations such as Mesopotamia and Egypt invented the term ancient globalisation. The overland Silk Road that connected Asia, Africa, and Europe is a good example of the transformative power of trans-local exchange that existed in the "Old World". Philosophy, religion, language, arts, and other aspects of culture spread far and wide and mixed as nations exchanged goods and ideas. The concept of globalisation was taken forward with the Romans. Furthermore, Italian city-states such as Venice and Florence created a merchant-driven "Renaissance globalisation". The larger context of globalisation emerged with the expansion of industrialisation and capitalisation in the 15th and 16th century. With the expansion of industrialisation, Europeans made important discoveries in their exploration of the oceans, including the beginning of transatlantic travel discovering new world. Early in the 19th century, the development of new forms of transportation (such as the steamship and railroads) and telecommunications that "compressed" time and space allowed the increasingly rapid rates of global interchange.

Thomas Friedman has characterised three phase of globalisation. The first phase is from 1492 to 1800, which was the age of mercantilism and colonialism. The driving force was brawn not brain—how much muscle, how much horsepower, wind power or later steam power—your country had and how creatively you could deploy it. The second phase was from 1800 to the mid-twentieth century till the end of World War II. This period was dominated by age of Pax Britannica. The colonial powers of countries such as Spain, the Netherlands, France and Britain built a new form of globalisation colonising across the globe. Global mega-companies exploited the dramatic drop in transportation and then communication costs to weave the world together into a seamless web of global products, capital and labour. Finally, during the second half of the 20th century the world started shrinking from its size to a tiny and flattening playing field where the United States reinvented and popularised a new model of globalisation. This is the age of Pax Americana, where the driving force is electronic communications the new find for individuals to collaborate and compete globally.[1] The US not only projected its military power throughout the world (Korea in the early 1950s; disastrously in Vietnam in the 1960s and early 1970s, Iraq in 2003), it extended its reach in the economic realm as it became the dominant industrial power when World War II decimated most of its competitors militarily and/or economically. Many other aspects of America's "soft power" and global reach accompanied these changes.[2] In the 20th century, road connectivity and airlines made transportation even faster. Above all, the advent of information communications technology, most notably mobile phones and the Internet connected billions of people in a number of new ways. Globalisation could be seen as the common evolutionary tree of mankind, which may end up with positive outcomes or dismal ones, depending upon how choices are made.[3] Thus, managing globalisation focuses upon international organisations and regional coordination mechanisms that generate opportunities for state cooperation.

The establishment of United Nations Union in 1945 and the agreement on economic and political fields like the establishment of International Monetary Fund (IMF), World Bank, General Agreement on Tariff and Trade (GATT) and other international organisations have provided the ground for new age of globalisation. On the other hand, the expansion of GATT to World Trade Organisation (WTO) and countries joining this organisation are considered as the expansion of globalisation. Especially the wonderful growth of technology in some areas such as transportation, telecommunication and more importantly, informatics revolution in 1980s and following the spread of internet and network provided proper tools for development of this phenomenon.

Further, environmental challenges such as climate change, cross-boundary water issues, air pollution, and over exploitation of fishing in the ocean are linked with globalisation. Globalising processes affect and are affected by business and work organisation, economics, socio-cultural resources, and the natural environment.

Defining Globalisation

Globalisation and transnationalism are often used interchangeably, but transnationalism is clearly more of a declining process than globalisation. Transnationalism is limited to interconnections that cross geo-political borders, especially those associated with two, or more, nation states.[4] For instance Indian immigrants in the Gulf countries or United States sending remittances home to family members in India. Globalisation includes such connections, but is not restricted to them and encompasses a far wider range of tans-planetary process (e.g. direct relationships between people in many places in the world networking via the Internet). Further, geo-political borders are only one of the barriers encountered, and often overcome by globalisation. Trans-nationalism is the one most often thought about and researched on, as immigrants who move from one country to another, but also continue to involve in various ways with country from which they came.[5]

The case of baseball is useful in clarifying the distinction between globalisation and trans-nationalism. Baseball is a transnational sport because many of its fundamental techniques, strategies, etc. and players have spread across the borders of a small number of nations, especially Japan, Taiwan, Cuba, the Dominican Republic and the US. However, it cannot be considered global because it has not followed a trans-planetary path to a large portion of the world. In contrast, soccer or football would be much more clearly a global sport because it exists in virtually every area of the world. For example, over 200 of the world's nations are members of a global organisation, the Federation Internationale de Football Association (FIFA). Another example of globalisation in the realm of sports is the summer and winter Olympics, sponsored by the International Olympic Committee (IOC), in which about the same number of nations participate.[6]

Globalisation has become a popular word in academic debates around the world. The expression globalisation primarily connotes greater interconnectedness and expression of social geography, aptly described in the "time space compression" thesis. In other words, it is widening, deepening and speeding up of worldwide interconnectedness in all aspects of life. The compression has been possible because of flexible accumulation of the capital and its flow is controlled by increasing electronic networks. The term globalisation is used in many ways, for example to describe a set of phenomenon—the transfer of money around the world, the development of information technology, international production, increased tourism and the declining of nation states. It is also used as a discourse in which the acceptance of globalisation as being inevitable, irresistible and irreversible. As such globalisation becomes a sort of natural process outside the control of human agency.

Globalisation involves the diffusion of ideas, practices and technologies. It is something more than internationalisation and universalisation. Anthony Giddens has described globalisation as the "intensification of worldwide social relations which link distant localities in such a way that local happenings are shaped by events occurring many miles away and vice versa".[7] This involves a change in the way we understand geography and experience localness. According to Jan Aart Scholte, "Globalisation is an ensemble of developments that makes the world a single place changing the meaning of importance of distance and national identity in world affairs".[8] International Monetary Fund, defines globalisation as the growing economic interdependence of countries worldwide through the increasing volume and variety of cross-border transactions in goods and services and of international capital flows, and also through more rapid and widespread diffusion of technology".[9] David Held and Anthony McGrew have defined globalisation as growing world interconnectedness, it denotes the expanding scale, growing magnitude, speeding up and deepening impact of inter-regional flows and patterns of social interaction. It refers to a shift or transformation in the scale of human social organisation that links distant communities and expands the reach of power relations across the world's major regions and continents.[10] In this conceptualisation, globalisation can be understood through the following four concepts:

- Stretching of social relations, so that events and processes occurring in one part of the world have significant impact on other parts of the world. For instance, civil wars and conflicts in the world's poorest regions increase the flow of asylum seekers and illegal migrants into the world's affluent countries.
- Intensification or growing magnitude of interconnectedness in almost every sphere of social existence from political, economic to the ecological interaction across the globe. On the other side, there is an increasing interpretation of economic and social practices, bringing distant cultures face to face.
- The accelerating pace of global interactions and processes as the evolution of worldwide systems of transport and communication increases the rapidity with which ideas, news, information, capital and technology move around the world.
- The growing extensity, intensity and velocity of global interactions is associated with a deepening enmeshment of the local and global; in so far as local events may come to have global consequences and global events can have serious

local consequences, creating a growing collective awareness or consciousness of the world as a shared social space.[11] Globalisation, therefore, denotes a significant shift and must be seen as a multi-dimensional phenomenon, involving highly intricate interactions between a whole variety of social, political and economic institutions across a spectrum of geographical scales. It is also a discourse of knowledge that elevates awareness that links between various scales of social life. It is a contested discourse of exhibiting many variants transcending across the continents.

Globalisation embodies a process of de-territorialisation as social, political, and economic activities are increasingly stretched across the globe, they become in a significant sense no longer organised solely. Terrorist and criminal networks for instance operate, both, locally and globally. National political and economic space under conditions of globalisation is no longer conterminous with national territorial space.

Theoretical Perspective of Globalisation

The theoretical perspective and inter-paradigm issues of globalisation can be debated under Realist, Liberalist and Marxist views. The three theories focus on different aspects of world politics. Realism on the power relations between states, Liberalism on wider set of interactions between states and non-state actors and Marxist theory emphasise on the patterns of the world economy. The rise of globalisation offers some ideas on its strengths and weaknesses as a description of contemporary international politics.

Realist Explanation

For realist the main actors on the world stage are states, which are legally sovereign actors. Realist explanations of globalisation emphasise the relative distribution of power. They see trade and economic activities flourishing only under favourable security conditions and in turn on the relative distribution of power. The two most favorable security conditions are alliance and hegemony or imperialism. As Joane Gowa explains "free trade is more likely within than across political-military alliance and... alliances have had a much stronger effect on trade in a bipolar than in a multipolar world".[12] Realist sees human nature as fixed and crucially is selfish. To think otherwise is to make a mistake and it was such a mistake that the Realists accuse the Idealists in making. As a result world politics represents a struggle for power between states each trying to maximise their national interests. Such an order exists in world politics and that as results in the working mechanism known as the balance of power, whereby state act so as to prevent any one state from dominating.

Realism provides the most influential tools for understanding the way globalisation affects international politics, while constructivism puts more emphasis on building it into a broader context of social interaction. For realists, globalisation is a reflection of great powers' struggle for supremacy. It helps exploit great powers' advantages and is being promoted by those which benefit more than others. As a result globalisation is just another context for struggle for hegemony.[13] The concept of globalisation needs to be defined more strictly within a context of international security. Realists rely on two core beliefs which shape their view on globalisation. First, they place the state in the centre of international politics. Secondly, they prioritise 'high politics' over 'low politics'. Thus, globalisation is mainly seen as a process which transforms the context of inter-state relations. The effects are seen at political level even if the nature of changes tends to be predominantly economic.[14]

The world had already experienced the sharp growth in trade and direct investment at the end of the 19th and the beginning of the 20th century. Just as the growing economic interdependence was unable to prevent the outbreak of World War I, the current globalisation (mainly economic) cannot fundamentally change the political structure of the international system.[15] As in ancient times (pre-globalisation era), international outcomes are determined by the distribution of forces and balances of power among states. Globalisation can accelerate structural changes by providing more opportunities for some states, but it is not a structural change itself. To some it may be a reason to claim globalisation as a destabilising factor in world politics, since it challenges the balance of power mechanisms of international order. However, bringing more inequality to the international system does not necessarily mean making it less stable.

Realists tend to limit the scope and significance of globalisation. Basically there are two primary ways which impacts global security: 1) by leading to economic changes, which are converted into balance of power shifts; and 2) by changing the environment in which nation states operate transforming patterns of cooperation and competition among them. The former usually works by changing the relative economic power of the states. Since economy is a key power indicator realist assume that changes in relative economic capabilities inevitably lead to shifts in distribution of power globally.[16] The anarchy of international system, the principles of self-help in a struggle for survival, and centrality of the nation-state as a key decision maker remain fundamental for realist analysis of globalisation. Globalisation can be analysed as an intervening variable between international structure and state action.[17] Realists argued that globalisation is a critical factor because the changing structure of world production significantly increased the opportunity costs for being isolated from the world's political economy.

Liberal Explanations

For Liberals globalisation is seen as the end product of a long running transformation of world politics. For them, globalisation fundamentally undermines realist accounts of world politics since it shows that states are no longer such central actors as they once were. From this perspective the most important historical events driving globalisation are: (1) the agricultural and industrial revolutions that launched the modern world, (2) the discovery of market institutions and free trade rules that propelled Pax Britannica, (3) the Bretton Woods institutions and their spillover or path-dependence effects that characterised the first phase of Pax Americana and (4) the Internet or information revolution that extended Pax Americana to the developing world.[18] Liberals are particularly interested in the revolution in technology and communications represented by globalisation. This increased interconnectedness between societies economically and technologically, result in a very different pattern of world political relations.

Liberals believe that globalisation brings social and political benefits. The free flow of information and ideas around the world widens opportunities for personal development and creates more dynamic and vigorous societies. From a liberal stand point, the spread of market capitalism is invariably associated with the advance of liberal democracy, economic freedom and demand for political freedom. For liberals, globalisaton marks the end of nation states which was the dominant global actor. States are no longer sealed units and as a result the world looks more like a cobweb of relations.[19] The global era is charaterised by a tendency towards peace and international cooperation as well as by the dispersal of global power through the emergence of global civil society and the growing importance of international organisations.[20] Liberals also argue that globalisation will inevitably lead to the dissemination of global political identity and then creation of a global civil society.

Marxist Explanation/Critical Views

Marxist critique of capitalism portrays the essence of globalisation as the establishment of a global capitalist order. Like the liberals, Marxist theorists usually accept that globalisation marks historically a significant shift. States have lost power over the economy, being reduced to little more than instruments for restructuring of national economies in the interest of global capitalism. For the Marxist, globalisation is viewed as an uneven, hierarchical between the rich and the poor, explained by world system theorist like Immanuel Wallerstein in terms of a structural imbalance between 'core', 'semi-peripheral' and 'periphery' areas in the global economy.[21] For them globalisation deepens the existing world system, weakening of the democratic accountability and popular responsiveness due to increase activities of corporate power.[22] Critical theorists like Anthony Gramci argue that the capitalist class system is upheld not simply by unequal economic and political power but what he termed the hegemony of bourgeois ideas and theories. Neo-Marxist highlight inequalities in the global capitalist system, through which developed countries operate or sometimes are operating through Transnational Corporations (TNCs) or linked to hegemonic powers such as the USA, who dominate and exploit developing countries. The revolution in information technology has changed the economic and political meaning of globalisation. Borders are transcended and has become increasingly supra-territorial as geographic space itself loses economic and political significance.[23] This has brought imbalance between the nation states and within the nation itself.

Competing Perspective on Globalisation

Globalisation consists of the multiplicity of linkages and interconnections that transcend the nation-state and by implication the societies which make up the modern world system. David Held and Anthony McGraw identify three distinct perspectives toward globalisation. The three perspectives are labelled as hyperglobalist, skeptical and transformationalist.

Hyperglobalist

Hyperglobalist focuses on the economic dimension of globalisation and include both neoliberal and Marxist theorists. The new epoch in human history is characterised by the declining relevance and authority of nation states, brought about largely through economic logic of global market. In their view, globalisation has produced a single global market in which transnational corporations from many countries vigorously compete with one another and where capital is immensely mobile. Hyperglobalisers argue that economic globalisation is bringing about a denationalisation of economies through the establishment of transnational networks of production, trade, and finance, a borderless economy in which national governments are relegated to little more than transmission belts for global capital.[24] Guided by the self-enforcing growth of global market and technology progress, globalisation inexorably destroys all previously established hierarchical structures. The role of the nation-state in this context is also significantly diminishing. Multinational corporations concentrated vast resources, and become the main carriers of economic activities on a global level. This creates a global civilisation in which the market is integrated on the world level, multinational companies are becoming major actors in the economic process and international institutions substitute the role of national states. Multinational companies have fundamental influence on the economy and represent natural response to the borderless economy that is characterised by homogeneous consumer tastes.[25]

Instead of distinctive local cultures and traditional values, globalisation promotes a globalised wealthy, highly educated and upwardly mobile sector, which places a premium on possessive individualism, consumerism, secularism, and neoliberal capitalism. Its members are psychologically closer to others like themselves who may be geographically remote, but with whom they regularly communicate by email, fax, mobile phones, Whatsapp, and Facebook and share a common taste, norms, and values. Hyperglobalist also content that the growth of a single global market and the declining capacity for states to determine their economic destiny are among the most important factors characterising contemporary globalisation. Transnational corporations, capital markets and related activities no longer have a true territorial home, and many are cross-border and transnational in nature.[26] The hyperglobalisers claim that the degree of contemporary economic interdependence is unprecedented.

All the variety of heterogeneous cultures withdraw in front of the unique social pattern, based on markets and institutions derived from the radically liberal cultural framework. In this sense, Fukuyama's interpretation of the "end of history" is generated, which implies that the modern, global capitalism with liberal democracy as the political framework represents the last word of socio-economic evolution.[27]

Hence for hyperglobalist, globalisation is seen as a kind of final stage in the spontaneous and self-enforcing process of creating a global society, which is the most efficient model that stops any further process of selection of types of socio-economic order.

Skeptics

Skeptics argue that contemporary globalisation is neither new nor revolutionary. They focused only on the economic dimension of globalisation, arguing that it features high levels of interstate trade and the expansion of regional common markets such as the European Union (EU), and the North American Free Trade Agreement (NAFTA) which reduce global economic integration. In their view, states retain a dominant role in these activities, including an ability to regulate and even unravel globalised economic processes. In other words, the state government has not ebbed; state sovereignty has not eroded; and transnational corporations remain under national control.[28] All the governments will retain the formal authority to regulate the global economy. According to P. Hisrt and G. Thompson, highly internationalised economy is one of a number of distinct conjunctures of states of the international economy that have existed since the economy based on modern industrial technology began to be generalised from the 1860s. The current international economy is less open and integrated than the regime that prevailed from 1870 to 1914. According to them, the prospects for regulation by international cooperation, the formation of trading blocs and the development of new national strategies that take account of internationalisation are by no means exhausted.[29] There are very few truly global transnational corporations and many multinational corporations continue to operate from distinct national bases. They advocate close coordination between the major capitalist powers to promote employment in the advanced countries.

For Scholte, economic liberalisation has generally ranked as policy orthodoxy in respect of contemporary globalisation because of its hold on elite circles. Corporations are organising their own supply chains and negotiating a wide range of accommodations directly with governments and their counterparts abroad.[30]

Nation states, especially the US, China and the members of the European Union, are responsible for and could undermine higher levels of economic intercourse. Major states have supported and are responsible for the existence of global institutions such as the IMF, World Bank and World Trade Organisation. Within this direction of thought, assessments of the non-sustainability of the current unification of the world raises radical resistance within individual cultures which in the end lead to a 'clash of civilisation'.[31] Thus, skeptics have expressed doubts, both in terms of impacts of globalisation and its ubiquity, as well as in terms of sustainability of unification influence which it produces.

Transformationalist

Transformationalists are convinced that globalisation is a central driving force behind the rapid social, political and economic changes that are reshaping modern societies and world order. According to transformationalists, one consequence of growing interconnectedness is a merging of the foreign and domestic arenas. They perceive a growing de-territorialisation of economic activity as production and finance increasingly acquire a global and transnational dimension. For them, the indisputable fundamental changes in the organisation of society that globalisation brings are the growing overall integration and acceleration of socio-economic dynamics through compression of space and time. Anthony Giddens, considers globalisation as a phenomenon shaped by forces of modern capitalism: politics, military power and industrialism.[32] The specific dimensions of modernity have enabled western countries to become the leading force in the world. According to Giddens, spreading dimensions of modernity to all countries in the world is identified as the process of globalisation. For transformationalists, international, sub-national, and transnational groups and organisations are growing more important as state authority and power wane. And with the declining capacity of states and the reduced importance of territory, the role of identity based features such as religion and ethnicity has grown and spread in global politics.[33]

However, according to sociologists modernity brings forth the risk of a new global threat. In order to avoid this risk it is necessary to create institutions of democracy and bring about cosmopolitan confidence, as an important dimension of reality. Without it, globalisation represents only a façade for the game of imperialist powers. The global financial, political and economic crises of recent years have led some observers to conclude that globalisation was a phenomenon of the 1980s and 1990s.

Radical Approach to Globalisation

Moderate accounts of globalisation acknowledge that nation states continue to be key players in the contemporary global economy. However, radical approach stress on the decline of the state as an autonomous decision making body. For the radicals it is multinational companies and not states that are most effective providers of economic prosperity. The radical globalisation perspective stresses on the following:

- The development and wide availability of low-cost telecommunication technology such as fiber-optic cables, fax machines, digital transmission and satellites, which has meant that the populations of the states are increasingly becoming subjected to a global culture that is beyond the power of individual governments to control.
- The rise of MNCs which have the resources to rival many states, but unlike the state are not rooted in geography and are easily able to relocate their plants/factory according to shifting demand and the availability of local advantages such as cheap wages, low business taxes and weak trade unions.
- The increasingly global nature of trade has rendered states unable to develop effective economic policies. States increasingly have to respond to factors beyond their control such as imperatives of MNCs and the fluctuations of the

world's financial markets. Overall, it is claimed that world markets and MNCs are more powerful forces in international affairs than states. These new forces of globalisation cannot be effectively dealt with by the states.[34]

Ohmae defines global change in terms of "four I's": Investment, Industry, Information technology and Individual consumers. He argues that investment through financial markets has grown rapidly in recent years, as technology has greatly increased the opportunity for speculators to bypass national government controls. Opportunities for investment are provided by globalised corporations, which unlike the old geographically bound firms are able to move quickly into newly developing markets.[35] Large successful companies attract individual's investments via large pension funds, which target well-known, global companies whose reputation is a guarantee for a good return.

Additionally, innovations in information technology have increased the mobility of capital and have made expertise in engineering, medicine or design more widely available across states' borders using sophisticated platforms. These developments are supported by a growing consumer awareness of the variety of lifestyles and products open to them in the world markets.

For Ohmae, the key to development is the rapid expansion of the global economy. It increased prosperity and opportunity across and within national cultures. Individuals have already begun to assert their consumer sovereignty above their bonds to national sovereignty. The well informed citizens of a global marketplace will not wait passively until nation states deliver tangible improvements. People want direct access to the global economy. The sheer speed of technological advancement is creating a deep change in the mindset of those who are exposed to it. Life opportunities can, like the interactive computer games, reshape their consciousness, be explored, rearranged, and reprogrammed.[36] Ohmae welcomes the changes brought by multimedia and echoing the position of evolutionary liberals, he suggests that nationalism must be reduced if not eliminated to improve the quality of individuals. He argues that nationalism is a cover for bureaucratic expansion and the protection of inefficient industries, leading to demands for equity from political regions that act as a drag on the dynamic economic regions, which drive economies.[37]

The Debates of Globalisation

Liberals and neoliberals believe that globalisation is inevitable, involving a fundamental transformation of global politics away from state control moving towards market control of global economic life, partly due to technological changes. Others, especially realists and neo-realists, argue that globalisation is the consequence of power arrangements, political and ideological preferences, and policy choices and that it is reversible if those arrangements, preferences, and choices are altered, just as global interdependence before World War I and freed trade cease during the Great Depression. Most believe that globalisation will persist only so long as major states find it in their interest to promote the free movement of persons, things, and ideas across borders and to maintain the liberal economic system that has prevailed since World War II.[38]

Two major concepts define the political struggle in the West today. One termed 'globalism' and other 'territorialism'.[39] At the core of the debate is whether borders should be porous or tightly controlled. For globalist, interconnectedness is a good thing because it drives progress towards more prosperity and freedom. For territorialist, interconnectedness is mainly a threat. For them what is good and healthy is attributed to the natives and danger comes from outside: unfair Chinese competition, dangerous immigrants and terrorists from the Middle East.[40]

Globalist wants to manage the cross-border streams and minimise disruptive character of borders to maximise the gains from connected markets and societies. Governments need to co-operate and set up regional and global institutions; they need to set rules and make sure these rules are upheld. Globalists argue among themselves about how to police the wider space but not about the principle. Terrritorialists, by contrast like realist, don't believe in international and transnational institutions –they believe in national strength and power. The world outside the borders is anarchical and dangerous and the way to deal with threat is to fight them by using force. For them, allies are not an asset; they are a burden because they are free riders, cheating on government tax payers. Territorialists believe that they can prosper economically even while interrupting, diminishing and shutting cross-border flows. Jobs must be brought back, free trade agreement renegotiated because they are unfair. Territorialists suggest that it is beneficial for the common man; they can disrupt globalistation and stay rich, minimise investment in international affairs and alliances and remain safe and free. They fail to understand that gains in prosperity depend on massive investments of nation states in international order, and that globalisation is based on open societies and increasingly easy cross-border flows of goods, people and information. In other words, if territorialism wins, globalisation is under threat in the international system.[41]

Globalists are actually at a crossroads; the refugee crisis is part of a larger challenge of globalisation. But the key challenge is how to keep globalisation afloat in spite of increasing geo-political conflicts and tensions. For them globalisation equals progress, open spaces and increased interaction across borders is a good thing as they unleash opportunity, secure freedom and prosperity. Globalists argue that in an open world they have to take responsibility for what happens outside their borders.

An Alternative Perspective on Globalisation
In the era of globalisation, the imposition of free trade policies and the increasing privatisation of social services have facilitated the accumulation of tremendous wealth for the owners of capital at the expense of working people. However, the neoliberal globalisation agenda does not serve the interest of the vast majority of the people. The key to struggle on globalisation lies in the contest between the sovereignty of capitalism which is based on privilege and domination versus socialist democracy based on the principles of liberty, unity and social justice. The Socialist, alternatively, offers a coherent strategy for action on both the national and international levels.

The efficacy of the market or capitalist economy was questioned by economists like Karl Marx and J. M Keynes. Marx theorised that a state driven by proletariat would be the best agency for efficient economic administration.[42] Socialism refers to various forms of economic organisation advocating public or direct ownership by workers and administration of the means of production and allocation of resources to society characterised by equal access to resources for all individuals with an egalitarian method of compensation.[43] Most socialists share the view that capitalism unfairly concentrates power and wealth among a small segment of society that controls capital and derives its wealth through exploitation, creates an unequal society, does not provide equal opportunities for everyone to maximise their potentialities and does not utilise technology and resources to their maximum potential. According to Socialist, the aim of both developed and developing economies is to have sustainable, equitable, democratic, diverse and genuinely free societies, based on largely self-reliant and local economies, in harmony with their environment. The important point is to empower nations and communities to retake control over their local economies and to make them as diverse which suits local needs. This moves from the situation in which all economies compete with each other to one in which goods and services are supplied more locally. This is the socialist alternative to free trade and market policies which currently dominate economic and political thoughts.

Some of the alternative perspectives on globalisation according to Socialist are:
- **The local economy:** The aim of the local and regional economies would be to produce as much goods and services as they own primary products. Long

distance trade should be the last resort. To this end controls such as tariff barriers and quotas should be gradually introduced.

- **Capital and investment:** Access to capital at local and regional level should be the key to funding investment by enterprises and communities to improve social and environmental conditions and job opportunities. This is not achieved by the free market which encourages even larger and more distant institutions and capital flows. There is no encouragement of local activity and the assertion of democratic control of larger capital flow. Encouragement must be given to financial institutions on mutual principles, including the re-mutualisation of building societies. The promotion of local and regional financial institutions is essential and should include de-merger of larger institutions. Community banks and credit unions can also play a major role in enabling local people.

  According to socialists, it will be necessary to reintroduce national controls of capital movements and to regulate finance capital more broadly. The aim must be to encourage productive investment, particularly community reinvestment. This will be best achieved by the application of stakeholder principles at local and regional levels, supported by national regulation of corporate investments in a manner which involves the wishes of the affected communities.

- **Transnational corporations:** Transnational institutions of similar size must be used to assert the primacy of the common interest over those of the corporations. They should encourage the breakup of such organisation to more manageable units, through regulations, anti-trust legislation and fiscal policies. The aim must be to encourage productive investments in goods and services.

- **Limiting market access:** A limit should be set for market at regional and national level for any company. Where such a market is dominated by a particular company, new firms should be encouraged through grants, loans and subsidies to enter it to maintain the impetus for improved products, more efficient use of resources and the provisions of choice. The transfer of information and technology would be encouraged to improve the efficiency of local industry. The advantages enjoyed by very large organisations must be countered. They must be rendered more accountable to their stakeholders through greater transparency, internal democracy and public regulation.

- **Multinational agreements:** According to Socialist, this approach, while sustainable and equitable, runs very much contrary to existing and proposed international arrangements such as the General Agreement on Tariffs and

Trade (GATT), World Trade Organisation (WTO) and the proposed Multilateral Agreement on Investment. According to them all these serve the interests of the large transnational corporations and capitalists, at the expense of the rest of the world, including regions and communities of the countries in which they are based. Such arrangements must be replaced with ones that promote cooperation for self reliance. Financial aid policies and capital flows, technology transfer and residual international trade should be on fair trade.. These should be geared to the promotion of sustainable local economies. The aim is to foster sustainable industry and prosperity through local and regional self-reliance.

There are also a number of practical alternatives to counter the onslaught of globalisation:

Promotion of self-reliance: The economy may be viewed at various levels from the family to the village to the state to the nation. At each level, there has to be relative self-reliance. The cooperative efforts of members and participatory decision-making are very significant. Women should be given equal status in the family. Similarly, at the village level whatever is required by the people should be produced as far possible within its geographic terrain. At the state and national levels it would be preferable to phase out the dependence on foreign aid and borrowing. Foreign debt is a trap to facilitate imperialist globalisation.

Avoid bad consumerism: The TNCs are the main beneficiaries of globalisation. Through various ways they domesticate the potential consumers in order to maintain their market. Most of the products of TNCs may not be necessary for ordinary people but due to consumerism they are forced to buy all these. Consumerism has been leading people to indebtedness and even to suicide.

IT to rebuild community: Globalisation fragmentises community. But the information media evolved through globalisation could be effectively used to rebuild the community.

Decentralised planning: If properly steered decentralised politics and planning can be a potential weapon to fight globalisation. Grassroots social and economic institutions like the Self-Help Groups, Micro-Financing, etc. can empower people enabling them to avert globalisation.[44]

Conclusion

The advance of globalisation and the progressive de-territorialisation of economic, cultural and political life have gradually weakened the idea that society should be understood merely in domestic or national terms. If societies are fashioned out as as a stable set of relationships between and among their members involving mutual awareness, then the consequence has been the emergence of transnational or 'world society'.[45]

No doubt, globalisation has brought in new opportunities to developing and developed countries. It is the leading process in global politics since the Cold War, which reflects the change and continuity. Globalisation is a mega trend which significantly shapes contemporary economy. Greater access to developed markets and technology transfer hold the promise of improved productivity and higher living standard. But globalisation has also thrown up new challenges like growing inequality across and within nations, volatility in financial market and environmental deteriorations. Another negative aspect of globalisation is that a great majority of developing countries refrain from the process. Globalisation holds the promise of enormous benefits for the people of the world. To make this promise a reality, we must find a way to carefully manage the process. Better attention must be paid for reducing the negative effects and ensuring that the benefits are widely and fairly distributed. The growing extensity, intensity, and velocity of global interactions create a growing collective awareness or consciousness of the world as a shared social space.

Notes

1. Thomas L. Friedman, *The world is Flat: A Brief History of the Twenty-First Century* New York: Farrar, Stauss and Giroux, (2005),pp.9-11. Also see Nau, Henry R., *"Perspective on International Relations"* (Washington: CQ Press,2009), pp.277-287.
2. Ritzer, George , *Globalization: The Essentials* (Sussex, Wiley- Blackwell, 2010),p.20.
3. Erik Lane and Jan, *Globalization and Politics: Promises and Dangers* (Hampshire, Ashgate Publishing Limited, 2006), p.1.
4. Ritzer, n.2, p3.
5. Portes, Alejandro, ed., *"New Research and Theory on Immigrant Transnationalism"* (London, Global Networks, 2001), p.1.
6. Ritzer, n. 2, p5.
7. Gidden, Anthony, *The Consequences of Modernity* (Stanford: Stanford University Press, 1990), p.21.
8. Scholte, Jan Aart, "Globalisation and Collective Identities", in J. Krause and N. Renwick (eds.), *Identities in International Relations* (New York: St. Martin's Press, 1996), p.44.
9. International Monetary Fund (May 1997) "World Economic Outlook, A Survey by the staff of the International Monetary Fund", A Meeting of the Challenges of Globalisation in the Advanced Economies", in the World Economic and Financial Surveys, at http://www.imf.org/external/pubs/WEOMAY/Weocon.htm, accessed on October 9, 2015.
10. Held, D and McGrew, A, *Globalisation Anti Globalisation* (Cambridge: Cambridge University Press, 2002).
11. McGrew, Anthony, "Globalisation and Global Politic" in John Baylis, et. al., *The Globalization of World Politics* (Oxford: Oxford University Press, 2008), p.18. Also see, Cochrane, A and Pain,

K, "A globalising Society?" in David Held, ed., *A Globalizing World? Culture, Economics, Politics* (London: Routledge,2000).

12. Joanne Gowa, *Allies, Adversaries, and International Trade* (Princeton: Princeton University Press, 1994), p.7.

13. Gilpin, Robert, *The Challenge of Global Capitalism* (Princeton: NJ: Princeton University Press, 2003). Also see Mearheimer, John , *The Tragedy of Great Power Politics* (New York: W.W. Norton, 2003).

14. Waltz, Kennet, "Globalization and Governance" in *PS: Political Science and Politics*, vol. 32, no.4, 1999, pp. 693-700.

15. Krasner, Stephen, *Sovereignty: Organized Hypocrisy* (Princeton, NJ: Princeton University Press, 1999).

16. Mearsheimer, John, *The Tragedy of Great Power Politics* (New York: St. Martin's Press, 1999).

17. Brooks, Stephen G. and William C. Wohlfoth, "Power, Globalization and the End of the Cold War: Reevaluating a Landmark Case for Ideas", *International Security*, vol. 23, 2000, pp.5-53.

18. Nau, Henry R, *Perspective on International Relations* (Washington D.C: CQ Press, 2009), p.298.

19. McGrew, n.11, p.7.

20. Heywood, Andrew, *Global Politics* (New York, Palgrave Macmillan, 2011), p.12.

21. 'World-systems refers to the inter-regional and transnational division of labour , which divides the world into core countries, semi-periphery countries and periphery countries, Core countries focus on higher skill, capital intensive production, and the rest of the world focuses on low-skill, labour-intensive production and extraction of raw materials. This constantly reinforces the dominance of the core countries. For detail see, Wallerstein, Immanuel , *World system Analysis: An Introduction* (Durham: Duke University Press, 2004).

22. Ibid.

23. Scholte, n. 8, pp.427-52.

24. Mansbach, Richard W. and Kirsten L. Taylor, *"Introduction to Global Politics"* (London, Routledge, 2014), p.190.

25. Ohmae, Kenichi, *Borderless World: Power and Strategy in the interlinked World* (New York, Harper Business, 1990).

26. Ferguson, Yale H. and Richard W. Mansbach, *Globalization: The return of borders to a borderless world?* (London: Routledge, 2012), p. 25.

27. Fukuyama, Francis, *The End of History and the Last Man*, (New York: Free Press, 1992).

28. Mansbach, n. 24, p.190.

29. Hirst, Paul and Grahame Thompson, *Globalization in Question*, (Cambridge: Polity Press, 2009).

30. Scolte, Jan Art *Globalization: A Critical Introduction*, (London, Palgrave, 2005), p.39.

31. Huntington, Samuel, *The Clash of Civilizations and the Remaking of World Order* (New York: Simon & Schuster, 1996).

32. Giddens, Anthony , *The Consequences of Modernity* (Cambridge: Polity Press, 1990).

33. Mansbach, n.24, p.191.

34. Khan, Z., "Globalisation: Radical Theories on Globalisation", at http://www.yourarticlelibrary.com/essay/globalisation-radical-theories-on-globalisation/45266/, accessed on November 15, 2015.

35. Ohmae, Kenichi , *The End of the Nation-State: The Rise of Regional Economies* (New York: Simon and Schuster Inc. 1995).

36. Ibid., p.16.

37. Ibid.

38. Mansbach., n.24, p.202.

39. Globalism is prominently represented by German Chancellor, Angela Merkel and Territorialism

view represents Republican candidate Donald Trump for US election in November 2016.

40. "From Trump to Merkel: how the world is divided between fear and openness", *The Guardian*, UK, March 6, 2016, at http://www.theguardian.com/commentisfree/2016/mar/06/donald-trump-angela-merkel-territorial-global-ulrich-speck?CMP=share_btn_fb, accessed on June 3, 2016.

41. Ibid.

42. Kurian, Mathew V, "Alternative to Globalisation: A Search" , *Mainstream Weekly*, Vol XLV (35), 2007, http://www.mainstreamweekly.net/article287.html, accessed on November 16, 2015.

43. "Socialism", Oxford English Dictionary. Also see, Newman, Michael , Socialism: A Very Short Introduction, (Oxford, Oxford University Press, 2005).

44. Kurian, n. 42.

45. Buzan, Barry, *From International to World Society?* (Cambridge: Cambridge University Press, 2004).

CHAPTER 2

Political Debates on Sovereignty and Territoriality, Cultural and Technological Dimension of Globalisation

Globalisation is a multi-dimensional phenomenon which is irreversible in character. It is a process characterised by stretching the political, economic, socio-cultural and technology activities across political frontiers so that events, decisions, and activities in one region of the world have significance for individuals and societies. It has also been conceived as a process of shrinking world, global integration, the reordering of interregional power relations, consciousness of the global condition and the intensification of interregional interconnectedness. Globalism is a state of the world involving networks of interdependence at multi-continental distances. The linkages occur through flows and influences of capital and goods, information and ideas, and people and forces as well as environmentally and biologically relevant. It is a shift or transformation in the spatial scale of human social activities that links distant communities and expands the reach of power relations across the globe. The path of globalisation has changed by the force of ideas and experience (ideas about whether trade or capital market liberalisation will improve and the actual experiences with these reforms) but also global events. In the recent years, 9/11 and the war on terrorism, the war on Iraq, Arab Spring and the global shift have redefined the globalisation. Globalisation and de-globalisation refers to the increase or decline of globalism.

Political Dimension

The basis of the interstate system is often viewed as having its origins in the peace of Westphalia (1648), which followed the thirty years of war, when Europe's monarchs agreed to recognise each other's right to rule their own territories, without external intervention. The Westphalian model of international system gave primacy to sovereign territorial nation states, which place their own national interests above all others, subject to no higher authority and thus pursuing their interests by force if deemed necessary.

The recent transformations in international relations have meant a movement away from these Westphalian principles, with a progressive undermining of exclusive territoriality, the strict division between domestic and international affairs and the haphazard relationships between states.[1] The Westphalia system was a framework of state governance. The core of governance stood on the principles of statehood and sovereignty. It exercised comprehensive, supreme unqualified and exclusive control over its designated territorial domain. Sovereignty has two dimensions: internal and external. Internal sovereignty is where the sovereign or government exercise absolute authority over a particular society. Externally, there is no absolute authority above and beyond the state. Thus, state should determine their direction and policies.[2]

Political globalisation refers to the growing importance of the international organisations. These organisations are transnational in character and they exert influence not within a state, but within an international area comprising several states. The process of globalisation has questioned the Westphalia system. However, the nature of political globalisation and its implications for state varies depending on how it is modelled on the principle of inter-governmentalism or supra-nationalism.[3] The globalist argues that political power or governance has been or is progressively being altered in a movement of politics from primarily national scale towards an increasingly transnational or global scale. According to Ulrich Beck, national spaces have become de-nationalised so that the national is no longer national, just the international is no longer international. This entails that the foundations of the power of the nation state are collapsing both from the inside and the outside.[4] The powerful forces of the global economy prevent states from pursuing independent economic or social policies. The spread of neoliberal common sense and the powerful forces exerted on states by financial markets, MNCs and international organisations such as the WTO and the IMF mean states are increasingly forced to develop policies that leave the market as free as possible. A supra-state body such as the EU, which came into being in 1950 around regulation of German and French steel production, is also viewed as an important development of the forthcoming changes to governance in future. Apart from this, there has also been a rise in number of intergovernmental organisations, non-governmental organisations (NGOs), and multilateral treaties. In the case of intergovernmental organisation such as the World Health Organisation or the IMF, the numbers have multiplied.[5]

David Held argues that a new mode of global governance is emerging as governments struggle to control the flows of ideas and commodities, as transnational processes expand, and as multilateral treaties and international organisations increase in number. The emerging tansnationalisation[6] of politics as state power is reconfigured and it is increasingly enmeshed in global processes and flows.[7] Scholte argues the demise of sovereignty in the Westphalian sense–supreme, comprehensive, unqualified and exclusive rule over its territory.[8] If globalisation has been associated with the internationalisation of the state, it has also facilitated and encouraged a corresponding transnationalisation of politics, that is, activity which transcends or cuts across societies. There has been a remarkable institutionalisation of intergovernmental and transnational networks of political interaction.

It is clear that globalisation entails not only the intensification of interactions and interconnections that have led to the shrinking of our world but also the emergence of a system of global governance that seeks to regulate and manage various areas of transnational activity. With the global governance comes increased intergovernmental interaction and transnational networks, new centres of political power alongside the state, and the growth of transnational civil society (such as NGOs). This pluralisation of global governance is theorised by Anthony McCrew into three layers: (1) the supra-state layer, which includes intergovernmental agreements and international institutions created by intergovernmental agreement (for example, the EU, the G8, NAFTA and APEC); (2) the sub-state layer, where the tendency in recent years has been towards devolution and expansion of power at local levels; (3) the transnational layer, which consists of arenas in which people across the world are able to make themselves heard (for example, The International Red Cross, and the WWF).[9]

Globalisation and Nation State

The Debate

The genesis of the modern state can be located in Western Europe in the 18th and 19th centuries, and is linked to industrial, economic, and military changes to an increasingly firm demarcation of national borders and to the spread of rationalisation and bureaucracy.[10] The French Revolution of 1789 is often viewed as a key moment in the development of the modern nation-state. This Revolution led to the centralisation of the French state, the citizen army and the key modern dynamics of nationalism.

There has been much debate about whether globalisation is undermining state sovereignty in the study of global politics. There are two distinct arguments in this debate. Hyperglobalist like Ohmae and Scholte hold pessimistic view and argue that globalisation brings about the demise of the sovereign nation state. Global forces undermine the ability of governments to control their own economics and societies.[11] Rosenau also argues that the cumulative scale, scope, velocity and depth of contemporary interconnectedness in dissolving the significance of borders and boundaries that separate the world into many constituent states or national economic and political spaces.[12] Thus, agrees to the notion that globalisation is undermining the sovereign state. In contrast, the Sceptics reject the idea of globalisation by emphasising the continuing importance of states in world politics. Krasner and Robert Gilpin argue that the states and geopolitics remain the principal agents and forces shaping world order today.[13]

Globalisation signals the end of sovereignty because a state can only be sovereign if it exercises authority over a given territory. In order to exercise power over its citizenry, the state needed to established itself as legitimate, that is to justify its power (through reference to religion or ancestry in the case of monarchy, or through elections, in the case of democracies). And nationalism as an ideology binds people to their country through shared history, language, symbols (for instance flags, emblems), or rituals. Through nationalism, individuals would integrate the nation as a major component to their identity. However, with globalisation, as a reflexive process, undermine national identity by promoting identification from below as in the case of the local nationalism.[14] For instance, in the 1990s, a few nations have entered a process of acute fragmentation, multiple polarisations and disintegration. When Communism ended, we have seen how Soviet Union disintegrated and balkanisation of Yugoslavia created into ethnic groups and later gained momentum for independence. Further, the pressure exercised by such extreme ethnic identifications resulted in a humanitarian catastrophe and years of conflict. Therefore, globalisation has promoted the rise of localised ethnic solidarities. As international conflicts (conflicts between nations) expanded, globalisation also gave birth to new wars within states itself.

Similarly, globalisation undermines national identity "from above." In this case, sources of identifications are based on transnational loyalties. For instance, in *Globalized Islam*, Olivier Roy has shown that members of many Islamist movements find their source of identity and solidarity in a global Muslim community connected through religious ideology and not territorially.[15] For instance, a global Islamist militant organisation like Al-Qaeda, Boko Haram and ISIS is attached to brotherhood of Islam. In the global context, non-territorial identities are also reflected in global movements which focused on gender, race, social class or sexual orientation.

At the same time states are undermined by globalisation by agreeing to dismantle national policies on trade, financial regulations, labour protections and welfare guarantees in the name of global competition. Many have also agreed and submit to regional (agreements between states in a common area) or global regulations. For instance, the creation of regional blocs such as the European Union (EU), the Association of South East Asian Nations (ASEAN), and North Atlantic Free Trade Association (NAFTA) whose rules take precedence over national legislation is a product of globalisation. In addition, many of the nation states are embedded within the multiple agencies of the United Nations and other transnational organisations.

Brown also argues that political aspect of globalisation is the focus on the global structures and processes of rule making, problem solving, the maintenance of security and order in the world system. This clearly undermines the characteristic of state sovereignty in relation to having supreme legitimacy over politics within its state.[16] Although these global structures acknowledge the continuing centrality of states and geopolitics, it does not give them the authority to decline laws that are employed on them. Under condition of political globalisation, states are increasingly embedded in worldwide webs of: multilateral institutions and multilateral politics from NATO and the World Bank, G-8, transnational associations and networks like the International Chamber of Commerce. There is a concern with the eroding of power and significance of nation states in the face of global capital. Transnational organisations are setting the agenda such as the World Trade Organisation (WTO), the International Monetary Fund (IMF) and the World Bank. These organisations are increasingly taking on world government roles to protect the interests of capital in general and transnational co-operations in particular. These transnational organisations sometimes overrule many decisions that are taken by governments within nation-states.[17] Just as modernisation was the era of the nation-state, globalisation is the era of multilayered governance. Power is differentially exercised at the local, national, regional, or global level. In addition non-state actors, such as corporations and non-governmental organisations (such as human rights or environmental organisations)— what is called the global civil society, demands their inclusion when treaties are negotiated. Under such conditions, the new world order frequently looks like global chaos. But such change has allowed transnational issues such as human rights and environmental degradation occupy the forefront of global political issues. Hence, it is the de-territorialisation or the growth of supranational relations between the people, in other words the demise of the nation state.

Cosmopolitan democracy can be conceived as basis for combining the democratisation of global governance with the pursuit of global social justice. It seeks to nurture and institutionalise some of the core values of social democracy—the rule of law, political equality, democratic governance, social justice, social solidarity and economy efficiency— within global power system.[18] Globalisation has undermined state sovereignty by exerting influences, in the form of ideas into the state. This can lead to the people questioning the legitimacy of the government to exert absolute power over the state. The Arab Spring 2011 is a vivid example of the dominance of global political dynamism over static state. The Arab uprising indicates that the world is drawing together as single a society, marked by common institutions and organisations by a shared culture and political consciousness. The external forces give communities and culture groups the confidence to fight against their current regime. They feel united and supported to do so by other fellow international community members after communicating with them through the advance technology and increased communication system present due to globalisation. Thus, globalisation has undermined state sovereignty domestically in the state.

However, there are counter arguments to proponents of hyperglobalist theories. Hirst argues that although there are changes in supra-national organisation (such as the World Trade Organisation) and global governance, the sovereign territorial state is not being undermined even if its role is changing. The new standardised rules, reached by agreement between states, can only work if there are territorial agencies that enforce them locally and have the power to do so. Those agencies can only be and are states. Moreover, for international treaties to be implemented, they have to be deliberated, signed and delivered domestically and internationally by the states. [19] Hirst emphasises the significant importance of the state as a key actor in globalisation in relations to global governance and economics. The states play a vital role in resisting the supra-national tyranny and their influence. Due to their territory and legitimacy states still hold the authority to speak on behalf of their populations on global issues and sustain the global order.[20] Hirst ideas of state sovereignty in relations to globalisation are strongly based on the assumption that it is the Wesphalian state sovereignty which can perform the responsibilities of keeping the international system stable and cooperative. The recent United Kingdom referendum (Brexit) to exit from the European Union signifies the importance of state sovereignty. Britain is concerned about the diminishing of its state sovereignty and rampant immigration in Europe.[21] Therefore, Krasner and Robert Gilpin argument holds true that the states remain the principal agents shaping the world politics.

But we can see that Westphalian state sovereignty has indeed, to a large extent been undermined by globalisation. It has transformed the nature of politics, from state-centric geopolitics to geocentric global politics. It has definitely changed the process of governance and accountability in the modern state. Cohen argues that rather than undermining the state, globalisation is a product of a rearrangement of the purposes, boundaries, and sovereign authority of the state. Domestically, the sovereignty of the state is seen with realist view and a self-sufficient unit with exclusive political power.[22] But due to external influences through globalisaiton people within the state are more aware of contemporary issues and ideas other than the ethos and norms exerted to them by the current regime in the state. This leads to the diminishing authority of the political actors/elites in the state. Internationally, state sovereignty defined by its territorial borders is wearing away because of the increasing impact of global governance and the international global community. Having looked at the impact of many aspects of globalisation domestically and internationally on state, globalisation undermines state sovereignty to a large extent. There will be increase as the impact of globalisation politically, culturally and economically continues to accelerate in the modern age, particularly with the advance of ICT.

Economic Dimension

Economic globalisation is the result of human innovation and technological progress. It refers to the increasing integration of economies around the world, particularly through the movement of goods, services, and capital across borders. It also refers to the process whereby all national economies have to a greater or lesser extent been absorbed into an interlocking global economy. In other words, it is a shift from the world of distinct national economies to a global economy in which production is internationalised and financial capital flows freely and instantly between two countries.[23] The patterns of worldwide trade, finance and production are creating global markets and in the process a single capitalist economy—what Castells calls "global informational capitalism".[24] Multinational Corporations organise production and marketing on global basis while operation of global financial markets, determines which countries get credit and upon what terms. Sometimes economic globalisation also refers to the movement of people (labour) and knowledge (technology) across international borders. It is the driving force behind the various changes bound up with culture and politics in the contemporary world.

The economic globalisation came into being in the late 19th century with European states colonising across Asia and Africa. The development of trans-border and transnational economic structures has been a central feature of imperialism. The modern globalised economy came into existence in the second half of 20th century. The Bretton Woods system created after the Second World War rested on the foundation of fixed exchange rates and regulations of capital accounts. But this began to change in 1973 with the breakdown of the Bretton Woods system. Throughout the 1970s, trade liberalisation within the framework of the General Agreement on Trade and Tariffs (GATT) involved primarily the industrialised countries. The disproportionate influence that the USA is exercising in transforming the GATT into a more strongly pro-free-trade World Trade Organisation demonstrate the extent to which economic globalisation was structured in line with the requirements of developed countries. The WTO system has sponsored numerous trade negotiations lowering trade barriers and extending agreements into other areas such as intellectual property and foreign investment. This system relies on reciprocity, attempting to balance countries' gains and losses. The WTO is now focusing on new round of trade negotiations which is intended to address the problems of the developing countries more directly.[25] Moreover, developing countries are frequently seen as the real losers, forced away more easily from measures that might protect and develop their domestic economies, while protectionism remains heavy in certain sectors in the economies of more developed nations.[26]

During the 1980s world trade was organised as a series of competing trade blocs (e.g. ASEAN, EU, NAFTA) that sought to remove trade barriers between members but were protectionist. Liberal trade environment provided by American hegemony after 1950 allowed certain Least Developing Countries (LDCs) to take advantage of neo-mercantilist division of labour. The Asian newly industrialised countries (NICs) (Hong Kong, Singapore, South Korea, Taiwan and later Malaysia and Thailand) have generally used export-oriented measures while the Latin American NICs (Brazil, Chile and Mexico) prefer import- substitution measures. Specific policy initiative includes tax incentives to investors, duty-free import of components and capital goods, wage suppression and depressed currency values.[27]

Generally, in the 1990s, trade liberalisation began to accelerate in the developing countries. The national economies in the world are becoming more open and integrated with one another. With the emerging market there is the explosive growth in private financial flows from North to South. The information and communications technology (ICT) revolution coupled with declining transport costs made the growth of multi-country based production of goods and services both technically and economically feasible.[28] Global economic resources are circulated among countries through continuing growth of economic linkages. The increase of global linkages narrows the gap among countries and creates a closer interdependence in terms of production and market through dynamics of flow of capital and technology.[29] Some emerging countries, in particular China, India, Brazil and others developed into significant economies, the bulk of countries in the South were unable to liberate themselves from underdevelopment and poverty through integration in world markets.

The new economy is truly global because it is non-territorial. Investors can choose where and when to invest or withdraw capital from any part of the world. In terms of financial investment and trade, the world is now a single place. This is the case because states agreed to dismantle their economic regulations (such as tariffs or investment limits) and most regional blocs such as the EU have practically eliminated their borders when it comes to trade. This deregulation of the trade and financial transactions further undermined the sovereignty of states who can no longer control flows of goods or finances and gave more power to new forms of economic organisations: transnational corporations. In addition, the Bretton Woods institutions (IMF, World Bank and WTO) have also been pushing for economic reforms in most countries in the direction of more deregulations.[30]

Globalisation is an effective erasure of national boundaries for economic purposes. National boundaries become totally porous with respect to goods and capital and increasingly porous in respect to people, viewed in this context as cheap labour, or cheap human capital.[31] Transnational corporations spread wealth, widen employment opportunities and improve access to technology in the developing world. Transnational corporations (TNCs) are different from multinational corporations (MNCs). MNC is a corporation with outlets in different countries. For instance, McDonalds and Kentucky Fried Chicken (KFC) has outlets in different countries.[32] A TNC treats the world as a single space and distribute its networks of production, distribution and consumption where conditions are most favourable. Economic globalisation helps market based economy and also brings social and political benefits. Social mobility increases as people are able to take advantage of wider working career and educational opportunities and the despotism of custom and tradition is weakened as individualism and self expression are given wider rein. The growth of trans-border production, the proliferation of global products, the multiplication of supra-territorial monies and the expansion of trans-world financial flows have shown little sign of heralding an end of cultural differences in the world economy.[33]

With enormous consequence in terms of production, consumption, and social welfare, finance has perhaps become the backbone of new global economy. This new centrality of finance is connected to the liberalisation of financial flows after the demise of Bretton Woods system, deregulation of the financial sector, development of a new communications infrastructure that allows round the clock and instantaneous transactions of enormous amounts of money, and the emergence of new financial instruments.[34] Financial and commodities markets are closely interlinked that cross-border trade and capital flows which shape the global economy become risky. The global financial and world economic crisis of 2008-09 has made this evident.[35] The crisis which emerged in the global North has made things even worse in many of these countries. Combating this crisis, which was triggered by prolonged global economic imbalances in combination with radically deregulated international financial markets, has consumed vast sums worldwide and has once more mired many countries in debt in a dramatic fashion.

The development and implementation of ideas on how to eliminate global economic imbalances and to limit the risks in the international financial system must be the efforts to shape globalisation in terms of democracy and the social dimension.[36] International dialogue on the various economic policy issues and its consequences of the crisis requires while dealing with economic globalisation. There are clear winners and drivers of corporate-led globalisation that represent powerful ideology which clearly benefits the already wealthy, and that presents a threat to democracy.

Cultural Dimension
Cultural globlalisation involves a mix of homogenisation and increase in heterogeneity given the global diffusion of popular culture, global media corporations, communications network and simultaneously the assertion of nationalism and ethnicity.[37] In other words, it is the process whereby information, commodities and images that have been produced in one part of the world enter into a global flow that tends to override cultural differences between nations, regions and individuals.[38] The process of globalisation has triggered forces of change which have set people thinking about the political institutions such as the state, the democracy and the civil society. In their functioning, the role of cultural pluralism and protection of the local cultures is now particularly recognised both in terms of institutional mechanism as an element of political morality or value system. The cultural dimension draws attention to the fact that there are two approaches to the cultural issue, and that they are contradictory, one is the recognition and appreciation of cultural differences, while the other is the homogenisation and the merger of different cultures into one overall global culture.[39]

In the pre-modern period cultural globalisation was most importantly about globalising religions— Buddhism, Christianity and Islam. In the modern period, with the enlightenment and the spread of capitalism, industrialisation, democracy, cultural globalisaton has been predominantly about the movement of secular ideologies— nationalism, liberalism, socialism— the diffusion of the values and practices associated with modern science. Today cultural globalisation is mostly cantered around the impact of the growing volume of exchanges of cultural products. [40] The rising power and visibility of cultural industries, the apparent ubiquity of Western popular culture diffuse and transform the cultural context of almost every society on the planet.

Cultural identities are shaped by a complex set of factors which are associated with the processes of evolution of cultural practices and beliefs of people in course of their historical experiences. Cultural identities constitute a dynamic process which is ever responsive to changes in the historical, social, economic and techno-ecological situations encountered by a community.[41] Globalisation process in this respect constitutes a very special kind of manifestation of inter-cultural encounters and reciprocities.

In the Indian context we can correlate with the notion of sanskritisation in which M.N Srinivas explained the process of cultural mobility. In his study of the Coorgs, he found that the lower castes adopted some customs of the Brahmins and gave up some their own, which were considered to be impure by the higher castes in order to raise their position in the caste hierarchy.[42] For example they gave up meat-eating, consumption of liquor and animal sacrifice to their deities. They imitated the Brahmins in matters of food, dress and rituals. Therefore, the cultural dimension invasion through globalisation has changed the life patterns of the people. For instance celebrating the Valentine's Day (which is considered westernisation) or people are adapting easily to the lifestyle of Western culture.

One of the effects of globalisation is to attenuate the link between a cultural phenomenon and its geographic location by transporting distant events, influences and experiences into our immediate vicinity. In a globalising world, cultural identities often derive from multiple sources; the increasing plasticity of cultural identities reflects the growing complexity of the globalised flows of people, goods and information. The increasing intercultural contact gives rise to new forms of cultural diversity and linguistic practices due to advances in digital technology. Cultural diversity, like cultural identity is about innovation, creativity and receptiveness to new influence.[43]

Globalisation also leads to homogenisation of cultures in some significant aspects throughout the world. It involves inter dependency, reciprocity and exchange of mutual skills and resources in large measures. The result is that homogenisation of cultures takes place in several aspects of cultural life of the people due to globalisation, but this process also accelerates the growth of cultural self-consciousness and cultural identities.[44]

Samuel Huntington put forward the thesis of clash of civilisation which underlines the enormous cultural differences in the world both in terms of geography and religion, and perceives that such differences would be the major basis of global conflict in the post Communist era. He also pointed out that the modern revolution in information and communication technology and the increasing mobility of the people bring into limelight hitherto invisible differences between different cultures.[45] Culture itself changes over time and can influence others. Many factors including technology mould this change, as the relative success or failure of a particular ideology or system. With the twin forces of economic globalisation and technological innovation there are enough indications that exchange of views, values, habits and the use of internet lead to fusion of culture with increasing collective like environment, individualism, human rights and tolerance.[46]

On the other side, some scholars portray cultural globalisation as a top-down process, the establishment of a single global system that imprints itself on all parts of the world; in effect, a global monoculture. From this perspective, cultural globalisation amounts to a form of cultural imperialism, emphasising that cultural flows are between unequal partners and are used as means through which powerful states exert domination over weaker states. Therefore, cultural globalisation can be portrayed as 'westernisation' or more specifically 'Americanisation'.[47]

The era of cultural globalisation unfolded in 1990s. Western culture was undoubtedly the predominant stream, but the development of globalising cosmopolitan culture drew on many influences and has become increasingly multicultural. The never ending quest of global and local capitalists to entertain did much to further cultural synthesis, in the realm of dress, art, entertainment and food. Western-originated images and aspirations are transported to the Middle East and Asia. Chinese, Indians and French culinary culture coexist with McDonald's and Kentucky Fried Chicken (KFC). The rising giants China and India would begin exerting a much more sustained cultural influence across the world.[48] Globalisation did create a cosmopolitan consumer culture which was apt to make different parts of the world uniform but it wouldn't become an identical entity. However, local ethnic and religious culture survives along with globalised culture as people and ideas increasingly flow around the world.

Technological Dimension

The other most important element of globalisation is the revolutionary changes in information technology communication which for the first time in human history has brought inter-cultural interactions among people to a level beyond human imagination. The satellite communications has reached people strengthening the inter-cultural contacts among diverse settings of culture and civilizations. The impact is not uniform and differs from level of cultural contact and the context in which globalisation process takes place. But these have truly globalised the means for sharing cultural experiences and interactions across the globe.

Globalisation offers a new opportunity for knowledge dissemination. Developing countries benefit from globalisation of technology if they implement polices designed to increased learning and improve access to knowledge. The new technology, either embodied or disembodied has a negligible learning impact *per se*, unless it is accompanied by local policies to promote learning, human capital and technological capabilities. The accelerating pace of global interactions and processes as the evolution of worldwide systems of transport and communications increase the rapidity or velocity with which ideals, news, goods, information, capital, and technology mover around the world.[49] Routine telephone banking transactions in the United States are dealt with by Business Processing Outsourcing (BPO) or Knowledge Processing Outsourcing (KPO) in developing countries like India.

Information technology is a driving factor in the process of globalisation. The revolution of Information Communication Technology (ICT) in the 1990s greatly increased people's ability to access information and economic potential. While advancement in Internet based tools over the past five to ten years, such as social networking websites are changing the way people use and share information for personal, political and commercial purposes. IT drives the innovative use of resources to promote new products and ideals across nations and cultures, regardless of geographic location.[50] Creating efficient and effective channels to exchange information through ICT has been the catalyst for global integration. Freedom of communication, access to information, political participation and leverage on decision-making process individuals are interested in shaping future. They are vigorously fighting independence or rights from state manipulation. They are building a virtual nation without states, a map without borders via ICT— facebook, instagram, twitter, other information sharing platforms gradually challenging state supremacy.[51]

Furthermore, another empowerment brought on by technological dimension of globalisation is rapid exchange of ideas, range and sophistication of propaganda materials used by the global terrorist network. Through the ICT, terrorist supporters and sympathisers build their own websites. Terrorists groups have utilised technologies and other innovations to maintain their activities tactically and strategically. They operate without any borders and have developed a virtual global network exchanging information to coordinate and conduct lethal attack. The technologies associated with globalisation have enabled terrorist cells and groups to mount coordinated attacks in different countries. Globalisation has improved the technical capabilities of terrorist and given them global reach but the same technologies also enable more effective means to states to combat them.[52] Therefore, one can say that the benefits that globalisation provides global network is neither one-sided nor absolute.

Globalisation is one of the many faces affecting our societies and our economies. Even with it, there would be increasing inequality. Changes in technology have increased the premium market places on certain skills, so that the winners in today's economy are those who have or can acquire those skills. These changes in technology may in the end be more important than globalisation in determining the increase in inequality, and even the decline in unskilled wages. Voters can do little about the technology but they can through their elected representatives –do something about globalisation.

Critical Assessment

Thomas L. Friedman argues that globalisation and technology have flattened the world, creating a level playing field in which developed and less developed countries can compete on equal terms. He is right that there have been dramatic changes in the global economy, in the global landscape in some direction, the world is much flatter than it has even been, with those various parts of the world being more connected than they have even been, but the world is not flat. Countries that want to participate in the new world of high-tech globalisation need new technologies, computers, and other equipment in order to connect with the rest of the world. Individuals who want to compete in this global economy have to have the skills and resources to do so. Parts of India, such as Bangalore and Hyderabad, have both the technology and the people with skills to use it, but Africa does not. As globalisation reduces the gap between parts of India and China and the advanced industrial countries, the gap between Africa and the rest of the world is actually increasing. Within countries too, the gap between the rich and the poor is increasing and, with it, the gap between those who can effectively compete globally and those who can't. High technology is a high-stakes game, in which large investments (by governments and countries) are required. The advanced industrial countries and their large firms have the resources; many others do not.[53]

Not only is the world not flat, in many ways it has been getting less flat. The countries of East Asia made globalisation work for them, their success is the best argument for the good that globalisation can do for other developing countries. But for some of the poorest countries of the world, dependent as they are on aid from World Bank, the IMF, or donors from Europe, America, and Japan, conditions imposed in order to receive aid though less onerous than in the past may still be precluding them from following economic policies of their own. It is bad enough that the developing countries are at a natural disadvantage but the rules of the game are tilted against them, and in some ways increasingly so. The global trade and financial regime give the advanced industrial countries a marked advantage.

Conclusion

The advance of globalisation and the progressive de-territorialisation of economic, cultural and political life have gradually weakened the idea that society should be understood merely in domestic or national terms. If societies are fashioned out of usually stable set of relationships between and among their members involving mutual awareness, then the consequence has been the emergence of transnational or 'world society'.[54] No doubt, globalisation has brought in new opportunities to developing countries. Greater access to developed country markets and technology transfer hold out promise of improved productivity and higher living standard. But globalisation has also thrown up new challenges like growing inequality across and within nations, volatility in financial market and environmental deteriorations. With globalisation, borders become more fluid with the impact of electronic developments on money transfers, satellite communications, computer data flow, capital flow and trade. The modern state is unable to control phenomena such as global companies, global production and trade. Another negative aspect of globalisation is that a great majority of developing countries remain removed from the process. Globalisation holds the promise of enormous benefits for the people of the world. To make this promise a reality, we must find a way to carefully manage the process. Better attention must be paid to reduce the negative effects and ensuring that the benefits are widely and fairly distributed. The growing extensity, intensity, and velocity of global interactions of the local and global create a growing collective awareness or consciousness of the world as a shared social space.

Globalisation is not an event but a gradual and continuous expansion and integration of relations. It is difficult to make predictions for the future of the nation state. Changes associated with globalisation have significant affects on states. However, it is not evident that it will reach and fully integrate global economy or lead to a decline of state. In the future state sovereignty might be eroded by supranational authority but as of now in the 21st century, nation states remain the dominant form of political organisation in the global perspective. Despite the challenges to state sovereignty and autonomy in the process of globalisation, states hesitate to submit all control to new forces. Thus the end of the state approach is little deterministic. It gives the impression that it is an inescapable process. State sovereignty might be affected by the transformation taking place in the world, yet it is not intended and depends on unknown circumstances. There are also structural obstacles to the withering away of the state. Votes have to be cast and taxes have to be paid to respective authorities, which can be held accountable for public services such as education and health. States have to continue to create a regulatory environment for their economies.

However, the effect and challenges of globalisation is likely to vary under different national and international conditions. Nation states will have to make different policy choices in response to the same global phenomena. Each nation-state takes pride in historical, political economic, socio-cultural and its accomplishments. Global politics is ever shifting, if anything, the pace of change accelerating over time. Debates have emerged about the changing nature of power and the shifting configuration of global power, whether national security has been displaced by the process of globalisation.

Notes

1. Held, David, *Democracy and Global Order*(Cambridge: Polity Press, 1995).
2. Held, David, *Political Theory and the Modern State* (Stanford, California: Stanford University Press, 1989), p. 215.
3. Intergovernmentalism refers to interaction among states which takes place on the basis of sovereign independence. Supranationalism is the existence of an authority that is higher than that of the nation-state and capable of imposing its will on the states.
4. Beck, U. "The Terrorist Threat: World Risk Society Revisited" in *Theory, Culture and Society*, vol. 19, 2002, pp.3-55.
5. Held, D. and McGrew, A, *Globalization/ Anti- Globalization* (Cambridge: Polity Press,2002).
6. It refers to the growth of contacts, networks and organisations which link people, business and communities across national boundaries.
7. Held, D, " Realism Versus Cosmopolitanism",in *A Debate Between Barry Buzan and David Held*, at https://www.polity.co.uk/global/realism-vs-cosmopolitanism.asp, accessed on June 4, 2016.
8. Scholte, J. A, *Globalization: A Critical Introduction* (Basingtoke: Palgrave Macmillan, 2000), p.135.
9. McGrew, A, "Power Shift: From National Government to Global Governance?' in D. Held (ed.), *A Globalising World? Culture, Economics, Politics* (London: Routledge, 2000).
10. Giddens, A., *The Consequences of Modernity* (Stanford, Palo Alto: Stanford University Press,1990).
11. Ohmae, K. , *The End of the Nation State*, New York: Free Press, 1995). Also see, Scholte, J.A. , *Globalization: A Critical Introduction* (London: Macmillan, 2000).

12. Rosenau, J, *Along the Domestic- Foreign Frontier* (Cambridge: Cambridge University Press, 1997).

13. Krasner, S.D. , *Sovereignty: Organized Hypocrisy*(Princeton, NJ: Princeton University Press, 1999). Also see, Gilpin, R. *Global Political Economy*(Princeton, NJ: Princeton University Press,2001) .

14. Monnier, Christine, *Dimension of Globalization,* at https://globalsociology.pbworks.com/w/page/14711172/Dimensions%20of%20Globalization,accessed on April 11, 2015.

15. Roy, Olivier, *Globalised Islam: The Search for a New Ummah,* (New York: Columbia University Press, 2004).

16. Brown, S, *International Relations in a Changing Global System*(Boulder, Co: Westview, 1999).

17. Rikowski, Glenn, *Transfiguration: Globalisation, the World Trade Organisation and the National Faces of the GATS,* at http://firgoa.usc.es/drupal/files/rikowski-transfiguration-gats.pdf, accessed on April 12, 2016.

18. Anthony, n 9, p.31.

19. Hirst, P, "Globalization and the Nation State", *Review of International Political Economy* vol.4, no. 3, 2002, p.474.

20. Ibid.

21. Erlanger, Steven, "Brexit: Explaining Britain's Vote on European Union Membership", *The New York Times,* June 21 2006, at http://www.nytimes.com/interactive/2016/world/europe/britain-european-union-brexit.html?_r=0 , accessed on June 28, 2016.

22. Cohen, E.S, "Globalization and the Boundaries of the State: A Framework for Analysing the Changing Practice of Sovereignty", *Governance* vol. 14 no. 1, 2001,pp.75-97.

23. Heywood, Andrew, *Global Politics* (New York: Palgrave Macmillan, 2011) p.94.

24. Castells, M, *The Rise of the Network Society* (Oxford: Blackwell, 2000).

25. Milner, Helen V, "Globalization, Development and International Institutions: Normative and Positive Perspective", *Review Essay,* vol. 3 no.4, December, 2005, p. 836.

26. Wallach, L. and Woodall, P., *Whose Trade Organization? A Comprehensive Guide to the WTO* (New York: The New Press, 2004).

27. Walters, R. and Blake, D., *The Politics of Global Economic Relations* (Englewood Cliffs, New Jersey: Prentice Hall,1992), p. 190.

28. "Globalization and its Impact", International Labour Organization, at http://www.ilo.org/public/english/wcsdg/docs/rep2.pdf, accessed on April 12, 2015.

29. Cap, Chu Van, "Marx and Engels on Economic Globalization", *Nature, Society and Thought,* vol. 15 no.2,2002, p.242.

30. Christine., n 14, p. 2.

31. Daly, Herman E., "Globalisation and Its Discontent", *Minnesotans For Sustainability,* (August 2000) at http://www.mnforsustain.org/daly_herman_globalism_and_its_discontents.htm, accessed on April 12, 2016.

32. "BBC- GCSE Bitesize: Transnational Corporations", *BBC news,* at http://www.bbc.co.uk/schools/gcsebitesize/geography/globalisation/globalisation_rev3.shtml, accessed on April 12, 2016.

33. Scholte, Jan Aart "Regionalism in International Affairs", in John Baylis, et al, *The Globalization of World Politics,*(Oxford: Oxford University Press, 2008), p.465.

34. Castells, M. , *The Information Age: Economy, Society and Culture: The Rise of the Network Society*(Oxford: Blackwell, 1996). Also see, Khor, M, *Rethinking Globalization: Critical Issue and Policy Choices* (London: Zed,2001).

35. 2008 witnessed the worst financial crisis since the Great Depression of 1929-30. See, Dullien, Sebastian, et al. (eds.), (*The Financial And Economic Crisis of 2008-2009 and Developing Countries*(New York: United Nations, December, 2010).

36. "Global Economic, Trade and Finance Policy", *Freidrich Ebert Stiftung*, at http://www.fes.de/gpol/en/globalisation1.htm, accessed on April 12, 2016.

37. Ibid.

38. Heywood, n.23, p. 147.

39. Glenn, n. 17, p. 1.

40. Held, David et.al., *Global Transformations: Politics, Economics and Culture*(Cambridge: Cambridge University Press, 1999).

41. "Cultural Diversity and Globalisation", A document for reflection on the subtheme of culture from the Millennium Forum of the United Nations, at http://www.forumsocialmundial.org.br/download/tconferencias_identidadecultural_prop_eng.pdf, accessed on April 15, 2015.

42. Mondal, Puja " Sanksritisation: Characteristics and Criticisms of Sanksritisation", at http://www.yourarticlelibrary.com/sociology/rural-sociology/sanskritisation-characteristics-and-criticisms-of-sanskritisation/31939/, accessed on April 18, 2015.

43. "Investing in Cultural Diversity and Intercultural Dialogue", UNESCO World Report, at http://www.un.org/en/events/culturaldiversityday/pdf/Investing_in_cultural_diversity.pdf, accessed on April 16, 2015, p.6-7.

44. Yeung, Henry Wai-chung *Capital, state and space: contesting the borderless world*, Royal Geographical Society (with The Institute of British Geographers, 1998).

45. Huntington, S. P, *The Clash of Civilisation and the Breaking of World Order*(New York: Simon and Schuster, 1996).

46. Mukherjee, Subrata and Sushila Ramaswamy, Democracy in Theory and Practice (New Delhi: Macmillan, 2005), pp.247-51.

47. Heywood, n.23, p. 145.

48. Murden, Simon "Culture in World Affairs" in John Baylis, et al, *The Globalization of World Politics* (Oxford: Oxford University Press, 2008) p. 423.

49. Anthony, n.9, p.22.

50. "Information Technology", *Globalization 101*, at http://www.globalization101.org/information-technology/. accessed on April 12, 2015.

51. Ayvazyan, Vahram, "Political Globalization—Global Politicization", *Diplomatic Courier,* at http://www.diplomaticourier.com/blog/2012/10/political-globalization-global-politicization/, accessed on April 12, 2015.

52. Kiras, James D " Terrorism and Globalisation" in John Baylis, et al, *The Globalization of World Politics*(Oxford: Oxford University Press, 2008), pp. 374-384.

53. Sitglitz, Joseph E. *Making Globalisation Work* (New York, W. W Norton & Company, Inc.,2006), p.58.

54. Buzan, Barry, *From International to World Society?* (Cambridge: Cambridge University Press, 2004).

CHAPTER 3

Global Economy: Its Significance and Anchors of Global Political Economy (IMF, World Bank, WTO, TNCs)

The global economy is considered as the international exchange of goods and services that is expressed in monetary units of account. It is a world-wide economic activity between various countries intertwined and thus can affect other countries negatively or positively. In a nutshell, the global economy refers to the economy of the world, comprising several countries, with each economy related to the other in one way or the other. A key concept in the global economy is globalisation, which is the process that leads to individual economies around the world being closely interwoven such that an event in one country is bound to affect the state of other world economies. In the past century or so, the focus on globalisation has intensified a lot. More trade has been conducted among different countries, and restrictions on movement and business across borders have reduced a great deal. This resulted in global economy. People are now able to sell their commodities in any market across the world. Likewise, consumers also enjoy a much wider choice of goods and services since they can sample them from other places and not just their own countries.[1]

The global political economy has changed dramatically since the Industrial Revolution of the late 18th and early 19th centuries. The study of the global political economy involves thinking reflectively about how and why changes in one dimension of the global political economy interconnect and overlap with others. Past experiences have helped us gain a better and more dynamic understanding of the evolution of trade in terms of changing forms of governance, authority, relationships and outcomes in the global political economy. International Political Economy (IPE) has developed since the 1970s to understand the modern world economy based on relations between the states and markets.

The Genesis and Growth of Global Economy

In the past, there did not exist a global economic system. Trade was mainly local and based on barter- the direct exchange of goods without money. When barter became inadequate owing to distance or the bulk of goods for trade, precious metals like gold and silver were used to make payment. Rome established a monetary system throughout its empire, and even after that empire collapsed its gold coins remained in use and were accepted everywhere.

Europe's medieval world economy evolved slowly under the influence of social and economic changes. In Flanders, Belgium, and northern Italy, self governing city states emerged as commerce flourished. Growing trade required money and banks came into existence. By the end of the 13th century, Florence had become Europe's banking center with 80 banks, and as money replaced other forms of exchange, banking system expanded to other lands. Florentine bankers such as the Bardi and Peruzzi families established branches around Europe and became immensely rich, involved in trading grain, wool and silk as well as in lending and exchanging currency. The most important Florentine banking family was the Medicis, later to become the city's rulers. The Medicis loaned money at high interest rates to European rulers.[2]

As commerce spread northwards, merchant groups from commercial cities along the northern Europe formed the Hanseatic League in the middle of the 13th century. It continued for 300 years. The league provided security for merchants, standardised weights and measures, and fostered trade among Russians, Scandinavians, Germans, Polish, and the English. Its network of alliance grew to 170 cities and it protected its interest from interfering rulers and rival traders using powerful fleet financed by its members.[3] Therefore, Europe's voyages of discovery created new economic links with distant people and places in the course of establishing empires and planting European colonies on distant shores. As territorial states emerged in the form of principal global actors in the 17th and 18th centuries, they assumed the role of providing money and regulating trade. Along with the state, the first international monetary system developed the gold standard, under which gold and money were equivalent.

Immanuel Wallerstein presented an account of the structure of world economy as necessarily divided into cores, peripheries and semi-peripheries. The 'core' in north-west Europe was able to develop comparatively effective and powerful states and to dominate politically and economically. It reflects the importance of communication and transportation in determining the power of states relative to their size.

The agricultural revolution in England significantly increased productivity, and the spread of its empire generated important commodities particularly tea and slavery. In the Atlantic, the 'Golden Triangle' brought together basic commodities from Britain, slaves from West Africa and sugar from the Caribbean Islands. In the early 19th century, in the East the demand for tea from China, the non-availability of products desired by the Chinese Empire led to the development of another triangle, involving British colonial cotton goods, Indian opium and Chinese tea.[4] With the emergence of the industrial revolution/society in the second half on 19th century large scale division of labour existed worldwide, especially after the two world wars.

Theoretical Perspective of Political Economy

There are four dominant theoretical traditions in global political economy – Mercantilism, Liberalism, Marxism and Constructivism, each with distinctive analytic and normative elements on global economy. Mercantilism dominated economic thinking between the 16th and late 18th centuries. Mercantilism influences many countries where it takes the form of protectionism for home industries. In the second perspective, economic liberalism or free market capitalism rose in the 18th and early 19th centuries, spread by imperialist. Marxism developed in the 19th century as an alternative to liberalism, with socialist and communist ideas advocating as an alternative to capitalism.

The Mercantilism

The Scottish political economist Adam Smith (1723-90) coined the term "mercantile system" which he defined as the "encouragement of exportation and the discouragement of importation". Mercantlism's normative premise was that economic policy should advance state power. The mercantilist era was one of intense colonial rivalry among Europe's powers. This system dominated Western European economic thought and policies from 16th to the late 18th centuries. Spain's conquest of South and Central America in the 16th century and its access to precious metals made it the leading power of its age and its new world colonies became part of a great imperial trade bloc. The goal of the mercantilist system was to achieve a favourable balance of trade that would bring gold and silver into the country and also to maintain domestic employment.[5] Jean Baptiste Colbert (1617-83) argued that states should accumulate gold and silver as well as build a strong central government. According to mercantilist states should be self sufficient in industries, especially those needed to wage war. Leaders did not allow skilled labourers to transfer capital goods (goods used to produce other goods) to be exported. Mercantilist argued that infant industries even if inefficient, should be nurtured and protected behind a protectionist wall. They assume that the world economy is an arena of competition among states seeking to maximise relative strength and power. In other words, the international system is like a jungle in which each state has to do what it can to survive. In this sense, mercantilists share the presumptions of realists in international system. For them, the aim of every state must be to maximise its wealth and independence. States will seek to do this by ensuring their self-sufficiency in key strategic industries and commodities and by using state protectionism (tariffs and other limits on exports and imports), subsidies and selective investments in the domestic economy. The most powerful states define the rules and limits of the system through hegemony, alliances and balances of power.[6] Mercantilists also support imperial expansion and establishment of overseas colonies to obtain larger exclusive markets for their products and access to raw materials. Mercantilist also encouraged population growth to provide colonies with labourers, development of bigger markets and armies. In this way, the English dominated during the colonisation period. They encouraged the building of merchant ships and navies.

England's mercantilist policies played a key role in relations between the American colonies and the mother country. The 1651 Navigation Act required that goods shipped to and from colonies use only English vessels manned by English crew. This law was directed principally against England's arch rival Holland and later against France. Similarly, the Staple Act of 1663 extended the Navigation Act by requiring that all colonial exports to Europe be landed through an English port before being re-exported to Europe. Mercantilism began to give way to economic liberalism during the Industrial Revolution and Britain's conversation to free trade. The Industrial Revolution (1760-1830) transformed Britain from an agrarian to an industrial society. Industrialisation and accompanying urbanisation empowered a commercial middle class, greatly enlarged the number of urban workers and advanced the spread of democracy.[7] Hence in this system stability and order will only achieved where one state can play the role of hegemony.

The Liberal Tradition
The liberal tradition is the free market in which the role of voluntary exchange and markets is emphasised both as efficient and as morally desirable. The assumption is that free trade and the free movement of capital will ensure the investment flows to where it is most profitable to invest (for example, flowing capital to underdeveloped areas where maximal gains might be made). David Ricardo (1772-1823) developed a theory that states should engage in international trade

according to their comparative advantage. The state should produce and export those products which they can produce most efficiently (or specialise), relative to other states. Thus, gains from trade are maximised for all because each state minimises its opportunity cost. National currencies should be bought and sold in a free market system. In such a system of floating exchange rates, the market determines the value of one currency as compared to other currencies. Floating exchange rates will lead to market equilibrium.[8] The economy is pushed forward by freely exchangeable currencies and open markets which create a global system to ensure an efficient and equitable distribution of goods and services across the world economy. The optimal role of governments and institutions is to ensure the smooth and relatively unfettered operation of markets.[9]

Today's giant corporations are rivals in markets that often have too few competitors to assure genuine competition based on comparative advantage. Success is measured by a corporation's share of the global market as well as the profit it earns. Neoliberal economists still favour free markets, elimination of trade barriers, and minimal government interference in markets, but they see a greater role for international economic institutions than did classical economic liberals. They argue that free movement of investment capital and labour produces greater wealth for the world as a whole, even though inefficient countries and industries may suffer. They believe that economic efficiency matters more than economic equality. With free markets, there may be inequality but even the poor become absolutely better off because of the overall growth in wealth. Moreover, concentrations of wealth provide the needed capital investment for further economic growth. Unfettered competition may trigger speculation that drives up the price of assets above their value and such bubbles burst, resulting in economic distress.[10] The critics of economic liberalism or "casino capitalism"[11] view unregulated capitalism as a source of economic inequality. Out of this critique emerged a competing economic perspective of Marxism.

Marxism

In the backdrop of the injustice towards the working class during the Industrial Revolution, Karl Marx and Friederich Engels offered a revolutionary alternative to capitalism that conceived the global history as a struggle between different economic classes rather than among nation state. Marx believes that history evolved owing to changes in the modes of production that allowed some economic classes to dominate and exploit others. The historical process, Marx argued was inevitable, evolving through a clash of opposing forces in a process called dialectical materialism. Economic conditions Marx argued determine politics, not the other way round. The world-economic relations are best conceived as a class struggle between the oppressor and the oppressed. The oppressor or capitalist are those who own the means of production (trade and industry). The oppressed are the working class. The struggle between the two arises because capitalists seek to increase their profits and this requires them to exploit even more harshly the working class. In Europe's Middle Ages, a feudal class dominated economic and political life and was overthrown by a new capitalist class, which in turn would be overthrown by the working class as industrialissation changed the way goods were produced.[12]

In international relations this description of class relations within a capitalist system has been applied to describe relations between the core (industrialised countries) and periphery (developing countries), and the unequal exchange which occurs between the two. Under development and poverty in many countries is explained as the result of economic, social and political structures within countries which have been deeply influenced by their international economic relations. The global capitalist order within which these societies have emerged reflects the interests of those who own the means of production.[13]

Andre Gunder Frank claims that unequal exchange and appropriation of economic surplus by the few at the expense of the many are inherent in capitalism.[14] As long as the capitalist system exists there will be under development in developing countries. A similar view is taken by Immanuael Wallerstein, who has analysed the overall development of the capitalist world system since its beginning in the 16th century.[15] Wallerstein allows the possibility that some developing countries can move upwards in the global capitalist hierarchy based on the exploitation of the poor by the rich and it will remain that way unless and until it is replaced.

The Post Second World War Economy

Making of Bretton Woods System
During the last phase of the Second World War the institutions and framework of the world economy found a new economic order. In August 1944, policy makers gathered at Bretton Woods in the United States to consider how to resolve economic instability and chaos of the interwar period. The US and UK, along with 42 other states, met at the small resort town of Bretton Woods, New Hamsphire, to formulate the institutional architecture for the postwar international and monetary system. They needed to ensure that the Great Depression of the 1930s would not happen again. They had to find ways to ensure a stable global monetary

system and open world trading system.[16] The significanct outcome of the Bretton Woods discussions was the establishment of the three new bodies, known as the Bretton Woods System or Washington Consensus.

Major outcomes of the Bretton Woods Conference was the promotion of a new world economic order. This included the formation of the International Monetary Fund to ensure a stable rate regime and the provision for emergency assistance to countries facing a temporary crisis in their balance of payment regime. International Bank for Reconstruction and Development (IRBD), later called World Bank, was created to facilitate private investment and reconstruction in Europe. The Bank was also charged with assisting development in other countries. And lastly, the General Agreement on Trade and Tariff (GATT) later called World Trade Organisation was created which became an institution for negotiations on trade liberalisation.[17] The IMF, World Bank and the GATT became pillars of the global economic system. They reflect the economic interdependence of actors in a globalising world, play a critical role in reinforcing neoliberal norms and provide global economic governance system.

The United States announced the Marshall Plan[18] in 1947, which directed massive financial aid to Europe and permitted to set conditions on it. The planned gold standard was replaced by the dollar standard which the US managed directly, backing the dollar with gold. Unsurprisingly, the IMF, World Bank and GATT which began to function in the 1950s were distinctly Western bloc organisations dependent on the US. Meanwhile, other countries in the world economy were enhancing their positions; European allies were benefiting from the growing and deepening economic integration in Europe. By the 1960s, the development of the European Economic Community (EEC) provided a springboard for European policy makers to diverge from the US domination.

The new protectionism in industrialised countries further fuelled the anger of developing countries which launched a New International Economic Order (NIEO). The agenda of the NIEO covered trade, aid, investment, the international and monetary system and institutional reforms. Developing countries sought better representation in international economic institutions, a fairer trading system, more aid, the regulation of foreign investment, the protection of economic sovereignty, and reforms to ensure a more stable and equitable financial and monetary system. The developing countries' push for reform of the international economic system reflected dependency theory and structuralist theories of international economic relations which highlighted negative aspects of inter dependence. Their central concern was to answer why so many countries within the world economy remained under developed in spite of the promises of modernisation and global growth.[19] Meanwhile, the US and European policies had facilitated the rapid growth of global capital markets and financial flows during the 1960s and 1970s.

The 1990s brought the end of Cold War and faced the challenge as to how to integrate Eastern European countries and former Soviet Union into the global economy. The IMF and World Bank became deeply involved. Both the institutions began to embrace a broader and deeper view of conditionality aimed at promoting good governance in member countries.[20] The newly rechristened World Trade Organisation began operations in 1995 opening up a new forum within which a broad range of international issues are being negotiated including trade issues, intellectual property rights, trade related investment measures and food safety standards. The Asian financial crisis of 1997 and the world financial crisis of 2007-08 have opened up a new dimension for a new international financial architecture. Global economy is important as each country's economy interact with other countries. Globalisation has become a trend for different countries with economic growth and technology advancement.

Anchors of Global Economy

The most important institutions of global governance in the present world economy are the international economic institutions. The Bretton Woods agreement is a clear example of the multilateralism that became prominent in the post Second World War period. The three major international economic organisations are the World Bank, the International Monetary Fund (IMF), and the World Trade Organisation (WTO). The WTO emerged out of the General Agreement on Tariffs and Trade in 1995; it is an arrangement across countries that serve as a forum for negotiations on trading rules as well as mechanism for disputes and resolution on trade issues.[21] By contrast, the World Bank and IMF deal with their member countries and have little influence with industrial countries but can affect developing countries. The Transnational Companies (TNCs) have existed for centuries and some have enjoyed the perquisites of sovereignty. Transnational National Companies are the engines of global capitalism knitting peoples together in a vast economic system. The process of globalisation breaks down barriers of nation-states, labour markets or national economies the same way the global economy has seemingly beat down the barriers between and among the various academic disciplines.

I. International Monetary Fund

The International Monetary Fund was designed to promote economic stability by regulating monetary policy and currency exchange rates. The main purpose was to encourage international cooperation in the monetary field by removing foreign exchange restrictions, stabilising exchange rates and facilitating a multilateral payment system between member countries. The International Monetary Fund (IMF) is an organization with 188 countries, working to foster global monetary cooperation, secure financial stability, facilitate international trade, promote high employment and sustainable economic growth, and reduce poverty around the world. The IMF has played a part in shaping the global economy since the end of the World War II. The current Managing Director of IMF is Christine Lagarde from France.

Each country has a representation on the Board of Governors, usually the Minister of Finance or Central Bank Chairman. The Board meets once a year and designates policy overview to the International Monetary and Finance Committee (IMFC). The Executive Board consists of 24 Executive Directors from the IMFC who are assigned duty on regular basis in Washington D.C., the Headquarters of IMF. The IMF has about 2700 civil servants, led by a Managing Director and 3 Deputy Managing Directors. By convention, the European members select the Managing Director, although that could change as members seek more equitable representation for developing countries. [22]

Voting in the IMF is based on quotas, and quotas in turn are based on a country's economic power, including its GDP, current account transactions and official reserves. An IMF quota represents the maximum amount of money a country provides to the IMF for lending to correct the balance of payments problems. The United States has the largest vote with 16.8 percent. IMF quotas are recalculated every five years. Increasing and redistributing quotas are controversial steps that require an 85 percent majority vote.[23]

The founders aimed to build a framework for economic cooperation that would avoid a repetition of the disastrous economic policies that had contributed to the Great Depression of the 1930s and the global conflict that followed. During the Great Depression of the 1930s, countries attempted to shore up their failing economies by sharply raising barriers to foreign trade, devaluing their currencies to compete against each other for export markets, and curtailing their citizens' freedom to hold foreign exchange. World trade declined sharply and employment and living standards plummeted in many countries.

Promoting economic stability became necessary for avoiding economic and financial crises, large swings in economic activity, high inflation and excessive volatility in foreign exchange and financial markets. Instability can increase uncertainty, discourage investment, impede economic growth, and hurt living standards. A dynamic market economy necessarily involves some degree of volatility, as well as gradual structural change. The challenge for policy makers is to minimise instability in their own country and abroad without reducing the economy's ability to improve living standards through rising productivity, employment and sustainable growth. Economic and financial stability is both a national and multilateral concern. As 2007-08 financial crises have shown, economies have become more interconnected. Vulnerabilities can spread more easily across sectors and national borders. [24]

Role of IMF

The IMF's main goal is to ensure the stability of the international monetary and financial system. It helps resolve crises, and works with its member countries to promote growth and alleviate poverty. It has three main tools at its disposal to carry out its mandate: surveillance, technical assistance and training, and lending. These functions are supported by the IMF's research and statistics.[25]

Surveillance

When a country joins the IMF, it agrees to subject its economic and financial policies to the scrutiny of the international community. It also makes a commitment to pursue policies that are conducive to orderly economic growth and reasonable price stability, to avoid manipulating exchange rates for unfair competitive advantage, and to provide the IMF with data about its economy. The IMF's regular monitoring of economies and associated provision of policy advice is intended to identify weaknesses that are causing or could lead to financial or economic instability. This process is known as surveillance and divided into three zones: Country surveillance, Regional surveillance and Global surveillance. Surveillance covers a range of economic policies, with the emphasis varying in accordance with a country's individual circumstances. It helps the international monetary system serve its essential purpose of sustaining economic growth by facilitating the exchange of goods, services and capital among countries and ensuring the conditions necessary for financial and economic stability.

IMF economists visit member countries annually to exchange views with the government and the central bank and consider whether there are risks to domestic and global stability. Discussions are mainly focused on exchange rate, monetary, fiscal, and financial policies as well as macro critical structural reforms. During their missions, IMF staff meets with stakeholders such as parliamentarians, representatives of business, labour unions and civil society to help evaluate the country's economic policies and outlook.

The IMF also monitors global and regional economic trends, and analyses spillovers from members' policies onto the global economy. The key instruments of multilateral surveillance are the regular publications such as the World Economic Outlook (WEO), Global Financial Stability Report (GFSR), and Fiscal Monitor. The WEO provides a detailed analysis of the world economy and its growth prospects, addressing issues such as the macroeconomic effects of global financial turmoil. It also assesses key potential global spillovers with a particular focus on the cross-border impact of economic and financial policies in systemic economies. The GFSR assesses global capital market developments and financial imbalances and vulnerabilities that pose risks to financial stability. The Fiscal Monitor updates medium-term fiscal projections and assesses developments in public finances.[26]

The IMF also publishes Regional Economic Outlook reports, providing more detailed analysis for major regions of the world. It cooperates closely with other groups such as the Group of Twenty (G20) industrialised and emerging market economies. The IMF provides analysis as to whether policies pursued by member countries are consistent with sustained and balanced global growth. Since 2012, it has prepared Pilot External Sector Reports, which analyse the external situations of systemically large economies in a globally consistent manner. Twice a year, the IMF also prepares a Global Policy Agenda that pulls together the key findings and policy advice from multilateral reports and defines a future agenda for the Fund and its members. The IMF regularly reviews its surveillance activities. The 2014 Triennial Surveillance Review (TRS) built on reforms by identifying five operational priorities for strengthening surveillance: integrate and deepen risk and spillover analysis; mainstream macro-financial surveillance; pay more attention to structural policies, including labour market issues; deliver more cohesive and expert policy advice; and a client focused approach to surveillance supported by clear and candid communication. The regular surveillance review has been moved to a five year cycle with progress assessed in a mid-point review in 2017.[27]

Technical Assistance and Training

Technical assistance helps countries develop more effective institutions, legal frameworks, and policies to promote economic stability and inclusive growth. Training through practical policy-oriented courses, hands-on workshops, and seminars strengthen officials' capacity to analyse economic developments and formulate and implement effective policies. Work on technical assistance and training is managed from the IMF's headquarters in Washington, DC, and through a network of regional technical assistance centers (RTACs), regional training centers and programs (RTCs and RTPs), trust funds, and numerous bilateral donor-supported activities.[28] The IMF works in close cooperation with other providers of training and technical assistance and with donor partners.

New training is offered in the areas of inclusive growth, financial inclusion, and external vulnerabilities. In 2015, low income and developing countries received about half of all IMF technical assistance, while emerging market countries received the largest share of IMF training. IMF also provides technical assistance in its areas of core expertise: macroeconomic policy, tax policy and revenue administration, expenditure management, monetary and fiscal policy, the exchange rate system, financial sector stability, legislative frameworks, and macroeconomic and financial statistics. The IMF has also significantly scaled up online learning as a vehicle to deliver training in macro-economics and finance to government officials. Since 2013, about 5,500 government officials and 5,400 non-government participants have successfully completed an online course.[29] IMF is also adopting a result-based management framework to facilitate systematic planning and improved monitoring of capacity in development activity.

The technical assistance provided to emerging and advance economies keeps the institution up-to-date on innovations and risks to the global economy. It also helps address crisis-related challenges and spillovers. The IMF has given advice to countries that have had to reestablish government institutions following severe civil unrest or war.

Lending

A country in severe financial trouble, unable to pay its international bills, poses potential problems for the stability of the international financial system, which the IMF was created to protect. Any member country, whether rich, middle-income, or poor, can turn to the IMF for financing if it has a balance of payments need—that is, if it cannot find sufficient financing on affordable terms in the capital markets to make its international payments and maintain a safe level of reserves.

The volume of loans provided by the IMF has fluctuated significantly over time. The oil shock of the 1970s and the debt crisis of the 1980s were both followed by sharp increase in IMF lending. In the 1990s, the transition process of Central and Eastern Europe and the crises in emerging market economies led to further surges of demand for IMF resources. Deep crises in Latin America and Turkey kept demand for IMF resources high in the early 2000s. IMF lending rose again since late 2008 in the wake of the global financial crisis. In recent years IMF has supported Greece and has called on Euro-zone Ministers to offer debt relief.[30]

IMF loans are meant to help member countries tackle balance of payments problems, stabilise their economies, and restore sustainable economic growth. Upon request by a member country, IMF resources are usually made available under a lending arrangement; specify the economic policies and measures a country has agreed to implement to resolve its balance of payment problems. The economic policy programme underlying an arrangement is formulated by the country in consultation with IMF and is presented to the Fund's Executive Board.[31]

The IMF's concessional facilities for Low Income Countries (LICs) under the Poverty Reduction and Growth Trust (PRGT) were reformed in 2013 as part of broader efforts to make the Fund's financial support more flexible and better tailored to the diverse needs of LICs. The norms and limits for concessional facilities were expanded in 2015 to maintain their levels to increasingly production, trade and capital flows. The Standby Credit Facility (SCF) provides financial assistance to LICs with short term or potential balance of payments needs. The Rapid Credit Facility (RCF) also provides rapid financial assistance with limited conditionality to LICs facing urgent balance of payments need. Financing under the RCF carries a zero interest rate, has grace period of 5 ½ years and a final maturity of 10 years.[32] The IMF is not a development bank and, unlike the World Bank and other development agencies, it does not finance projects.

At the same time, the global financial crisis has highlighted the need for effective global financial safety nets to help countries cope with adverse shocks. A key objective of recent lending reforms has therefore been to complement the traditional crisis resolution role of the IMF with more effective tools for crisis prevention.

Critics argue that IMF policies serve primarily the interests of advanced countries. Like the bankers, the G-8 is more concerned about getting their money back. IMF conditionally squeezes developing countries to pay debts, which reduces resources for domestic growth. Developing countries have to keep borrowing, debts accumulate, and the pernicious cycle persists. For the first time in 1995, the IMF and World Bank set up a programme to reduce the debts of heavily indebted poor countries (HIPCs). The HIPC programme targeted 41 deeply distressed developing countries for debt relief. In 2005, the G-8 countries supplemented the HIPC program with the Multilateral Debt Relief Initiative (MDRI). MDRI cancels the complete debt owed to multilateral institutions as countries fulfill their obligations under the HIPC programme. By 2008, 33 countries, 27 from the African continent, received debt relief totaling US$ 49 billion.[33]

II. World Bank

The International Bank for Reconstruction and Development (IBRD and later World Bank) was originally established 1944 at the Bretton Woods to fund post-World War II reconstruction and development in Europe but soon turned to the task of economic development. The bank assisted development activities in other countries. Like IMF, the World Bank is an intergovernmental grouping with a Board of Governors and Executive Board. Funded by contributions from members and borrowing on global capital markets, the bank makes lending decisions on market principles — loan rates and prospects for repayment. For many years, the bank funded large, mega infrastructure projects such as dams that critics argued provided little help to the poor and ignored environmental consequences.[34] In recent years, the bank has focused more on the problems of the poorest countries, has raised additional funds for development. It provides borrowers with low-interest loans to alleviate poverty and stimulate sustainable economic development. The World Bank's official goal is the reduction of poverty. According to its Articles of Agreement (as amended and effective from February 16, 1989), all its decisions must be guided by a commitment to the promotion of foreign investment and international trade and to the facilitation of capital investment.

Since its inception in 1944, the World Bank has expanded from a single institution to a closely associated group of five development institutions. Its mission evolved from the International Bank for Reconstruction and Development as a facilitator of post-war reconstruction and development to the present-day mandate of eradication of poverty, worldwide. The World Bank is a vital source for financial and technical assistance to developing countries around the world. The bank is having a unique partnership with poor countries to reduce poverty and support development. The World Bank group is headquartered in Washington D.C. The current President of the World Bank is Jim Yong Kim.

The World Bank group consists of five institutions and is managed by their member countries:[35]

• The International Bank for Reconstruction and Development (IBRD): It lends to governments of middle income and credit worthy low-income countries. As a part of the World Bank Group, IBRD aims to end extreme poverty by 2030 and to promote shared prosperity in a sustainable manner. It seeks to achieve these objectives by providing loans, guarantees, risk management products, and expertise on development related discipline, as well as by coordinating responses to regional and global challenges. New lending commitments by IBRD were to the extent of US$ 23.5 billion in fiscal 2015 for 112 operations.[36]

- The International Development Association (IDA): It provides interest-free loans- called credits and grants - to governments of the poorest countries. IDA's funding supports countries' efforts to increase economic growth, reduce poverty, and improve the living conditions of the poor. In 2015, 77 countries were considered eligible to receive IDA assistance. India has graduated from IDA assistance at the end of the fiscal 2014 but will receive transitional support on an exceptional basis. IDA commitments for infrastructure includes energy and mining; transportation; water, sanitation and flood protection; and information and communication. IDA commitments amounted to US$19.0 billion in fiscal 2015, including US$15.9 billion in credits, US$2.4 billion in grants, and US$600 million in guarantees. The largest share of resources was committed to Africa, which received US$10.4 billion.[37]
- The International Finance Corporation (IFC): The IFC a member of the World Bank groups, is the largest global development institutions focused exclusively on the private sector. IFC help developing countries achieve sustainable growth by financing investment, mobilising capital in international financial markets, and providing advisory services to businesses and governments.
- The Multilateral Investment Guarantee Agency (MIGA). The MIGA was created in 1988 as a member of the World Bank Group to promote foreign direct investment into developing countries to support economic growth, reduce poverty, and improve people's lives. MIGA fulfils this mandate by offering political risk insurance (guarantees) to investors and lenders.
- The International Centre for Settlement of Investment Disputes (ICSID): It provides international facilities for conciliation and arbitration of investment disputes.

World Bank's adjustment programmes were usually wider in scope than those promoted by the IMF having a more long-term development focus. However, in emphasising the need to promote growth by expanding trade, World Bank helps in maintaining dependency and poverty. Development disparities thus became entrenched and during the 1990s even widened, through a structural imbalance in trade that allowed developed countries to grow rich by selling high price and capital intensive goods, while developing countries sold low price and labour intensive goods, often in highly volatile markets. In this way, the World Bank, together with the IMF, presided over a substantial transfer of wealth from peripheral areas of the world economy to its industrialised core.

Since 2002, World Bank poverty reduction programmes have been increasingly formulated through negotiations with recipient countries, accepting the need for higher local control and accountability and for projects to be tailored better, according to the needs of recipient countries. The desire to demonstrate a greater willingness to take on board the ideas of the developing world, particularly in the light of 2007-09 global crises, led the Bank in the spring of 2010 to boost its capital by US$ 86 billion, the first increase in 20 years.[38]

The World Bank Group has set two goals for the world to achieve by 2030: [39]

- End extreme poverty by decreasing the percentage of people living on less than US$ 1.90 a day to no more than 3 percent.
- Promote shared prosperity by fostering the income growth of the bottom 40 percent in every country.

The World Bank provides low income interest loans, zero to low interest credits, and grants to developing countries. They support a wide array of investments in areas such as education, health, public administration, infrastructure, financial and private sector development, agriculture, environmental and natural resource management. The World Bank also co-finances with governments, multilateral institutions, commercial banks, export credits agencies and private sector investors. It also provides support to the developing countries through policy advice, research and analysis. To ensure that countries can access the best global expertise and help generate cutting-edge knowledge, the Bank is constantly seeking to improve the way it shares its knowledge and engages with clients and public at large.[40] The World Bank continues to play an integral role in helping countries reduce poverty and improve the well being of their citizens. Their funding provides a resource to countries to utilise the services of global companies to accomplish their objectives. Its focus is on helping countries to achieve the Millennium Development Goals.

III. World Trade Organisation

The World Trade Organisation was established in 1995, succeeding the GATT which emerged as the basis of the postwar international trading order in 1948. Before GATT was created, an initiative to establish International Trade Organisation was proposed in 1945 by the UN Economic and Social Council. UN Conference on Trade and Employment was held in Havana, Cuba, in 1947 to establish ITO. Unfortunately, the ITO treaty was not approved by the US and a few other countries. The World Trade Organisation (WTO) is the only global international organisation dealing with the rules in respect of trade between nations. The most vital part of WTO are the WTO agreements, negotiated and signed by the bulk of the world's trading nations and ratified by their Parliaments. The objective of WTO is to facilitate producers of goods and services, exporters, and importers conduct their business.[41]

In the first place, GATT existed only as a set of norms and rules, acquiring the semblance of an institutional character. The early Dillon (1960-1961) and Kennedy (1964-67) rounds reduced trade and non-tariff barriers in key industrial sectors, and the Tokyo Round (1973-79) achieved deep tariff cuts and launched efforts to confront controversial issues such as favorable trade treatment for poor countries. The Uruguay Round, which concluded in 1993 proposed to establish the WTO. The emergence of the WTO was a response to the changing imperatives of the international trading system in the 1980s, linked to the wider triumph of neo-liberalism and the acceleration of globalisation. The WTO is stronger than GATT, particularly in the field of settlement of disputes. Under the GATT, the settlement of disputes required the agreement of all members of a disputes panel, which comprised the members of the GATT Council, as well as the parties to the dispute itself. Under the WTO, settlement on judgments in the case of disputes can only be rejected if they are opposed by all members of the Dispute Settlement Body, to which all member states belong.[42] This has made the WTO the primary instrument of international law.

The World Trade Organisation (WTO) is intended to provide, the common institutional framework for the conduct of trade and relations among its members. Its main function is to ensure that trade flows as smoothly, predictably and freely as possible. It has 159 member countries and is based in Geneva, Switzerland. Currently, Roberto Azevedo from Brazil is the Director General.

Decisions on various issues are made by the entire membership. This is usually by consensus. A majority vote is also likely but it has never been made use of in the WTO, and it is extremely rare under the WTO's predecessor, GATT. The WTO's agreements have been ratified by all countries through their Parliaments. The WTO's top level decision-making body is the Ministerial Conference which meets at least once every two years.

Role of WTO

The WTO is run by its member governments. All major decisions are made by the members as a whole, either by Ministers (who usually meet at least once every two years) or by the Ambassadors or delegates of member countries (who meet regularly in Geneva).

While the WTO is made use of by its member states, it needs a Secretariat to coordinate its activities. The Secretariat employs over 600 staff and has experts with different backgrounds such as lawyers, economists, statisticians and communications experts to assist WTO members regularly to ensure, *inter-alia* , that negotiations progress smoothly, and that the rules of international trade are correctly applied and enforced.

Trade Negotiations

The WTO agreements cover goods, services and intellectual property. They spell out the principles of liberalisation, and the exceptions which are admissible. They include the commitments of individual countries to lower customs tariffs and other trade barriers, and to open up and keep open markets in the services sector. They set up a prescribed procedure for settling disputes. These agreements are not static; they are renegotiated from time to time and new agreements can be added to the package. Many are being negotiated under the Doha Development Agenda, launched by WTO Trade Ministers in Doha, Qatar, in November 2001.

Implementation and Monitoring

WTO agreements require governments to make their trade policies transparent by notifying the WTO about laws in force and measures adopted. Various WTO councils and committees seek to ensure that these requirements are being followed and that WTO agreements are being properly implemented. All WTO members must undertake periodic scrutiny of their trade policies and practices, each review containing reports by the country concerned to the WTO Secretariat.

Dispute Settlement

The WTO's procedure for resolving trade disputes under the Dispute Settlement Understanding is vital for enforcing the rules and for ensuring that trade flows smoothly. Countries bring disputes to the WTO if they think their rights under the agreements are being infringed. Decisions by specially appointed independent experts are based on interpretations of the agreements and commitment of individual countries who are parties to the dispute.

Building Trade Capacity

WTO agreements have included special provision which allow developing countries, longer period of time to implement agreements and commitments, measures to increase their trading opportunities, and necessary support to help them build their trade capacity, to handle disputes and to implement technical standards. The WTO organises a number of technical cooperation missions to developing countries annually. It also holds several courses each year in Geneva for government officials in order to enable them understand various aspects pertaining to WTO and how the respective countries would be able to benefit from it. WTO aims to help developing countries develop the skills and infrastructure needed to expand their trade.

Outreach

The WTO maintains regular dialogue with non-governmental organisations, parliamentarians, other international organisations, the media and the general public on various aspects of the WTO and the ongoing Doha negotiations, with the aim of enhancing cooperation and increasing awareness of WTO activities.

World Trade Organisation and the Principles of the Trading System

Trade without Discrimination

Most-favoured-nation (MFN): WTO stipulates that all contries should be treated equally.   Under the WTO agreements, no country can normally discriminate between their trading partners. If a special favour is granted to any country (such as a lower customs duty rate for one of their products) then similar benefits will have to be extended to all other WTO members.

No country should discriminate between trading partners (giving them equal benefits or treating them as most favoured nation or MFN status). And it should not discriminate between its own and foreign products, services or nationals (giving domestic products any special treatment at national level).[43]

Free Trade through Negotiation

Lowering trade barriers is one of the most obvious means of encouraging trade. The barriers could include customs duties (or tariffs) and measures such as import bans or quotas that restrict quantities selectively. From time to time other issues such as red tape and exchange rate policies have also been discussed. Opening markets can be beneficial, but it also requires adjustment. The WTO agreements allow countries to introduce changes gradually, through "progressive liberalisation". Developing countries are usually given a longer period of time to fulfill their obligations.

Predictability through Binding and Transparency

Sometimes, promising not to raise a trade barrier can be as important as lowering one, because the promise gives businesses a clearer view of their future opportunities. With stability and predictability, investment is encouraged, jobs are created and consumers can fully enjoy the benefits of competition through better choice and lower prices. The multilateral trading system is an attempt by governments to make the business environment stable and predictable. Transparency is the pillar of WTO. WTO members are required to publish their trade regulations and to make sure any decisions affecting trade are notified to other WTO members and to the WTO Secretariat itself.

Promoting Fair Competition

The WTO is sometimes described as a "free trade" institution, but that is not entirely accurate. The system does allow tariffs and, in limited circumstances, other forms of protection. More accurately, it is a system of rules dedicated to open and fair competition, without distortion.

The rules pertaining to non-discrimination—MFN and lack of special treatment on a national scale to help domestic products—are designed to secure fair conditions of trade. So too are those pertaining to dumping (resorting to export at below cost to gain market share) and subsidies. The issues are complex, and the rules try to lay down what is fair or unfair, and how governments can respond, in particular by charging additional import duties calculated to compensate the damage caused by unfair trade.

Many of the other WTO agreements aim to support fair competition: in agriculture, intellectual property, services, etc. The agreement on government procurement ('plurilateral'[44] agreement because it is signed by only a few WTO members) extends competition rules on purchases made by government entities in many countries to protect their farmers and supply to the poor at below market prices.

Safety Valves

In certain circumstances governments are allowed to restrict trade. For instance under the "Agreement on Safeguards", a country is allowed to restrict, temporarily, products from which a surge in imports have resulted due to any reason or is becoming a threat or serious injury to a specific domestic industry.[45]

Encouraging Development and Economic Reform

WTO tries to extend more beneficial terms for less developed countries— such as giving them more time to adjust, greater flexibility and special privileges. The WTO system contributes to development. On the other hand, developing countries need flexibility in terms of the time they need to implement the system's agreements. And the agreements themselves inherit the earlier provisions of GATT that allow for special assistance and trade concessions for developing countries.

Over three quarters of WTO members are developing countries and countries in transition to market economies. During the seven and a half years of the Uruguay Round, over 60 of these countries implemented trade liberalisation programmes autonomously. At the same time, developing countries and transition economies were more active and influential in the Uruguay Round negotiations than in any previous round, and they are even more so in the current Doha Development Agenda.

At the end of the Uruguay Round, developing countries were prepared to take most of the obligations that are required of developed countries. The agreements did give them transition periods to adjust to the more unfamiliar and, perhaps, difficult WTO provisions—particularly for the poorest, "least-developed" countries. More recently, developed countries have started to allow duty-free and quota-free imports for almost all products from least-developed countries. On all these, the WTO and its members are still going through a learning process. The current Doha Development Agenda includes developing countries' concerns about the difficulties they face in implementing the Uruguay Round agreements.

Assessment

The WTO has reviewed a variety of complaints, although trade in agriculture has generated the most disputes. Most have been brought by developed countries against one another or against Least Developed Countries (LDCs), but LDCs also use the WTO to correct what they view as trade injustice by rich states. For poor countries, poverty reduction and economic growth are more important than environmental and safety concerns.

In some respects, the WTO appears to be a more democratic body than the IMF or the World Bank. Decisions are made within the WTO on a one country one vote basis, and usually on a simple majority. This gives considerable weight to the views of developing countries which constitute more than two-thirds of the WTO's members. However, the WTO is a highly controversial organisation, which has often been the primary target of anti-globalisation or anti-capitalist protests, as in the case of the 1999 Battle of Seattle.

Criticism of World Trade Organisation (WTO)

Critics of the WTO argue that subtle biases operate within the decision making structures that systematically favour developed countries over developing ones. These include a general emphasis on consensus-based decision making, which tends to be disadvantageous for developing countries which may have no permanent representation at the WTO's Geneva headquarters or have delegations smaller than those of developed countries. However the economic rise of China, which became a WTO member in 2001, and the growing influence of emerging countries such as India, Brazil, Egypt and South Africa have started to alter the balance within the WTO. This was demonstrated in the Doha round of negotiations, which were initiated in 2001 but where suspended in 2009, largely due to disagreement over agriculture and textiles, where the USA and EU were unwilling to abandon protectionism.[46]

Nevertheless, the main ideological debate about the benefits of the WTO concentrates on its underpinning philosophy of free trade. While some argue that free trade brings prosperity to all and in the process, makes war less likely, others view fair trade as blatantly unfair and a cause of structural inequality.[47] The WTO has failed the world's poor. Trade related issues such as rich country subsidies and the ambiguity of trade rules have been ignored or intensified by the powerful countries. Pro-development policies such as special treatment and improved access to vital medicines have been deliberately neglected. Developing countries have been completely sidelined by the economic and political interests of global powers.[48] Serious and democratic debate on the purpose and powers of the WTO is long overdue. Rich countries do not want to give way to emerging economies and often circumvent WTO rules by engaging in bilateral talks to create deals, severely hampering the progress of developing nations. Developed countries have a steadfast adherence to free trade policies and find it beneficial to ignore social issues such as climate change and food security. The WTO must view trade "not as a goal in itself but as a means to achieving broader social, environmental and development goals", by demanding accountability from rich nations and increasing consultation with civil society.[49] If an agreement can't be reached on measures to help developing countries as a part of development agenda, then the relevance of the WTO and the multilateral trading systems need to be questioned. The inability of the WTO to adapt and adjust to emerging global trade priorities could create a new institution that can deal with the urgent global issues.

IV. Transnational Corporations (TNCs)

Transnational Corporation is any enterprise that undertakes foreign direct investment, owns or controls income gathering assets in more than one country, produces goods or services outside its country of origin, or engages in international production. TNCs are engines of global capitalism, knitting people together in a vast system of economic exchange. Transnational economic enterprises have existed for centuries and some enjoyed many of the prerequisites of sovereignty. For instance, British East India Company or the John Company was at its height, virtually ruling India with an army of 150,000 men.[50] A transnational or multinational corporation has its headquarters in one country and operates wholly or partially owned subsidiaries in one or more other countries.

The role of TNCs has expanded in recent decades. Their numbers grew from 7,000 in 1970 to over 82,000 in 2009. TNCs employ 77 million people, producing a quarter of the gross world product. By 2007, the 100 largest TNCs had assets of US$10.7 trillion, had sales in 2008 worth over US$8.5 trillion and employed over 15 million.[51]

Although TNCs may have a national center, they are transnational because they engage in direct foreign investment and conduct business in more than one country. Some have many subsidiaries. Ford, for example, employs about 159,000 employees and has some 70 plants worldwide.[52] TNCs are organised to pursue a coherent global strategy that permits units to poor knowledge, technology and financial resources. Most TNCs are located in the developed world while many of their foreign affiliates are in LDCs and they have immense economic clout. Of the world's 50 largest corporations in 2010, 18 have American roots, 6 Chinese, 5 French and 5 British, and 4 German. The net value of Walmart's in 2009 sales alone was more than the gross national income of Sweden. Walmart employs 2,100,000 people of whom 700,000 are non-American; making it the largest employer in Canada and Mexico and it has 8,300 stores and warehouse of which 4,000 are outside the US in 14 countries. Its net worth is US$261.3 billion.[53] General Electric with foreign assets of over US$401 billion ranks first among TNCs.[54]

Role of Transnational Corporations (TNCs)

The TNCs provide an inflow of capital into the developing country. Multinational Corporations provide employment and boost the local economy. Although wages seem very low, people in developing countries often see these new jobs as preferable to working as a subsistence farmer with even lower income. Multinational firms may help improve infrastructure in the economy. They may improve the skills of their workforce.[55] Foreign investment may stimulate spending on infrastructure such as roads and transport. The corporate firms help to diversify the economy away from relying on primary products and agriculture which are often subject to volatile prices and supply.[56]

The role of TNCs or MNCs has created wealth, new job opportunities and new tax revenues that arise from multinational corporations' generated income. By increasing the efficiency of capital flows, MNCs will contribute in reducing poverty in developing countries, improve their infrastructure, strengthen their human capital and always encourage countries to corporate and seek peaceful solutions for conflicts. TNCs have responsibilities on its employers, customers, governments, suppliers and communities as well as towards shareholders. Corporate social responsibility (CSR) that take part in protecting TNCs' business where business must include duty, do business honestly, legally and with integrity, make deals fairly, do not be corrupt and always obey the laws' of host countries.[57]

Developing new technology provides great opportunities to countries' economic growth as there will be a change in technology advance by improving information flows rapidly and increase the speed to integrate national economies in global economy. Countries that have relations with transnational corporation will be able to access to more advanced technology such as information technology as well as increasing their competencies and get a stronger position in the world market.[58]

Criticism of TNCs

There are several criticisms of TNCs. One is that they expropriate local resources and export them for their own benefit so that poor countries lose control over their assets. Critics also argue that TNCs create little local employment and reward executives for employing fewest possible number of workers. And while TNCs do create jobs, they hire few locals for senior positions and create privileged urban elites with little stake in helping local development. TNCs increase local demand for useless, unhealthy or dangerous products like cigarettes. One case involved the chemical giant Union Carbide that was implicated in an industrial disaster in Bhopal, India, in which thousands died. The plant was build in a densely populated neighbourhood, produced the pesticide carbaryl and the organic compound methyl isocynate.[59]

Another criticism is that TNCs meddle in local politics in ways ranging from outright bribery to illicit campaign contributions. In 1997, the world's developed countries agreed to ban bribery by companies seeking contracts, and several major corporations signed an agreement which show zero tolerance for paying bribes. Finally, TNCs have been accused of human rights abuses. In November 1997, a leaked internal audit of Nike, the maker of sports equipment, revealed the company was using child labour in unsafe conditions at its Vietnam facility.

In May 1998, Nike agreed to end its use of child labour and introduced US health safety standard in its Asian factories.[60]

The dominance of TNCs is most visible in developing countries that rely primarily on a narrow range of exports, usually primary goods. It has the ability to disrupt traditional economies, impose monopolistic practices, and assert a political and economic agenda on a country. TNCs are becoming more independent from the control and regulations of both the parent and the host economy. The position of corporations in the performance of world economy and the stimulation of growth and the economic efficiency, the stimulation of restructuring, the reinforcement of the market competition, the integration of enterprises and economies needs to be watched.

Conclusion

In conclusion, we can say that the interaction of international politics and economics are widely appreciated and its implications are very much visible in the global economy. It attempts to understand international and global problems using interdisciplinary tools and theoretical perspectives. The growing prominence of global political economy is the result of the continuing breakdown of boundaries between economics and politics. With the end of the Cold War, TNCs behaviour quickly spread to issues well beyond their role in geopolitics. The rise of Asia's newly industrialising countries and the increasing globalisation of production and finance spurred research on the role of MNCs in the allocation of capital and the control of information technology. The process of globalisation has generated an array of social and environmental problems as well. Growing inequality has had profound influence on quality of democracy and social stability. The rise of China, India and the creation of the Euro currency has reshaped geopolitics. Most importantly, globalisation has helped produce serious threats and crises that states and international institutions seem incapable of controlling, such as global warming, financial turmoil and refugee flows.

Notes

1. "The Global Economy" at http://www.whatiseconomics.org/the-global-economy, accessed on March 19, 2016.
2. Mansbach, W. Richard and Kirsten L. Taylor, *Introduction to Global Politics* (New York, Routledge, 2014), p.456.
3. "The First Common Market? The Hanseatic League", *History Today*, at http://www.historytoday.com/stephen-halliday/first-common-market-hanseatic-league, accessed on March 20, 2016
4. Brown, Chris and Kirsten Ainley, *Understanding International Relations* (New York, Palgrave Macmillan, 2009) p.156.

5. Lahaye, Laura , *Mercantilism* at http://www.econlib.org/library/Enc/Mercantilism.html, accessed on March 20, 2016.

6. Baylis, John, Steve Smith and et al., *The Globalization of World Politics: An introduction to International relations*(Oxford, Oxford University Press, 2008), , p.248.

7. Mansbach, n.2. p. 460.

8. *Essential of International Relations*, Available online at http://www.wwnorton.com/college/ polisci/essentials-of-international-relations5/ch/09/summary.aspx., accessed on March 20, 2016.

9. Baylis, n.6. p. 249.

10. Mansbach, n.2., p.462.

11. Strange, Susan, *Casino capitalism* (Manchester: Manchester University Press, 1997).

12. Mansbach, n.2. p.464.

13. Baylis, n.6. p. 2.

14. Frank, A. G, *Capitalism and Underdevelopment in Latin America* (New York: Monthly Review Press,1967).

15. Wallerstein, I, *The Modern World System* (New York: American Press, 1975).

16. Heywood, Andrew, *Global Politics* (New York, Palgrave Macmillan, 2011), p.460.

17. Baylis, n.6. pp.244-45.

18. The George C. Marshall Plan, also known as the European Recovery Program, Channeled over $13 billion to finance the economic recovery of Europe between 1948 and 1951. The Marshall Plan successfully sparked economic recovery, meeting its objective of restoring the confidence of the European people in the economic future of their own countries and of European as a whole.

19. Baylis., n.6. p.247.

20. Baylis., n.6 p.248.

21. Krueger, Anne O, " International Economic Organisation, Developing Country Reforms, and Trade", *The International Bureau of Economic Research*, March 26, 2016, at http://www.nber. org/reporter/winter00/krueger.html , accessed on March 26 , 2016.

22. Nau, Henry R, *Perspective on International Relations* (Washington D.C: CQ Press, 2009), p.520.

23. Ibid., p. 521.

24. "How the IMF promotes Global Economic Stability", *International Monetary Fund*, March 10, 2016, at https://www.imf.org/external/np/exr/facts/globstab.htm, accessed on March 27, 2016.

25. "Globalization 101", *The Levin Institute, The State University of New York*, at http://www. globalization101.org/uploads/File/IMF/imfall.pdf, accessed on March 27, 2016.

26. "IMF Surveillance", *International Monetary Fund*, March 23, 2016, at https://www.imf.org/ external/np/exr/facts/surv.htm, accessed on March 27, 2016.

27. Ibid.

28. "Technical Assistance and Training", *International Monetary Fund*, March 23, 2016, at https:// www.imf.org/external/np/exr/facts/tech.htm, accessed on March 28, 2016.

29. Ibid.

30. "Greece Crisis: IMF calls for Greek debt relief after bailout approved", August 15, 2015, *BBC News*, http://www.bbc.com/news/world-europe-33945263, accessed on March 28, 2016.

31. "IMF Lending", *International Monetary Fund*, March 22, 2016, https://www.imf.org/external/ np/exr/facts/howlend.htm, accessed on March 28, 2016.

32. Ibid.

33. Nau., n.22.,p.521.

34. Mansbach, n.2., p. 478.

35. *About The World Bank*, at http://www.worldbank.org/en/about, accessed on April 04, 2016.

36. "The Roles and Resources of IBRD and IDA", *The World Bank*, Annual Report 2015, Available online at http://www.worldbank.org/en/about/annual-report/roles-resources,accessed on April 04, 2016.

37. Ibid.

38. Heywood, n.16., p.470.

39. *The World Bank*, http://www.worldbank.org/en/about/what-we-do, accessed on April 04, 2016.

40. Ibid.,

41. *World Trade Organization*, https://www.wto.org/english/thewto_e/whatis_e/whatis_e.htm, accessed on April 10, 2016.

42. Heywood, n.16. pp. 471-72.

43. "Basic Principles of WTO", China Trade in Services, *Beijing Time*, Sunday April 10, 2016, at http://tradeinservices.mofcom.gov.cn/en/h/2007-10-24/7836.shtml, accessed on April 10, 2016.

44. A plurilateral agreement is a multinational legal or trade agreement between countries. It is an agreement between more than two countries but not a great many, which would be multilateral agreement.

45. "Principles of the WTO Trading System," Available online at http://moci.gov.af/en/page/8772, accessed on April 10, 2016.

46. Heywood, n.16. p.473.

47. Ibid.

48. Walker, Aurelie, "The WTO has Failed Developing Nations" *Global Policy Forum*, November 14, 2011, at https://www.globalpolicy.org/global-taxes/51022-the-wto-has-failed-developing-nations-.html?itemid=id#959, accessed on April 10, 2016.

49. Bergan, Ruth, "WTO Fails the Poorest Again", *Global Policy Forum* , at https://www.globalpolicy.org/global-taxes/50514-wto-fails-the-poorest--again.html?itemid=id#959, accessed on April 10, 2016.

50. Mansbach, n.2. p.480.

51. *World Investment Report 2009: Transnational Corporations, Agricultural Production and Development*, at http://unctad.org/en/docs/wir2009_en.pdf ,accessed on April 12, 2016.

52. Ford Motor Company, "Ford Global" (2010) at http://www.ford.com/about-ford/company-information/ford-international-websites. ,accessed on April 12, 2016.

53. *The World's Most Valuable Brands*, at http://www.forbes.com/companies/wal-mart-stores/, accessed on April 12, 2016.

54. Mansbach, n.2., p.483.

55. "Multinational Organisation", *Business Management*, at http://www.bbc.co.uk/bitesize/higher/business_management/business_enterprise/business_contemporary_society/revision/13/, accessed on April 14, 2016.

56. Pettinger, Tejvan, "Multinational Corporations in Developing Countries", March 17, 2009, at http://www.economicshelp.org/blog/1413/development/multinational-corporations-in-developing-countries/, accessed on April 14, 2016.

57. Role of Transnational Corporations (TNCs), at http://www.essay.uk.com/free-essays/marketing/role-of-transnational-corporations.php, accessed on April 15, 2016.

58. Ibid.

59. Mansbach, n.2. p.484.

60. Ibid.

CHAPTER 4

Global Resistances: Global Social Movements and Non Governmental Organisations

Since the end of the Cold War, a number of resistance movements have taken place in different parts of the world. We have seen the rise of popular movements all over the world, a resistance to the forces of imperialism, capitalism, and to subjugation. The global community has been a witness to the most recent Arab Spring, the world's largest coordinated anti-war protest against Iraq, to the rise of the occupation movement and the rise of indigenous resistance movement across the world. Some cases of global resistance movements have an anarchist undercurrent. The intensification of trans-border or transnational economic interaction, including global financial flows, require a corresponding transnational social and political response from social forces. It is precisely why the neoliberal elites and governments are constraining the ability of governments and conventional political parties to pursue substantive democracy and social justice so that neoliberal globalisation can be understood to be activating new social movements across the globe. So widespread and deep are the deleterious effects of neo-liberalism that it worked to stimulate people into action in defence of their own interests. Therefore, the new political economy of neoliberal globalisation encourages a great diversity of movements and creates both the objective need and the material conditions for these movements to unify at a global level.[1] Thus, the globalisation of capitalism leads directly to the globalisation of political activism.

The Concept of Global Civil Society

The advance of globalisation and the progressive de-territorialisation of economic, cultural and political life have also generally weakened the idea that society should be understood merely in domestic or national terms. Civil society groups are not formally part of the state apparatus; nor do they seek to gain control of state office.[2] One of the consequences of globalisation has been the emergence of 'transnational' or 'world society'.[3] Interest in the idea of a global civil society grew during the 1990s, as a mosaic of new groups organisation and movements started to appear, which both sought to challenge or resist what was seen as 'corporate' globalisation and articulate alternative models of social, economic and political development. This has happened against a backdrop of the spread of demands for democratisation around the world, in the aftermath of the Cold War, and in the light of the intensifying process of global interconnectedness. In some case, these groups and organisation rejected globalisation altogether, projecting as 'anti-globalisation' movement but in other cases they supported a reformed model of globalisation and seen as 'social democratic or 'cosmopolitan' globalisation.[4]

The emergence of a global civil society can best be explained through the theory of "countervailing power" developed by J.K Galbraith.[5] In his view, emergent global civil society is a direct reaction to the perceived domination of corporate interests within the globalisation process. The rise of global civil society is therefore part of a backlash against the triumph of neo-liberalism.[6] This helps to explain the ideological orientation of most of these new groups and movements, which broadly favour a global social justice or world ethics agenda, reflected in a desire to extend the impact and efficacy of human rights. This has deepened international law, develop citizen networks to monitor and put pressure on states and international organisations. The growth of such groups has been facilitated by the emergence of a framework of global governance, which has both provided civil society groups with sources of funding and given them the opportunity to engage in policy formulation and implementation. Other factors include the wider availability of advanced ICT to facilitate transnational communication and organisation and the development of a pool of intellectuals or educated professionals in both developed and developing countries which feel alienated by the globalised capitalist system.[7] The global civil society has emerged as a third force between TNCs and international organisations, representing neither the market nor the state.

In the context of globalisation, it is often said that civil society has assumed a significant global dimension on the basis of transnational networks of non-state actors, especially NGOs such as Amnesty International, Greenpeace, Oxfam International, and *Medecins sans Frontieres* whose memberships, common purpose, and organisational activities have spread across national borders. Global civil society has served as a source of governance through dissemination of information, formation of open forums for dialogue and debate, and advocacy of greater democracy, transparency and accountability in governmental and multilateral institutions. In this way, global civil society or global public spheres can help to prevent the powerful from owning power privately.[8] This expanding transnational or civil society layer has often been greeted as enhancing democracy and providing a counterbalance to the power of markets and transnational institutions.

Resisting Globalisation

The debate on the politics of globalisation and resistance is being simplified by advocates of neo-liberalism into binary opposition between pro-globalisation and anti-globalisation forces. Resistance to globalisation refers to the gamut of struggles and actions of social groups and individuals in response to the dislocating consequences of neoliberal reforms and its effects in the sphere of the economy, politics and identity/culture.[9] It is not a coincidence that the new global social movements of resistance are led primarily from the South, i.e. from the global periphery and semi-periphery. This composition of social forces of resistance reflects the fact that much of the gains of neoliberal economic globalisation have been the expense of the South and among its poor or working majority. The advent of better global communications has served not only the expansion of the global capital but also the expansion of global solidarity among resistance forces. With a broad array of social forces coming into action and able to communicate with one another, even to meet physically, it is natural that global solidarity movements pursue a politics that is not only more participatory and direct but also more inclusive. This is useful in order to mobilise the maximum strength of global social forces in opposition to corporate led neoliberal globalisation and in opposition to neo-imperialist war. Opposition to corporate control of the global economy and globalisation is over-arching them to unify the social movements of resistance.[10] Positive values also characterised these movements, which are ultimately about reinvigorating a politics based on grassroots motivation, participation, democracy, decentralisation and autonomy while at the same time striving to build bridges and solidarities.

The core values of the new global social movements of resistance include non-violent struggle, democratic practice, social justice, inclusiveness, secularism, peace, solidarity (in opposition to localism, parochialism and narrow nationalism or chauvinism) and equality (including opposition to patriarchal forms of oppression against women as well as class, caste and ethnic based discrimination). There is a more diffused pattern of ideas and organisation that characterises the new social movements with higher participation by women. For instance, the World Social Forum continues to argue for an open and plural process that works with a great diversity of resistances, organisation and proposals. It reflects an extremely broad agenda of the new social movements of resistance.[11] The new social movement continues to fight for social justice, citizenship, participatory democracy, universal rights and the right for people to decide their own future.

Politics of resistance call for the need to bring the state back to act as a countervailing force to neoliberal globalisation, but also of suitable new governance institutions to cope with the challenges of an interconnected world economy. This perspective is inspired by Karl Polanyi's notion of resistance as "counter- movement". This concept refers to the self-protective measures taken by society to cope with the disruptive and polarising effects of industrial capitalism in England during the 18th and 19th centuries. Neoliberal globalisation led to a new great counter-movement, a societal contestation to the effect of a market- driven integration.[12] Resistance to globalisation is about the struggles to overturn the trend towards a capitalist economy disengaging from socially defined functions. It is about reclaiming control of the market. Antonio Gramsci has introduced the notion of "counter-hegemonic resistance" which the resistance is about the actions of oppressed groups, or subaltern forces, directed at undermining the power strategy used by ruling classes to create and maintain social order in conditions of uneven capitalist development. The legitimacy of social order is secured with a combination of consent and domination. In its original inception, counter hegemony was directed at seizing control of the state apparatus through its direct control of the state apparatus through its direct assault or through long-term strategy to transform the social attitudes and values reproduced in civil society organisations.[13]

From this perspective, resistance to globalisation is about gaining control of the state by democratic means in order to advance a national popular political project and thereafter realign international political relations to transform globalisation. It is also about contesting the accepted and institutionalised knowledge and ideology that legitimates the common sense of neoliberal globalisation and its faith in the market.[14] The idea that wealth is generated at the expense of deprived people of their rights, leading to unprecedented levels of social inequality, disempowerment and ecological destruction.

Globalisation is seemingly omnipresent and resisting it has only grown dramatically. Anti-globalisers argue that globalisation has created a democratic deficit by empowering institutions in which people have no vote and unleashes economic and cultural forces over which they have no control. Globalisation is eroding the rights and capacity of people to determine their own future. The result is alienation and anxiety as losses are buffeted by forces beyond their control or understanding. Therefore, a wide variety of specific aspects of globalisation have become the focus of resistance movements. These include the exploitation of indigenous labour by MNCs, the adverse effect on the actions taken by the developed world on the environment (e.g. global warming) and threats posed by global culture to indigenous culture.[15] Resistance must be seen as being highly complex, contradictory and ambiguous, ranging from the radically progressive (the positions taken by the World Social Forum and its participation) to reactionary and conservative (including frontier style self-determination, isolationism, fundamentalism, neo-fascism and ultra-nationalism). In addition to making immediate gains, the resistance movement could constitute the beginning of a global civil society of a new public sphere that might uphold progressive values such as autonomy, democracy, peace, ecological sustainability and social justice.[16] The social movements are against the globalising efforts and policies of neo-liberal economic system of MNCs, of aggressively expanding nation-states, of large proselytising religions and McDonaldisation.

The construction of alternatives to neo-liberalism is also a form of resistance to globalisation that has been shaped by the expanding power of transnational corporations. Alternatives are seen in the emergence of new form of flexible organisation for resistance, such as transnational advocacy networks like "Our World Is Not for Sale" (OWINS) against neo-liberal agenda in the WTO; the Global Union organisation reflecting a renewed internationalism of the labour movement and transnational social movements.[17]

Characteristics of Social Movements

A social movement has the following characteristics: network of groups and activists, with an emerging identity, involved in conflicting issues, using mainly unconventional forms of participation. Large number of social movements identify themselves with a movement that is critical to the process of globalisation and define themselves as global citizens who have knowledge about global developments and express a sense of solidarity with the deprived. They also engage in unconventional actions such as street protests which increasingly aim at global targets. They have also used the internet as a platform to develop global organisational structure.[18] The heart of social movements is protests, which is based on three logics. Firstly, protest has the potential to cause material damage and has great symbolic value. Secondly, protests require great number of people to participate. Finally, there is the logic of witnessing violent moves from the authority on those who are engaged in acts of civil disobedience and also constitute potential risks to public and to their lives.

Contemporary Social Movements of Resistance

The heart of the resistance to globalisation lies in individuals, groups and organisations. It arises among those who are, or feel they are, wronged or oppressed by globalisation (e.g. the Zapatistas in Chiapas, Mexico) or among organisations supported more by those who come from the same social classes as those involved in globalisation (e.g. the members of an INGO like the Rainforest Alliance or Greenpeace), but which seeks to represent the interest of those who are adversely affected by it. Their actions often translate into opposition to neo-liberal globalisation or the "Washington Consensus"[19]. They involve opposition to economic globalisation. There is opposition against main organisations involved in globalisation such as The World Bank, the IMF, the WTO and also against regional efforts such as North American Free Trade Agreement (NAFTA).[20] The movement seeks a more democratic process of globalisation and seeks greater justice in the process of globalisation.

Globalisation from below also occurs at various other levels. Individuals can take an array of actions that serve to resist the aspects of globalisation they oppose. For example Jose Bove of France opposed the expansion of McDonald's, individuals refusing to buy global products (e.g. Coca-Cola), refusing to buy coffee in global chains of coffee shop (e.g. Starbucks), or refusing to ship in Wal-Mart because its ruthless commitment to low prices often translates into low-wage work in South. There are small, locally active, groups at the grassroot level that oppose globalisation.[21] There are religious fundamentalists such asthe Taliban in Afghanistan, Boko Haram, ISIS, Rashtriya Swayamsevak Sangh and its affiliates in India, who seek a return to a pure version of their religion, and resist global processes that they think are a threat to their purity.

Of great and growing importance today is the techno-politics of global resistance especially with the use of the Information and Communication Technology. There are new terrains for political struggle and places where new voices can be heard. Use of these technologies tend to be highly democratic and generally decommodified. They create domains where campaigns can be waged against global corporations. There are internet "hackers" who create havoc on the internet about government policies.[22]

Zapatista Movement

Since colonial era the voice of the indigenous people in Mexico have either been ignored or brutally silenced. Indigenous lands and resources have been repeatedly stolen and people themselves were exploited under some of the worst labour conditions in Mexico. In January 1994, the indigenous farmers of southern

Mexico took up arms and declared autonomy from the Mexican state; they call themselves the Zapatista, in honour of the leader of the 1910 Mexican Revolution, Emilliano Zapata. This uprising was a response to globalisation and free trade, especially the North American Free Trade Agreement (NAFTA). The demands of the Zapatistas could be called modest as they struggle for democracy and land reform in Chiapas.[23] They wanted dignity, land, liberty and the ability to decide their own future. After the Zapatista Army of National Liberation occupied the southern city of San Cristobal and engaged in a bloody street battle with the Mexican military, a cease-fire was reached and peace talks began. In 2003, they unveiled an ambitious project in anarchistic democracy. They developed Juntas of good government, governing bodies with rotating membership that are response to the bad governments i.e. the official Mexican state government structure. The Juntas are made up of representatives from autonomous Zapatista communities and make important decision.[24] Thus, the Zapatista movement ensured that all the members of their communities have a voice and through rotation of representatives and power distribution system does not stagnate.

The Zapatista movement attracted and inspired thousands of people around the world which have been influential on the global anti-capitalist movement or anti-globalisation. While the concrete implementation of autonomy, collective organising and self government are grounded in local cultures unique to Chiapas. The movement showed to the global community who are building their own local alternatives to neo-liberalism.

World Social Forum

People's movements around the world are working to demonstrate that the path to sustainable development, social and economic justice lies in alternative models for people-centered and self-reliance progress, rather than in neo-liberals globalisation. Indeed the origins and roots of the anti-globalisation movement can be traced at the WTO meetings in Seattle in late November 1999. The first World Social Forum (WSF) was organised in Porto Alegre, Brazil, from January 25 to 30, 2001, marking an opposition to the World Economic Forum held in Davos. A key overall focus was the lack of democracy in global economic and political affairs. Its slogan has been "Another World is Possible".[25] This means that there must be, and there is, an alternative to the neo-liberalism that dominates the world economically and politically. The Forum made evident the capacity of mobilisation that civil society has when faced with a new methodology, characterised by a guarantee of diversity and co-responsibility in the process of constructing the event. The success of the first WSF led to assessing the need of continuity. The forum offers an arena beyond formal politics, a space where activities and civil society groups can explore alternative pathways to social, economic and climate justice. In order to make possible international articulation of the WSF process, the International Council (IC) of the WSF was established in 2001. The IC was mandated to enhance and expand the diversity of the WSF process at the global level. The IC is a group of international networks from different regions of the world. It is constituted by several organisations working on issues including economic justice, human rights, environmental issues, labour, youth and women. Since the establishment of IC, the Secretariat of the WSF has been working on strengthening it as a political and operational stage of the WSF that contribute both defining strategic paths of the WSF as in mobilising and in other activities of an organisational nature.[26] The action of the International Council has favoured a greater interlocution among the organisations, both on a national and international level and has been fundamental for laying down the foundation for the WSF process in several countries.

The WSF 2004 in Mumbai marked a major step in the global advance of the WSF process and saw the participation of approximately one lakh delegates. It was followed by the next edition of the Forum in Porto Alegre, Brazil, in January 2005 attended by more than 1,20,000 delegates. Clearly, the WSF process has grown over the years and is able to attract increasingly larger participation from across the globe. The WSF meeting brings together social movements from around the world to discuss grassroots struggles for political change. It is a meeting place for social movements, freedom of expression, citizen exchanges, artistic demonstrations, advocacy and inspiration. It creates concrete commitments and leads to the development of action strategies by strong networks. Its mission is to build together in a movement of international solidarity, a better world founded on social and environmental justice of social economy, a participative democracy and the acknowledgement of equality for all.[27]

The World Social Forum was conceived as an open meeting space for deepening the reflection, the democratic discussion of ideas, the formulation of proposals, the free exchange of experiences and the articulation of civil society organisations and movements that are opposed to neoliberal globalisation and the domination of the world capital and by any other form of imperialism. In accordance with its "Charter of Principles" WSF is constituted as a plural and diversified, non-confessional, non-governmental and non-partisan. Some of its principles are:[28]

- The World Social Forum is an open meeting place for reflective thinking, democratic debate of ideas, formulation of proposals, free exchange of experiences and interlinking for effective action, by groups and movements of civil society that are opposed to neo-liberalism and to domination of the world by capital and any form of imperialism, and are committed to building a planetary society directed towards fruitful relationships among humankind and between it and the Earth.

- The World Social Forum at Porto Alegre was an event localised in time and place. Porto Alegre's declaration that "another world is possible" becomes a permanent process of seeking and building alternatives.

- The World Social Forum is a world process. All the meetings that are held as part of this process have an international dimension.

- The alternatives proposed at the World Social Forum stand in opposition to a process of globalisation commanded by the large multinational corporations and by the governments and international institutions at the service of those corporations' interests, with the complicity of national governments. They are designed to ensure that globalisation in solidarity will prevail as a new stage in world history. This will respect universal human rights and those of all citizens – men and women – of all nations and the environment and will rest on democratic international systems and institutions at the service of social justice, equality and the sovereignty of peoples.

- The World Social Forum brings together and interlinks only organisations and movements of civil society from all the countries in the world, but it does not intend to be a body representing world civil society.

- The meetings of the World Social Forum do not deliberate on behalf of the World Social Forum as a body. No one, therefore, will be authorised, on behalf of any of the editions of the Forum, to express positions claiming to be those of all its participants. The participants in the Forum shall not be called on to take decisions as a body, whether by vote or acclamation, on declarations or proposals for action that would commit all, or the majority, of them and that propose to be taken as establishing positions of the Forum as a body. It thus does not constitute a locus of power to be disputed by the participants in its meetings, nor does it intend to constitute the only option for interrelation and action by the organisations and movements that participate in it.

- Nonetheless, organisations or groups of organisations that participate in the Forum's meetings must be assured the right, during such meetings, to deliberate on declarations or actions they may decide on, whether singly or in coordination with other participants. The World Social Forum undertakes to circulate such decisions widely by the means at its disposal, without directing, hierarchising, censuring or restricting them, but as deliberations of the organisations or groups of organisations that made the decisions.

- The World Social Forum is a plural, diversified, non-confessional, non-governmental and non-party context that, in a decentralised fashion, interrelate organisations and movements engaged in concrete action at levels from the local to the international, to build another world.
- The World Social Forum will always be a forum open to pluralism and to the diversity of activities and ways of engagingthe organisations and movements that decide to participate in it, as well as the diversity of genders, ethnicities, cultures, generations and physical capacities, providing they abide by this Charter of Principles. Neither party representations nor military organisations shall participate in the Forum. Government leaders and members of legislatures who accept the commitments of this Charter may be invited to participate in a personal capacity.
- The World Social Forum is opposed to all totalitarian and reductionist views of economy, development and history and to the use of violence as a means of social control by the State. It upholds respect for human rights, the practices of real democracy, participatory democracy, peaceful relations, in equality and solidarity, among people, ethnicities, genders and peoples, and condemns all forms of domination and all subjection of one person by another.
- As a forum for debate, the World Social Forum is a movement of ideas that prompts reflection, and the transparent circulation of the results of that reflection, on the mechanisms and instruments of domination by capital, on means and actions to resist and overcome that domination, and on the alternatives proposed to solve the problems of exclusion and social inequality that the process of capitalist globalisation with its racist, sexist and environmentally destructive dimensions is creating internationally and within countries.
- As a framework for the exchange of experiences, the World Social Forum encourages understanding and mutual recognition among its participant organisations and movements and places special value on the exchange among them, particularly on all that society is building to centre economic activity and political action on meeting the needs of people and respecting nature, in the present and for future generations.
- As a context for interrelations, the World Social Forum seeks to strengthen and create new national and international links among organisations and movements of society, that – in both public and private life – will increase the capacity for non-violent social resistance to the process of dehumanisation that the world is undergoing and to the violence used by the State, and

reinforce humanising measures being taken by the action of these movements and organisations.

- The World Social Forum is a process that encourages its participant organisations and movements to shift their actions, from the local level to the national level and seek active participation in international contexts, as issues of planetary citizenship and to introduce the global agenda of change-inducing practices experimented in building a new world in solidarity.

The WSF is by design, not a political movement or an actor, but merely an arena in which like-minded people can exchange ideas on global issues. The very diversity of those involved in the WSF makes the development of concrete political proposals. The WSF continues to struggle with its identity and role in globalisation.[29] The WSF is a huge social network based on "cyberactivism" which is a cultural logic of networking-- the creation of horizontal ties and connections among diverse and autonomous elements; the free and open communication of information among and between elements; coordination among the elements that is decentralised and involves directly with democratic decision making; and networking that is self-directed.[30] An important aspect of the WSF is that of decentralisation. The forum is meant to be plural, diversified, non-concessional, non-governmental and non-party.

World Social Forum 2016

World Social Forum, Montreal 2016 as an event and a process included the wider process of WSF promoting convergence of people energies and solutions for building another world.[31] The WSF-2016 will make history as the first event of its kind to take place in a developed country. Beyond the North-South divide and facing the context of global crisis affecting all of humanity and actors for solutions from all continent act together. The WSF-2016 is designed as a collective and human process which is based on five core values: inclusion and openness, transparency, horizontally, self management and independence. It is addressed to all citizens and activities organisations who believe that another world is not only possible, but especially necessary. The WSF 2016 is based on three fundamental principles: First, the WSF is an open process whose function is to facilitate beyond the 2016 event, the meeting and collaboration of organisation and individuals around the world who are working to build another world. Second, participation in the WSF is a chance for all social transformation actors, beyond the exchange and discussions, to develop or strengthen common sustainable actions and to disseminate source of inspiration. And finally beyond the time of assembly, the

WSF event allows for the creation of a strong symbolic space which materialises an original occupation of spaces that give visibility to practices heralding other possible world.[32] There are countless alternatives that flourish locally around the world to build communities more cohesive and respectful of the human being and the limits of the planet. The challenge is to bring these agents of change across the North- South divide, enabling them to exchange, their messages and actions and fuel positive momentum for change. Think global and act local.

Criticism to World Social Forum

The most common criticisms of the forum is that it is simply too chaotic and disorganised. Some people believe that the presence of too many participants means that there is no clearly defined agenda and therefore, no real ability to implement any change. Owen Worth argues that the Forum has already made itself useless because of its exclusivity, rather than being inclusive. He calls it as "elitist tool for NGOs and certain developing nations". Worth argues that the agenda of the WSF has been developed by only a small group of people participating in the Forum.[33] Furthermore, those people who are able to participate in the Forum are themselves, from fairly privileged background. Nearly 30 percent of the participants have university education and 80 percent have daily access to the internet. WSF seeks to limit top down leadership by the elite and is characterised by its plurality and diversity. The WSF does not issue a political platform or an agenda at the conclusion of its events. Another common criticism of the WSF comes in the form of its repetitiveness and failure to move toward. Some argue that every year the same arguments are expounded, yet it does not seem to be progressing. Proponents of WSF believe that it is heading in the correct direction.[34] The issues addressed by WSF participants seem redundant to the outside, but the topics discussed continue to remain relevant year after year.

Significance of Resistance to Globalisation

Powerful social and environmental movements which claim alternative policies seeking social and environmental justice have erupted around the world. People have come together from around the world to consolidate efforts to reverse the global rush to oligarchic rule and environmental catastrophe.[35] Global efforts to defend the environment, end poverty and marginalisation, advance in women's rights, protect human rights, and promote fair and dignified employment are all being undermined as a consequence of the concentration of wealth and power in the hands of a few. The current clampdown on civil society taking place in many parts of the world is precisely because it represents a challenge to the nexus of money and power.[36] Activists at the WSF have shown that different issues have unified them to bring social justice or climate justice, economic rights or civil rights. These are all part of a common struggle for a world in which everyone matters and in which the power of ordinary people can challenge the people with power.[37] Resistance to globalisation is occurring in the form of extreme right political movements that seek to defend ideas such as frontier style self-determination, national isolationism and fundamental culture against imposition of total global governance or modern liberal and secular culture.

Non-Governmental Organisation

Non-Governmental Organisations are viewed as the key actors within global civil society. Many of the NGOs are institutionalised and professionalised and many of the international NGOs constitute a significant group of political actors on the global stage. The politics of an individual country cannot be understood without knowing what groups lobby the government and what debate has been there in the media. Similarly, international diplomacy does not operate on the consultation from the global civil society.[38] Advocacy NGOs have had a variety of high profile successes, often constraining the influence of TNCs and altering the policy direction of national governments and international organisations. NGOs' pressure during the UN's Earth Summit in Rio in 1992 contributed to a treaty to control the emission of greenhouse gases. The International Campaign to Ban Land Mines, a network of more than 14,000 NGOs working in 90 countries was effective in 1997 in getting the agreement of some 120 states to ban the production, use and stockpiling of anti-personnel landmines. The Multilateral Agreement on investment negotiated by OECD aimed at liberalising foreign investment and reducing domestic regulation was pushed off its political agenda by a sustained NGO campaign.[39] As a result of pressure, primarily from American groups, the United Nations Charter contains Article 71, providing for the Economic and Social Council (ECOSOC) to consult the NGOs.

Role of NGOs

Non-Governmental Organisation cannot be a profit making body and cannot use or advocate violence. It must respect the norm of non-interference in the international affairs of states. And NGOs concerned with human rights should not restrict their activities to a particular group, nationality or country.

NGOs can facilitate communication from people to the government and from the government to the people. Communication upward involves informing government about what local people are thinking, doing and feeling and while communication downward involves informing local people about what the government is planning and doing. NGOs become spokespersons or ombudsmen for the poor and attempt to influence government policies and programmes on their behalf. It plays roles of advocates for the poor and implementers of government programmes; from agitators and critics to partners and advisors; from sponsors of pilot projects to mediators. NGOs can communicate to the policy-making levels of government, information about the lives, capabilities, attitudes and cultural characteristics of people at the local level.[40]

Expansion of NGOs and Globalisation

NGOs are seen as one of the key actors in the global economy, together with governments and firms. The creation of a complex global economy has had effects way beyond the international trade in goods and services. It leads to globalisation of unions, commercial bodies, the professions which participate in the relevant international regimes. Most companies, in each distinct area of activity have formed organisations to facilitate communication, to harmonise standards and to manage adaptation to complex change. Equally, the employees have faced common problems in different countries and so trade unions and professional bodies have developed their own transnational links. Any form of international regime to formulate policy for an industry, whether it is non-governmental or intergovernmental will encourage the strengthening of the global links among the NGOs concerned with its activities. The technical revolution increased density, speed and reduced the cost of communication. The political revolution lies in these changes bringing rapid global communication within the capabilities of most people. Changes in communication constitute a fundamental change in the structure of world politics.[41] Global authority is highly decentralised, and independent states control all functions of the government, including security. States might differ in terms of how much independence they give to civil society groups and individuals. But global balance of power system generally regards non-governmental actors where they exist, as subordinate to national actors.[42] Governments can no longer control the flow of information across the borders of their country. NGOs from each country may combine in four ways: as international NGOs, as advocacy networks, caucasus and as governance networks. NGOs can directly affect governments, directly affect firms, indirectly (moderate or mediate) the business-government relationship, and/ or act as nodes with business-government-NGO network.[43] It also influences the major decision process of the international organisation. The growth and interaction of NGOs and Inter-Governmental Organisations (IGOs) constitute the central arena of emerging global governance.

Conclusion

The most important theoretical and practical question facing the new social movements of global resistance is whether they are capable of acting as a counter hegemonic bloc in global politics and achieving significant transformation of the global system. The real challenge in this new wave of resistance to capitalist globalisation is to maintain the impetus to action and to global solidarity and achieve more concrete political results. It is the diversity of the movement and their insistence on participation, inclusiveness, and autonomy that gives the new movements their real strength. These same qualities now challenge the global movement to solve the problem of political representation and organisation in the new global politics of resistance.[44] Global civil society and non-state actors constitute one pillar of global governance. Supporters of global civil society argue that it has effectively reconfigured global power, providing a kind of bottom up democratic vision of civilising world order. NGOs populate a large space in global affairs across many sectors - commercial, environment, human rights, etc. and increasingly affect relations with and among governments. NGOs in this space also increasingly agree on basic human rights and urge all governments to respect them.

Notes

1. Gills, Barry K. (ed)., *Globalization and the Politics of Resistance*(New York: St. Martin's Press,2000).
2. Scholte, Jan Aart, "Global Civil Society: Changing the World?", Centre for the Study of Globalization and Regionalization, University of Warwick, at http://home.aubg.edu/faculty/mtzankova/POS%20102%20Readings/Scholte_Global%20Civil%20Society.pdf, accessed on April 15, 2016.
3. Buzan, Barry, *From International to World Society?* (Cambridge: Cambridge University Press, 2004).
4. Heywood, Andrew, *Global Politics* (New York: Palgrave Macmillan, 2011), p.150.
5. Countervailing power was a term coined by Galbraith to describe the ability of large buyers in concentrated downstream markets to extract price concessions from suppliers.
6. Buzan, n.3. p.90.
7. Heywood, n.4. p.152.
8. Kean, J, *Global Civil Society?* (Cambridge: Cambridge University Press, 2003).
9. Saguier, Marcelo, "Resistance to Globalization" in George Ritzer, *The Wiley Blackwell Encyclopedia of Globalization*, Blackwell Publishing Ltd. at https://www.academia.edu/2643851/Resistance_to_globalization?auto=download, accessed on April 16, 2016.

10. Broad, Robin (ed.) (2002), *Global Backlash: Citizen Initiative for a Just World*, (Lanham, MD: Rowman and Littlefiled, 2002).

11. Chase, Dunn, Christopher and Barry Gills *Understanding Waves of Globalization and Resistance in the Capitalist World: Social Moments and Critical Globalization Studies*, at http://irows.ucr. edu/papers/irows12/irows12.htm, accessed on April 16, 2016.

12. Munck, R. , *Globalization and Contestation: the New Great Counter- Movement* (New York: Routledge, 2007).

13. Saguier, n.9.

14. Mittelman, J.H. *Whither Globalization? The Vortex of Knowledge and Ideology* (London: Routledge, 2004).

15. Kahn, Richard and Douglas Kellner . "Resisting Globalization" In George Ritzer , (ed.) *The Blackwell Companion to Globalization* (Malden, MA: Blackwell, 2007).

16. Ritzer, George ,*Globalization: The Essentials* (UK: Willey Blackwell, 2011), p.301.

17. Saguier,n.9.

18. Ritzer, n.16. , p.301.

19. The policy movement in the 1990s advocating market oriented ideas for developing nations.

20. Brooks, Thom, (ed.) *The Global Justice Reader*, (Malden, MA : Blackwell, 2008).

21. Ritzer, n.16. p.303.

22. Mention may be made about Edward Snowden and Julian Assange who have exposed the US government's secret classified document.

23. *Brief Historical Background to the Zapatista Movement*, Available at http://hemisphericinstitute. org/hemi/en/su10-tourism/item/879-su10-brief-historical-background-zapatista-movement, accessed on April 18, 2016.

24. "A Brief History of the Zapatista Movement and the Other Campaign in Mexico", *Media House*, at https://mediamousearchive.wordpress.com/2006/03/06/a-brief-history/, accessed on April 18, 2016.

25. Teivainen, Teivo "World Social Forum " In Jan Aart Scholte and Roland Robertson , eds., *Encyclopedia of Globalization* (New York: MTM Publishing, 2007).

26. "About WSF", at http://www.wsfindia.org/?q=node/2, accessed on April 19, 2016.

27. "Information", *World Social Forum 2016*, at https://fsm2016.org/en/sinformer/, accessed on April 19, 2016.

28. "About the World Social Forum", at https://fsm2016.org/en/sinformer/a-propos-du-forum-social-mondial/, accessed on April 19, 2016.

29. Ritzer, n.16. p. 307.

30. Juris, Jeffrey "The New Digital Media and Activist Networking within Anti -Corporate Globalization Movements." Annals 597 (January 2005), pp.189-208.

31. "2016 WSF", at https://fsm2016.org/en/sinformer/fsm-2016/, accessed on April 20, 2016.

32. "World Social Forum, Montreal, August 9-14, 2016", at https://fsm2016.org/wp-content/uploads/2015/11/One-pager-EN.pdf, accessed on April 20, 2016.

33. Worth, Owen , " The World Social Forum: Post Modern Prince or Court Jester?",(Paper Presented at *ISA's 49th Annual Convention, Bridging Multiple Divides*, San Francisco, US, March 23, 2008).

34. Corbeil, Jessica (2009), " A Movement of Ideas: The World Social Forum, is it a Model for Political Change?" *Canadian Centre for Policy Alternatives*, at http://www.policyalternatives.ca/sites/default/files/uploads/publications/Saskatchewan_Pubs/2009/Movement_of_Ideas_World_Social_Forum.pdf, accessed on April 20, 2016.

35. Campolina, Adriano, "World Social Forum can inspire activists to unite against the global power grab", *The Guardian*, March 23, 2015, at http://www.theguardian.com/global-

development/2015/mar/23/world-social-forum-tunis-activists-united-against-global-power-grab, accessed on April 20, 2016.

36. "World Social Forum 2015: Another World Is Possible", at http://350.org/world-social-forum-2015-another-world-is-possible/, accessed on April 20, 2016.

37. Ibid.

38. Baylis, John, Steve Smith and et al., *The Globalisation of World Politics:An Introduction to International Relations* (Oxford: Oxford University Press ,2008) p.339.

39. Heywood, n.4. p.154.

40. "Role of NGOS", at http://www.gdrc.org/ngo/ngo-roles.html, accessed on April 28, 2016.

41. Baylis, n.38. p.340.

42. Nau, Henry R. *Perspective on International Relations* (Washington D.C: CQ Press, 2009), p. 487.

43. Doh, Jonathan P., and Hildy Teegen , "Globalization and NGOS: Transforming Business, Government, and Society", *Journal of International Business Studies,* 2003, pp.565-66.

44. Chase Dunn n.11.

CHAPTER 5

The United Nations Organisation in a Globalising World

The growth in the number and importance of international organisations has been one of the most prominent features of world politics particularly since 1945. The formation of international organisation can be traced after the Napoleonic Wars which included the Congress of Vienna (1814-15) that created the Concert of Europe. Following the end of World War I, there was a surge in new international organisations. The League of Nations failed to maintain peace, leading to the outbreak of the Second World War in 1939. The outbreak of the Second World War revealed to the world the weaknesses of the League of Nations. It was felt that a much stronger international organisation should be created, if the world has to maintain peace. The significance of the phenomenon of international organisation has nevertheless been hotly disputed. Some see international organisations as a little more than a mechanism for pursuing traditional power of politics by other means, others claim that they contain the seeds of supranational or world government. The process of globalisation has affected the working system of the United Nations Organisation. Globalisation restraints the capacity of nation-states to perform as fully sovereign entities in a world where there is still no true global governance. As the world's only universal global organisation, the United Nations has become the foremost forum to address issues that transcend national boundaries and cannot be resolved by any one country acting alone.

To its initial goals of safeguarding peace, protecting human rights, establishing the framework for international justice and promoting economic and social progress, the United Nations has added new challenges, such as climate change, international terrorism and newly emerging diseases. While conflict resolution and peacekeeping continue to be among its most visible efforts, the UN, along with its specialised agencies, is also engaged in a wide array of activities to improve people's lives around the world – from disaster relief, through education and advancement of women, to peaceful uses of atomic energy. With the end of the Cold War, the globalisation process plunged the UN into another existential crisis. The UN has to rethink its approach, guiding principles, and operational tools to collective security, development and human rights.

Evolution of the United Nations Organisation

The World War I led to the formation of the League of Nations. The World War II led to the establishment of the United Nations Organisation. The victorious powers felt after World War I that there was a need for establishment of the League of Nations to institute a calming down effect , so that states would not enter unwisely into destructive wars. Similarly, the allied countries of World War II believed that a stronger world organisation was needed, one with a Security Council that has the authority to take binding decisions to oppose calculated aggression and cope with other threats to peace. In each case, the aim was to develop ways and means for maintaining peace and stability after a destructive world war. The UN was established in 1945 and aimed to correct the League of Nations Covenant's deficiencies. The intention of the major powers in formulating the UN Charter was to rectify the fundamental weakness of the League such as the absence of collective security arrangements for the maintenance of international peace and security and ultimate freedom of a member state to use force to effect a settlement.[1] The League of Nations broke down and international community was driven to World War II although the formal dissolution of the League occurred in 1946. League of Nations assets, property and some of its function were transferred to the UN.[2]

The Atlantic Charter

Even before the end of the war, in August 1941, the U.S. President, Franklin Roosevelt, and the British Prime Minister, Winston Churchill, met on a battleship, 'the Cruiser', in the mid-Atlantic and drew up the Atlantic Charter which was released on August 14, 1941.

United Nations Declaration or the Washington Declaration

On January 1, 1942, representatives of 26 Allied countries met in Washington and signed a Declaration of the United Nations. The signatories endorsed the principles of the Atlantic Charter. This was the first time that the term 'United Nations' was used. The UN Charter finally emerged after three major conferences—the Dumbarton Oaks Conference (1944), the Yalta Conference (1945) and the San Francisco Conference (1945). At the Dumbarton Oaks Conference the representatives of four major powers (Britain, the United States, the Soviet Union and China) agreed on proposals for the aims, structure and functioning of the United Nations. They voted for an Assembly, a Security Council, a Secretariat and an International Court. The Yalta Conference decided on the voting procedure to be followed by the Security Council.

Membership of the United Nations was to be opened to all peace-loving states. Representatives of 50 nations met at San Francisco to sign the Atlantic Charter. Poland signed it later and became one of the original 51 member states. The United Nations Organisation officially came into existence on October 24, 1945. The Charter had been ratified by the 5 big powers - Britain, China, France, the Soviet Union, and the United States and by a majority of the other signatories. The 24th of October is celebrated as United Nations Day. Today, the organisation has 193 members. The headquarters of the United Nations is located in New York, USA. The organisation has six official languages - English, French, Spanish, Russian, Chinese and Arabic. Its flag bears its emblem, a map of the world encircled by two bent olive branches.

The aim and objectives of the United Nations according to its Charter are:
- To maintain international peace and security.
- To develop friendly relations among nations on the basis of equality and the principle of self-determination.
- To foster worldwide cooperation in solving economic, social, cultural and humanitarian problems.
- To promote human rights and fundamental freedom for the people of the world.
- To serve as a centre where various nations can coordinate their activities towards the attainment of the objectives of the United Nations.
- To save succeeding generations from the scourge of war.

The UN has six principal organs to carry out its functions
- The General Assembly
- The Security Council
- The Economic and Social Council
- The Trusteeship Council
- The International Court of Justice 6. The Secretariat

United Nation Millennium Development Goals
The Millennium Development Goals are a UN initiative. The Millennium

Development Goals (MDGs) are the eight international development goals that were established following the Millennium Summit of the United Nations in 2000, following the adoption of the United Nations Millennium Declaration.

The Millennium Development Goals (MDGs) are the eight international development goals that were established following the Millennium Summit of the United Nations in 2000, following the adoption of the United Nations Millennium Declaration. All 189 United Nations member states at that time (there are 193 currently), and at least 23 international organisations, committed to help achieve the following Millennium Development Goals by 2015:[3]

1. To eradicate extreme poverty and hunger:
   - Extreme poverty has declined significantly over the last two decades. In 1990, nearly half of the population in the developing world lived on less than US$1.25 a day; that proportion is to be brought down to 14 percent by 2025.
   - Globally, the number of people living in extreme poverty has declined by more than half, from 1.9 billion in 1990 to 836 million in 2015. Most of the progress occurred since 2000.
   - The number of people in the working middle class—living on more than US$ 4 a day- has almost tripled between the period from 1991 and 2015. This group now makes up half of the workforce in the developing regions, up from just 18 percent in 1991.
   - The proportion of undernourished people in the developing regions has fallen by almost half since 1990, from 23.3 percent in 1990-1992 to 12.9 percent in 2014-2016.

2. To achieve universal primary education:
   - The primary school net enrolment rate in the developing regions has reached 91 per cent in 2015, up from 83 percent in 2000.
   - The number of children of primary school age who are not in schools worldwide has fallen by almost half, to an estimated 57 million in 2015, down from 100 million in 2000.
   - Sub-Saharan Africa has had the best record of improvement in primary education of any region since the MDGs were set. The region achieved a 20 percentage point increase in the net enrolment rate from 2000 to 2015, compared to a gain of 8 percentage points between 1990 and 2000.
   - The literacy rate among youths of age between 15 to 24 years has increased globally from 83 percent to 91 percent between 1990 and 2015. The gap between women and men has narrowed.

3. To promote gender equality and empower women:
   - As compared to 15 years ago, more girls are now attending schools. The developing regions as a whole have achieved the target to eliminate gender disparity in primary, secondary and tertiary education.
   - In Southern Asia, only 74 girls were enrolled in primary school for every 100 boys in 1990. Today, 103 girls are enrolled for every 100 boys.
   - Between 1991 and 2015, the proportion of women employed in the vulnerable sectors as a proportion of total females employed has declined by 13 percentage points. In contrast, employment in the vulnerable sectors among men fell by only 9 percentage points.
   - Women have gained ground in parliamentary representation in nearly 90 percent of the 174 countries with data available over the past 20 years. The average proportion of women in parliament has nearly doubled during the same period. Despite this, only one in five members are women.

4. To reduce child mortality:
   - The global under-five mortality rate has declined by more than half, dropping from 90 to 43 deaths per 1,000 live births between 1990 and 2015.
   - Despite population growth in the developing regions, the number of deaths of children under five has declined from 12.7 million in 1990 to almost 6 million in 2015 globally.
   - In sub-Sahara Africa, the annual rate of reduction of under-five mortality was over five times faster during 2005-2013 than it was during 1990-1995.
   - Measles vaccination helped prevent nearly 15.6 million deaths between 2000 and 2013. The number of globally reported measles cases declined by 67 percent during the same period.
   - About 84 percent of children worldwide received at least one dose of measles vaccine in 2013, up from 73 percent in 2000.

5. To improve maternal health:
   - Since 1990, the maternal mortality ratio has declined by 45 percent worldwide, and most of the reduction occurred since 2000.
   - In Southern Asia, the maternal mortality ratio declined by 64 percent between 1990 and 2013, and in sub-Saharan African it fell by 49 percent.
   - More than 71 percent of births were assisted by skilled health personnel globally in 2014, an increase from 59 percent in 1990.

- In Northern Africa, the proportion of pregnant women who received four or more antenatal visits increased from 50 percent to 89 percent between 1990 and 2014.
- Use of contraceptives among women between the age of 15 to 49, married or single, increased from 55 percent in 1990 worldwide to 64 percent in 2015.

6. To combat HIV/AIDS, malaria, and other diseases:
   - New HIV infection fell by approximately 40 percent between 2000 and 2013, from an estimated 3.5 million cases to 2.1 million.
   - By June 2014, 13.6 million people living with HIV were receiving antiretroviral therapy (ART) globally, an immense increase from just 800,000 in 2003. ART averted 7.6 million deaths from AIDS between 1995 and 2013.
   - Over 6.2 million malaria deaths have been averted between 2000 and 2015, mainly children under five years of age in sub-Saharan Africa. The incidence rate of malaria at global level has fallen by an estimated 37 percent and the mortality rate by 58 percent.
   - More than 900 million insecticide-treated mosquito nets were delivered to malaria-endemic countries in sub-Saharan African between 2004 and 2014.
   - Between 2000 and 2013, tuberculosis prevention, diagnosis and treatment interventions saved an estimated 37 million lives. The tuberculosis mortality rate fell by 45 percent and the prevalence rate by 41 percent between 1990 and 2013.

7. To ensure environmental sustainability:
   - Ozone- depleting substances have been virtually eliminated since 1990, and the ozone layer is expected to recover by the middle of this century.
   - Terrestrial and marine protected areas in many regions have increased substantially since 1990. In Latin America and the Caribbean, coverage of terrestrial protected areas rose from 8.8 percent to 23.4 percent between 1990 and 2014.
   - In 2015, 91 percent of the global population is using an improved drinking water source, compared to 76 percent in 1990.
   - Of the 2.6 billion people who have gained access to improved drinking water since 1990, 1.9 billion gained access to piped drinking water on premises. Over half of the global population (58 percent) now enjoys this higher level of service.

- Globally, 147 countries have met the drinking water target, 95 countries have met the sanitation target and 77 countries have met both.
- Worldwide, 2.1 billion people have gained access to improved sanitation. The proportion of population practicing open defection has fallen almost by half since 1990.
- The proportion of urban population living in slums in the developing regions fell from approximately 39.4 percent in 2000 to 29.7 percent in 2014.

8. To develop a global partnership for development:
   - Official development assistance from developed countries increased by 66 percent in real terms between 2000 and 2014, reaching US$135.2 billion.
   - In 2014, Denmark, Luxembourg, Norway, Sweden and the United Kingdom continued to exceed the United Nations official development assistance target of 0.7 percent of gross national income.
   - In 2014, 79 percent of imports from developing to developed countries were admitted duty free, up from 65 percent in 2000.
   - The proportion of external debt service to export revenue in developing countries fell from 12 percent in 2000 to 3 percent in 2013.
   - As of 2015, 95 percent of the world's population is covered by a mobile-cellular signal.
   - The number of mobile-cellular subscriptions has grown almost tenfold in the last 15 years, from 738 million in 2000 to over 7 billion in 2015.
   - Internet penetration has grown from just over 6 percent of the world's population in 2000 to 43 percent in 2015. As a result, 3.2 billion people are linked to a global network of content and applications.

The Declaration committed nations to a new global partnership to reduce extreme poverty, and set out a series of eight time-bound targets - with a deadline of 2015 - that have come to be known as the Millennium Development Goals (MDGs). The final MDG Report found that the 15-year effort has produced the most successful anti-poverty movement in history:[4]
- Since 1990, the number of people living in extreme poverty has declined by more than half.
- The proportion of undernourished people in the developing regions has fallen by almost half.
- The primary school enrolment rate in the developing regions has reached 91 percent, and many more girls are now in school compared to 15 years ago.

- Remarkable gains have also been made in the fight against HIV/AIDS, malaria and tuberculosis.
- The under-five mortality rate has declined by more than half, and maternal mortality is down by 45 percent worldwide.
- The target of halving the proportion of people who lack access to improved sources of water was also met.

Although significant achievements have been made on many of the MDG targets worldwide, progress has been uneven across many regions and countries, leaving significant gaps. Millions of people are being left behind, especially the poorest and those disadvantaged because of their sex, age, disability, ethnicity or geographic location. Targeted efforts will be needed to reach the most vulnerable people. The concerted efforts of national governments, the international community, civil society and the private sector have helped expand hope and opportunity for people around the world. Yet the job is unfinished for millions of people—need to go the last mile on ending hunger, achieving full gender equality, improving health services and getting every child into school. Now there is a need to shift the world onto a sustainable path. The global Sustainable Development Goals (SDGs), or Global Goals, will guide policy and funding for the next 15 years, beginning with a historic pledge on September 25, 2015, to end poverty everywhere permanently.[5]

United Nations and Global Conflict
The United Nations work to maintain international peace and security in a world where security threats have become extremely complex. The principal aim of the UN is to maintain international peace and security (Article 1) with responsibility for this being vested in the Security Council. Since its creation, the UN has often been called upon to prevent disputes from escalating into a war, or to help restore peace when armed conflict does break out, and to promote lasting peace in societies emerging from wars. The Security Council, the General Assembly and the Secretary-General, all play a major and complementary role in fostering peace and security. The Departments of Political Affairs, Peacekeeping Operations and Field Support as well as the Peace building Support Office work to maintain international peace and security in the areas of conflict prevention and mediation, peacemaking, peace enforcement and peace building. Promoting peace and justice is one of 17 global goals that make up the 2030 Agenda for Sustainable Development. An integrated approach is crucial for progress across the multiple goals.[6] Indeed, the performance of the UN can largely be judged

in terms of the extent to which it has saved humankind from deadly military conflict. This, nevertheless, is difficult to judge. On the other hand, the fact that the two World Wars of the 20th century have not been followed by World War III has sometimes been seen as the supreme achievement of the UN, demonstrating a clear advance on the performance of the League of Nations. On the other hand, realist theorists in particular have argued that the absence of global war since 1945 has had little to do with the UN, being more a consequence of the 'balance of terror' that developed during the Cold War as well as nuclear stalemate developed between the US and the Soviet Union. Ultimately, how global and regional conflict would have developed and whether 'cold' wars would have become 'hot' ones in the absence of the UN is questionable. It is nevertheless, evident that the UN has only had limited and intermittent success in establishing a system of collective security that can displace a reliance on violent self-help.[7]

Promotion of International Peace and Security

The UN works to maintain international peace and security in a world where security threats have become more complex. Since its creation, the UN has often been called upon to prevent disputes from escalating into war, or to help restore peace when armed conflict does break out, and to promote lasting peace in societies emerging from wars. The Security Council, the General Assembly and the Secretary- General all play major, complementary roles in fostering peace and security.[8] Although the Organisation has had many successes, there are also, unfortunately, several recent tragic cases where the United Nations has not been so successful. Hundreds of thousands have died around the world as conflicts have recently mounted. The breakdown of the State security apparatus in intra-State and inter-communal conflicts now poses tremendous security challenges and tests the Organisation's capacity to carry out its mandates and programmes. And the UN, as a relatively soft target, has been the victim of attacks resulting in the tragic loss of life.

With the mounting complexity and growing costs of addressing crisis situations, the imperative of conflict prevention is higher than ever. In its conflict prevention and mediation work, the United Nations continues to face challenges regarding how best to engage with sometimes amorphous movements or fractured armed groups and how to ensure inclusivity. The Organisation has strengthened its relationships with regional and sub-regional organisations, which play a significant role in fostering conflict prevention and mediation partnerships, in addition to rapid responses to regional crises.

There is continued political will to prevent the scourge of conflict-related sexual violence, exemplified by the Declaration of Commitment to End Sexual

Violence in Conflict, and the Global Summit to End Sexual Violence in Conflict, in 2014. The Security Council has also called for sustained monitoring and reporting on the violations affecting children in armed conflict and for perpetrators to be brought to account. The global campaign "Children, Not Soldiers" is aimed at ending and preventing the recruitment and use of children by all national security forces in conflict by 2016.[9]

Member States have demonstrated their continued interest in using peacekeeping and continue to recognise it as an effective and cost-effective tool, without which the human and material costs of conflict and chances to relapse into conflict would be unquestionably higher. Although the situation and circumstances for the conduct of United Nations peacekeeping operations have always been challenging, we face today a heightened level and new types of security threat, requiring new approaches and strategies. Peacekeeping operations are being increasingly deployed earlier in the conflict continuum, before any peace or ceasefire agreement. Creating the political and security space necessary for successful negotiations is crucial. Ensuring that United Nations troops are properly supported and equipped is a high priority. The complexity of contemporary peacekeeping environments require strengthened partnerships with all stakeholders, including regional and sub-regional organisations, the wider United Nations family, international and regional financial institutions and donors and multilateral and bilateral partners. Only through such collaboration can we collectively address the international peace and security challenges we face now and in the coming years.[10]

Global Challenge to Armed Conflict

Preventing armed conflict, keeping peace, and rebuilding war torn states remain among the most intractable challenges facing the international community. Each year, at least 250,000 people die in armed conflicts, most of which occur within, rather than between, states and in the past three years an especially brutal civil war in Syria has killed more than 100,000 people. Armed conflict and its aftermath corrode virtually every aspect of society: law and order, human rights, socioeconomic development, education, basic health services, and the environment. The global economic costs of insecurity generated by conflicts amount to an estimated of US$400 billion each year. At the same time, conflict prevention, mitigation and response are global concerns, because instability often spills across borders and triggers piracy, drug trafficking, small-arms sales, environmental exploitation, and terrorism.[11]

After the shocking mass atrocities in Rwanda and Bosnia in the 1990s, the UN and several regional organisations mandated new initiatives to address violence.

The UN reforms improved its ability to monitor political developments, plan and support peacekeeping operations, and coordinate mechanisms charged with peace building. Meanwhile, new arrangements within the European Union (EU), African Union (AU), Organisation of American States (OAS), and other regional organisations have increased responsiveness to instability and violence within their regions—albeit with varying levels of engagement, capabilities and effectiveness.

But these international instruments have had a mixed record of success. In many cases, international institutions charged with promoting peace and stability lack the political consensus and financial resources to fulfill their mandates. Moreover, these institutions remain disproportionately reactive, and often neglect conflict prevention as a critical tool for managing armed conflicts. Most peacekeeping efforts still have insufficient manpower, money, and equipment to meet their overstretched mandates. And the international community too frequently fails to foster peace and recovery in war-torn countries. Multilateral action can be an effective response to outbreaks of armed conflict, but international and regional approaches need to be enhanced and coordinated if they are to effectively address the range of conflict management problems facing the global community.[12]

UNO and Intervention within State

There are a number of occasions where a UN resolution justified intervention due to gross infringement of the rights of individuals has remained limited. The justification of intervention in Kosovo represented a break from the past in that it included a clear humanitarian element. Kosovo was arguably the first occasion in which international force were used in defiance of a sovereign state in order to protect humanitarian standards. NATO launched the air campaign in March 1999 in Kosovo against the Republic of Yugoslavia without a mandate from the Security Council, since Russia had declared that it would veto such action. Nonetheless, NATO states noted that by intervening to stop ethnic cleansing and crimes against humanity in Kosovo they were acting in accordance with the principles of the UN Charter.[13]

The War on Iraq in 2003 was questionably another case although the legality of intervention under existing Security Council resolution is contested, especially in view of the failure to obtain UN Security Council resolution to give an explicit mandate for the action. The US action against Afghanistan in 2001 is an exceptional case in which the UN Security Council acknowledged the right of a state which had been attacked—referring to the events of September 11, 2001 in the United States—to respond in its own defence.

The difficulty in relaxing the principle of non-intervention should not be underestimated. For instance, the UN has been reluctant to send peacekeepers to Darfur without the consent of the Sudanese government. Some fear a slippery slope whereby a relaxation of the non-intervention principle by the UN will lead to military action by individual states without UN approval.[14] It could be argued that the action against the Iraq in 2003 illustrates the danger. There are significant numbers of other international and regional organisations involved in peace operations, and several countries are suspicious of what appears to be the granting of a licence to intervene in their affairs.

On Syria, Iraq and the war against the Islamic State of Iraq and the Levant (ISIS), UN has clearly fallen short of laudable aim. Four of the five permanent members are themselves involved militarily in the fight in one way or the other. The UN Security Council is supposed to be international guarantor of the new world order. The United Nations Supervision Mission in Syria (UNSMIS) is a United Nations peacekeeping mission in Syria, set up in 2012 as a result of United Nations Security Council Resolution 2043 in response to the Syrian Civil War.[15] With human rights violations at the heart of the Syrian crisis, the UN has called for an immediate end to violence; release of political prisoners; impartial investigations to end impunity, ensure accountability and bring perpetrators to justice and reparations for the victims. The Intra-Syrian Talks facilitate by UN Special Envoy for Syria took place from April 13-27, 2016 in Geneva. Talks focused on political transition, governance and consultation principles. Two task forces created by the International Syria Support Group (ISSG) are overseeing the delivery of much needed humanitarian aid to thousands of Syrians in besieged and other hard-to-reach areas.[16]

An increased readiness by the UN to intervene within states in order to promote internal justice for individuals would indicate a movement towards global governance and away from unconditional sovereignty or what we term as political globalisation. There have been some signs of movement in this direction, but principles of state sovereignty and non-intervention remain important. There is still some support for the view that Article 2(7) of the UN Charter should be interpreted strictly: that there can be no intervention within a state without the express consent of the government of that state. Others believe that intervention within a country to promote human rights is justifiable on the basis of a threat to international peace and security. Evidence of a threat to international peace and security could be the appearance of significant numbers of refugees, or the judgment that other states might intervene militarily. Some liberals argue that the condition is flexible enough to justify intervention to defend human rights whenever possible.[17] However, most operations of the United Nations were justified in the traditional way as a response to a threat to international peace and security. While handling conflicts, the UN had to break traditional principles and norms such as non-use of force in peacekeeping operations, non-intervention into domestic affairs and state sovereignty.

Economic Growth and Sustainable Development

Sustainable development, which balances current needs with the needs of future generations, is at the core of UN's development agenda. The UN has shifted to the idea of sustainable development in part because of climate change. According to the Intergovernmental Panel on Climate Change, if climate change is left unchecked, it will increase the likelihood of severe, irreversible changes to our ecosystems. Sustainable development, because it is less harmful to our ecosystems, can help in the fight against climate change. Sustainable development will also help the development needs of the poor and most vulnerable, who have contributed the least to the climate change problem. The Millennium Development Goals have been a great success in many ways. The global extreme poverty rate has been halved and continues to decline. More children, than ever, are attending primary school. Child deaths have dropped dramatically. About 2.6 billion people gained access to an improved drinking water source.[18] Targeted investments in fighting malaria, HIV/AIDS and tuberculosis have saved millions around the globe.

Plans are now being made within the UN system to ensure that sustainable development goals can be met which ultimately aim to eradicate poverty, improve people's lives and rapidly transit to a low-carbon, climate-resilient economy. The 2030 Agenda for Sustainable Development was adopted at a high-level summit in September 2015, where a set of action-oriented and universal sustainable development goals were presented, leading to a renewed global partnership for development, backed by civil society, the private sector, parliamentarians and the scientific and academic community.

Sustained economic growth and sustainable development are dependent on the development of sustainable energy sources. Secretary-General Ban Ki-Moon's "Sustainable Energy for All" initiative brings together top-level leadership from all sectors of society (governments, business and civil society). The goal of this initiative is to transform the world's energy systems by ensuring universal access to modern energy services, doubling global energy efficiency, and doubling the share of renewable energy sources in the global energy mix.[19] Sustainable economic growth will also require societies to create the conditions that allow people to have quality jobs that stimulate the economy while not harming the environment.

Reform of United Nations Organisation

Since the end of the Cold War, the old patterns of interaction have broken down or changed significantly. Old methods to solve the problems are not sufficient anymore, and they are being challenged, but the new ones have not yet emerged. Although the member states are dissatisfied with the past experiences of the UN, they have not yet obtained the necessary political will for a new UN to manage world politics after the Cold War. The UN is ill-equipped to respond adequately to the crises of the present era. As a result, the UN needs reforms to perform its function as it was designed in the Charter. Without reforms, it will lack both the credibility and capacity to meet the challenges of the contemporary world.

The ability of the UN to meet adequately the demands of the present and future world depends on the policies of its member states. The UN can only do what the member states want it to do. As an inter-governmental organisation, its reform heavily depends on the member states, especially the more powerful ones. Thus, the sole remaining superpower US polices for political, military and financial reasons would mainly determine the main parameters of the UN's future operations. We have seen in cases of Somalia, Haiti and Yugoslavia that the US support for UN peacekeeping is worthwhile.

Reforming the UN to expand its role in international politics brought the Security Council on the agenda as well. Since the Charter of the UN gives the Council a primary responsibility for the maintenance of international peace and security, its reform is regarded as unavoidable. Reform proposals to the Security Council put on the future international peace and security focuses on the size, composition and the decision making of the Council. The number of both permanent and non-permanent members of the Security Council should be increased, and the privilege of veto power should be abolished to have a more democratic and better functioning reforms. However, if the UN desires to be an important instrument of international politics, it is essential to find ways to reform the Council.

Since the late 1990s there have been many calls for reform of the UN. However, there is little clarity or consensus about what reform might be made in practical terms. Those who want the UN to play a greater role in world affairs and those who want its role confined to humanitarian work or otherwise reduced the use of the term "UN reform" to refer to their ideas. The range of opinion varies from those who want to eliminate the UN entirely, to those who want to make it into a full-fledged world government.

On June 1, 2011, UN Secretary-General Ban Ki-Moon appointed Atul Khare of India to spearhead efforts to implement a reform agenda aimed at streamlining and improving the efficiency of the world body. Khare led the Change Management Team (CMT) at the UN, working with, both, departments and offices within the Secretariat and with other bodies in the UN system and the 193 member states.[20] The CMT is tasked with guiding the implementation of a reform agenda at the UN that starts with devising a wide-ranging plan to streamline activities, increase accountability and ensure that the organisation is more effective and efficient in delivering its many mandates and protocols.[21]

Security Council Reforms

The reforms of the United Nations Security Council (UNSC) encompasses five key issues: categories of membership, the question of the veto held by the five permanent members, regional representation, the size of an enlarged Council and its working methods, and the Security Council-General Assembly relationship. Member states, regional groups and other member state interest groupings developed different positions and proposals on how to move forward on this contested issue. Any reform of the Security Council would require the agreement of at least two-thirds of UN member states, and that of all the permanent members of the UNSC enjoying the right to veto.

Draft Resolution for Expansion of Council

At a meeting held on September 14, 2015, nearly 200 member countries of the United Nations have agreed that over the next year, they will negotiate the wording of a document that will call for reforming the Security Council, the top decision-making body, which has 15 members.

For the first time, different countries have submitted written suggestions for what the resolution should contain. In what was seen as an attempt to thwart Security Council's expansion bid, the US, China and Russia did not participate in that exercise. China has been strongly opposing the expansion of the Security Council; it reportedly wanted to force a vote on whether the UN should proceed with a one-year discussion on how the reform should be framed, but failed to muster enough support. The draft resolution calls for next year's UN agenda to discuss the "Question of equitable representation on and increase in the membership of the Security Council." Once the draft is agreed on, it will be put to vote at the General Assembly, where a two-thirds vote is needed to clear it.[22]

New Permanent Member Proposal

One proposed change is to admit more permanent members. The candidates usually mentioned are Brazil, Germany, India, and Japan. By 1992, Japan and

Germany had become the second and third largest contributor to the United Nations and started to demand a permanent seat. Also Brazil (fifth largest country in terms of territory) and India (second largest country in terms of population) as the most powerful countries within their regional groups and key players within their regions saw themselves with a permanent seat. They comprise the group of G4 nations, mutually supporting one another's bids for permanent seats. The United Kingdom, France and Russia support G4 membership in the U.N. Security Council. This sort of reform has traditionally been opposed by the Uniting for Consensus group, which is composed primarily of nations who are regional rivals and economic competitors of the G4. The group is led by Italy and Spain (opposing Germany), Mexico, Colombia and Argentina (opposing Brazil), Pakistan (opposing India), and South Korea (opposing Japan) in addition to Turkey, Indonesia and others. Since 1992, Italy and other members of the group have proposed semi-permanent seats or the expansion of the number of temporary seats as an alternative.[23] The four countries (G4) also said that Africa, the poorest continent in the United Nations, must also be represented as a permanent member in the Security Council. African leaders are also debating which country from that vast continent might get a permanent Security Council seat if one is made available.[24] However, Algeria, Egypt, Ethiopia, South Africa and Nigeria are seen as the strongest choices.

Most of the leading candidates for permanent membership are regularly elected into the Security Council by their respective groups: Japan was elected for eleven two-year terms, Brazil for ten terms, and Germany for three terms. India has been elected to the council seven times in total, with the most recent successful bid being in 2010 after a gap of almost twenty years since 1991–92. According to the Stockholm International Peace Research Institute (SIPRI) the current "P5" members of the Security Council, along with the G4, account for eight of the world's ten largest defence budgets. They also account for nine of the ten largest economies by both nominal GDP and Purchasing Power Parity GDP.[25]

The UNSC, created in the post-War context, doesn't actually reflect the changes that have occurred in the international sphere after the end of the Cold War. In a quarter century, the global economic architecture has undergone massive changes. The developing nations, including India, now play a bigger role in international affairs. But within the UN, the five permanent veto-wielding members still effectively take all the crucial decisions. The Indian position is that this "democracy deficit in the UN prevents effective multilateralism" in the global arena. The way the UNSC handled or failed to handle some of the recent crises would underscore the soundness of the Indian position. Libya and Syria being typical examples of this kind of scenario. While the western nations are accused of distorting the UNSC mandate in Libya, the Security Council failed to reach a consensus on how the Syrian crisis may be resolved. This clearly points to a worsening institutional crisis within the UNSC.[26]

Meaningful reform of the Council to make it more representative and democratic would strengthen the UN to address the challenges of a changing world more effectively. India's demand for a permanent seat has to be looked into, duly considering the merits of the case. It is the world's largest democracy and Asia's third largest economy. The Indian Army is the largest contributor to the UN peacekeeping mission since the inception of the mission. More important, India's foreign policy has historically been aligned with world peace, and not with conflicts. As a permanent member of the UNSC it will be able to play a larger role on the pressing international issues. But the latest development shows the path will not be smooth. New Delhi should continue its efforts to build a democratically evolved global consensus on restructuring of the Security Council, at the same time pursuing bilateral diplomacy with the big powers.[27] The permanent members ought to realise that there are much more serious issues globally than their own so-called prerogatives, and they should be flexible in addressing those issues. Security Council is the most important UN organ and its geographical centre of gravity. But its expanded powers have steadily reduced the role and relevance of the General Assembly which should be the major source of its authority and legitimacy.

The Challenges for United Nations

There are questions about the relevance of the world body in dealing with new challenges confronting global security. The world has changed enormously since the creation of the UN in 1945. Despite the fact that the number of UN members has quadrupled to 193 states, the Security Council that virtually controls the decision making still comprise only the victors of the Second World War. Its structure does not reflect the diversity of the present member states. It is the biggest failure of the UN, when faced with some of the most critical issues, leaving it open to allegations of being a powerless body. While not denying the role of the UN in preventing many crises threatening world peace, its failure to protect and defend the interest of the weaker and smaller nations has become much more apparent. Many skeptics see the UN as having been reduced to a debating forum, not a problem solving entity. Too often it has demonstrated failure to tackle urgent collective action on problems due to its structural inability and inertia.[28]

The much delayed critical structural and procedural reforms further highlight the question of its legitimacy and performance. The crisis of confidence in the world body as a symbol of multilateralism has intensified with Washington's unilateral US military action in Iraq and the inability of the UN to play a more active role in the West Asian conflict, especially in the Syrian civil war. The United Nations, in its present form does not meet the requirements of a truly representative multilateral organination in a fast changing world that is confronted with complex security challenges.[29] Over the past seven decades, the UN has survived various phases – from the bipolarity of the Cold War period to a uni-polar order in 1990s and now to the transition to a sort of fragmented multi-polar order.

Global human rights challenges, such as migration, disabilities, rights of women and children, sexual orientation, and the rights of various minorities, are being addressed through promotion of equality and countering discrimination. A higher number of ratifications in the past year of the Convention on the Rights of Persons with Disabilities demonstrate that States are receptive to new approaches on this issue. There are more international migrants on the move now than ever before in human history, many of them facing unacceptable levels of human rights abuses throughout the migration cycle, in countries of origin, transit and destination. In response, the United Nations has appealed for protection of the human rights of all migrants and called on Governments to embrace migration as essential for inclusive and sustainable social and economic development.[30]

The UN should strive continuously to improve its capabilities according to new circumstances and changes in the world agenda. Its future success depends on creating new ways to overcome prospective crises. The changed face of conflict today requires use to be perceptive, adaptive, creative, and courageous, and to address simultaneously the immediate as well as the root causes of conflict, which all too often lie in the absence of economic opportunities and social inequalities. The UN should be made a more representative of a broader constituency of interests.

Conclusion

The United Nations is the only truly global organisation ever established. It is a hybrid body configured around the competing need to accept the realities of great power politics and to acknowledge the sovereign equality among the member states. Its principal aim is to maintain international peace and security, with the responsibility vested in Security Council. However, the UN has been restricted in carrying out this role particularly by the veto powers of the permanent members. The UN also faces a range of important challenges and pressure for reform. These are generated by the changing location of global power in an increasingly multi-polar world. The UN is not a world government rather a forum for the world's sovereign states to debate issues and determine collective course of action. Promoting respect for human rights is the core purpose of the United Nations and defines its identity as an organisation for people around the world. Reform of the economic and social arrangements of the UN aimed at improving coordination, eliminating duplication and clarifying spheres of equal responsibility is a necessity. These efforts helped and strengthened the norms of the UN as a multilateral system.

The process globalisation also shaped state into a direction to promote peace, democracy and social justice. The United Nations represents multilateral and inter-state processes in which non-state actors and security issues are gaining importance. Since the end of the Cold War, the capacity of the UN in its economic and social work, its developmental work, and its management of peace keeping and post-conflict reconstruction has expanded immensely. The UN needs to determine how best to respond to world developmental needs while also serving the goal of sustaining peace and security.

Notes

1. Latif, Dilek, "United Nations' Changing Role in the Post-Cold War Era," *Turkish Year Book* , Vol. XXX, 2000, p. 26.
2. *Everyone's United Nations* (New York: Department of Public Information Press, 1995), p.5.
3. "The Millenium Development Goals Report 2015", United Nations, New York, 2015, at http://www.un.org/millenniumgoals/2015_MDG_Report/pdf/MDG%202015%20Summary%20web_english.pdf, accessed on May 31, 2016.
4. "Millennium Project", at http://www.unmillenniumproject.org/goals/ ,accessed on May 31, 2016.
5. "End Poverty: Millennium Development Goals and Beyond, 2015", at http://www.un.org/millenniumgoals/, accessed on May 31, 2016.
6. "Peace and Conflict Resolution", at https://academicimpact.un.org/content/peace-and-conflict-resolution, accessed on June 1, 2016.
7. Heywood, Andrew, *Global Politics* (New York, Palgrave Macmillan, 2011), p.440.
8. "Peace and Security", *Global Issues*, at http://www.un.org/en/globalissues/peacesecurity/, accessed on June 1, 2016.
9. "International Peace and security", *United Nations*, at http://www.un.org/en/sections/priorities/international-peace-and-security/, accessed on June 1, 2016.
10. Ibid.
11. "The Global Regime for Armed Conflict", *Council on Foreign Relations*, at http://www.cfr.org/peacekeeping/global-regime-armed-conflict/p24180, accessed on June 1, 2016.
12. Ibid.
13. Baylis, John, Steve Smith and et al., *The Globalization of World Politics: An Introduction to International Relations* (Oxford: Oxford University Press, 2008), pp.324-325.
14. Ibid.

15. Spencer, Richard "How Syria and the bloody conflict has torn the UN Security Council apart", *The Telegraph*, October 7, 2015, at http://www.telegraph.co.uk/news/worldnews/middleeast/syria/11915649/How-Syria-and-the-bloody-conflict-has-torn-the-UN-Security-Council-apart.html, accessed on June 2, 2016.

16. "Syria" *UN News Centre*, at http://www.un.org/apps/news/infocusRel.asp?infocusID=146, accessed on June 2, 2016.

17. Baylis, n.13. pp. 323-24.

18. "Economic Growth and Sustainable Development", *United Nations*, athttp://www.un.org/en/sections/priorities/economic-growth-and-sustainable-development/index.html, accessed on June 2, 2016.

19. Ibid.

20. "Indian to lead UN change management team', *Deccan Herald*, June 1, 2011, at http://www.deccanherald.com/content/165568/indian-lead-un-change-management.html, accessed on June 2, 2016.

21. " Ban appoints experienced UN official to lead change management team", *UN News Centre*, May 31, 2011, at http://www.un.org/apps/news/story.asp?NewsID=38563&Cr=khare&Cr1=#.V1HXSpF97IU, accessed on June 2, 2016.

22. Razdan, Nidhi, "India's Big Step Forward in Bid for UN Security Council", NDTV, New Delhi, September 14, 2015, at http://www.ndtv.com/india-news/big-win-for-india-at-un-general-assembly-agrees-to-negotiate-on-text-for-reforms-1217521, accessed on June 3, 2016.

23. "What is latest about United Nations security Councils Reform?", at https://www.researchgate.net/post/What_is_latest_about_United_Nations_Security_Councils_reforms, accessed on June 3, 2016.

24. "G4 Nations Bid for Permanent Security Council Seat", *Global Policy Forum*, at https://www.globalpolicy.org/the-dark-side-of-natural-resources-st/water-in-conflict/41186.html, accessed on June 4, 2016.

25. "UN Security Council Reform", *World Heritage Encyclopedia*, at http://www.gutenberg.us/Article.aspx?Title=UN_Security_Council_reform, accessed on June 4, 2016.

26. "Much- needed reform", *The Hindu*, New Delhi, August 18, 2015, available at http://www.thehindu.com/opinion/editorial/restructuring-the-unsc-muchneeded-reform/article7550930.ece, accessed on June 2, 2016.

27. Ibid.

28. Hussain, Zahid "Reforming the United Nations", *Dawn*, September 30, 2015, at http://www.dawn.com/news/1209833, accessed on June 3, 2016.

29. Ibid.

30. "Human Rights", *United Nations*, at http://www.un.org/en/sections/priorities/human-rights/index.html, accessed on June 4, 2016.

Contemporary Global Issues

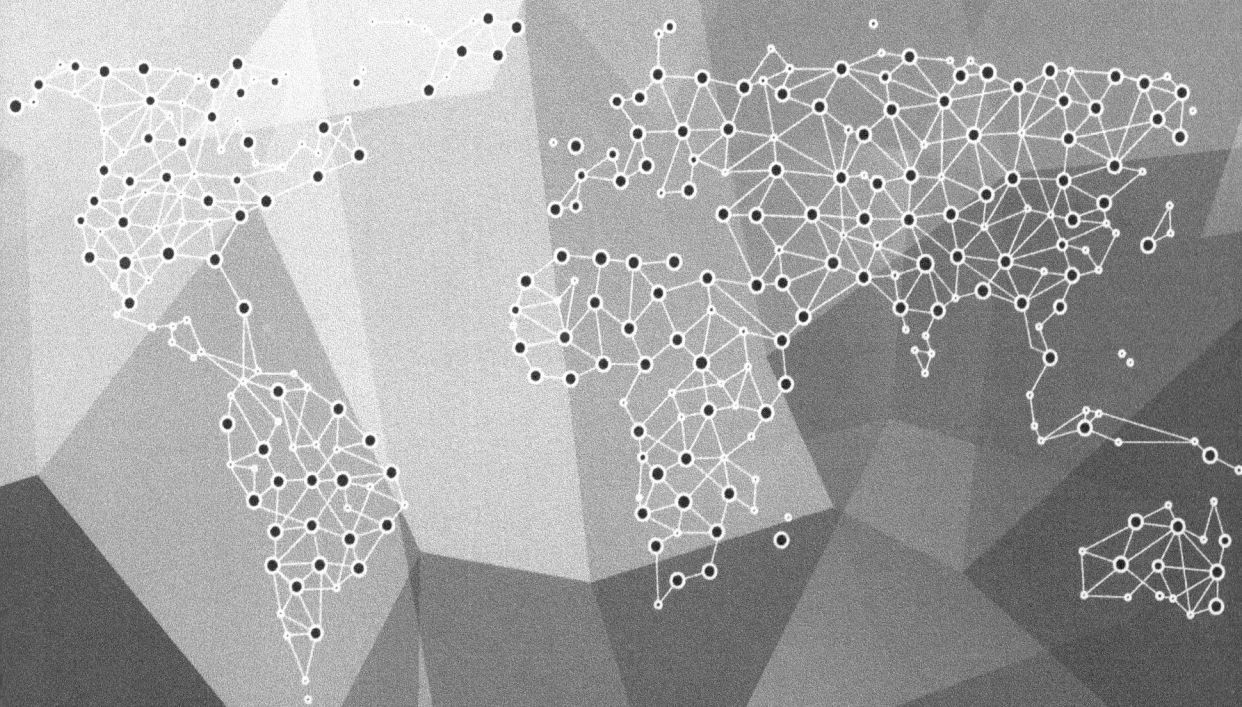

CHAPTER 6

Ecological Issues: Historical Overview of International Environmental Agreements, Climate Change, Global Commons Debate

Introduction

The 21st century has seen the complex human activities which have been undertaken to achieve good lifestyle and maintaining the environmental harmony. The human activities in the last many centuries have degraded the environment drastically. The massive development projects undertaken ever since the Industrial Revolution in Europe, US and Asia have been emitting enormous amounts of greenhouse gases (GHGs). For a very long time, development projects based on the western model were considered to be the panacea to all human miseries, particularly in the poor countries of Africa, Latin America and Asia. By the second half of the 20th century it was clear that environmental damage, caused primarily by the mindless search for development, is endemic to human existence itself. It was realised that it needs urgent environmental movement in the 1970s. The growing concern for the future of the earth has forced the states in the world to come forward and cooperate. However, this cooperation has given way to debates regarding the extent of sacrifice one country is ready to make in order to save the Earth. Today this debate is the central focus in all the international environmental regimes. This debate has given birth to numerous grass-root movements worldwide for ecological protection.

What is Ecology?

The term ecology was first used by German Zoologist Ernst Haeckel in 1869 to describe the "*relations of the animal both to its organic as well as its inorganic environment.*" The term itself has been drawn from the Greek word *oikos*, meaning household, home or place to live. Hence, the interaction between individuals, between populations and between organisms and their environment form ecological systems or ecosystems. In simple words the term ecology can be defined as *"the study of the inter-relationships of organisms with their environment and with each other."* The surroundings or environment consists of other living organisms (biotic) and physical (abiotic) components. Modern ecologists believe that an adequate definition of ecology must specify some unit of study and one such basic unit described by Tansley (1935) was ecosystem. An ecosystem is a self-regulating group of biotic communities of species interacting with one another and with their non-living environment, exchanging energy and matter. Now ecology is often defined as *"the study of ecosystems"*.

"Ecology is the scientific study of the processes regulating the distribution and abundance of organisms and the interactions among them, and the study of how these organisms in turn mediate the transport and transformation of energy and matter in the biosphere (i.e., the study of the design of ecosystem structure and function)". In fact most of the problems which affect the human beings such as expanding population, food scarcities, environmental pollution and all the attendant sociological and political problems are ecological in nature. Unlike ecology, environment means the non-living elements of ecology necessary for the survival of the living beings in different ways. For example, atmosphere or different layers of air contain different gases, elements etc which are necessary to maintain living conditions. Ecology has assumed a much broader meaning since 1960s. It has become a politics of environment or 'green' movement. Environment-related issues became a prominent part of the political system first in developed countries like Germany where apolitical party called Green Party was formed (1980) to raise environmental issues. Today it has become a global movement. There are a number of environmental NGOs in the world today working both at the national and international levels. The ecological changes which have taken place during the past few decades have posed a serious threat to the future mankind. In fact, the indiscriminate use of natural resources by the developed countries during the past centuries has given rise to serious problem of environmental degradation. This problem assumed serious dimension in the 70s of the 20th century.

Environmental Issues at Global Level

'Environment' is a term derived from the French word '*Environner*' that means '*to surround*'. There was a time when environment just meant the surroundings. It was used to describe the physical world surrounding us including soil, rocks, water and air. Gradually it was realised that the enormous variety of plants, animals and micro-organisms on this earth, including human beings are an integral part of the environment. Hence, to make a sensible definition of the environment, it was necessary to include the interactions and inter-relationships of all living organisms with the physical surroundings. Later, it was further recognised that all types of social, cultural and technological activities carried out by human beings also have a profound influence on various components of the environment. Thus various built-in structures, materials and technological innovations also became a part of the environment. All biological (biotic) and non-biological (abiotic) entities surrounding us are included in the term *'environment'*. The impact of technological and economic development on the natural environment may lead to degradation of the social and cultural environment. Thus, environments are to be considered in a broader perspective where the surrounding components as well as their interactions are to be included.

The problem of the environment cannot be treated as a single problem. There are several different kinds of problems that interact but at the same time can be separated. The problem of population leads to the problem of the environment and with it fears not just of pollution but of a continued chronic food scarcity and famine. The population at the beginning of the third millennium is around 6300 million. If it continues to grow at the present rate of slightly under 2 percent a year, it will be about 8300 million by 2020 and around 11 billion by 2084. It will bring further serious strains on the environment. There is a lot of scientific evidence to suggest that the world is getting warmer primarily because of the side effects of industrial production. This is the so-called greenhouse effect. Various gases, particularly carbon dioxide, are released into the atmosphere. Water vapour is also significant. This will have a number of consequences, some of them unpleasant, such as rising of the sea-level and the probable increase in violent and destructive storms.

Some important global environmental issues which raise concern are:
- *Depletion of natural resources.*
- *Water pollution.*
- *Air pollution.*
- *Ground water pollution.*
- *Toxic chemicals and soil pollution.*
- *Ozone layer depletion.*
- *Global warming.*
- *Loss of bio-diversity.*
- *Extinction of wildlife and loss of natural habitat.*

- *Nuclear wastes and radiation issues.*

Most people feel that global warming and energy crisis are the only main global environmental issues that the planet faces today. These people are not aware of the fact that there are several other issues of global concern, each of which is equally hazardous. More importantly, all these issues are related to each other some way or the other, and hence, tackling them one by one has just become difficult.

Climate Change

Climate change has become more than obvious over the past decade, with nine years of the decade making it to the list of hottest years the planet has ever witnessed. The rise in temperature has also ensured that the equations on the planet have gone for a toss. Some of the most obvious signs of this include irregularities in weather, frequent storms, melting of glaciers, rising levels of sea, etc. Going by the prevailing conditions, it is not difficult to anticipate that the planet is heading for a dramatic climate change in, the near future. Climate change is a term that refers to major changes in temperature, rainfall, snow, or wind patterns lasting for decades or longer. Both human-made and natural factors contribute to climate change:

- **Human causes** include burning fossil fuels, cutting down forests, and developing land for farms, cities and roads. These activities all release greenhouse gases into the atmosphere.
- **Natural causes** include changes in the Earth's orbit, the sun's intensity, the circulation of the ocean and the atmosphere, and volcanic activity.[1]

Climate change is a change in the space and time distribution of weather patterns or conditions or properties of a region or some regions or the entire earth. It is caused by natural processes like biotic processes, variation in Earth's orbit, variation in *albedo* or reflexivity of the oceans and continents, continental drift and formation of mountain, variation in solar radiation on earth, melting of glaciers, floods, volcanic eruptions and plate tectonics or anthropogenic activities like deforestation, burning of crop residues, use of fossil fuel and high energy consumption through electronic gadgets (use of air conditioners, aeroplanes, refrigerators, vacuum cleaners, industrial machines, etc.). While the term "*global warming*" means specific increase in surface temperature due to human activities, the "climate change" is very comprehensive and includes global warming as well as other changes in weather patterns/conditions resulting into more emissions of greenhouse gases due to both human activities and natural processes. Many natural scientists have found in their researches that there are internal and external force mechanisms for climate change - internal force mechanisms are natural processes within the climate system (e.g. thermohaline circulation) while external force mechanisms may be either natural (e.g. changes in solar output) or anthropogenic (human activities leading to more emission of greenhouse gases). The year 2014 was the hottest year in recorded history of climate and July 2015 was the hottest month in past 1627 months since January, 1880. There are three categories of nations in terms of per capita carbon emission in the world:

- *There are 60 countries with average per capita GDP of US$1768 that emit up to 2.3 tons carbon per capita;*
- *74 countries with average per capita GDP of US$3058 emit up to 4.5 tons carbon per capita;*
- *13 countries with average per capita GDP of US$ 33700 emit above 10 tons carbon per capita (as per World Bank, 2014).[2]*

Global climate change is caused by the accumulation of greenhouse gases in the lower atmosphere. The global concentration of these gases is increasing, mainly due to human activities, such as the combustion of fossil fuels (which release carbon dioxide) and deforestation (because forests remove carbon from the atmosphere). The atmospheric concentration of carbon dioxide, the main greenhouse gas, has increased by 30 percent since pre-industrial times. There is now clear evidence that the Earth's climate is warming:

- *Global surface temperatures have risen by 1.3 degrees Fahrenheit (ºF) over the last 100 years.*
- *Worldwide, the last decade has been the warmest on record.*
- *The rate of warming across the globe over the last 50 years (0.24ºF per decade) is almost double the rate of warming over the last 100 years (0.13ºF per decade).*

Projections of future climate change are derived from global climate model or general circulation model (GCM) experiments. Climatologists of the Intergovernmental Panel on Climate Change (IPCC) review the results of these experiments for global and regional assessments. It is estimated that global mean surface temperature will rise by 1.5° to 3.5° C by 2100. This rate of warming is significant. Large changes in precipitation, both increases and decreases, are forecast, largely in the tropics. Climate change is very likely to affect the frequency and intensity of weather events, such as storms and floods, around the world. Climate change will also cause sea level rise due to the thermal expansion of the oceans and the melting of the mountain glaciers. Global mean sea level is anticipated to rise by 15 to 95 centimeters by 2100. Sea level rise will increase vulnerability to coastal flooding and storm surges. The faster the climate changes, the greater will be the risk of damage to the environment. Climatic zones (and thus ecosystems and agricultural zones) could shift toward the poles by 150 to 550 kilometers by 2100. Many ecosystems may decline or fragment and individual species may become extinct. The IPCC Second Assessment report concludes that climate change has probably already begun.

As the world is getting hotter, many of the world's plants and animals, on land and in the oceans, have begun moving toward the poles. Where possible, some terrestrial species are moving up to mountain sides, and marine species are moving to deeper depths and higher latitudes. These changes are happening on every continent and in every ocean.[3] In some places, seasonal behaviours are occurring two or three weeks earlier than they did just a few decades ago.[4] The organisms that cannot adapt to the new climate conditions—because they cannot move fast enough or run out of room—will be worse off. Extinctions are likely to increase as climate change combines with other human-related environmental pressures. Moreover, the impacts of climate change on ecosystem processes such as decomposition, plant production, and nutrient cycling—processes that determine how much fossil fuel–derived CO_2 the land and ocean will continue to sequester in coming decades—remain largely unknown.

The rise in sea level has also accelerated, making possibilities of storms higher and pushing salt water into the aquifers that coastal communities depend on for fresh water, and increasing the extent of coastal flooding. Over the past two decades, sea levels have risen almost twice as fast as the average during the 20th century.[5] Salt-water intrusion can be witnessed in Southern Florida, where sea level rise is contributing to salt-water infiltration of coastal wells.[6] Global warming has changed the pattern of precipitation worldwide.[7] Flooding in the northern half of eastern United States, the Great Plains, and over much of the Midwest has been increasing, especially over the past several decades. Since 1950, worldwide heat waves have become longer and more frequent.[8] Climate change has amplified the threat of wildfires in many places. In the western United States, the area burnt by wildfires and the length of the fire season have increased substantially in recent decades. Climate disruption is already affecting human health and well-being in many ways, and health threats are expected to intensify.[9] Some well-understood impacts include the direct effects of heat and the effects of other weather conditions such as droughts, floods, and severe storms. Heat waves cause deaths and illness, with urban dwellers, the elderly, the poor and certain other especially vulnerable groups.[10]

According to NASA:
- *Carbon dioxide levels were at 399.2 ppm as of November, 2015.*
- *The global temperature has risen 14 F (7.8 C) since 1880.*
- *The global Arctic ice minimum (the extent of sea ice in warm months) is decreasing by 13.3 percent each decade.*
- *Land ice is decreasing by 258 billion tons (234 million kilo tons) each year.*
- *Due to melting ice, the sea level has risen by 0.12 inches (3.17 millimeters) per year.*

Some air pollutants increase with climate change, with the potential to aggravate heart and respiratory diseases. Some plant products such as ragweed pollen reach higher concentrations for longer stretches each year, affecting people with allergies.[11] Scientists have extensively studied the impact of climate change on the risk of infectious diseases.[12] Climate change affects the life cycle and distribution of disease-carrying "vectors"—mosquitoes, ticks, and rodents, which transmit diseases such as West Nile virus, equine encephalitis, Lyme disease, Rocky Mountain spotted fever, and Hantavirus Pulmonary Syndrome.[13] There is uncertainty about how climate change will affect infectious disease risk, because many factors other than climate affect the spread of disease. The role of climate change on the ranges of vector-borne diseases in the United States, such as Lyme disease, West Nile virus, and dengue, is an active area of research.[14]

According to the IPCC, given the current pathway for carbon emissions the high end of the "likely" range for the expected increase in global temperature is about 8° F by the end of the century.[15] This is similar to the roughly 9° F warming that ended the last ice age. It is important to remember that temperature change due to CO_2 emissions is essentially irreversible for several hundred years because this CO_2 is removed from the atmosphere only very slowly by natural processes.[16] Climate change threatens the collapse of some ecosystems and amplifies extinction pressures on species, which have already elevated extinction rates well above natural background rates.[17] The rate of climate change now may be as fast as any extended warming period over the past 65 million years and it is projected to accelerate in the coming decades.[18] When rapid climate change is added to other sources of extinction pressure such as ocean acidification, land use, invasive species, and/or exploitation, the resulting rates of extinction are likely to place our era among a handful of severe biodiversity crises in the Earth's geological record.

Climate change has posed a major threat to the pace of development firstly due to increased frequency and intensity of hydro-meteorological hazards such as floods, droughts, heat waves, cyclones, storm surges, etc. and secondly, due to degradation or alteration of ecosystems (structure, extent and services), decreased food production, reduced availability of water and negative impact on livelihoods etc., and thereby increasing people's vulnerability to the impacts of natural and human-induced disasters.

At present, we have two major global ecological crises: first, the climate change; and the second, the extinction of species of flora and fauna. Since the Industrial Revolution in Western Europe, there has been a substantial increase in earth's surface temperature and if no proactive mitigation steps are taken in time, we may experience up to 4°C increase in temperature by the end of 21st century. There have been many extreme weather events (in both means and spread) as, in 2015, 2/3^{rds} of India faced droughts and at global level glacier melting, shrinkage of lakes, rise in sea level, floods, droughts, cyclones, global warming, acid rains, longer and colder winter, etc., are pronounced. A glimpse of such major extreme weather events at global level may be perused in *Table 1* below:

Table 1: Major Global Events of Climate Change

S. No.	Major extreme climate events	Country/ Continent	Time	Climate Effects
1	Shrinkage of Lake Chad	Chad, Africa	1960-2002	Persistent drought has shrunk Lake Chad (once world's sixth largest Lake) to 1/20th of its size in 1960- now wetland in place of open water.
2	Shrinkage of Lake Toshka	Egypt	1984-2001	From Lake Nasser reservoir (on Nile river) water passed to Toshka Depression in Western Desert, but flow to Toshka ceased in 2001, so many lakes almost lost.
3	Floods in Mississippi river	U.S.	28th Jan 2011- 3rd May, 2011	Due to snowiest winters and violent early spring rainstorms, Mississippi and its tributaries overflowed their banks inundating lakhs of homes, crops, woodland with muddy water.

4	Flood in Indus river	Pakistan	August, 2010	More than a million acres of land were flooded destroying crops, devastating towns (Sukkar, Dadu and Mehar), 1800 persons were killed and one crore persons lost their shelters.
5	Yellow river's course change	China	2001-2009	Yellow river was the cradle of Chinese civilization but frequent devastating floods have changed its course and now it is known as "China's sorrow"
6	Shrinkage of Lake Mead, Nevada/ Arizona	U.S.	2000-2010	Lake Mead supplies water to California, Arizona, Nevada, Las Vegas and Mexico; since 2000 water level is dropping due to lower snowfall and by July, 2010 it is at 38 percent of its capacity between 2001-2004 it dropped 18 mtrs.
7	Global Warming	World over	1880-2009	Earth's surface temperature increased by 0.7°C since 1880; 2/3rd of warming since 1975. 0.15 degree Celsius to 0.20°C per decade.
8	Helheim Glacier melting	Greenland	2001-2005	Helheim Glacier is crumbling into icebergs; glacier's flow to the sea has speeded up.
9	Inja Glacier Melting	Himalayas		Major retreat and collapse of the lower tongue of the glacier and formation of new ponds formed as a result of melting.
10	Ice melting Mount Kilimanjaro	Tanzania (Africa)	1993-2000	Kilimanjaro is the tallest free standing mountain, is made up of three volcanic cones, there is major decline in its ice cap during 1993-2000.
11	Flood in KedarNath	Uttarakhand, India	June, 2013	Cloudburst led to death of 10,000 persons and huge property loss.

Source: *"Climate Change Mitigation: Proactive Approach"*, Subhash Sharma, Yojana, December, 2015, p.63

These and other extreme weather events have caused massive losses to human, animals, plants and properties. In 1995, United Nations Leipzig Conference on Plant Genetic Resources pointed out that 75 percent of world's biodiversity disappeared in agriculture due to Green Revolution and industrial farming. On the other hand, another UN agency, Food and Agriculture Organisation (FAO), has estimated that 70 to 90 percent of global deforestation is caused by industrial agriculture which has promoted monoculture into forests to grow commodities for export, not for food. Further, according to grain.org report, transnational food industry contributes to 44 to 57 percent of all anthropogenic greenhouse gas emission. Furthermore, fossil fuel consumption is also largely responsible for increase in emissions.

In this regard, Inter-governmental Panel on Climate Change (IPCC) has published many comprehensive reports (in 1990, 1995, 2001, 2007 and 2014). It's Synthesis Report of *(Assessment Report)* AR5 found the following major trends:

- Anthropogenic emissions of GHGs are highest in history; climate changes have widespread impact on both human and natural systems.
- Oceanic uptake of carbon dioxide (CO_2) resulted in acidification of oceans; warming of 0.85°C increased during 1882-2012 and sea level rose by 0.19 m during 1901-2010.
- Due to continued emission of GHGs, there is likelihood of severe, pervasive and irreversible impacts for human ecosystems.
- Limiting total human induced warming to less than 2°C relative to the period 1861-1880 with a probability of more than 66 percent would require cumulative CO_2 emissions from all anthropogenic sources since 1870 to remain below 2900 $GtCO_2$, about 1900 $GtCO_2$ had already been emitted by 2011.
- Risks are unevenly distributed and are generally greater for disadvantaged people and communities in all countries at all levels of development.
- Adaptation and mitigation are complementary strategies for reducing and managing the risks of climate change.
- Without additional mitigation efforts beyond those in place today, warming by the end of 21st century will lead to high to very high risk of severe, widespread and irreversible impacts globally.
- Multiple mitigation pathways would require substantial emission reductions over next few decades and near zero emissions of CO_2 and other GHGs by the end of 21st century. To implement these would pose technological, economic, social and institutional challenges.
- During 2001-2100 relatives to 1986-2005 (FAO circular no. 1066), the rise in sea level ranges for 0.26 to 0.55 m for RCP 2.6, and from 0.45 to 0.82 m for RCP 8.5. By the end of 21st century sea level will rise in more than 95 percent of the ocean area.

- Emission scenarios leading to GHG concentrations in 2010 of about 450 PPM CO_2 or lower are likely to maintain warming below 2°C over 21st century relative to pre-industrial levels. These scenarios are characterised by 40 percent to 70 percent global anthropogenic GHG emissions reduction by 2050 compared to 2100 and emission levels near zero or below in 2100.

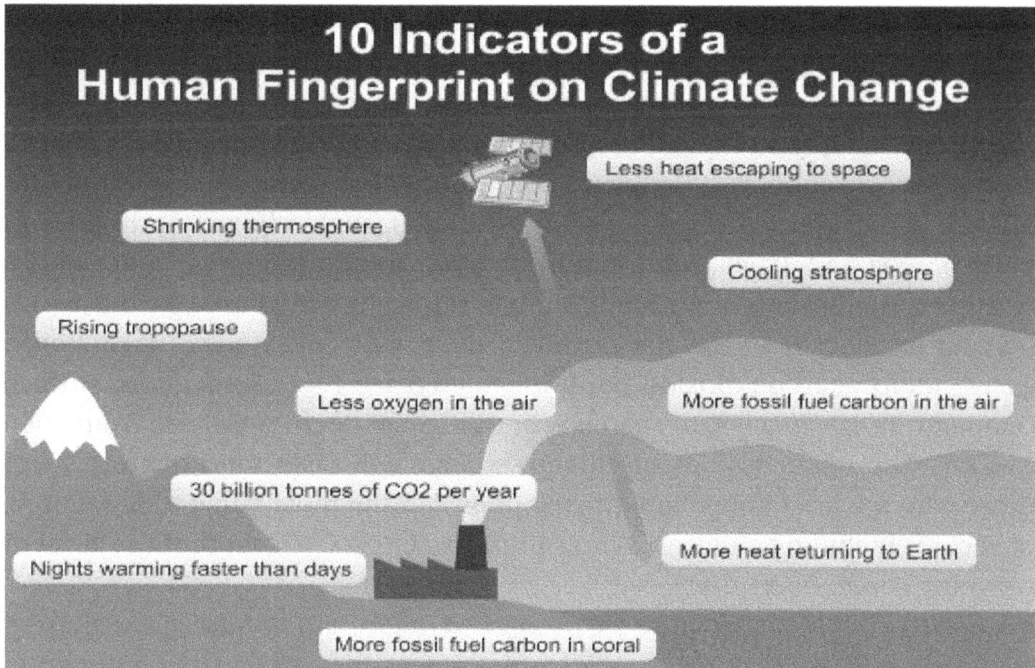

10 Indicators of a Human Fingerprint on Climate Change

- Less heat escaping to space
- Shrinking thermosphere
- Cooling stratosphere
- Rising tropopause
- Less oxygen in the air
- More fossil fuel carbon in the air
- 30 billion tonnes of CO2 per year
- More heat returning to Earth
- Nights warming faster than days
- More fossil fuel carbon in coral

Source: "10 Indicators of a Human Fingerprint on Climate Change", John Cook, July 30, 2010 Skeptical Science,http://www.skepticalscience.com/10-Indicators-of-a-Human-Fingerprint-on-Climate-Change.html

Thus, many credible researches have confirmed that climate is changing over the last few decades and humans are realising and experiencing such changes in their everyday life. Now this phenomenon cannot be brushed aside by the utilitarian's, develop mentalists and political leaders of different hue. Hence, mitigation and adaptation measures are to be taken well in time.

Ecosystems and their responses to environmental change may play various roles in a climate and global change context. Ecological control of reservoir size or rates of flux for climate-influencing materials such as CO_2 is a potentially important factor. In relation to human society, ecosystem sensitivity-or-vulnerability is an important issue; ecosystem collapse in response to environmental change may result in loss of resources; degradation could, in principle, serve as an early warning of increasing stress. From a scientific standpoint, large-scale environmental changes represent a natural experiment that may permit investigation and understanding of ecosystem structure and function not possible on a laboratory scale or in a stable environment.

It is now widely recognised that global warming over the past 50 years is largely due to human activities that have released greenhouse gases into the atmosphere. The most recent assessment report by the Intergovernmental Panel on Climate Change (IPCC) concludes that the global average surface temperature has increased by about 0.6°C during the 20th century. The seemingly small rise of mean temperature is already showing adverse effects. One of the consequences has been a rise in the global average sea level another effect has been more frequent and intensified droughts in recent decades in parts of Asia and Africa. Additionally, in most mid and high latitudes of the Northern Hemisphere continents, precipitation has increased by 0.5 to 1.0 percent per decade in the 20th century. The world's emissions of greenhouse gases, notably carbon dioxide, continue to increase. As a result, global surface temperature is expected to increase by 1.4 to 5.8 degrees Celsius from 1990 to 2100. The repercussions of climate change will disproportionately affect those who are least able to adapt- the poor and the most vulnerable sections of society, including children. For example, scientists project that this level of warming could, *inter-alia*:

- *Greatly exacerbate the range, frequency and intensity of natural disasters, from flooding, to droughts, to torrential rains, ice storms, tornadoes and hurricanes;*
- *Cause sea levels to rise by between 9 and 80 centimeters by 2100 due to the expansion of warming waters and the melting of polar icecaps and other glaciers, which in turn may produce deadly flooding in many low-lying areas and small island States, displacing millions from their homes;*
- *Increase the number of environmental refugees resulting from weather-related disasters;*
- *Augment the risk of disease migration and disease out-breaks; and*
- *Render large areas of the world "uninsurable" due to the magnitude of property damage from disasters.*

It is widely recognised that climate change, by altering local weather patterns and by disturbing life-supporting natural systems and processes, has significant implications for human health. While the range of health effects is diverse, often unpredictable in magnitude, and sometimes slow to emerge, children remain among the most vulnerable to these threats.

Higher temperatures, heavier rainfall, and changes in climate variability would encourage vectors of some infectious diseases (such as malaria, schistosomiasis, dengue fever, yellow fever and encephalitis) to multiply and expand into new geographical regions, intensifying the already overwhelming threats to children from such diseases. There is also evidence that El Nino, a vast natural climatic phenomenon that can bring intense floods and droughts in many parts of the globe is becoming more frequent as a result of global warming and could further aggravate health problems in many parts of the world. Excessive flooding is, for example, a prime cause of cholera and other water-borne and food-borne infections to which children are particularly susceptible. While heavy rains will become more frequent, there will also be more periods of drought and increased spreading of the deserts. Scientists predict that lack of rain, warmer temperatures and increases in evaporation could have severe implications in terms of water availability and food security, reducing crop yields in Africa, further compromising child nutrition. There are also numerous health effects, both in terms of disease and injury, associated with extreme weather events, such as heat waves, storms and floods. Extreme weather events can exacerbate health issues such as asthma and respiratory problems due to worsening air pollution, precisely those diseases that most children suffer from.

Effects on Ecosystems
Climate change holds the potential of inflicting severe damage on the ecosystems that support all life, from hazards to coral reefs due to warmer and more acidic ocean waters to threats to polar bears because of declines in sea ice. Ecosystems around the world already are reacting to a warming world. For example, one study found that 130 species, including both plants and animals, have responded to earlier spring warming over the last 30 years. These organisms have changed their timing of flowering, migration and other spring activities. The changes occurred regardless of regional difference and were linked directly to enhance greenhouse warming.[19] Researchers also have established that climate change is driving some species to extinction. For instance, in the past 20 years dozens of species of mountain frogs in Central America have disappeared because of a disease that formerly did not occur where they live. The greenhouse gases that are already in the atmosphere because of human activity will continue to warm the planet for several centuries. In other words, some level of continued climate change is inevitable, meaning that humanity is going to have to take action to adapt to a warming

world. The consensus among climate scientists is that worldwide emissions of greenhouse gases need to start a long-term decline within the next decade or two. According to the Intergovernmental Panel on Climate Change, the world needs to reduce total emissions by about 50 to 80 percent (compared to a business-as-usual scenario) in order to stabilise atmospheric greenhouse gas concentrations and avoid dangerous climatic change.[20] The effects of global warming are already visible in many areas of the world. For example, in Montana's Glacier National Park, where about 150 glaciers were once located, only 25 glaciers larger than 25 acres remain, according to the U.S. Geological Survey (USGS). A commonly accepted guideline for identifying a glacier — a body of snow and ice that moves — is that the object must be about 101,000 square meters or about 25 acres in size.[21]

Global Temperature, 1880 - 2014
Land - Ocean Index: 1951-1980 Base

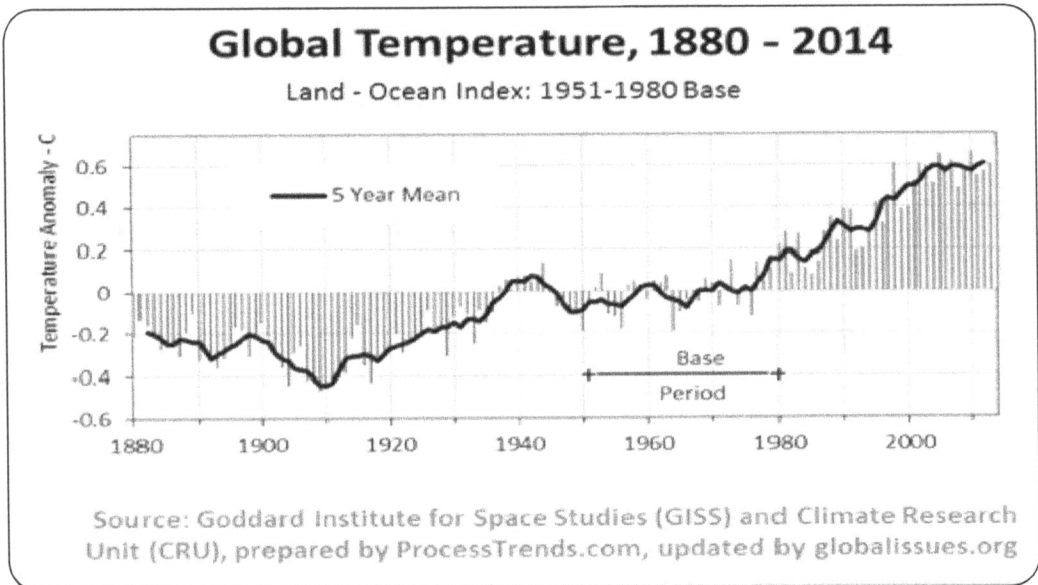

Source: Goddard Institute for Space Studies (GISS) and Climate Research Unit (CRU), prepared by ProcessTrends.com, updated by globalissues.org

Source: GISS Surface Temperature Analysis, NASA, accessed on January 25, 2015 http://www.globalissues.org/article/233/climate-change-and-global-warming-introduction

Greenhouse Effect

Human caused global warming occurs when human activity introduces too much of certain types of gases into the atmosphere. More of this gas equals more warming. The atmospheric gases primarily responsible for the greenhouse effect are known as *"greenhouse gases"* and include water vapour, carbon dioxide (CO_2), methane (CH4) and nitrous oxide (N2O). The most prevalent greenhouse gas is CO_2. The term greenhouse is used in conjunction with the phenomenon known as the greenhouse effect. The phenomenon in brief is:

- Energy from the sun drives the earth's weather and climate, and heats the earth's surface;
- In turn, the earth radiates energy back into space;
- Some atmospheric gases (water vapour, carbon dioxide, and other gases) trap some of the outgoing energy, retaining heat like the glass panels of a greenhouse;
- These gases are therefore known as greenhouse gases;
- The greenhouse effect is the rise in temperature on Earth as certain gases in the atmosphere trap energy.

Six main greenhouse gases are *carbon dioxide (CO_2), methane (CH4) (which is 20 times as potent a greenhouse gas as carbon dioxide) and nitrous oxide (N2O),* plus three fluorinated industrial gases: *hydro fluorocarbons (HFCs), per fluorocarbons (PFCs) and sulphur hexafluoride (SF6).* Water vapour is also considered a greenhouse gas. Many of these greenhouse gases are actually life-enabling also, for without them, heat would escape back into space and the Earth's average temperature would be a lot colder. However, if the greenhouse effect becomes stronger, then more heat gets trapped and the Earth might become less habitable for humans, plants and animals. It is, therefore, necessary to control greenhouse emissions and reduce it to desirable limits to save the earth.

Annual Greenhouse Gas Emissions by Sector

Industrial processes 16.8%

Power stations 21.3%

Transportation fuels 14.0%

Waste disposal and treatment 3.4%

Agricultural byproducts 12.5%

Land use and biomass burning 10.0%

Fossil fuel retrieval, processing, and distribution 11.3%

Residential, commercial, and other sources 10.3%

Carbon Dioxide (72% of total)
20.6% 29.5% 8.4% 9.1% 12.9% 19.2%

Methane (18% of total)
40.0% 4.8% 6.6% 18.1% 29.6%

Nitrous Oxide (9% of total)
62.0% 1.1% 1.5% 2.3% 5.9% 26.0%

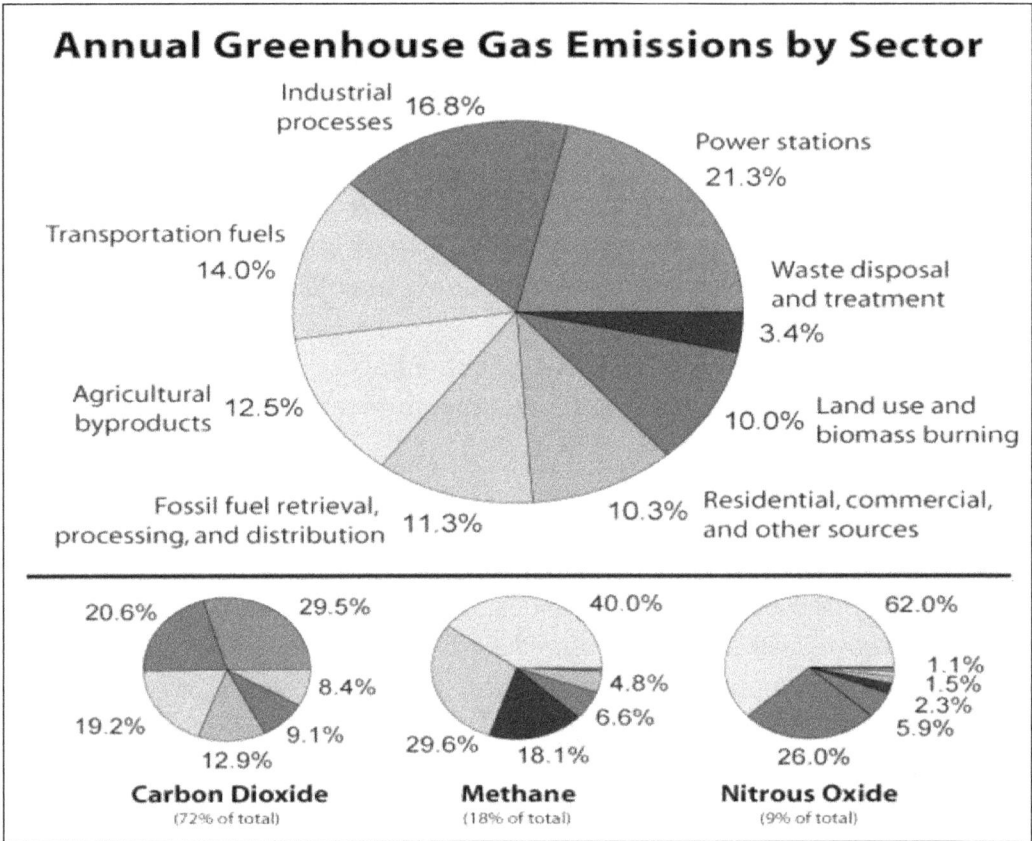

Source: Wikipedia File: Greenhouse Gas by Sector.png (link is external) / CC BY-SA 3.0 https://www.e-education.psu.edu/geog438w/node/364

Some atmospheric CO_2 is natural. For example, before the Industrial Revolution, there were about 280 parts per million (ppm) of CO_2 in the atmosphere, and during most of the past 800,000 years, CO_2 fluctuated between about 180 ppm during ice ages and 280 ppm during interglacial warm periods. Since the Industrial Revolution the amount of CO_2 has dramatically increased. Currently, the increase is 100 times faster than that when the last ice age ended, according to the National Oceanic and Atmospheric Administration (NOAA). CO_2 makes its way into the atmosphere through a variety of routes. Burning fossil fuels, for example, releases CO_2. Deforestation is also a large contributor to excessive CO_2 in the atmosphere. In fact, deforestation is the second largest anthropogenic (human-made) source of carbon dioxide, according to research published by Duke University. When trees are destroyed, they release the carbon they have stored for photosynthesis. According to the 2010 *Global Forest Resources Assessment*, deforestation releases nearly a billion tons of carbon into the atmosphere per year. But fossil fuel combustion is the number one anthropogenic source of carbon dioxide. The Environmental Protection Agency (EPA) lists this source as the cause of 32 percent of total U.S. CO_2 emissions and 27 percent of total U.S. greenhouse gas emissions in 2012. Methane is the second most common greenhouse gas, but it is much more destructive. In 2012, the gas accounted for about 9 percent of all U.S. greenhouse gas emissions, according to the EPA. There may be less methane in the atmosphere, but this gas is much more efficient at trapping radiation. The EPA reports that methane has 20 times more impact on climate change over a 100-year period. Methane can come from many natural sources, but humans cause a large portion of methane emissions through mining, the use of natural gas, the massive raising of livestock and the use of landfills. In fact, according to the EPA, humans are responsible for more than 60 percent of methane emissions.[22]

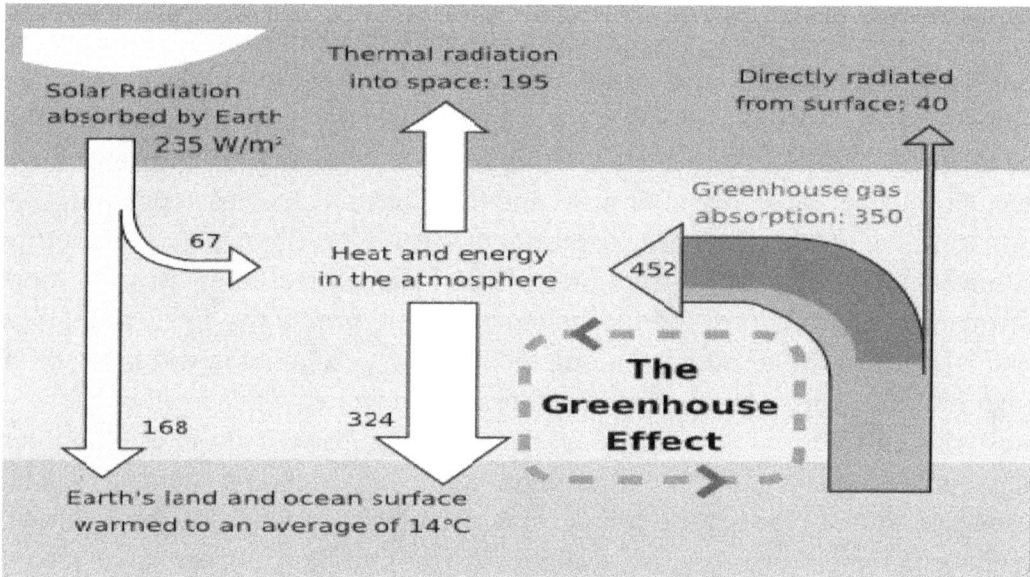

Source: "Climate Change and Global Warming Introduction", Robert A. Rohde, Global Issues, February 1, 2015

Rising Sea Level

Among the most serious and potentially catastrophic effects of global warming is rise of sea level, caused by a combination of melting of glaciers all over the world and the *"thermal expansion"* of the seas as oceans warm. By the end of the century, if nothing is done to rein in emissions of greenhouse gases, global sea level may be three feet higher than it is today and rising.[23]Rising sea level will have severe impacts in low-lying coastal communities throughout the world. In Bangladesh, for example, even a one-meter rise would inundate 17 percent of the country. In the United States where 54 percent of the population lives in close proximity to the ocean, the most vulnerable areas are the Southeast and Mid-Atlantic coasts. Also at risk are low-lying areas and bays such as North Carolina's Outer Banks, the Florida Coast, and much of southern California. It is noticed that melting Polar ice is having an impact on environment. In November 2004 an international team of 300 scientists from 15 countries, including the United States, issued a report on the impacts of climate change in the Arctic. In addition to painting a stark picture as to of how climate change already is affecting the region, the report of the Arctic Climate Impact Assessment predicted that at least half the summer sea ice in the Arctic will melt by the end of this century, along with a significant portion of the Greenland Ice Sheet.[24]

Using new satellite-based measurements, researchers showed that the second largest land-based ice sheet in the world is losing ice twice as fast as scientists had estimated. A complete melting of this ice sheet could raise global sea level by almost 20 feet within a few hundred years, a level that would permanently flood virtually all of America's major coastal cities. Other weather impacts from climate change include a higher incidence of drought and flooding and changes in precipitation patterns. According to the Intergovernmental Panel on Climate Change, future changes in weather patterns will affect different regions in different ways. In short term, for instance, farms and forests may be more productive in some regions and less productive at others. Among the reasons: precipitation will increase in high-latitude regions of the world in summer and winter, while southern Africa, Australia and Central America may experience consistent declines in winter rainfall.[25] As a result of these changes, agriculture in developing countries will be especially at risk. Wheat, for example, may virtually disappear as a crop in Africa, while experiencing substantial declines in Asia and South America.[26]A recent United Nations report blamed climate change, along with worsening air and water quality and poor disposal of solid waste, for an increase in malaria, cholera and lower respiratory tract infections in African societies.[27]

Biodiversity

The variety of life on Earth, its biological diversity, is commonly referred to as biodiversity. Biodiversity is defined as the sum variation of all living organisms (animal, plant, fungal and microbial) on earth, including their genetic diversity, species diversity and the diversity in the ecosystems they help build and regulate. Biodiversity is the variety and differences among living organisms from all sources, including terrestrial, marine, and other aquatic ecosystems and the ecological complexes of which they are a part. In essence, biodiversity represents all life. The presence of this biodiversity is extremely important to human welfare in the sense that it is the basic foundation of the food chain where in, every organism is dependent on one other. It provides immense direct benefits to humans, with at least 40 percent of the world's economy being derived from biological resources. Maintaining biodiversity provides greater food security, opportunities for economic development and provides a foundation for new pharmaceuticals and other medical advances. Ironically, maintaining biodiversity levels and functioning ecosystems is critical to ameliorate climate change.

The number of species of plants, animals, and micro-organisms, the enormous diversity of genes in these species, the different ecosystems on the planet, such as deserts, rainforests and coral reefs are all part of a biologically diverse Earth. Appropriate conservation and sustainable development strategies attempt to recognise this as being integral to any approach. In some way or form, almost all cultures have recognised the importance of nature and its biological diversity for their societies and have therefore understood the need to maintain it. Yet, power, greed and politics have affected the precarious balance.

Biodiversity and climate change are issues of concern worldwide and both directly and indirectly affect the living things on earth. It is now widely recognised that climate change and biodiversity are interconnected. Although throughout Earth's evolution, the climate has always changed with ecosystems and species had been developing and disappearing with rapid climate change and affects ecosystems and species' ability to adapt so biodiversity loss increases. Biodiversity is affected by climate change, with negative consequences for human well-being, but biodiversity, through the ecosystem services it supports, also makes an important contribution to both climate-change mitigation and adaptation. The earth is full of astonishing things including vast diversity of flora and fauna. There are 17 countries in the world which have rich floral and faunal diversity. Most of the plant and animal species are endemic to that region only. The particular species is found in that region on the basis of climatic, geographical habitat and availability of prey. For example, cheetah, the fastest animal on land is normally found in the savannah grassland which is truly suitable for its existence. And the polar bear are found in Arctic Regions.

The present global biota has been affected by fluctuating Pleistocene (last 1.8 million years) concentrations of atmospheric carbon dioxide, temperature, precipitation and has coped through evolutionary changes, and the adoption of natural adaptive strategies. Habitat fragmentation has confined many species to relatively small areas within their previous ranges, resulting in reduced genetic variability. Warming beyond the ceiling of temperatures reached during the Pleistocene will stress ecosystems and their biodiversity far beyond the levels imposed by the global climatic change that occurred in the recent evolutionary past. Human activities have already resulted in the loss of biodiversity and thus, may have affected goods and services crucial for human well-being. The rate and magnitude of climate change induced by increased greenhouse gas emissions has and will continue to affect biodiversity either directly or in combination with other drivers of change. According to the Millennium Ecosystem Assessment, climate change is likely to become one of the most significant drivers of biodiversity loss by the end of the century. Climate change is already forcing biodiversity to adapt either through shifting habitat, changing life cycles, or the development of new physical traits. As per the convention on Biological Diversity Goals, conserving natural terrestrial, freshwater and marine ecosystems and restoring degraded ecosystems (including their genetic and species diversity) is essential for the overall Convention on Climate Change because ecosystems play a key role in the global carbon cycle and in adapting to climate change, while also providing a wide range of ecosystem services that are essential for human well-being and the achievement of the Millennium Development Goals.

One hundred and fifty years ago, the Native American leader, Chief Seattle, is reported to have said *we humans are but a thread in the web of life*. He added whatever we do to the web, "*We do to ourselves*" The web is unraveling at an increasing rate. Both plant and animal species have been disappearing at 50 to 100 times the natural rate, due to such factors as the large-scale clearing and burning of forests, over-harvesting of plants and animals, indiscriminate use of pesticides, draining and filling of wetlands, destructive fishing practices, air pollution and the conversion of wild lands for agricultural and urban uses. Recent studies suggest that this high rate of extinction will accelerate even faster, taking an increasing number of living plants and animals away from us forever. This species loss and ecosystem disruption is causing a complex range of circumstances with consequences to human health. In response, governments and communities worldwide are now concerned with the purification of air and water, maintenance of soil fertility, mitigation of floods and droughts, detoxification and decomposition of wastes, maintaining concentrations of vital gases and water vapour in the atmosphere, and controlling infectious agents in the environment. In addition, the loss of biodiversity obstructs the discovery of new medicines to treat various diseases. Another emerging modern health concern is bio-safety and the effects of advances in and increased use of biotechnology to genetically modify foods. Public concern about the health and ecological risks of foods made with biotechnology has intensified in Europe and has spread rapidly to other parts of the world, including the United States. Proponents contend that biotechnology could help feed the developing world, cut costs and reduce the need for pesticides. The United Nations Convention on Biological Diversity (UNCBD), which was adopted at UNCED in 1992 and has since been ratified by more than 175 countries, establishes three main goals: *the conservation of biological diversity, the sustainable use of its components, and the fair and equitable sharing of the benefits from the use of genetic resources.* In May 2000, the Convention's Cartagena Protocol on bio-safety was opened for signature. The Protocol seeks to protect the planet's species and ecosystems from the potential risks posed by living modified organisms, commonly referred to as genetically modified organisms, and to establish an advanced informed agreement procedure for ensuring that countries are provided with the information necessary to make informed decisions before agreeing to the import of such organisms. The Protocol has been hailed as a breakthrough from a health and environment perspective in that it is the first global treaty that formally enshrines the "precautionary approach", as set forth in the 1992 Rio Declaration on Environment and Development, as a principle of international environmental law.

Ozone Layer Depletion

Ozone in the atmosphere's upper layer, the stratosphere, protects humans, animals and plants from the damaging effects of UV-radiation from the sun. Without it, all life on earth would cease to exist. However, the use of chlorofluorocarbons (CFCs) and other Ozone Depleting Substances (ODS) are slowly eating away at the stratospheric ozone layer, creating a major potential health hazard. While the concentrations of ODS in the lower atmosphere peaked in about 1994 and is now slowly declining due to worldwide efforts to phase out the use of CFCs and other damaging substances, significant health threats relating to ozone depletion persist. Past and current emissions of ODS result in increase of ultraviolet radiation reaching the Earth's surface which can pose several health effects:

- *Increase of melanoma and non-melanoma skin cancers;*
- *Cause or acceleration of eye cataracts development;*
- *Reduce effectiveness of the immune system;*
- *Impact on nutrition (e.g. reduced plant yield);*

- *Damage to ocean ecosystems and reduced fish yield (by killing microbial organisms in the ocean).*

Skin cancer is the most worrisome health impact of ozone depletion. Over exposure to the sun's harmful Ultra-Violet (UV) lights damage children's skin. Recent studies indicate that excessive sunburns experienced by children 10 to 15 years of age increase by threefold the chance of developing malignant melanoma, the most deadly kind of skin cancer, later in life. In Europe, evaluations of ultraviolet-related skin cancers suggest that, despite the decline in ODS concentrations, skin cancer incidences will not begin to fall until about 2060. The stratosphere has an ozone layer which protects the earth's surface from excessive ultraviolet (UV) radiation from the Sun. Chlorine from chemicals such as chlorofluorocarbons (CFCs) used for refrigeration, air conditioning, fire extinguishers, cleaning solvents, aerosols (spray cans of perfumes, medicine, insecticide) cause damage to ozone layer chlorine contained in the CFCs on reaching the ozone (O3) layer split the ozone molecules to form oxygen (O2). Amount of ozone, thus gets reduced and cannot prevent the entry of UV radiation. There has been a reduction of ozone umbrella or shield over the Arctic and Antarctic regions. This is known as ozone hole. This permits passage of UV radiation on earth's atmosphere which causes sunburn, cataract in eyes leading to blindness, skin cancer, reduced productivity of forests, etc. Under the "*Montreal Protocol*" amended in 1990 it was decided to completely phase out CFCs to prevent damage of ozone layer. The international response to this issue is embodied in the Convention for the Protection of the Ozone Layer, which was concluded in Vienna in 1985. The Vienna Convention set an important precedent because nations for the first time agreed in principle to tackle a global environmental problem before its effects were felt. The Convention's 1987 Montreal Protocol on Substances that Deplete the Ozone Layer has been remarkably successful. Production of the most damaging ozone-depleting substances was eliminated, except for a few critical uses, by 1996 in developed countries and should be phased out by 2010 in developing countries. Thanks to these measures, it is currently estimated the CFC concentration in the ozone layer is expected to recover to pre-1980 levels by the year 2050.

Pollution

Pollution occurs when pollutants contaminate the natural surroundings; which brings about changes that affect our normal lifestyles adversely. Pollutants are the key elements or components of pollution which are generally waste materials of different forms. Pollution disturbs our ecosystem and the balance in the environment. With modernisation and development in our lives pollution has reached its peak; giving rise to global warming and human illness. Pollution occurs in different forms; air, water, soil, radioactive, noise, heat/ thermal and light. Pollution has existed for centuries but started to be significant only following the industrial revolution in the 19th century. Pollution occurs when the natural environment cannot destroy an element without creating harm or damage to itself. The elements involved are not produced by nature, and the destroying process can vary from a few days to thousands of years (that is, for instance, the case for radioactive pollutants). In other words, pollution takes place when nature does not know how to decompose an element that has been brought to it in an unnatural way. Pollution, in whatever form, whether it is air, water, land or noise is harmful for the environment. Air pollution pollutes the air that we breathe which causes health issues. Water pollution degrades the quality of water that we use for drinking purposes. Land pollution results in degradation of earth's surface as a result of human activities. Noise pollution can cause irreparable damage to our ears when exposed to continuous large sounds like honking of vehicles on a busy road or machines producing large noise in a factory or a mill.

Human activities directly or indirectly affect the environment adversely. A stone crusher adds a lot of suspended particulate matter and noise into the atmosphere. Automobiles emit from their tail pipes oxides of nitrogen, sulphur dioxide, carbon dioxide, carbon monoxide and a complex mixture of un-burnt hydrocarbons and black soot which pollute the atmosphere. Domestic sewage and excess water from agricultural fields, laden with pesticides and fertilizers, pollute water bodies. Effluents from tanneries contain many harmful chemicals and emit foul smell. These are only a few examples which show how human activities pollute the environment. Pollution may be defined as addition of undesirable material into the environment as a result of human activities. The agents which cause environmental pollution are called pollutants. A pollutant may be defined as a physical, chemical or biological substance unintentionally released into the environment which is directly or indirectly harmful to humans and other living organisms.

Types of Pollution
Pollution may be of the following types:
- *Air pollution.*
- *Noise pollution.*
- *Water pollution.*
- *Soil pollution.*

- *Thermal pollution.*
- *Radiation pollution.*

Air pollution is a result of industrial and certain domestic activity. An ever increasing use of fossil fuels in power plants, industries, transportation, mining, construction of buildings, stone quarries had led to air pollution. Air pollution may be defined as the presence of any solid, liquid or gaseous substance including noise and radioactive radiation in the atmosphere in such concentration that may be directly and indirectly injurious to humans or other living organisms, plants, property or interferes with the normal environmental processes. Air pollutants are of two types (1) suspended particulate matter, and (2) gaseous pollutants like carbon dioxide (CO_2), NO_2 etc. Particulate matter suspended in air is dust and soot released from the industrial chimneys. Major source of SPM (suspended particulate matter) are vehicles, power plants, construction activities, oil refinery, railway yard, market place, industries, etc. Fly ash is ejected mostly by thermal power plants as byproducts of coal burning operations. Fly ash pollutes air and water and may cause heavy metal pollution in water bodies. Fly ash affects vegetation as a result of its direct deposition on leaf surfaces or indirectly through its deposition on soil. Fly ash is now being used for making bricks and as a land fill material. Power plants, industries, different types of vehicles – both private and commercial - use petrol, diesel as fuel and release gaseous pollutants such as carbon dioxide, oxides of nitrogen and sulphur dioxide along with particulate matter in the form of smoke. All of these have harmful effects on plants and humans.

Noise is one of the most pervasive pollutants. Noise by definition is *"sound without value"* or *"any noise that is unwanted by the recipient"*. Noise in industries such as stone cutting and crushing, steel forgings , loudspeakers, shouting by hawkers selling their wares, movement of heavy transport vehicles, railways and airports leads to irritation and an increased blood pressure, loss of temper, decrease in work efficiency, loss of hearing which may be first temporary but can become permanent if the noise stress continues. It is therefore of utmost importance that excessive noise is controlled. Noise level is measured in terms of decibels (dB). W.H.O. (World Health Organisation) has prescribed optimum noise level as 45 dB by day and 35 dB by night. Anything above 80 dB is hazardous. The problem of noise pollution is increasing. All human activities contribute to noise pollution to varying degrees. Sources of noise pollution are several and could be located indoors or outdoors. Indoor sources include noise produced by radio, television, generators, electric fans, air coolers, air conditioners, different home appliances, and family conflict. Noise pollution is available more in cities due to a higher concentration of population and industries and activities such as transportation. Noise like other pollutants is a byproduct of industrialisation, urbanisation and modern civilisation. Outdoor sources of noise pollution include indiscriminate use of loudspeakers, industrial activities, automobiles, rail traffic, airplanes and activities such as those at market place, religious, social and cultural functions, sports and political rallies. In rural areas farm machines, pump sets are main sources of noise pollution. During festivals, marriage and many other occasions, use of fire crackers contribute to noise pollution. Noise pollution is highly disturbing and irritating. Noise disturbs sleep, causes hypertension (high blood pressure), emotional problems such as aggression, mental depression and annoyance. Noise pollution adversely affects efficiency and performance of individuals.

Water pollution is one of the most serious environmental problems. Water pollution is caused by a variety of human activities such as industrial, agricultural and domestic. Agricultural run-off laden with excess fertilizers and pesticides, industrial effluents with toxic substances and sewage water with human and animal wastes pollute our water thoroughly. Natural sources of pollution of water are soil erosion, leaching of minerals from rocks and decaying of organic matter. Rivers, lakes, seas, oceans, estuaries and ground water sources may be polluted by point or non-point sources. When pollutants are discharged from a specific location such as a drain pipe carrying industrial effluents discharged directly into water body it represents point source pollution. In contrast non-point sources include discharge of pollutants from diffused sources or from a larger area such as runoff from agricultural fields, grazing lands, construction sites, abandoned mines and pits, roads and streets. Water pollution is the major source of water borne diseases and other health problems. Sediments brought by runoff water from agricultural fields and discharge of untreated or partially treated sewage and industrial effluents, disposal of fly ash or solid waste into or close to a water body cause severe problems of water pollution. Increased turbidity of water because of sediments reduces penetration of light in water that reduces photosynthesis by aquatic plants. Pesticides like DDT and others used in agriculture may contaminate water bodies. Aquatic organisms consume pesticides from water get into the food chain (aquatic in this case) and move up the food chain. At higher tropic level they get concentrated and may reach the upper end of the food chain. Metals like lead, zinc, arsenic, copper, mercury and cadmium in industrial waste waters adversely affect humans and other animals. Arsenic pollution of ground water has been reported from West Bengal, Orissa, Bihar, and Western U.P. Consumption of such arsenic polluted water leads to accumulation of arsenic in the body parts like blood, nails and hairs causing skin lesions, rough skin, dry and thickening of skin and ultimately skin cancer. Pollution of water bodies by mercury causes Minamata disease in humans and dropsy in fish. Lead causes displexia, cadmium poisoning causes Itai – Itai disease, etc. Oil pollution of sea occurs from leakage from ships, oil tankers, rigs and pipelines. Accidents of oil tankers spill large quantity of oil in seas which kill marine birds and other marine life. It also adversely affects beaches.

Addition of substances which adversely affect the quality of soil or its fertility is known as soil pollution. Generally polluted water also pollutes soil. Solid waste is a mixture of plastics, cloth, glass, metal and organic matter, sewage, sewage sludge, building debris, generated from households, commercial and industries establishments add to soil pollution. Fly ash, iron and steel slag, medical and industrial wastes disposed on land are important sources of soil pollution. In addition, fertilizers and pesticides from agricultural use which reach soil as run-off and land filling by municipal waste are a growing cause of soil pollution. Acid rain and dry deposition of pollutants on land surface also contribute to soil pollution. Plastic bags made from low density polyethylene (LDPE), is virtually indestructible, create colossal environmental hazard. The discarded bags block drains and sewage systems. Leftover food, vegetable waste etc., on which cows and dogs feed may die due to the choking by plastic bags. Plastic is non-biodegradable and burning of plastic in garbage dumps release highly toxic and poisonous gases like carbon monoxide, carbon dioxide, phosgene, dioxine and other poisonous chlorinated compounds. Industrial sources include fly ash, chemical residues, metallic and nuclear wastes. Large number of industrial chemicals, dyes, acids, etc. find their way into the soil and are known to create many health hazards including cancer. Agricultural chemicals especially fertilizers and pesticides pollute the soil. Fertilizers in the run-off water from these fields can cause eutrophication in water bodies. Pesticides are highly toxic chemicals which affect humans and other animals adversely causing respiratory problems, cancer and death.[28]

Power plants - thermal and nuclear, chemical and other industries use lot of water (about 30 percent of all extracted water) for cooling purposes and the used hot water is discharged into rivers, streams or oceans. The waste heat from the boilers and heating processes increase the temperature of the cooling water. Discharge of hot water may increase the temperature of the water body to which it is discharged by 10 to 15 °C above the ambient water temperature. This is thermal pollution. Increase in water temperature decreases dissolved oxygen in water which adversely affects aquatic life. Unlike terrestrial ecosystems, the temperature of water bodies remains steady and does not change very much.

Accordingly, aquatic organisms are adapted to a uniform steady temperature of environment and any fluctuation in water temperature severely affects aquatic plants and animals. Hence discharge of hot water from power plants adversely affects aquatic organisms. Aquatic plants and animals in the warm tropical water bodies live dangerously close to their upper limit of temperature, particularly during the warm summer months. It requires only a slight deviation from this limit to cause thermal stress to these organisms. Discharge of hot water in water body affects feeding in fishes, increases their metabolism and affects their growth. Their swimming efficiency declines. Running away from predators or chasing prey becomes difficult. Their resistance to diseases and parasites decreases. Due to thermal pollution biological diversity is reduced.

Radiation is a form of energy travelling through space. The radiations emanating from the decay of radioactive nuclides are major sources of radiation pollution. Radiations can be categorised into two groups namely the non-ionizing radiations and the ionizing radiations. Non-ionizing radiations are constituted by the electromagnetic waves at the longer wavelength of the spectrum ranging from near infra-red rays to radio waves. These waves have energies enough to excite the atoms and molecules of the medium through which they pass, causing them to vibrate faster but not strong enough to ionize them. In a microwave oven the radiation causes water molecules in the cooking medium to vibrate faster and thus raising its temperature. Ionizing radiations cause ionization of atoms and molecules of the medium through which they pass. Electromagnetic radiations such as short wavelength ultra violet radiations (UV), X-rays and gamma rays and energetic particles produced in nuclear processes, electrically charged particles like alpha and beta particles produced in radioactive decay and neutrons produced in nuclear fission, are highly damaging to living organisms. Electrically charged particles produced in the nuclear processes can have sufficient energy to knock electrons out of the atoms or molecules of the medium, thereby producing ions. The ions produced in water molecules, for example, can induce reactions that can break bonds in proteins and other important molecules. An example of this would be when a gamma ray passes through a cell, the water molecules near the DNA might be ionized and the ions might react with the DNA causing it to break. They can also cause chemical changes by breaking the chemical bonds, which can damage living tissues. The ionizing radiations cause damage to biological systems and are, therefore, pollutants. Large amounts of radiation can kill cells that can dramatically affect the exposed organism as well as possibly its offspring. Affected cells can mutate and result in cancer. A large enough dose of radiation can kill the organism.

Radiation damage can be divided into two types: (a) somatic damage (also called radiation sickness) and (b) genetic damage. Somatic damage refers to damage to cells that are not associated with reproduction. Effects of somatic radiation damage include reddening of the skin, loss of hair, ulceration, fibrosis of the lungs, the formation of holes in tissue, a reduction of white blood cells, and the induction of cataract in the eyes. This damage can also result in cancer and death. Genetic damage refers to damage to cells associated with reproduction. This damage can subsequently cause genetic damage from gene mutation resulting in abnormalities. Genetic damages are passed on to the next generation.

Deforestation

Deforestation is the cutting down of trees to make way for more homes and industries. Rapid growth in population and urban sprawl are two of the major causes of deforestation. Apart from that, use of forest land for agriculture, animal grazing, harvest for fuel wood and logging is some of the other causes of deforestation. Deforestation contributes to global warming as decreased forest size puts carbon back into the environment. Deforestation is the conversion of forest to an alternative permanent non-forested land use such as agriculture, grazing or urban development.[29] Deforestation is primarily a concern for the developing countries of the tropics as it is shrinking areas of the tropical forests[30] causing loss of biodiversity and enhancing the greenhouse effect.[31] Forests cover almost a third of the earth's land surface providing many environmental benefits including a major role in the hydrologic cycle, soil conservation, and prevention of climate change and preservation of biodiversity.[32] Forest resources can provide long-term national economic benefits. For example, at least 145 countries of the world are currently involved in wood production.[33] Sufficient evidence is available that the whole world is facing an environmental crisis on account of heavy deforestation.

The main causes of deforestation are:
- agriculture;
- shifting cultivation;
- demand for firewood;
- demand of wood for industry and commercial purposes;
- urbanisation and developmental projects and
- other causes.

Deforestation is a major contributor to global warming[34] and is often cited as one of the main causes of the enhanced greenhouse effect. Tropical deforestation is responsible for approximately 20percent of world greenhouse gas emissions.[35] According to the Intergovernmental Panel on Climate Change deforestation, mainly in tropical areas, could account for up to one-third of total anthropogenic carbon dioxide emissions.[36] But recent calculations suggest that carbon dioxide emissions from deforestation and forest degradation (excluding peat land emissions) contribute about 12percent of total anthropogenic carbon dioxide emissions with a range from 6 to 17percent.[37] Expanding cities and towns require land to establish the infrastructures necessary to support growing population which is done by clearing the forests.[38] The construction of roads, railways, bridges, and airports needs land for development which lead to destruction of forests and brings increasing numbers of people out of forest cover.

Acid Rain

"Acid rain" refers to the additional acidity in rain as a result of the emissions of sulfur dioxide (primarily from coal-burning utility plants) and nitrogen oxides (dominantly from vehicles). "Acid rain" is a popular term referring to the deposition of a mixture from wet (rain, snow, sleet, fog, cloud water, and dew) and dry (acidifying particles and gases) acidic components. When sulfur dioxide and nitrogen oxides are emitted into the atmosphere, they come into contact with water where they are chemically converted to acidic compounds of sulfates and nitrates. These strong acids are deposited on the earth's surface as rain, snow and fog and through dry deposition. While acidic deposition is the more accurate term, acid rain is used more commonly. To define acidity the chemist uses a "pH scale," in which each unit of pH represents a tenfold difference in acid concentration. A pH of 7 means a solution is neutral, a pH of 14 is highly basic, and a pH of 1 is highly acidic. The bulk of the acidity in rain comes from the reaction of sulfur dioxide ($SO2$) with hydrogen peroxide in clouds, a reaction that produces sulfuric acid. This is an important mechanism in summer, when most of acid rain happens. The hydrogen peroxide is formed from the photochemical reactions of volatile organic compounds derived from such divergent sources as trees and automobile exhaust. It can have harmful effects on plants, aquatic animals and infrastructure. Acid rain is caused by emissions of sulfur dioxide and nitrogen oxide, which react with the water molecules in the atmosphere to produce acids. Some Governments have made efforts since the 1970s to reduce the release of sulfur dioxide and nitrogen oxide into the atmosphere with positive results. Nitrogen oxides can also be produced naturally by lightning strikes, and sulfur dioxide is produced by volcanic eruptions. The chemicals in acid rain can cause paint to peel, corrosion of steel structures such as bridges, and weathering of stone buildings and statues. The principal cause of acid rain is sulfur and nitrogen compounds from human sources, such as electricity generation, factories, and motor vehicles. Electrical power generation using coal is among the greatest contributors to gaseous pollutions that are responsible for acidic rain. The gases can be transported hundreds of kilometers in the atmosphere before they are converted to acids and deposited. In the past, factories had short chimneys to let out smoke but this caused many problems locally; thus, factories later on started having taller smoke chimneys. However, dispersal from these taller stacks caused pollutants to be carried farther, causing widespread ecological damage.[39] West Virginia streams are experiencing killing of fish and changes in their insect populations as a result of chronic and episodic acidity. Roughly 10 percent of the total streams are affected by acid rain.[40] Limestone and marble, the stones used in many buildings and monuments around the world, are especially vulnerable to acid rain. With regard to these stones, strong acids easily dissolve calcium carbonate – the dominant mineral. When a sculpture or building is damaged by acid rain, restoration is not possible and there is no chance of recovering. The composition of the stone is permanently altered. The most disastrous effects of acid rain that are visible to the naked eye are the effects on old monuments and buildings of historical importance. These include the Taj Mahal in India, the Acropolis in Greece and many others around the world. High concentrations of fine-particulate sulfate and nitrate can enter the cardiovascular and respiratory systems of living beings, resulting in disease or even death. Metals, such as mercury and cadmium from soil deposits in lakes, streams, and reservoirs, can accumulate in the tissues of fish, making them toxic to humans. Metals also can be leached from the soil into reservoirs, or from old lead and copper pipes directly into domestic water supplies, causing serious illness.[41]

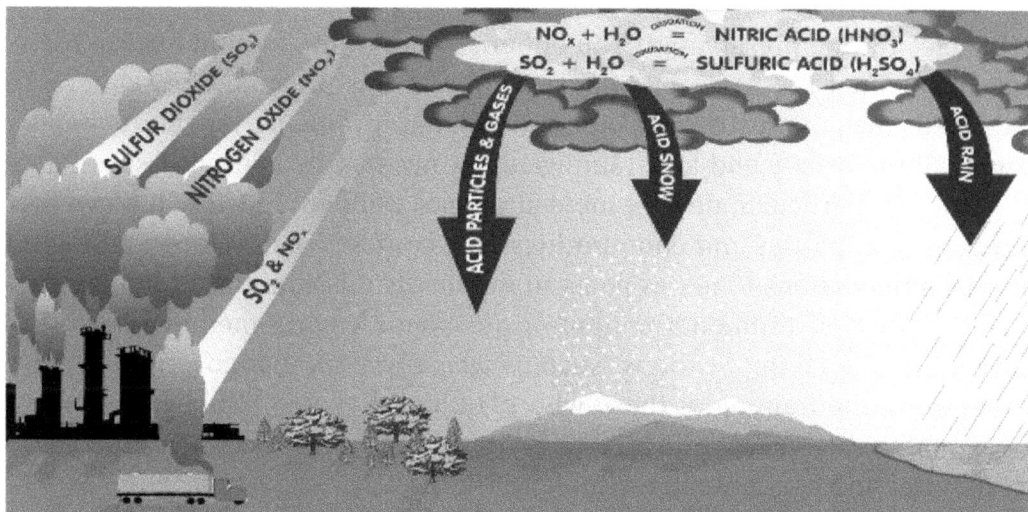

$$NO_x + H_2O \overset{\text{oxidation}}{=} NITRIC\ ACID\ (HNO_3)$$
$$SO_2 + H_2O \overset{\text{oxidation}}{=} SULFURIC\ ACID\ (H_2SO_4)$$

SULFUR DIOXIDE (SO₂)

NITROGEN OXIDE (NO₂)

SO₂ & NO₂

ACID PARTICLES & GASES

ACID SNOW

ACID RAIN

Source: "Acid Rain", Department of Environmental Conservation, New York State, http://www.dec.ny.gov/chemical/8418.html

International Environmental Agreements

International environmental agreements are important because they enable countries to work together to address vital environmental issues that are trans boundary or global in nature, such as air pollution, climate change, protection of the ozone layer, and ocean pollution. Countries have increasingly recognised this and have developed a wide range of international environmental agreements to enable them to work together on global environmental issues. International environmental agreements have been reached in some areas, such as the Montreal Protocol on substances that deplete the ozone layer and a number of agreements on marine pollution (e.g. the International Conference on Protection of the Marine Environment from Land-Based Sources, the International Convention for the Prevention of Pollution from Ships and the International Convention for the Prevention of Marine Pollution by Dumping of Wastes and Other Matter). Some important agreements are the following:

- **United Nations Conference on the Human Environment (UNCHE), Stockholm, Sweden (1972)**

The first United Nations Conference on the Human Environment (UNCHE) was held in Stockholm, Sweden, from June 5 to June 16, 1972.[42] Representatives from 113 countries were present, as well as representatives from many international non-governmental organisations, intergovernmental organisations, and many other specialised agencies. The Stockholm Declaration and Action Plan defined principles for the preservation and enhancement of the natural environment, and highlighted the need to support people in this process. The Conference indicated that "industrialised" environmental problems, such as habitat degradation, toxicity and acid rain, were not necessarily relevant issues for all countries. In particular, development strategies were not meeting the needs of the poorest countries and communities. The conference developed a long set of recommendations to act as goals to pursue its mission. Recommendations included that governments communicate about environmental issues that have international implications (such as air pollution), that governments give attention to the training of those who plan, develop, and manage settlement areas, and that agencies work together to address many issues, such as access to clean water and population growth.

- **United Nations Environment Programme**
   One of the greatest achievements of the UNCHE was the creation of the United Nations Environment Programme (UNEP), based in Nairobi, Kenya.[43] The mission of UNEP is "to provide leadership and encourage partnership in caring for the environment by inspiring, informing, and enabling nations and peoples to improve their quality of life without compromising that of future generations." UNEP is the voice for the environment within the United Nations system and works toward this mission by:
- *Encouraging international participation and cooperation in addressing environmental issues and environmental policy,*
- *Monitoring the status of the global environment and interpreting environmental data collected,*
- *Creating environmental awareness in governments, society, and the private sector,*
- *Coordinating UN activities pertaining to the environment,*
- *Developing regional programs for sustainability,*
- *Helping environmental authorities, especially those in developing countries, form and implement policy and*
- *Helping to develop international environmental law.*

Montreal Protocol (1987)

Montreal Protocol, formally Montreal Protocol on Substances that Deplete the Ozone Layer, international treaty, adopted in Montreal on Sept. 16, 1987, that aimed to regulate the production and use of chemicals that contribute to the depletion of Earth's ozone layer. Initially signed by 46 countries, the treaty has nearly 200 signatories. In 1985, with the discovery of a "hole" in the ozone shield over Antarctica by the British Antarctic Survey, representatives from 28 countries met to discuss the issue at the Vienna Convention for the Protection of the Ozone Layer. The meeting called for international cooperation in research involving ozone-depleting chemicals (ODCs) and empowered the United Nations Environment Programme (UNEP) to lay the groundwork for the Montreal Protocol. The initial agreement was designed to reduce the production and consumption of several types of CFCs and halons to 80 percent of 1986 levels by 1994 and 50 percent of 1986 levels by 1999. The protocol came into effect on January 1, 1989. Since then the agreement has been amended to further reduce and completely phase out CFCs and halons, as well as the manufacture and use of carbon tetrachloride, trichloroethane, hydro fluorocarbons (HFCs), hydro chlorofluorocarbons (HCFCs), hydrobromofluorocarbons (HBFCs), methyl bromide, and other ODCs.

In developed countries the production and consumption of halons formally ended by 1994, several other chemicals (such as CFCs, HBFCs, carbon tetrachloride, and methyl chloroform) were phased out by 1996, methyl bromide was eliminated in 2005, and HCFCs are scheduled to be completely phased out by 2030. In contrast, developing countries phased out CFCs, carbon tetrachloride, methyl chloroform, and halons by 2010; they are scheduled to phase out methyl bromide by 2015 and eliminate HCFCs by 2040.

Earth Summit (UNCED, 1992)

United Nations Conference on Environment and Development (UNCED), referred to as Earth Summit, was held at Rio de Janeiro, Brazil (June 3–14, 1992),[44] to reconcile worldwide economic development along with protection of the environment. The Earth Summit was the largest gathering of world leaders in history, with 117 Heads of State and representatives of 178 nations in all attending. The issues addressed at the summit included:

- *systematic scrutiny of patterns of production — particularly the production of toxic components, such as lead in gasoline, or poisonous waste including radioactive chemicals,*
- *alternative sources of energy to replace the use of fossil fuels which delegates linked to global climate change,*
- *new reliance on public transportation systems in order to reduce vehicle emissions, congestion in cities and the health problems caused by polluted air and smoke,*
- *the growing usage and limited supply of water.*

An important achievement of the summit was an agreement on the Climate Change Convention which in turn led to the Kyoto Protocol. Another agreement was to *"not to carry out any activities on the lands of indigenous peoples that would cause environmental degradation or that would be culturally inappropriate"*. The Convention on Biological Diversity was kept open for signature at the Earth Summit, and made a start towards redefinition of measures that did not inherently encourage destruction of natural Eco regions and so-called uneconomic growth. The main documents agreed upon at the Earth Summit are as follows. The Convention on Biological Diversity is a binding treaty requiring nations to take inventories of their plants and wild animals and protect their endangered species. The Framework Convention on Climate Change, or Global Warming Convention, is a binding treaty that requires nations to reduce their emission of carbon dioxide, methane, and other "greenhouse" gases thought to be responsible for global warming; the treaty stopped short of setting binding targets for emission reductions, however. The Declaration on Environment and Development, or Rio Declaration, laid down 27 broad, nonbinding principles for environmentally sound development. Agenda 21 outlined global strategies for cleaning up the environment and encouraging environmentally sound development. The Statement of Principles on Forests, aimed at preserving the world's rapidly vanishing tropical rainforests, is a nonbinding statement recommending that nations monitor and assess the impact of development on their forest resources and take steps to limit the damage done to them. The Earth Summit was hampered by disputes between the wealthy industrialised nations of the North (i.e., Western Europe and North America) and the poorer developing countries of the South (i.e., Africa, Latin America, the Middle East, and parts of Asia).

Kyoto Protocol (1999)

The Kyoto Protocol is an international treaty which extends the 1992 United Nations Framework Convention on Climate Change (UNFCCC) that commits State Parties to reduce greenhouse gases emissions, based on the premise that (a) global warming exists and (b) man-made CO_2 emissions have caused it. The Kyoto Protocol was negotiated in Kyoto, Japan in December 1997, kept open for signature on March 16, 1998, and closed on March 15, 1999. The agreement came into effect on February 16, 2005 following ratification by Russia on November 18, 2004. There are currently 192 Parties (Canada withdrew effective from December 2012)[45] to the Protocol. The Kyoto Protocol implemented the objective of the UNFCCC to fight global warming by reducing greenhouse gas concentrations in the atmosphere to "a level that would prevent dangerous anthropogenic interference with the climate system" (Art. 2). The Protocol is based on the principle of common but differentiated responsibilities: it puts the obligation to reduce current emissions on developed countries on the basis that they are historically responsible for the current levels of greenhouse gases in the atmosphere. The objective is the *"stabilszation of greenhouse gas concentrations in the atmosphere at a level that would prevent dangerous anthropogenic interference with the climate system."*[46] The Intergovernmental Panel on Climate Change (IPCC) has predicted an average global rise in temperature of 1.4°C (2.5°F) to 5.8°C (10.4°F) between 1990 and 2100. The protocol was developed under the UNFCCC - the United Nations Framework Convention on Climate Change. Participating countries that have ratified the Kyoto Protocol have committed to cut emissions of not only carbon dioxide, but of also other greenhouse gases, being: Methane (CH4), Nitrous Oxide (N2O), Hydro fluorocarbons (HFCs), Perfluorocarbons (PFCs), Sulphur hexafluoride (SF6). The main goal of the Kyoto Protocol is to control emissions of the main anthropogenic (i.e., human-emitted) greenhouse gases (GHGs) in ways that reflect underlying national differences in GHG emissions, wealth, and capacity to make the reductions. The ultimate objective of the UNFCCC is the "stabilisation of greenhouse gas concentrations in the atmosphere at a level that would stop dangerous anthropogenic interference with the climate system."[47]

According to a press release from the United Nations Environment Programme: *"The Kyoto Protocol is an agreement under which industrialised countries will reduce their collective emissions of greenhouse gases by 5.2 percent compared to the year 1990 (but note that, compared to the emissions levels that would be expected by 2010 without the Protocol, this target represents a 29 percent cut). The goal is to lower overall emissions of six greenhouse gases - carbon dioxide, methane, nitrous oxide, sulfur hexafluoride, HFCs, and PFCs - calculated as an average over the five-year period of 2008-12. National targets range from 8 percent reductions for the European Union and some others to 7 percent for the US, 6 percent for Japan, 0 percent for Russia, and permitted increases of 8 pecent for Australia and 10 percent for Iceland."*[48]

The Protocol's first commitment period commenced in 2008 and ended in 2012. A second commitment period was agreed to in 2012, known as the Doha Amendment to the protocol, in which 37 countries had binding targets: Australia, the European Union (and its 28 member states), Belarus, Iceland, Kazakhstan, Liechtenstein, Norway, Switzerland, and Ukraine. Belarus, Kazakhstan and Ukraine indicated that they might withdraw from the Protocol or not put into legal force the Amendment with second round targets. Japan, New Zealand and Russia have participated in Kyoto's first-round but have not taken on new targets in the second commitment period. The official meeting of all states party to the Kyoto Protocol is called the Conference of the Parties. It is held every year as part of the United Nations Climate Change conference, which also serves as the formal meeting of UNFCCC. The first Meetings of Parties of the Kyoto Protocol (CMP) was held in 2005 in conjunction with the eleventh Conferences of parties to UNFCCC (COP). Also parties to the Convention who are not parties to the Protocol can participate in Protocol-related meetings as observers.

Kyoto establishes the following principles:

- Kyoto is underwritten by governments and is governed by global legislation enacted under the UN's aegis. Governments are divided into two general categories: developed countries, referred to as Annex 1 countries (who have accepted GHG emission reduction obligations and must submit an annual greenhouse gas inventory) and developing countries, referred to as Non-Annex 1 countries (who have no GHG emission reduction obligations but may participate in the Clean Development Mechanism).

- Any Annex 1 country that fails to meet its Kyoto target will be penalised by having to submit 1.3 emission allowances in a second commitment period for every ton of GHG emissions they exceed their cap in the first commitment period (i.e, 2008-2012).

- By 2008-2012, Annex 1 countries have to reduce their GHG emissions by an average of 5 percent below their 1990 levels (for many countries, such as the EU member states, this corresponds to some 15 percent below their expected GHG emissions in 2008). While the average emissions reduction is 5 percent national targets range from 8 percent reductions for the European Union to a 10 percent emissions increase for Iceland. Reduction targets were to be met by 2013.

- Kyoto includes "flexible mechanisms" which allow Annex 1 economies to meet their GHG targets by purchasing GHG emission reductions from elsewhere. These can be bought either from financial exchanges (such as the new EU Emissions Trading Scheme) or from projects which reduce emissions in non-Annex 1 economies under the Clean Development Mechanism (CDM), or in other Annex-1 countries under the Joint implementation (JI).

- Only CDM Executive Board-accredited Certified Emission Reductions (CER) can be bought and sold in this manner. Under the aegis of the UN, Kyoto established this Bonn-based Clean Development Mechanism Executive Board to assess and approve projects ("CDM Projects") in Non-Annex 1 economies prior to awarding CERs. (A similar scheme called "Joint Implementation" or 'JI' applies in transitional economies mainly covering the former Soviet Union and Eastern Europe).[49]

The Kyoto Protocol allows for flexibility in terms of the methods the countries could use to meet their gas reduction commitments. Such methods include: [50]

- *Compensating for emissions by increasing the number of a country's carbon sinks. Carbon sinks are forests, which take up carbon dioxide from the atmosphere. Countries are allowed to create carbon sinks on suitable sites outside of their own territory.*

- *Emissions trading – trading of emission allowances between countries. The emissions trading method gives countries the opportunity to reduce emissions where it is most economically efficient to do so.*

- *Clean development mechanism – promotes environmentally-friendly foreign investments from industrialised countries to developing countries. The developing countries are thus aided at achieving sustainable development.*

- *Joint implementation – allows developed countries to sponsor foreign research to decrease emission levels in countries of economic transition. In exchange for the developed country's investment, the host country provides the investor with emission reduction units, also known as carbon credits. The developed economies can afterwards use their carbon credits towards meeting their emission-reduction requirements under the Kyoto Protocol.*

UN Climate Conference – Paris, France (November 30-December 11, 2015)

The 2015 United Nations Climate Change Conference, COP 21 or CMP 11 was held in Paris, France, from November 30 to December 12, 2015. It was the 21st yearly session of the Conference of the Parties (COP) to the 1992 United Nations Framework Convention on Climate Change (UNFCCC) and the 11th session of the Meeting of the Parties to the 1997 Kyoto Protocol.[51] The conference negotiated the Paris Agreement, a global agreement on the reduction of climate change, the text of which represented a consensus of the representatives of the 196 parties attending it.[52] The agreement will become legally binding if by at least 55 countries join which together represent at least 55 percent of global greenhouse emissions.[53] Such parties will need to sign the agreement in New York between April 21, 2016 (Earth Day) and April 22, 2017, and also adopt it within their own legal systems (through ratification, acceptance, approval, or accession). According to the organising committee at the outset of the talks, the expected key result was an agreement to set a goal of limiting global warming to less than 2 degrees Celsius (°C) compared to pre-industrial levels. The agreement calls for zero net anthropogenic greenhouse gas emissions to be reached during the second half of the 21st century. In the adopted version of the Paris Agreement, the parties will also "pursue efforts to" limit the temperature increase to 1.5°C.[54] The 1.5°C goal will require zero emissions sometime between 2030 and 2050, according to some scientists. On December 12, 2015, the participating 195 countries agreed, by consensus, to the final global pact, the Paris Agreement, to reduce emissions as part of the method for reducing greenhouse gas. In the 12-page document, the members agreed to reduce their carbon output "as soon as possible" and to do their best to keep global warming "to well below 2 °C".

Global Commons Debate

The term *'commons'* has been in vogue for quite some time and was commonly used for tract of ground shared by the residents of a village. It included the grazing grounds or village square which did not belong to any one person but to the whole community and was used by all. In the recent years 'global commons' has been used for the natural systems which maintain the biosphere of the world on which we live. It includes the atmosphere, hydrosphere, lithosphere and biosphere, which are shared by all. The indiscriminate use of the atmosphere by the advanced countries has created serious problems. The noxious gases and particles from our cooking, heating, industrial activities and various modes of transportation have given rise to problems like acid rain, persistent smog, increasing atmospheric carbon dioxide, and disturbance of the stratospheric ozone layer. The mining of water from underground, discharge of industrial effluents and sewage into streams or lakes etc. have also produced adverse effects. There has been dramatic drop in the level of water table under many key agricultural areas and cities. The problem of potable water has been further aggravated due to enormous increase in population.

The *'Global Commons'* refers to resource domains or areas that lie outside of the political reach of any one nation State. Thus international law identifies four global commons namely: the High Seas; the Atmosphere; Antarctica; and Outer Space. Despite efforts by governments or individuals to establish property rights or other forms of control over most of natural resources, the Global Commons have remained an exception. Historically, access to some of the resources found within the global commons, except for a few types fisheries, has been difficult and these resources have historically not been scarce to justify the attempt for exclusive control and access. However, with the advancement of science and technology in recent years it has made access to resources in the Global Commons easier, leading to an increase in activities in these resource domains, some types of which lack effective laws or policies to control and regulate such uses. Basically global commons is a phrase generally would always explain international, supranational, and global resource fields wherein common-pool resources can be found. Global commons include things like the earth's shared natural resources, like the deep oceans, the atmosphere, outer space and the Northern and Southern polar regions, the Antarctic in particular. Cyberspace may also fulfill the interpretation of a global commons.

Hence international law recognises four global commons particularly: *the High Seas; the Atmosphere; Antarctica; Outer Space and Cyber space.* All these zones have historically been guided by the principle of the common heritage of human being - the open access doctrine or the *mare liberum* (free sea for all) regarding the High Seas. Even though initiatives by governments or individuals to develop property rights or other forms of control over natural resources, the Global Commons have continues as an exception.

The United Nations Environment Program (UNEP) has recognised numerous areas of needs of countries in managing the global ocean: strengthen national capabilities for actions, particularly in developing countries; develop fisheries management; reinforcement of cooperation in semi-enclosed and regional seas; enhanced controls over ocean; disposal of hazardous and nuclear wastes; and also advancement of the Law of the Sea. Specified problems referred to are drawing particular attention include rising sea levels; contamination by hazardous chemicals (including oil spills); microbiological contamination; ocean acidification; harmful algael blooms; and over-fishing and other overexploitation.

The eight Arctic countries, Canada, Denmark (Greenland and the Faroe Islands), Norway, the United States (Alaska), Sweden, Finland, Iceland, and Russia, are all members of the treaty organisation, the Arctic Council, as are organisations representing six indigenous populations. The Council operates on consensus basis, mostly dealing with environmental treaties and not addressing boundary or resource disputes. At present, the Antarctic Treaty and associated agreements, jointly called the Antarctic Treaty System or ATS, manage international relations with reference to Antarctica, Earth's only continent without a native-born human population. The treaty came into force in 1961 and presently including 50 signatory nations, sets aside Antarctica as a scientific preserve, establishes freedom of scientific analysis and even bans military activity on that continent.

The Outer Space Treaty gives a primary structure for international space law. It includes the legal use of outer space by nation states. The treaty states that outer space is free for all nation states to explore and is not subject to claims of national sovereignty. It also prohibits the deployment of nuclear weapons in outer space. The treaty was passed by the United Nations General Assembly in 1963 and signed in 1967 by the USSR, the United States of America and the United Kingdom. As of mid-year, 2013 the treaty has been ratified by 102 states and signed by another 27 states.

The International Space Station (ISS) program is a combined project among five participating space agencies: NASA, the Russian Federal Space Agency (RSA), Japan Aerospace Exploration Agency (JAXA), European Space Agency (ESA), and Canadian Space Agency (CSA). National budget constraints led to the merger of three space station projects into the International Space Station.

The ISS is arguably the most expensive single item ever before developed, and may be the most essential instances of international cooperation in modern history. As per the original Memorandum of Understanding between NASA and the RSA, the International Space Station was intended to be a laboratory, observatory and factory in space. It was also planned to provide transportation, maintenance, and act as a staging base for possible future missions to the Moon, Mars and asteroids. In the 2010 United States National Space Policy, it was provided further specific roles of serving commercial, diplomatic and educational purposes.

As a global system of computers interconnected by telecommunication technologies consisting of millions of private, public, academic, business, and government resources, it is difficult to argue that the Internet is a global commons. These computing resources are largely privately owned and subject to private property law, although many are government owned and subject to public law. The World Wide Web, as a system of interlinked hypertext documents, either public domain (like Wikipedia itself) or subject to copyright law, is, at best, a mixed good.

The resultant virtual space or cyberspace, however, is often viewed as an electronic global commons that allows for as much or more freedom of expression as any public space. Access to those digital commons and the actual freedom of expression allowed does vary widely by geographical area. Management of the electronic global commons presents as many issues as do other commons.

The need to address environmental issues of the global commons has been debated among various stakeholders for a long time now. Furthermore, a number of legal and institutional frameworks exist to deal with the environmental issues of the global commons. For instance, parts of the United Nations Convention on the Law of the Sea (UNCLOS) are dedicated to environmental management of the world's oceans and various components of the Antarctic Treaty Systems (ATS) for Antarctica deal with the environment of the Antarctica. While some institutional and regulatory frameworks currently address natural resource issues in the Global Commons there are fundamental gaps and inconsistencies that require immediate attention.

Environmental security encompasses the interactive dynamics of the diverse human and natural networks that constitute the modern world.[55] Environment as a resource has strategic significance for nation-states who build power through natural resources like water, oil, gas, and various other minerals. Increasing state control over environment and natural resources has spillover effects such as environmental degradation, resulting in undue catastrophes. These include uncontrolled migration, high population growth, and human casualties. Such catastrophes have become real security concerns for the affected states. Traditionally, the realist understanding of security does not include the environment as a matter of concern. However, post-realist scholars do include the environment as an important security concern. Shaukat Hassan in Adelphi paper discusses the relationship between the environmental foundation of a nation and its effect on the economy. According to his argument, continuous environmental calamities decrease the economic growth of a nation, hamper its social cohesion, and destabilise its political structure.[56] Environmental change reduces economic opportunities for a country by causing demographic displacement within states and across international borders. An unexpected movement of population across the international border raises political tension between neighbouring countries. Environmental stress can also cause an affected sub-national group to shift its allegiance from the center to the periphery, increasing the possibilities of political disorder, civil strife, and even insurgency.[57] Environmental calamities trigger policy choices that can catalyse a potential conflict or aggravate an existing one. Environmental devastation faced by a country due to natural calamities, especially those originating from beyond its borders, eventually sour bilateral relations and hamper regional stability. In recent times, environmental challenges ranging from pollution, excessive carbon emissions and rapid population growth have led to increased scarcity of natural resources like water, energy, and food. The case of Darfur in Sudan is the most suitable example in this regard. Darfur faced relentless desertification over the past several decades. The process of desertification had eroded the surface clay and soils, and finally depleted the productivity of arable lands in the greater region of Darfur and particularly in northern Darfur.[58] This environmental degradation has forced ecological migration towards the southern part of Sudan. This internal displacement caused tensions in the issues of land use and resource sharing, which finally continued to threaten peaceful coexistence and the social cohesion of Darfur. Hence, the situation ignited local tensions and provoked violent resource-based conflicts since February 2003.

The global warming controversy concerns the public debate over whether global warming is occurring, how much has occurred in modern times, what has caused it, what its effects will be, whether any action should be taken to curb it, and if so what that action should be. In the scientific literature, there is a strong consensus that global surface temperatures have increased in recent decades and that the trend is caused by human-induced emissions of greenhouse gases. No scientific body of national or international standing disagrees with this view, though a few organisations with members in extractive industries hold non-committal positions. Disputes over the key scientific facts of global warming are now more prevalent in the popular media than in the scientific literature, where such issues are treated as resolved, and as more prevalent in the United States than globally.

Political and popular debate concerning the existence and cause of climate change includes the reasons for the increase seen in the instrumental temperature record, whether the warming trend exceeds normal climatic variations, and whether human activities have contributed significantly to it. Scientists have resolved many of these questions decisively in favour of the view that the current warming trend exists and is ongoing, that human activity is the primary cause, and that it is without precedent in at least 2000 years. Disputes that also reflect scientific debate include estimates of how responsive the climate system might be to any given level of greenhouse gases (climate sensitivity)[59] and what the consequences of global warming will be. Scientific consensus is normally achieved through communication at conferences, publication in the scientific literature, replication (reproducible results by others),[60] and peer review. In the case of global warming, many governmental reports, the media in many countries, and environmental groups, have stated that there is virtually unanimous scientific agreement that human-caused global warming is real and poses a serious concern.[61] On November 12, 2015, NASA scientists reported that human-made carbon dioxide (CO_2) continues to increase above levels not seen in hundreds of thousands of years: currently, about half of the carbon dioxide released from the burning of fossil fuels remains in the atmosphere and is not absorbed by vegetation and the oceans.[62]

There are debates on environment as the primary source of conflict or cause of war. Alan Dupont argues that environmental difficulties are unlikely to be the primary cause of major conflict between states.[63] Environmental issues, according to Dupont, interact with more direct causes of conflict to prolong or complicate existing disputes. For example, environmental degradation can create refugee crisis between two neighboring countries. Now, refugee issues may aggravate conflicts in between the neighbours. Thus environment is not the direct cause of a conflict. Daniel Deudney has also vehemently opposed considering environmental degradation as a reference object of international security. According to Deudney, the concept of national security, as opposed to national interest or well-being, has been centered upon organised violence. He gives the example of natural calamities like earthquakes or hurricanes that had caused excessive damage; he opposes the notion that such events are threats to national security.[64] However, Deudney's analysis is flawed as it is very biased to the natural disasters which have comparatively fewer effects on developed countries. He did not consider the lacking of capacity of underdeveloped countries to tackle these environmental disasters. For example, the February 2010 earthquake in Chile was stronger than the one that devastated Haiti just a month before. Yet, Haiti faced more casualties and damages than Chile, because of its poor and unprotected infrastructure; lack of preparation to face such disaster, and absence of emergency response to the post-earthquake situation.[65] On the contrary, Chile maintained its building codes and built its own emergency response system for such situations.[66] Chile is a wealthier nation with the experience of tackling such seismic catastrophes. While Haiti has experienced several catastrophic earthquakes over the course of its history, the country's lack of building codes, lack of preparation and disaster planning resulted in total crisis in the aftermath of the 2010 earthquake. Haiti still carries the devastation and is on a low path to recovery.

Another natural occurrence that has caused major changes in the Earth's climate in the past is shifts in the Earth's orbit. Consider the Sahara desert, for example. There is a wide acceptance among scientists that Sahara transformed from fertile grassland to a desert because of a change in the Earth's orbit. This shift as to how the Earth circled the Sun affected the amount of sunlight that region of Africa received.

The tilt in the Earth's orbit is said to vary between 22 and 25 degrees roughly every 41,000 years. While a natural event such as this could bring about major changes to the climate, some scientists are warning that there is a possibility for reverse feedback. In other words, instead of an orbital tilt causing climate change, such as the one that took place in the African continent, current changes in climate could end up causing changes in the Earth's axial tilt. In an article published in 2010, Astrobiology Magazine reported on such a prediction: "Scientists from NASA's Jet Propulsion Laboratory say that the current melting of ice in Greenland is already causing the tilt to change at a rate of approximately 2.6 centimeters each year. They predict that this change could increase in the years ahead."[67]

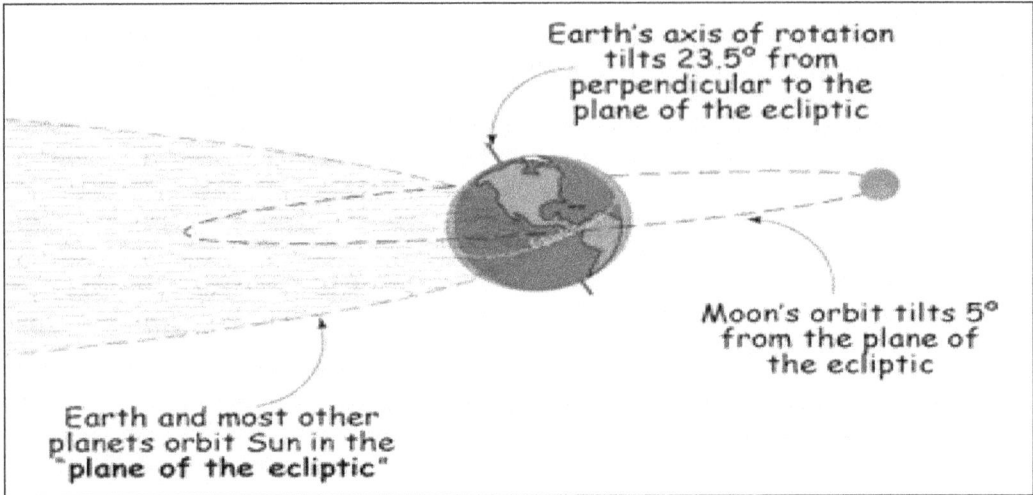

Source: Changes in the Earth's tilt cause changes in weather patterns. Such a change is believed to have made the "Green Sahara" go dry. Image credit: NASA - http://www.astrobio.net/news-exclusive/how-earths-orbital-shift-shaped-the-sahara/#sthash.W8WbdT3Y.dpuf

The environment-threat-vulnerability nexus plays a vital role in proving that environment is a real security threat. Two aspects of this nexus are significant. First, ecosystem integrity is crucial for the population's sustainable livelihood. Therefore, certain environmental conditions often resulting from environmental change such as pollution depletion, or natural disasters can pose an acute threat to security.[68] Environmental degradations and climate change increase an individual's vulnerability. Moreover, environment is linked with international security as it becomes evident that national solutions to environmental problems would not be sustainable in the long-run without international cooperation.[69] Chalecki has explained how the patterns of human behaviour and its interaction with the economic variables of society can bring climatic changes both regionally and globally.[70] The relevant example is the increase of carbon dioxide gas emissions due to industrialisation in many parts of the world. Climate change and ecological degradation hamper the natural flow of resource supply and lead to political disputes as well as ethnic and civil unrests. Due to the transnational nature of resources, conflict due to scarcity affects the regional or global level in the long-run. Homer-Dixon has investigated the relationship between population growth, renewable resource scarcities, migration, and violent conflict and thus has contributed in framing a nexus among environment, threat, and vulnerability. He mentions three reasons that connect the environment with conflict. These are the degradation and depletion of renewable resources, the increased consumption of those resources, and their uneven distribution.[71] This annotation establishes environment as the core referent object of security.

Climate change is a long-term problem. However, an increasing frequency of such extreme weather events can be another indication that climate change is in fact a reality. In this complex and seemingly never-ending debate, there is now an increasing number of scientists and other observers who say researchers and policymakers need to move on, to respond to the Earth's reactions to global warming instead of still debating whether or not it is a reality. Climate change affects nearly every other sector of society. Take, for example, public health. Some of the diseases that impact global populations the most, such as malaria and diarrhea that kill millions each year are highly sensitive to climatic conditions. Then there is the inequity of these risks. China is now the world's top emitter of greenhouse gases, but developed countries, primarily the United States, is still mainly responsible for causing climate change after having emitted the most pollution for the longest time. But the population that suffer the most from climatic changes will be those in developing countries – countries that have contributed the least to climate change and populations who have the least access to resources that could help them deal with the consequences.[72]

Global climate change is causing these areas to experience an increasingly sparse and erratic rainfall pattern and a long dry season, affecting the livelihood of thousands of villagers; some areas are also facing water shortages. People are becoming aware of global warming, as they have started cultivating more and more trees, planting mangrove forest by the coastal areas and reduced the usage of plastic. They have sowed more than 12 million seeds and half a million plants. Planting trees balances the carbon emissions and pollution. There are organisations that will help offset carbon footprint. The deforestation comes in as a close second in causes for global warming. There is still much that is unknown about the potential health effects of global climate change. The various phenomena that can be said to contribute to the rubric include stratospheric ozone depletion, global warming, acid aerosol formation, desertification, and deforestation. At the current time, these phenomena are being investigated separately, yet the case can and should be made that these things are happening concurrently and there are many instances where interactions are possible as well as likely. Thus, a more global view is required, particularly with regard to the science, but also with regard to policy.

These phenomena are not occurring independently. There is the need to analyse them to arrive at an optimum solution. Although it is sometimes helpful to divide a problem into components in order to analyse, at some point the analyst has to reassemble the parts and look for the total effect. This has not yet been done in the public health arena regarding global climate change, and there is very little evidence that it is being done in other important areas such as agriculture and natural resources. At last, global warming can be dealt with only through international agreements. The context is one of game theory, and the stress is on designing incentive systems for global cooperation. The Montreal Protocol on ozone may be an ineffective guide to the prospects for a greenhouse agreement. The most urgent need is to develop appropriate policy instruments and compensatory mechanisms for the best results. The growing recognition that greenhouse gas reductions are not the only option we have to slow and ultimately reverse global warming. Restoring and expanding global forests can also cool the planet.

Conclusion

At one point of time, the damage reaches a stage wherein the environment can't attain the required balance on its own. In such a situation, we humans need to step in, and ensure that the damage is curbed and balance is attained. Simple measures, such as conservation of electricity, use of alternative energy sources, avoiding the use of things that pollute the environment, soil conservation, etc., can help in saving the environment from the threat of degradation. Environmentalists, the world over, are trying their best to save our environment, and we need to do our bit to make sure that they succeed. The need of the hour is to identify the causes of environmental degradation, and eliminate them one by one. We need to understand the fact that we are a part of the interwoven life system on the planet, and any problems, like environmental degradation and environmental pollution, are bound to affect us directly or indirectly. Though the disaster is not expected to happen tomorrow or a hundred years from now, that doesn't mean it will never happen at all. That being said, the onus is on us - the most intelligent species on the planet, to make sure that such problems are kept at bay.

We can say that if the human race has to survive on the face of this earth, it is important that stringent measures be taken up to arrest further deterioration of the environment. One will have to work towards conserving air, water and soil and try to restore balance in the ecosystem, which has been destroyed or is on the verge of extinction or total destruction. In other words, one will have to work towards restoring natural habitats and make sure no further harm is done to the environment.

Notes

1. "Climate Change Science Facts" April, 2010, www.epa.gov/climatechange, Office of Air and Radiation (6207J), United States Environmental Protection Agency, 2010.
2. "The World Bank Annual Report 2014" Washington, DC. https://openknowledge.worldbank.org/handle/10986/20093, International Bank for Reconstruction and Development/ The World Bank, February, 2014.
3. Parmesan, C., "Ecological and evolutionary responses to recent climate change", *Annual Review of Ecology Evolution and Systematics*, Vol 37, 2006, pp. 637–69.
4. Linderholm, Hans W., "Growing season changes in the last century", *Agricultural and Forest Meteorology*, vol no. 137. http://research.eeescience.utoledo.edu/lees/papers_PDF/Linderholm_2006_AFM.pdf, accessed on March, 14, 2014..
5. IPCC. Summary for Policymakers, A report of Working Group I of the Intergovernmental Panel on Climate Change, Vol. No.II, Cambridge University Press, Cambridge, United Kingdom.
6. Langevin, C. D. and Zygnerski, M., "Effect of sea-level rise on salt water intrusion near a coastal well field in southeastern Florida, Ground Water", vol, or no.51, 2013, pp.781–803. doi: 10.1111/j.1745-6584.2012.01008. July, 2013.
7. Trenberth, K. E., "Changes in precipitation with climate change" in Climate Research, 2011, vol 47, pp.123–38.
8. Trenberth, K. E., et al "Surface and Atmospheric Climate Change" in *Climate Change 2007: The Physical Science Basis.* at https://www.ipcc.ch/publications_and_data/ar4/wg1/en/ch3.html. accessed May 10, 2015, Contribution of Working Group I to the Fourth Assessment Report of the Intergovernmental Panel on Climate , eds., Solomon, S., et al (eds.) (Cambridge University Press, Cambridge, United Kingdom and New York, NY, 2007).
9. Melillo et al., *Third National Climate Assessment Draft Report* (Washington, DC: United States Global Change Research Program,2013).
10. Ibid.
11. Ariano, R., G. W. Canonica, and G. Passalacqua, "Possible role of climate changes in variations in pollen seasons and allergic sensitizations during 27 years" in *Annals of Allergy, Asthma and Immunology*, vol. 104, pp. 215–22.
12. Altizer S. et al., Climate change and infectious diseases: From evidence to a predictive framework. *Science*, vol. 341 no.6145, 2013, pp. 514–19.
13. Karl, T. R., G. A. Meehl, and T. C. Peterson, Global *Climate Change Impacts in the United States* (Cambridge, UK: Cambridge University Press, 2009).
14. Ibid.
15. IPCC IPCC Guidance Note for Lead Authors of the IPCC Fifth Assessment Report on Consistent Treatment of Uncertainties. "Likely" defined by the IPCC as a probability of 66 percent to 100 percent.
16. IPCC Climate Change 2013: The Physical Science Basis, Contribution of Working Group I to the Fifth Assessment Report of the Intergovernmental Panel on Climate Change (Cambridge, UK: Cambridge University Press, 2013).
17. National Research Council, Strategy 2013-2018, National Research Council Canada, Montreal Road Building, Ottawa, Ontario K1A, 2013.
18. Ibid.
19. Impacts of a Warming Arctic, Arctic Climate Impact Assessment, http://www.acia.uaf.edu/pages/overview.html., (Paris, and Parthenon Publishing Group, New York and London, 261-278. 2007.
20. McMichael T., H. Montgomery, and A. Costello, "Health risks, present and future, from global climate change", *International Journal of Environmental Research and Public Health*, 2012, May; 11(5): pp. 5224–5240.

21. Alina Bradford, "*What Is Global Warming?*" Live Science, December 15, 2015,

22. Ibid.

23. Overpeck, J.T., et al. "Paleoclimatic Evidence for Future Ice-Sheet Instability and Rapid Sea-Level Rise". Science vol.311, pp.1747-1750.

24. Impacts of a Warming Arctic, Arctic Climate Impact Assessment, http://www.acia.uaf.edu/pages/overview.html.,accessed on May 5, 2015.

25. Intergovernmental Panel on Climate Change. 2001, *"Climate Change 2001: Synthesis Report; Summary for Policymakers".* http://www.ipcc.ch/pub/un/syreng/spm.pdf., May 21, 2007.

26. *Climate Change and Agricultural Vulnerability,* International Institute for Applied Systems Analysis, 2002 at http://www.iiasa. ac.at/Research/LUC/JB-Report.pdf. 2002, pp53-88.

27. Intergovernmental Panel on Climate Change Working Group III, *Climate Change 2001: Mitigation,* (Cambridge University Press: 2001).

28. "Environmental Pollution and Impacts on Public Health", United Nations Environment Programme http://www.unep.org/urban_environment/PDFs/DandoraWasteDump-ReportSummary.pdf accessed on August 2, 2005.

29. Van Kooten, G. C. and Bulte, E. H., The *economics of nature: managing biological assets.* (Oxford: Blackwells,2000).

30. Barraclough, S. and Ghimire, K. B., "Agricultural Expansion and Tropical Deforestation" (Earthscan, 2000).

31. Angelsen, A., "Agricultural expansion and deforestation: modeling the impact of population, market forces and property rights" in *Journal of Development Economics* 1999, vol.58, pp. 185-218.

32. Sheram, K., *The Environmental Data Book* (The World Bank, Washington DC, 1993).

33. "Deforestation Technical Support Package" (paper presented at the Third International Conference on Environment Enforcement, Oaxaca Mexico April 25-28, 1994) World Wildlife Fund; U. S. Environmental Protection Agency and U. S. Agency for International Development.

34. Philip M. Fearnside1 and William F. Laurance, "Tropical Deforestation And Greenhouse-Gas Emissions", Ecological Applications, vol. 14, no. 4 (August 2004) pp. 982–986.

35. Foundation Chirac *Deforestation and desertification* (Science Daily, August 14, 2007)

36. IPCC Fourth Assessment Report, Working Group I Report "The Physical Science Basis", Section 7.3.3.1.5, p. 527.

37. G.R. van der Werf et al., "CO2 emissions from forest loss". *Nature Geoscience* vol. 2 no. 11, 2009, pp.737–738. doi:10.1038/ngeo671.(Nature Geoscience, Vol. 2, No. 11. (01 November 2009).

38. Mather, A. S., *Global Forest Resources* (Dehra Dun :International Book Distributors, 1991).

39. Weathers, K. C. and Likens, G. E., "Acid rain", pp. 1549–1561 in: W. N. Rom and S. Markowitz (eds.). Environmental and Occupational Medicine. (Lippincott: Raven Publ., Philadelphia, 2006).

40. EPA, 2000. Mid-Atlantic highlands streams assessment, EPA- 903-R-00-015. http://www.epa.gov/maia/html/maha.html., accessed on February 3, 2010.

41. Savita Dubey, "Acid Rain-The Major Cause of Pollution: Its Causes, Effects and Solution" *International Journal of Scientific Engineering and Technology*, vol.2, no.8, August 1, 2013, pp: 772-775.

42. Buss, R., United Nations Conference on the Human Environment (UNCHE), 2007, Stockholm, Sweden. athttp://www.eoearth.org/view/article/156774, accessed on March 28, 2012.

43. ibid.

44. "United Nations Conference on Environment and Development (UNCED)", *Encyclopedia Britannica* at http://www.britannica.com/event/United-Nations-Conference-on-Environment-and-Development, accessed on April 6, 2010.

45. "Kyoto Protocol to the United Nations Framework Convention on Climate Change". *UN Treaty Database*, accessed on December 10, 2012.

46. "Status of ratification". UNFCC , details and accessed on January 23, 2011.

47. "Article 2". *The United Nations Framework Convention on Climate Change*. Such a level should be achieved within a time-frame sufficient to allow ecosystems to adapt naturally to climate change, to ensure that food production is not threatened and to enable economic development to proceed in a sustainable manner, accessed on November 15, 2005.

48. "Article 4", *The United Nations Framework Convention on Climate Change* at http://unfccc.int/essential_background/convention/background/items/1362.php accessed on April 6, 2010.

49. "Article 2", *The United Nations Framework Convention on Climate Change* at http://unfccc.int/essential_background/convention/background/items/1353.php. , accessed on November 15, 2005

50. *Buis Alan, Ramsayer Kate and Rasmussen, Carol,* "A Breathing Planet, Off Balance". November 12, 2015, NASA,(NASA Goddard Space Flight Center, and Carol Rasmussen).

51. Oreskes, Naomi, *"Beyond the Ivory Tower: The Scientific Consensus on Climate Change"*, University of California at San Diego, December 3, 2004.

52. *America's Climate Choices: Panel on Advancing the Science of Climate Change; National Research Council Advancing the Science of Climate Change. (Washington, D.C.: The National Academies Press, 2010).*

53. *Understanding and Responding to Climate Change* (United States National Academy of Sciences. *2008).*

54. Ibid.

55. Matthew and McDoland, Networks of Threats and Vulnerability: Lessons From Environmental Security Research, (2004), p. 36.

56. Shaukat Hassan, "Environmental Issues and Security in South Asia", *ADELPHI Paper*, no. 262, (Autumn 1991): pp. 5-6.

57. Ibid.

58. To know more about the environmental impact on Darfur's conflict situation, one can read: "Environmental Degradation as a Cause of Conflict in Darfur" (Conference Proceedings name of event, place, country name, month, date year), (Ethiopia: University for Peace, 2004), pp.12-13.

59. *Union of Concerned Scientists,* "World's Nobel Laureates And Preeminent Scientists Call On Government Leaders To Halt Global Warming". *ScienceDaily.com.*, accessed on October 2, 1997.

60. "List of Selected Prominent Signatories with awards and affiliations". *Dieoff.org.*, accessed on 14 January, 2009.

61. *Buis, n.50.*

62. Ritter, Karl, "UK: In 1st, global temps average could be 1 degree C higher". *AP News* .November, 9, 2015.

63. Alan Dupont,"The Environment and Security in Pacific Asia", *ADELPHI Paper* 319, (June 1998), pp. 75-76.

64. Daniel Deudney, "Environment and Security: Muddled thinking", *Bulletin of the Atomic Scientists* vol. 47, no. 3, (1991): pp.22-28.

65. Frank Bajak, "Chile-Haiti Earthquake Comparison: Chile Was More Prepared", *The Huffington Post,* February 27, 2010, http://www.huffingtonpost.com/2010/02/27/chile-haiti-earthquake-co_n_479705.html, February, 2010.

66. Ibid.

67. Anuradha K. Herath "How Earth´s Orbital Shift Shaped the Sahara" - December 20, 2010 *NASA Astrobiology* Portal, accessed on December 20, 2010.

68. Jon Barnett and W. Neil Adger,"Climate Change, human security and violent conflict", *Political Geography* 26 (2007): pp.639–655.

69. Lars Wirkus and Ruth Vollmer (Eds.), *Monitoring Environment and Security Integrating Concepts and Enhancing Methodologies,* (Bonn: Bonn International Center for Conversion, 2009), p.8.

70. Elizabeth Chalecki, "Environmental Security: A Case Study of Climate Change", (2009), p. 2.

71. Homer-Dixon in Betsy Hartmann, *Population, environment and security: a new trinity, Environment and Urbanization*, vol. 10, no 2, (October 1998), pp.116-117.

72. Anuradha K. Herath "The Climate Change Debate: Man vs. Nature" *Astrobiology Magazine*, October 05, 2011.

CHAPTER 7

Proliferation of Nuclear Weapons

Introduction

A primary security concern in today's world is the threat about the proliferation of nuclear weapons. Apart from states which are the five "*original*" nuclear weapons-possessing countries (Britain, China, France, Russia and the United States) many other states are also seeking to acquire, or have already acquired, nuclear materials, industrial systems etc., to produce plutonium or uranium, and delivery systems, such as missiles and aircrafts. Despite multilateral and bilateral efforts to control the spread of nuclear weapons, the international community seems to be fighting an uphill task.

Proliferation of nuclear weapons is one of the major challenges we face as a global society. Controlling the proliferation of nuclear weapons on priority basis—and ultimately abolishing them—must be our major goal. This could be achieved only by involving national governments, intergovernmental organisations, and nongovernmental (civil-society) organisations. The attempts of the respective governments towards this have so far has been through bilateral and multilateral treaties.[1] Non-political international organisations, such as the United Nations (UN), the International Atomic Energy Agency (IAEA) and the International Court of Justice (World Court) have also made attempts towards this objective. Nongovernmental organisations—including organisations of professionals, such as the Federation of American Scientists, the International Physicians for the Prevention of Nuclear War (IPPNW), and Physicians for Social Responsibility (IPPNW's US affiliate)—have worked towards this through education, dissemination of information, and advocacy aimed at governments and governmental organisations.[2]

The threat posed by the proliferation of nuclear weapons has three major dimensions:

- The development of capability for producing or acquiring nuclear weapons by countries that do not currently have nuclear weapons (horisontal proliferation).
- The increase of weapon stockpiles by countries that currently have nuclear weapons, the improvement of technical sophistication or reliability of these weapons, and the development of new weapons, such as "mini-nukes" or battlefield nuclear weapons (vertical proliferation).
- The acquisition of nuclear weapons or the materials and knowledge by individuals or non-state entities, often termed "terrorists," to produce nuclear weapons (another form of horisontal proliferation).

Arms Control and Disarmament

One of the major efforts being made to preserve international peace and security in the 21st century has been to control or limit the number of weapons and the ways in which weapons can be used. The means being adopted to achieve this goal include disarmament and arms control. Disarmament is the process of reduction in the number of weapons and troops maintained by a state. Arms control refers to treaties made between potential adversaries that reduce the likelihood and scope of war, usually imposing limitations on military capability. Although disarmament always involves the reduction of military forces or weapons, arms control does not mean all parties to the agreement are obliged to reduce military forces and weapons. In fact, arms control agreements sometimes allow increase of weapons by one or more parties to a treaty in certain instances.[3]

Arms control as a policy was developed both in theory and in practice during the Cold War, a period between the late 1940s and 1991 when the two military Super Powers, the United States and the Union of Soviet Socialist Republics (USSR), were forced to deal with one another from a position of mutual mistrust. Arms control was devised deliberately during the postwar period as an alternative to disarmament, which did not help as a means of reducing the likelihood of war. For instance, Germany which was forced to disarm itself following World War I became belligerent again during the 1930s, resulting in World War II. Although Germany's weapons were largely eliminated, the underlying factors pertaining to conflict remained intact. Germany's experience thus illustrated that no simple cause-and-effect rule could be applied between the possession of weapons by a nation and a tendency to go for war.[4]

Following World War II, advocates of arms control adopted a new approach to limit hostility between nations and emphasised that military weapons and power would continue to remain a part of modern life. It was, therefore, unrealistic and even dangerous, they felt, for a country to seek complete elimination of weapons, and it would not necessarily reduce the likelihood of war. Whereas disarmament had formerly been seen as an alternative to military strength, arms control was now viewed as an integral part of it. Arms control proponents sought to create a stable balance of power in which the forces that cause states to go to war could be controlled and regulated. The emphasis in arms control is on maintaining overall stability rather than elimination of arms, and proponents recognise that an increase in weaponry is sometimes required to preserve a balance of power.

The establishment of arms control regime owes a great deal to the existence of nuclear weapons as well. By the 1950s, when both the United States and the Soviet Union possessed nuclear weapons, the Super Powers were convinced that they could not safely disarm themselves of those weapons. In the absence of guaranteed verification—the process whereby participants in a treaty monitor each other's adherence to the agreement—neither side could disarm without making itself vulnerable to cheating by the other side. The goal of Super Powers and other nations possessing nuclear weapons, therefore, became not total elimination of those weapons, but exercise control over them so that a stable nuclear deterrent might be maintained. According to the idea of nuclear deterrence, a state possessing nuclear weapons would hesitate to use them , or prevented from using them against another nuclear power because of the threat of retaliation. No state is willing to attempt a first strike because it cannot prevent the other side from striking back. Nuclear deterrence is, therefore, predicated as a mutual abhorrence of the destructive power of nuclear weapons. This idea is termed as mutual assured destruction (MAD). Many experts see deterrence as the ultimate goal of nuclear arms control.[5]

Table -1

Nuclear Weapons: Who has what?				
Country	*First Test*	*Most Recent Test*	*Total Tests*	*Estimated Warheads*
United States	1945	1992	1,054	7,200
Russia	1949	1990	715	7,500
United Kingdom	1952	1991	45	215
France	1960	1996	210	300
China	1964	1996	45	260
India	1974	1998	6	110-120
Pakistan	1998	1998	6	120-130
North Korea	2006	2016 (claimed)	3	Fewer than 10

| Israel | No confirmed test | No confirmed test | No confirmed test | 80 |
| Iran | No confirmed test | No confirmed test | No confirmed test | 0 |

Sources: Federation of American Scientists, CIA World Fact book, Nuclear Threat Initiative, U.S. Census Bureau, January 6, 2015, CNN Frontier.

As many civilians generally assume that arms control and disarmament is one and the same, there has often been public disappointment when treaties have resulted in an increase in the number or power of weapons. An advantage of arms control over disarmament, however, is that even states with a high degree of suspicion or hostility toward each other can still negotiate agreements on arms control. Disarmament agreements, on the other hand, require a high degree of trust, and such an agreement is unlikely between hostile nations.

Arms control is used more often as a means to avoid an arms race—a competitive buildup of weapons between two or more powers. Such a race can be costly for both sides, and arms control treaties serve the useful purpose of limiting weapons stockpiles to a level that preserves deterrence while conserving the economic and social resources of a state for other uses.[6]

Evolution of Nuclear Weapons

American scientists, Albert Einstein and Leo Szilard warned about the developments taking place in Nazi Germany and urged President Franklin D. Roosevelt to begin a research programme on nuclear fission for military use in 1939.[7] It led to the establishment of the Manhattan Project[8] in 1941 with the objective to develop, produce, and test the first "atomic bombs," and J. Robert Oppenheimer was appointed as Director of the project.[9] The first "atomic bomb" was tested on July 16, 1945 at Alamogordo, NM,[10] and US military aircraft dropped atomic bombs on Hiroshima and Nagasaki, Japan on August 6 and 9 of the same year. These bombs, based on nuclear fission, each had an explosive power equivalent to about 20, 000 tons (20 kilotons) of TNT. It resulted in the death of approximately 2 lakh people immediately and the suffering of thousands more subsequently from blast and thermal injuries, radiation sickness, and malignancies.[11]

U.S. Nuclear Weapons Stockpile, 1962-2015

Since the late-1960s, the United States and Russia have signed a series of nuclear arms treaties that have contributed to steep cuts in their active and inactive nuclear warhead stockpiles.

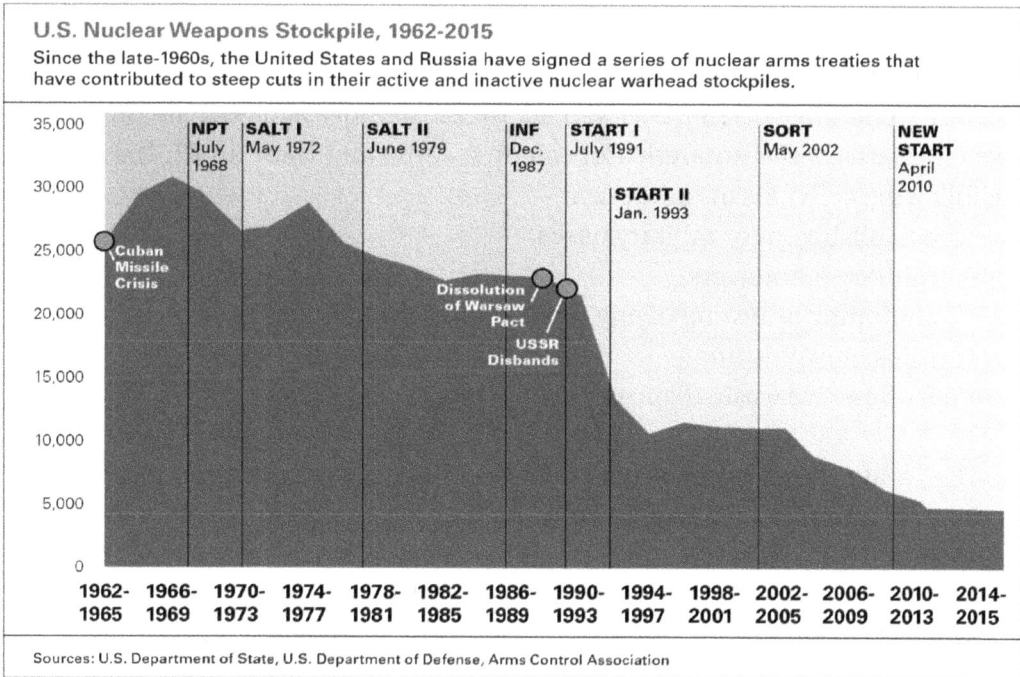

Sources: U.S. Department of State, U.S. Department of Defense, Arms Control Association

Source: Arms Control Association, Federation of American Scientists, International Panel on Fissile Materials, U.S. Department of Defence, and U.S. Department of State October 13,2015.

Despite opposition by Oppenheimer and other physicists, President Harry Truman ordered the development of bombs based on nuclear fusion—termed "thermonuclear weapons," "hydrogen bombs," or "H-bombs"—in 1951. The said research was carried out under the direction of Edward Teller, who had proposed the development of a fusion weapon while working on the Manhattan Project. The first test of the hydrogen bomb was carried out in 1952 at Eniwetok Atoll in the Marshall Islands. The blast had an explosive power equivalent to 104 lakh tons (10.4 megatons) of TNT—500 times greater than the power of the bombs dropped on Hiroshima and Nagasaki. The Soviet Union, which had exploded its first fission bomb in 1949, exploded its first fusion bomb.[12] The Soviet Union detonated a fusion bomb with a yield equivalent to 50 megatons of TNT in 1961. Its power was reported to be over 2000 times greater than the yield of the Hiroshima and Nagasaki bombs and greater than the total destructive power of all the bombs and explosives used in World War II.[13] The manufacture of weapons with such destructive power led to the initiation of a worldwide movement calling for nuclear disarmament and conclusion of several treaties as enumerated in succeeding paragraphs to prevent nuclear proliferation.[14]

Nuclear Proliferation Treaties concluded so far are explained below:

- **Antarctic Treaty 1959**

The Antarctic Treaty 1959 was signed by 12 nations agreeing to protect the peaceful status of the Antarctic Continent. It came into force on 23, 1961. It bans the following activities in Antarctica:

- establishment of military bases,
- military maneuvers,
- stationing or testing of any type of weapon,
- nuclear explosion,
- Radioactive waste disposal.

The Treaty allows each party to carry out full on-site and aerial inspection of all Antarctic installations in order to verify that these provisions are not violated.

- **The International Atomic Energy Agency (IAEA)**

The International Atomic Energy Agency was established in 1957 with the objective to assist nations in carrying out their nuclear programmes for peaceful purposes (primarily research and development of nuclear power programmes) and to safeguard the safety of nuclear materials used during such programmes. The establishment also is meant to ensure that nuclear materials are not diverted for manufacture of nuclear weapons. The system adopted by IAEA for complying with safeguards relies on collection of data, review, and periodic inspections of facilities declared by states. The IAEA may also inspect other facilities if it suspects that nuclear materials are being used or weapons-related activities are being carried out by anyone without filing the prescribe declaration. In fact, non-nuclear weapon member states (NPT members) are required to file a declaration and submit details of all nuclear materials in their possession for regular inspection of IAEA with a view to ensure that sensitive nuclear materials and technologies are not diverted from civilian to military purposes. Some of the states who are not parties to the NPT (India, Israel, and Pakistan) but are members of the IAEA and allow inspections of some, but not all, of their nuclear facilities. The IAEA also provides to its members technical assistance for peaceful application of nuclear technology in the field of energy, medicine, agriculture, and research. After the conclusion of Persian Gulf War in 1991, IAEA inspection teams conducted an inspection of nuclear facilities in Iraq. The team was working with the U.N. Special Commission on Iraq (UNSCOM). It was revealed that Iraq was conducting an extensive covert nuclear weapons programme that was virtually undetected during the annual inspections of Baghdad's facilities declared to IAEA. This revelation led to efforts for strengthening the authority of IAEA to conduct more intrusive inspections of a wider variety of installations, so as to provide the Agency with reliable information about suspected nuclear activities being conducted in secrecy and to provide the Agency with the resources and political support needed to increase confidence in its system of safeguards. The IAEA adopted an "*Additional Protocol*" in 1998 that would provide the agency greater authority and access to verify nuclear declarations. This protocol comes into effect when individual NPT states ratify the same. 146 countries have signed the additional protocol and 125 have made it applicable and effective by April 2015. With regard to United States, the US Senate gave its advice and consent to the protocol on March 31, 2004. The implementing legislation was passed in P.L. 109-401, as part of the Hyde Act on December, 18, 2006.The US President signed the instrument of ratification of the additional protocol on December 30, 2008. It was deposited with the IAEA and came into force on January 6, 2009.

- **The Hot Line Agreement 1963**

A hotline is a quick link for communication between Heads of States, with the objective to establish instant communication link to reduce the danger of an accident, miscalculation or a surprise attack and especially an event that might trigger a nuclear war. The United States and the Soviet Union signed the "*Memorandum of Understanding Between the United States of America and the Union of Soviet Socialist Republics Regarding the Establishment of a Direct Communications Link,*" also known as the hotline agreement, on June 20, 1963. This was designed to help speed up communication between the two governments and prevent the possibility of accidental nuclear war.

- **The Limited Test Ban Treaty or PTBT 1963**

The Limited Test Ban Treaty (LTBT) is a treaty prohibiting all detonations of nuclear weapons for testing on the surface of the earth. However, it permitted such tests underground. It was meant to slow the arms race (nuclear testing, at the time, was considered to be unavoidable for continued developments of nuclear weapons). The purpose of the treaty was to stop the excessive release of nuclear fallout into the planet's atmosphere. The treaty was signed and ratified by the Soviet Union, the United Kingdom, and the United States during the autumn of 1963.

It is officially known as the treaty banning nuclear weapon tests in the atmosphere, in outer space and under water, but is often abbreviated as the Partial Test Ban Treaty (PTBT), Limited Test Ban Treaty (LTBT), or Nuclear Test Ban Treaty (NTBT) – although the latter also refers to the Comprehensive Test Ban

Treaty. The treaty was signed by the Soviet Union, the United Kingdom, and the United States, named as the "*Original Parties*", in Moscow on August 5, 1963. It was kept open for signature by other countries subsequently. The said treaty was ratified by the U.S. Senate on September 24, 1963. The treaty came into effect on October 10, 1963.[15]

The first major nuclear arms control agreement was the Limited Test-Ban Treaty of 1963. The LTBT prohibited nuclear explosions in the atmosphere, in outer space, and under water. This treaty was motivated first of all by a desire to reduce and contain the health hazards caused by radioactive fall-out from nuclear explosions in the atmosphere. Many of the radioactive isotopes that were being spread around the globe in the wake of such explosions have a lifetime of many tens or hundreds or even thousands of years. Further nuclear explosions in the atmosphere could have resulted in more deaths due to cancer and other serious health problems on a large scale for many generations to come.

- **The Outer Space Treaty 1967**

The Multilateral agreement signed and ratified by the United States, Soviet Union and United kingdom in 1967 banned *interalia*:

- ...placement of nuclear weapons or "weapons of mass destruction" in orbit around the Earth.
- ...installation of nuclear weapons or "weapons of mass destruction" on the moon, on any other celestial body, or in outer space.
- ...use of the moon or any celestial body for military purposes, including weapons testing of any kind.

    This treaty was ratified by 95 nations. It came into force on October 10, 1963. The Outer Space Treaty, as it is known, was the second "*non-armament*" treaty. The concepts and some of its provisions were similar to that of its predecessor, the Antarctic treaty. Both the treaties sought to prevent "*a new form of colonial competition*" and the possible damage that self-seeking exploitation might cause.

In early 1957, even before the launch of Sputnik in October, keeping in view research and developments in technology with regard to rockets the United States proposed international verification of testing of space objects. The development of an inspection system for outer space was part of a Western proposal for partial disarmament put forward in August 1957. The Soviet Union, however, which was in the midst of testing its first ICBM and was about to orbit its first Earth satellite, did not accept these proposals. Between 1959 and 1962 the Western powers made a series of proposals to bar the use of outer space for military purposes. Their proposals placed before Soviet Union called for general and complete disarmament. It included provisions to ban the orbiting and stationing in outer space weapons of mass destruction. Addressing the General Assembly President Eisenhower proposed on September 22, 1960 that the principles of the Antarctic Treaty be applied to outer space and celestial bodies.

Soviet plans for general and complete disarmament between 1960 and 1962 included provisions for ensuring the peaceful use of outer space. The Soviet Union, however, would not separate outer space from other disarmament issues, nor would it agree to restrict outer space to peaceful uses unless U.S. foreign bases in which short-range and medium-range missiles were stationed were also eliminated. The Western powers declined to accept the Soviet approach. The linkage, they held, would upset the military balance and weaken the security of the West. After the signing of the Limited Test Ban Treaty, the stand of the Soviet Union changed. It ceased to insist on linking an agreement on outer space with the question of vacation of missiles from foreign bases. The Soviet Foreign Minister Gromyko told the General Assembly on September 19, 1963 that the Soviet Union wanted to conclude an agreement banning the orbiting of objects carrying nuclear weapons. U.S. Ambassador Stevenson also asserted that the United States had no intention of deploying weapons of mass destruction in orbit, deploying them on celestial bodies or stationing them in outer space. The UN General Assembly unanimously adopted a resolution welcoming the Soviet and U.S. statements and calling upon all states to refrain from introducing weapons of mass destruction into outer space on October 17, 1963. The United States supported the resolution, despite the absence of any provisions for verification. The capabilities of space-tracking systems of the United States, it was estimated, were adequate for detecting launchings and devices in orbit. Seeking to sustain the momentum for agreements on arms control, the United States pressed for a treaty in the years 1965 and 1966 that would give further substance to the U.N. resolution.

The United States and the Soviet Union submitted draft treaties on June 16, 1966. The U.S. draft dealt with only celestial bodies; the Soviet draft covered the whole outer space environment. The United States accepted the Soviet position on the scope of the treaty and by September agreement was reached through discussions at Geneva on most of the provisions of the treaty. Differences on a few remaining issues –chiefly involving access to facilities on celestial bodies, reporting on space activities, and the use of military equipment and personnel in space exploration were satisfactorily resolved in private consultations during the

General Assembly session by December. On the 19th of that month the General Assembly adopted a resolution commending the treaty. It was kept open for signature in Washington, London, and Moscow on January 27, 1967. On April 25 the US Senate gave consent for its ratification unanimously and the treaty came into effect on October 10, 1967.

- **The Nuclear Non-Proliferation Treaty 1968**

The Nuclear Nonproliferation Treaty (NPT), which came into force in 1970 and the validity of which was extended indefinitely from 1995 onwards, is the most important piece of legislation supporting the nuclear nonproliferation regime. The treaty currently has 190 member states as parties. The efforts of nuclear nonproliferation regime is supplemented by safeguards imposed by International Atomic Energy Agency (IAEA), national laws on export control and coordinated export control policies adopted under the Nuclear Suppliers Group, U.N. Security Council resolutions and *ad hoc* initiatives. The NPT recognises five nations (the United States, Russia, France, Britain, and China) as nuclear weapon states—a distinction that is maintained in other parts of the regime and in their national laws. As per NPT policy, the non-nuclear weapon states have to commit not to develop, acquire or possess nuclear weapons. The NPT has three *"pillars"* or main areas of operation, non-proliferation (stopping the spread of nuclear weapons and related technology), disarmament (getting rid of existing nuclear arsenals), and the right to use nuclear energy for peaceful purposes (including access to nuclear technology, which is the right of all states parties to the NPT).

In this connection it is to be noted that three nations which have not signed the NPT—India, Israel, and Pakistan—is known to possess capabilities to develop nuclear weapons. North Korea, which had initially signed the NPT withdrew from it in 2003. It is now thought to possess a small number of nuclear weapons. Several countries, including Argentina, Brazil, and South Africa, suspended their nuclear weapons programmes and joined the NPT in the 1990s. Others—Ukraine, Belarus, and Kazakhstan—gave up nuclear weapons deployed in their territories as part of Soviet Union and joined the NPT as non-nuclear weapon states in the 1990s.

The NPT was first signed by the United States, the United Kingdom, and the Soviet Union along with 59 other countries. China and France signed the treaty in 1992. Ukraine, Belarus and Kazakhstan gave up their nuclear weapons, left over from the Soviet Union when it fell apart in 1991-92, and signed the NPT as non-nuclear weapons state parties in 1966. The NPT is presently the most widely accepted arms control agreement. By June 2003, all members of the United

Nations except Israel, India, and Pakistan had signed the NPT. However, one signatory, North Korea, had recently threatened to withdraw from the treaty.

The Nuclear Nonproliferation Treaty is unique in its near universality—only India, Pakistan, Israel, and North Korea are now outside the treaty. In signing the NPT, non-nuclear weapon states (NNWS) pledge not to acquire nuclear weapons in exchange for a pledge by the nuclear weapon states (NWS) not to assist the development of nuclear weapons by any NNWS and to facilitate "the fullest possible exchange of equipment, materials and scientific and technological information for the peaceful uses of nuclear energy." (*NPT, Article IV-2*) The NWS, defined as any state that tested a nuclear explosive before 1967, also agree to "pursue negotiations in good faith on effective measures relating to cessation of the nuclear arms race at an early date and to nuclear disarmament." (*NPT, Article VI*). Many NNWS have often expressed dissatisfaction with the apparent lack of progress toward disarmament. Nuclear proliferation often has significant regional security repercussions, but there is also a growing realisation that the current challenges of proliferation risks may require further improvements to the system itself. The concern has shifted from keeping technology away from the states outside the NPT to stemming potential further proliferation, either from those states outside the regime or through black markets, such as the Pakistani A.Q. Khan network. Currently, member states of the NPT are grappling with ways to strengthen controls within the current system and through *ad hoc* complementary measures.

The NPT Review Conference 2010

The conference to review all aspects of the Treaty on the Non-Proliferation of Nuclear Weapons (NPT) was held at United Nations Headquarters in New York from May 3 to 28, 2010.[16] UN Secretary-General Ban Ki-moon used the opening of the conference to note that "*sixty five years later, the world still lives under the nuclear shadow*".[17] The said conference considered a number of issues, including: universality of the treaty; nuclear disarmament, including specific practical measures; nuclear non-proliferation, including the promoting and strengthening of safeguards; measures to advance the peaceful use of nuclear energy, safety and security; regional disarmament and non-proliferation; implementation of the 1995 resolution in the Middle East; measures to address withdrawal from the treaty; measures to further strengthen the review process; and ways to promote engagement with civil society in strengthening NPT norms and in promoting disarmament education. Conferences to review the operation of the treaty were held at five-year intervals since the treaty went into effect in 1970. Each conference has sought to find agreement on a final declaration that would assess the implementation of the treaty's provisions and make recommendations on measures to further strengthen it.[18]

The conference of the parties to the treaty on the Non-Proliferation of Nuclear Weapons, held in New York from 27 April to 22 May, 2015 was presided over by Ambassador Taous Feroukhi (Algeria). It ended without the adoption of a consensus substantive outcome. After a successful conference held in 2010 at which states parties agreed to a final document which included conclusions and recommendations for follow-on actions, including the implementation of the 1995 resolution on the Middle East, the absence of outcome in the conference held in 2015 constitutes a setback for the strengthened review process instituted to ensure accountability with respect to activities under the three pillars of the treaty as part of the package in support of the indefinite extension of the treaty in 1995.

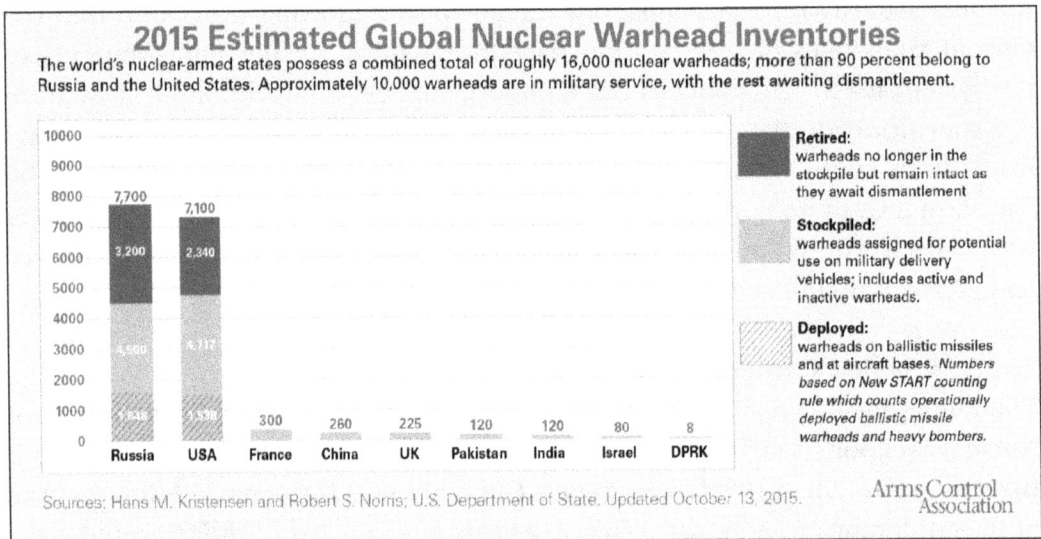

2015 Estimated Global Nuclear Warhead Inventories

The world's nuclear-armed states possess a combined total of roughly 16,000 nuclear warheads; more than 90 percent belong to Russia and the United States. Approximately 10,000 warheads are in military service, with the rest awaiting dismantlement.

	Russia	USA	France	China	UK	Pakistan	India	Israel	DPRK
Retired	3,200	2,340							
Stockpiled	4,500	4,117							
Deployed	1,548	1,538	300	260	225	120	120	80	8
Total	7,700	7,100	300	260	225	120	120	80	8

Retired: warheads no longer in the stockpile but remain intact as they await dismantlement

Stockpiled: warheads assigned for potential use on military delivery vehicles; includes active and inactive warheads.

Deployed: warheads on ballistic missiles and at aircraft bases. *Numbers based on New START counting rule which counts operationally deployed ballistic missile warheads and heavy bombers.*

Sources: Hans M. Kristensen and Robert S. Norris; U.S. Department of State. Updated October 13, 2015.

Arms Control Association

Source: Arms Control Association, Federation of American Scientists, International Panel on Fissile Materials, U.S. Department of Defence, and U.S. Department of State October 13, 2015.

The Nuclear Suppliers Group (NSG)

The Nuclear Suppliers Group (NSG) is a group of countries of nuclear suppliers which attempt to prevent nuclear proliferation by regulating the export of products, equipment and technology which can be used to manufacture nuclear weapons. The NSG was established after the Indian nuclear test in May 1974 and first met in November 1975. Nuclear Suppliers Group (NSG) is a group of 48 nuclear supplier states, including China, Russia, and the United States, who has voluntarily agreed to coordinate their export, controls governing transfers of civilian nuclear material and nuclear-related equipment and technology to non-nuclear-weapon states. The NSG aims to prevent nuclear exports made for commercial and peaceful purposes from being used to make nuclear weapons. NSG members are expected not to have trade in nuclear material and equipments with governments that do not subject themselves to scrutiny at international level and inspections by the authorised bodies to ensure that their imports of nuclear material and equipments are not used to develop nuclear arms. The NSG has formulated two sets of guidelines listing the specific nuclear materials, equipment, and technologies that are subject to export controls.

The NSG guidelines seek to ensure that trade in the nuclear field made for peaceful purposes does not contribute towards the proliferation of nuclear weapons or other nuclear explosive devices, while not standing in the way of international trade and cooperation in the nuclear field. The NSG guidelines facilitate the development of trade in nuclear field for peaceful purposes by providing the means. It facilitates peaceful nuclear cooperation in a manner consistent with international nuclear non-proliferation norms. NSG members commit themselves to the conditions of supply, in the context of the further development of the applications of nuclear energy for peaceful purposes.

- **The Strategic Arms Limitation Treaty I 1972**

The Strategic Arms Limitation Talks (SALT-I) began in November 1969 and ended in January 1972, with agreement on two documents: the *Anti-Ballistic Missile Treaty* (ABM Treaty) and the *Interim Agreement on the Limitation of Strategic Offensive Arms*. Both were signed on May 26, 1972. Interim Agreement between the U.S. and U.S.S.R. which was of five-year duration froze the number of strategic ballistic missiles at 1972 levels. Construction of additional land-based intercontinental ballistic missile (ICBM) silos was prohibited, while submarine-launched ballistic missile (SLBM) launcher levels can be increased if corresponding reductions are made in older ICBM or SLBM launchers. Modernisation of launchers is allowed, however, if kept within specific dimensions.

SALT I, the first series of Strategic Arms Limitation Talks, extended from November 1969 to May 1972. During that period the United States and the Soviet Union negotiated the first agreements to place limits and restraints on some of their central and most important armaments. In a Treaty on the Limitation of Anti-Ballistic Missile Systems, they moved to end an emerging competition in defensive systems that threatened to spur offensive competition to still greater heights. In an Interim Agreement on Certain Measures with respect to the Limitation of

Strategic Offensive Arms, the two nations took the first steps to check the rivalry in their most powerful land- and submarine-based offensive nuclear weapons.

Soviet and American weapons systems were far from symmetrical. The Soviet Union had continued its development and deployment of heavy ballistic missiles and had overtaken the U.S. lead in land-based ICBMs. During the period of SALT I alone the number of Soviet ICBMs rose from around 1,000 to around 1,500 and they were being deployed at the rate of about 200 annually. The number of Soviet submarine-based launchers had quadrupled. The huge payload capacity of some Soviet missiles (throw-weight) was seen as a possible threat to U.S. land-based strategic missiles even in heavily protected (hardened) launch-sites. The United States had not increased its deployment of strategic missiles since 1967 (when its ICBMs numbered 1,054 and it's SLBMs 656), but it was conducting a vigorous programme of equipping missiles with "*Multiple Independently-targeted Re-entry Vehicles*" (MIRV). MIRVs permit an individual missile to carry a number of warheads directed at separate targets. MIRVs thus gave the United States a lead in the number of warheads. The United States also retained a lead in long-range bombers. The Soviet Union had a limited ABM system around Moscow; the United States had shifted from its earlier plan for a "thin" ABM defence of certain American cities and instead began to deploy ABMs at two land-based ICBM missile sites to protect its retaliatory forces. Besides these asymmetries in their strategic forces, the defence needs and commitments of the two parties differed materially. The United States had obligations for the defence of allies overseas, such as Western Europe and Japan, while the Soviet Union's allies were its near neighbours. All these circumstances made difficulties in equating specific weapons, or categories of weapons, and in defining overall strategic equivalence. In a summit meeting in Moscow, after two and a half years of negotiations, the first round of SALT was brought to a conclusion on May 26, 1972, when President Nixon and General Secretary Brezhnev signed the ABM Treaty and the Interim Agreement on strategic offensive arms.

- **The Seabed Treaty 1971**

The Seabed Arms Control Treaty (or *Seabed Treaty*), formally the Treaty on the Prohibition of the Emplacement of Nuclear Weapons and Other Weapons of Mass Destruction on the Sea-Bed and the Ocean Floor and in the Subsoil there of, is a multilateral agreement between the United States, Soviet Union (now Russia), United Kingdom, and 91 other countries[19] banning the emplacement of nuclear weapons or "*weapons of mass destruction*" on the ocean floor beyond a 12-mile (22.2 km) coastal zone. It allows signatories to observe all seabed "activities" of any other signatory beyond the 12-mile zone to ensure compliance. Like the Antarctic Treaty, the Outer Space Treaty, and the Nuclear-Weapon-Free Zone treaties, the Seabed Arms Control Treaty sought to prevent the introduction of international conflict and nuclear weapons into an area hitherto free of them. Reaching agreement on the seabed, however, involved specific problems not faced while framing the other two agreements. The Seabed Arms Control Treaty was kept for signatures in Washington, London, and Moscow on February 11, 1971. It came into force on May 18, 1972, when the United States, the United Kingdom, the Soviet Union, and more than 22 nations deposited instruments of ratification. By May 2013, 94 states have become parties to the treaty, while another 21 have signed the treaty but have not completed ratification process.

- **The Anti-Ballistic-Missile Treaty 1972**

At the U.S.-Soviet summit held in Moscow on May 26, 1972, President Richard Nixon of the United States and President Leonid Brezhnev of the Soviet Union signed, the Anti-ballistic Missile (ABM) treaty along with the strategic arms limitation talks held during 1969–72 (SALT I). The treaty limited each country to two ABM sites, with no more than 100 ABM launchers and interceptors at each site. One of these sites could protect an ICBM silo deployment area, and the second could protect the national capital. The treaty prohibited the development, testing, or deployment of sea-based, air-based, space-based, or mobile land-based ABM systems. Furthermore, it excluded the transfer or deployment of ABM systems to or in other nations. The 15 articles of the treaty were not limited by any duration. It was provided that the treaty would come up for renewal every five years. The principles of the treaty explicitly reflected the policy of mutual assured destruction (MAD)—the belief that the best way to control nuclear arms is to allow both sides enough power to ensure the destruction of both nations in the event of war. In December 2001, however, the United States announced that it would no longer follow the ABM treaty. The United States withdrawal from the treaty was motivated by the desire to build and deploy a long-range missile defence system that would protect the nation from attacks by rogue nations such as North Korea. The deployment of the missile shield system was proposed for 2004.

- **The Threshold Test Ban Treaty 1974**

The Treaty on the Limitation of Underground Nuclear Weapon Tests, also known as the Threshold Test Ban Treaty (TTBT), was signed in July 1974. It establishes a nuclear "threshold," by prohibiting tests having a yield exceeding 150 kilotons (equivalent to 150,000 tons of TNT). The threshold is militarily important since it removes the possibility of testing new or existing nuclear weapons going beyond the fractional-megaton range. In the 1960s, many tests above 150 kilotons were conducted by both countries. The mutual restraint imposed by the treaty reduced the explosive force of new nuclear warheads and bombs which could otherwise be tested for weapons systems. Of particular significance was the relationship between explosive power of reliable, tested warheads and first-strike capability.

- **The Strategic Arms Limitation Treaty II 1979**

The negotiations for a second round of SALT began in late 1972. Since SALT I did not prevent each side from enlarging their forces through the deployment of Multiple Independently Targeted Re-Entry Vehicles (MIRVs) onto their ICBMs and SLBMs. SALT II initially focused on limiting, and then ultimately reducing, the number of MIRVs. Negotiations also sought to prevent both sides from making qualitative breakthroughs that would again destabilise the strategic relationship. The negotiations continued during the period of the Nixon, Gerald Ford, and Jimmy Carter administrations of United States.

At the Vladivostok Summit held in November 1974, Ford and Brezhnev agreed on the basic framework of a SALT II agreement. This included imposition of a limit of 2,400 on strategic nuclear delivery vehicles (ICBMs, SLBMs, and heavy bombers) for each side; a limit of 1320 on MIRV systems; a ban on new land-based ICBM launchers; and limitation on deployment of new types of strategic offensive arms. Bilateral, un-ratified agreement between the U.S. and U.S.S.R. provided for setting equal aggregate ceilings and sub ceilings on strategic offensive weapon systems and imposing qualitative restraints on existing and future strategic systems. Specifically, the SALT II equal ceilings include:

- 2,400 aggregate limit on strategic nuclear delivery vehicles (ICBMs, SLBMs, and bombers).
- 1,320 sub-ceiling on MIRV ballistic missiles.

The United States did not ratify the treaty after the Soviet Union invaded Afghanistan in December 1979. But President Carter, and later President Ronald Reagan, agreed to comply with the provisions of the treaty as long as the Soviet Union reciprocated. Soviet Premier Brezhnev made a similar statement regarding Soviet intentions. Although SALT II resulted in an agreement in 1979, the United States chose not to ratify the treaty in response to the Soviet war in Afghanistan, which took place later that year. The agreement expired on December 31, 1985 and was not renewed.

- **The Intermediate Range Nuclear Forces Treaty – INF 1987**

The Intermediate Range Nuclear Force Treaty (INF), ratified by US and USSR, which came into effect on June 1, 1988 is the first nuclear arms control agreement meant to actually reduce nuclear arms, rather than establish ceilings. It provided for the elimination of all missiles with ranges between 625 and 3,500 miles by June 1, 1991, and all missiles with ranges between 300 and 625 miles within 18 months. In all, 2,692 missiles were to be eliminated. In addition, all associated equipment and operating bases were to be closed from any further INF missile system activity.It resulted in the elimination of 846 U.S. INF missile systems and 1,846 Soviet INF missile systems. Compliance of the agreement is monitored using national technical means, five types of on-site inspection, and cooperative measures.

- **The Strategic Arms Reduction Treaty1991**

The Strategic Arms Reduction Treaty (START) was a bilateral treaty negotiated between the United States of America and the Union of Soviet Socialist Republics (USSR) on the reduction and limitation of strategic offensive arms. The treaty was signed on July 31, 1991 and came into force on December 5, 1994.[20]The treaty barred its signatories from deploying more than 6,000 nuclear warheads atop a total of 1,600 inter-continental ballistic missiles (ICBMs) and bombers. START negotiated the largest and most complex arms control treaty in history, and its final implementation in late 2001 resulted in the removal of about 80 percent of all strategic nuclear weapons then in existence. Proposed by United States President Ronald Reagan, it was renamed START I after negotiations began on the second START treaty.

The START I treaty expired on December 5, 2009. On April 8, 2010, a New START treaty was signed in Prague by U.S. President Barrack Obama and Russian President Medvedev. Following ratification by the U.S. Senate and the Federal Assembly of Russia, it came into force on January 26, 2011.

START I provides for the following:[21]
- It is valid for 15 years with an option to extend for successive periods of five years. Based on commitments made at the March 1997 Helsinki Summit, the sides agreed in principle to negotiate an agreement making the START treaties of unlimited in duration.
- Separate "politically binding" agreements limit the number of sea-launched cruise missiles with ranges above 600 to 880 kilometers for each side and the Soviet backfire bombers to 500 kilometers.

- To limit the number of deployable intercontinental ballistic missiles (ICBMs), submarine-launched ballistic missiles (SLBMs), and heavy bombers for each side to 1,600.
- The number of "accountable" warheads on ICBMs, SLBMs, and heavy bombers to be limited to 6,000, of which no more than 4,900 may be on ICBMs and SLBMs, 1,540 on heavy missiles (the Soviet SS-18), and 1,100 on mobile ICBMs.
- Ballistic missile throw-weight (lifting power) is limited to 3,600 metric tons on each side.

- **The Strategic Arms Reduction Treaty II 1993**

The START II treaty is a bilateral treaty negotiated by the United States and Russia and signed by Presidents Bush and Yeltsin on January 3, 1993. As per terms of the agreement, both sides would reduce the number of their strategic warheads to 3,800–4,250 by 2000 and to 3,000–3,500 by 2003. They would also eliminate multiple independent reentry vehicles (MIRVs) on their ICBMs—in effect eliminating two of the more controversial missiles of the Cold War, the U.S. Peacekeeper missile and the Russian SS-18. It would reduce the number of strategic delivery vehicles (ballistic missiles and heavy bombers) and the number of warheads deployed on them. Overall strategic forces would be reduced by 5,000 warheads in addition to the 9,000 warheads being reduced under START I.

By December 31, 2002, each party must have reduced the total number of its deployed strategic warheads so that it does not exceed 3,500. Of those, none may be on MIRVs, ICBMs, including heavy ICBMs. No MIRVs or ICBMs will be deployed by the end of the second phase. No more than 1,750 warheads may be on deployed SLBMs. There will be no prohibition on MIRVs SLBMs. Russia formally withdrew from the START II nuclear arms treaty with the United States on June 14, 2002, saying that it is no longer relevant in view of the expiry of the Anti-Ballistic Missile Treaty. The U.S. Congress ratified the treaty in 1996 and the Russian Parliament followed suit in 2000, but Russian lawmakers linked START II to the continuance of the ABM Treaty 1972. The U.S. Senate did not ratify the treaty until 1996, largely because the parallel process in the Russian Duma was moving so slowly. There the treaty became a hostage to growing Russian irritation with Western policies in the Persian Gulf and the Balkans and then to concerns over American attitudes toward the Anti-Ballistic Missile (ABM) Treaty. Thus, START II, it may be stated, was never implemented.

The Comprehensive Test-Ban Treaty (CTBT) 1996

The Comprehensive Test Ban Treaty, 1996 is a multilateral agreement signed by the US, CIS, UK, and 90 non-nuclear-weapon states which would ban any and all nuclear tests, big or small, above and below the Earth's surface. It established a worldwide monitoring system - including 170 seismic stations - to check air, water and soil for signals when someone set off a nuclear explosion. The 44 nations each having nuclear capability at different levels which is required to ratify the Comprehensive Test Ban Treaty for it to be effective are:

Algeria, Argentina, Australia, Austria, Bangladesh, Belgium, Brazil, Britain, Bulgaria, Canada, Chile, China, Colombia, Congo, Egypt, Finland, France, Germany, Hungary, India, Indonesia, Iran, Israel, Italy, Japan, Mexico, Netherlands, North Korea, Norway, Pakistan, Peru, Poland, Romania, Russia, Slovakia, South Africa, South Korea, Spain, Sweden, Switzerland, Turkey, Ukraine, United States and Vietnam.

The following 26 nations have already ratified the treaty:
Argentina, Australia, Austria, Belgium, Brazil, Britain, Bulgaria, Canada, Finland, France, Germany, Hungary, Italy, Japan, Mexico, Netherlands, Norway, Peru, Poland, Romania, Slovakia, South Africa, South Korea, Spain, Sweden and Switzerland.

The following 15 nations have signed but not yet ratified the treaty:
Algeria, Bangladesh, Chile, China, Colombia, Congo, Egypt, Indonesia, Iran, Israel, Russia, Turkey, Ukraine, Vietnam and the United States signed the treaty but failed to ratify the treaty. The names of three nations which have neither signed nor ratified the treaty are India, Pakistan and North Korea. Eventually, the Comprehensive Test-Ban Treaty (CTBT) was signed and made effective on October 24, 1996 that banned all nuclear explosions, including underground tests, for military as well as peaceful purposes. Both France and China were now ready to sign it. By June 2003, the CTBT was signed by 167 and ratified by 100 out of a total of 197countries. Among the countries that had still to sign and/or ratify the treaty were Afghanistan, Cuba, India, Iraq, Iran, Israel, North Korea, Pakistan, Saudi Arabia, Syria, and the United States. President Clinton signed the CTBT when it was opened for signature and submitted the treaty to the Senate for advice and consent in 1997. The Senate rejected the treaty through vote on October 13, 1999. Parties to the treaty agree "not to carry out any nuclear weapon test explosion or any other nuclear explosion."

The treaty establishes a Comprehensive Nuclear-Test-Ban Treaty Organisation (CTBTO) consisting of all member states to implement the treaty. The CTBTO oversees the functioning of the Conference of State Parties, Executive Council, and Provisional Technical Secretariat. The latter would operate an International Data Center to process and report on data from an International Monitoring System (IMS), a global network that, when completed, would consist of 321 monitoring stations and 16 laboratories. A Protocol details the monitoring system and inspection procedures. The CTBTO would come into effect when the treaty comes into force; until that time, the CTBTO Preparatory Commission conducts work towards implementing the provisions such as building and operating the IMS. The treaty would come into force, when 44 specified states ratify it. By May 1, 2015, 183 nations had signed the CTBT and 164 had ratified. Of the 44 required nations, 36 have ratified, 3 have not signed (India, North Korea, and Pakistan) and another 5 have not ratified (China, Egypt, Iran, Israel, and the United States). States that have ratified the treaty have held conferences every two years since 1999 to discuss as to how to accelerate the process of implementation and persuading the remaining members to sign and ratify the treaty to make the treaty truly comprehensive and meaningful.

- **The Chemical Weapons Convention (CWC) 1997**
The Chemical Weapons Convention (CWC), which was adopted in 1992 came into force in 1997. The CWC bans the development, production, stockpiling and use of chemical weapons. It requires state parties to destroy all stocks of chemical weapons within 10 years of its coming into force (by 2007) with a possible extension of up to five years (2012). To ensure that no clandestine development of prohibited weapons are being carried out, the CWC sets in place a stringent system of inspections, carried out by the Organisation for the Prohibition of Chemical Weapons (OPCW), which also ensures the safe destruction of weapons. The prohibition of the acquisition, production and use of chemical weapons set in place by the Convention has been a success. However, challenges remain, most importantly due to the slow rate of destruction of vast chemical arsenals by the United States and the Russian Federation. High costs as well as environmental concerns have contributed to these delays.

- **Biological Weapons**
During the Cold War period, a large number of countries conducted biological warfare research programmes, the largest of which were conducted by the then Soviet Union and the United States. Anthrax, smallpox, plague and tularemia were among the diseases which were made to be used as weapons. It was not until

the late 1960s that initiatives were made to control the manufacture of biological weapons. In 1969, United States President Richard Nixon announced the unilateral closure of the United States offensive biological weapons programme. As a result of prolonged efforts by the international community to establish a new instrument that would supplement the 1925 Geneva Protocol, the Biological Weapons Convention was drawn up and kept open for signature in 1972. The Convention came into force in 1975.[22]

As a result of the grave concern about the potential harm biological weapons could inflict, the Convention on the Prohibition of the Development, Production and Stockpiling of Bacteriological (Biological) and Toxin Weapons and on their Destruction was kept open for signature in 1972 and came into force in 1975. The Biological Weapons Convention (BWC) bans the development, production, stockpiling and acquisition of biological and toxin weapons and requires the destruction of such weapons or delivery means. The Convention has 163 State Parties and 13 signatories (as of June 2009). There are 19 States which have neither signed nor ratified the Convention.

- **The Strategic Offensive Reductions Treaty (SORT) 2002**

The Strategic Offensive Reductions Treaty signed by the United States of America and the Russian Federation on Strategic Offensive Reductions (SORT), also known as the Treaty of Moscow, was a strategic arms reduction treaty between the United States and Russia that came into force from June 2003 upto February 2011 when it was superseded by the New START treaty.[23] It was signed in Moscow on May 24, 2002. After ratification by the U.S. Senate and the State Duma, SORT came into force on June 1, 2003. It would have expired on December 31, 2012 if not superseded by New START.[24]At that time, SORT was positioned as a bilateral agreement between the U.S. and Russia. It contained the following provisions:

- The United States and Russia would be limiting strategic nuclear warheads to 1,700 to 2,200 apiece.
- Limits must be in place by 2012.
- Each country can withdraw from the treaty with three months' notice by citing "a supreme national interest."
- Verification procedures in the 1991 START I treaty, such as onsite inspections, will apply to the new deal, though they will not be spelled out in the treaty. A new U.S.-Russian commission will discuss how to implement the treaty.
- The agreement allows either side to decide what to do with the warheads removed from missiles, long-range bombers and submarines. No warheads would have to be destroyed.

- **The International Convention for the Suppression of Acts of Nuclear Terrorism 2005**

The Convention for the Suppression of Acts of Nuclear Terrorism, adopted on April 15, 2005 by the United General Assembly after seven years of preparatory work, was kept open for signature on September 14 at United Nations Headquarters in New York. The Convention came into force on July 7, 2007.[25] The idea for a treaty on the suppression of acts of nuclear terrorism originated in the 1990s in the wake of growing concerns about the threat of terrorists using nuclear or radiological material. The post-Cold War surge of fears about terrorism generally and more specifically, terrorism involving biological, chemical, nuclear, or radiological agents led to the creation of an Ad Hoc Committee by the United Nations (UN) General Assembly in December 1996 which was mandated "to elaborate an international convention for the suppression of terrorist bombings and subsequently, an international convention for the suppression of acts of nuclear terrorism, to supplement related existing international instruments, and thereafter to address the means of further developing a comprehensive legal framework of conventions dealing with international terrorism."[26]

- **The New Strategic Arms Reduction Treaty (New START) 2010**

The New Strategic Arms Reduction Treaty cited above was a bilateral agreement between the U.S and Russia signed in 2010. Under the Treaty, the U.S. and Russia would be limiting fewer types of strategic arms significantly within seven years from the date the Treaty come into force. [27] Each Party has the flexibility to determine for itself the structure of its strategic forces within the aggregate limits of the Treaty. It was signed on April 8, 2010 in Prague[28] and after ratification, [29] came into force on February 5, 2011.[30] It is expected to be valid at least until 2021. New START replaced the Treaty of Moscow (SORT), which was due to expire in December 2012. In terms of title, it is a follow-up to the START I treaty, which expired in December 2009and the proposed START II treaty, which never came into force. Under the terms of the treaty, the number of strategic nuclear missile launchers will be reduced by half. It does not limit the number of operationally inactive stockpiled nuclear warheads that remain in thousands in both the Russian and American inventories. Measures provided under the treaty include on-site inspections and exhibitions, exchanges of data and notifications related to strategic offensive arms and facilities covered by the treaty, and provisions to facilitate the use of national technical means for monitoring of treaty.. To increase confidence and transparency, the treaty also provides for the exchange of telemetry.

Aggregate limits provided under the treaty are as follows:

- 1,550 warheads. Warheads on deployed ICBMs and deployed SLBMs count toward this limit and each deployed heavy bomber equipped for nuclear armaments counts as one warhead toward this limit. The limit set was 74 percent lower than the limit of the 1991 START Treaty and 30 percent lower than the deployed strategic warhead limit of the 2002 Moscow Treaty.
- A combined limit of 800 deployed and non-deployed ICBM launchers, SLBM launchers, and heavy bombers equipped for nuclear armaments.
- A separate limit of 700 deployed ICBMs, deployed SLBMs, and deployed heavy bombers equipped for nuclear armaments. This limit is less than half of the corresponding strategic nuclear delivery vehicle limit of the START Treaty.

The United Nations Security Council Resolution 1540

In April 2004, the U.N. Security Council adopted Resolution 1540, which requires all states to *"criminalize proliferation, enact strict export controls and secure all sensitive materials within their borders."* UNSCR 1540 called on states to enforce effective domestic controls over WMD and WMD-related materials in production, use, storage, and transport; to maintain effective border controls; and to develop national export and trans-shipment controls over such items, all of which should help interdiction efforts. The resolution did not, however, provide for any enforcement authority, nor did it specifically mention interdiction. About two-thirds of all states have reported to the U.N. about their efforts to strengthen defences against WMD trafficking. United Nations Security Council Resolutions (UNSC) 1673 (2006), 1810 (2008), and 1977 (2011) extended the duration of the 1540 Committee. The 2011 resolution extended the committee's mandate for 10 years. The committee is currently focused on identifying projects for aasistance for states in need and matching donors to improve these WMD controls.

The Illegal Nuclear Weapons States

The NPT distinguished between nuclear weapons states and non-nuclear weapons states as parties of the Treaty. However, from the very beginning there was in fact a third category of countries as well, namely, non-nuclear weapons states that for one reason or another had decided not to become parties of the NPT. Some countries, like Cuba, dismissed the NPT as an instrument that served to maintain the existing and, in their opinion, thoroughly unjust world order. Others simply wanted to reserve the option of developing their own nuclear arsenal: either to enhance their regional or international status, to deter military aggression or to underpin their political independence. Not surprisingly, most of the threshold states belonged to this group.

The first country outside the NPT to cross the nuclear threshold was India, which exploded a nuclear device in an atmospheric test in 1974. In 1998, both India and Pakistan conducted several nuclear underground tests, inviting a storm of international protests and some short-lived economic and political sanctions as well. Meanwhile, the ending of white minority rule in South Africa in 1993[31]had led to the sensational disclosure that, in the mid-1980s, South Africa had developed and stockpiled a small number of nuclear weapons. The weapons had been dismantled and destroyed in the last years of apartheid because the white government feared that they might one day fall into the hands of militant black opposition groups and be used against the government. Subsequently, South Africa signed both the NPT (1991) and the CTBT (1996) as a non-nuclear weapons state. Allegations about a secret Israeli nuclear weapons programme were frequently heard in the 1960s and 70s. It was not until the mid-1980s, however, that the allegations were backed up with firm proof. In the fall of 1986, a former Israeli nuclear technician, Mordechai Vanunu, disclosed details of illegally possessed materials and gave evidence proving that Israel, by all meaningful definitions of the term, was indeed a nuclear weapons state and a powerful one as well. Today, Israel may possess as much as 150-200 nuclear weapons. Thus, by June 2003 there were at least three countries – India, Israel, and Pakistan – that were both in possession of nuclear weapons and are not parties to the NPT.

Iran's nuclear programme is clearly intended to develop nuclear weapons capability. For eighteen years, it was kept secret, even though international assistance was available to a civilian programme. In 2002, Iran's covert programme was exposed. On November 8, 2011 it released a report stating there is "credible" evidence that "Iran has carried out activities related to the development of a nuclear device." The IAEA's May 2013 report noted that Iran had a 182 kilogram stockpile of 20 percent enriched uranium and 6,357kilogram of 5 percent enriched uranium, enough to produce weapons-grade uranium for seven nuclear bombs using the same enrichment technology. Iran continued to install centrifuges at the deep underground, heavily defended Fordow installation, increasing its capability to quickly enrich to weapons-grade. On April 2, 2015, the P5+1 (the US, UK, China, Russia, France and Germany – with EU facilitation) announced a framework agreement, setting the parameters for a final Joint Comprehensive Plan of Action (JCPOA) agreement with Iran over its nuclear programme. Iran has agreed to:

- *Reduce the number of installed centrifuges from 19,000 to 6,104, with only 5,060 of those enriching uranium for 10 years (all of which will be located at the Natanz facility).*

- *Limit all uranium enrichment to 3.67 percent for 15 years.*
- *Reduce its current stockpile of low-enriched uranium from 10,000 kg to 300 kg.*
- *Cease enrichment of uranium at the Fordow facility for 15 years.*
- *Convert the Fordow facility into a nuclear, physics, technology research center. Approximately 1,000 centrifuges will be used for this purpose.*
- *Redesign and rebuild the Arak heavy water reactor so it can no longer produce weapons grade plutonium.*
- *Ship all spent fuel from the Arak reactor out of the country.*
- *Allow the International Atomic Energy Agency (IAEA) regular access to all nuclear facilities and suspected sites, as well as to the nuclear supply chain. Allow inspectors access to uranium mines and surveillance of uranium mills for 25 years.*
- *Implement the Additional Protocol of the IAEA to allow the Agency greater access and information regarding the nuclear program, including the program's possible military dimensions.*

Iran's decision to enter into negotiations with the P5+1 was a direct result of the pressure international sanctions created on Iran's economy.[32] In September 2007, Israel conducted an airstrike on Syria what U.S. officials have alleged was the construction site of a nuclear research reactor similar to North Korea's Yongbyon reactor.

The Democratic People's Republic of Korea (DPRK) has an active nuclear weapons programme and tested nuclear explosive devices in 2006, 2009, 2013, and 2016. The DPRK is also capable of enriching uranium and producing weapons-grade plutonium. North Korea deploys short and medium range ballistic missiles and successfully launched long-range rockets in 2012 and 2016. North Korea unilaterally withdrew from the Treaty on the Non-Proliferation of Nuclear Weapons (NPT) in January 2003 and is not a party to the Comprehensive Nuclear-Test-Ban Treaty (CTBT) or a member of the Missile Technology Control Regime (MTCR). The DPRK is not a party to the Chemical Weapons Convention (CWC), and is believed to possess a large scale chemical weapons programme. North Korea is a party to the Biological and Toxin Weapons Convention (BTWC) and Geneva Protocol, but is suspected to be maintaining an offensive weapons programme in defiance of the BTWC. On January 6, 2016 North Korea conducted its fourth nuclear detonation. North Korean media made announcements that the regime had successfully tested a hydrogen bomb.[33]On March 24, 2016; North Korea tested a solid-fueled rocket motor. This transition from solid to liquid-fueled technology is a major technological improvement, and is of significant proliferation concern, as solid-fueled missiles do not require the hours of preparation and fueling that liquid-fueled missiles require.[34] The Nuclear programme of North Korean and Iran has been a matter of concern for the international community.

Conclusion

The world should look towards peace and stability and not conflicts. Arms race threatens the serenity of the world. The world leaders supported the retention of nuclear weapons due to their effective function as deterrents. However, the endless supply of nuclear weapons has made leading research scientists to be worried about the destruction that category of weapons can cause and how the weapons are likely to fall into the wrong hands. The reality is that if we wish to protect the world and to keep the billions of people safe, we need to eliminate nuclear weapons.[35] Nuclear weapons have caused mass destruction and continue to be a significant threat on earth. Its power was demonstrated on Japan, which killed hundreds of thousands of civilians. Hundreds of thousands of civilians do not need to die again, so we need to stop the possibility of it from happening. Nuclear weapons are far too dangerous and there are too many possible threats. It is time that the world gave up nuclear weapons.

Notes

1. Schultz GP, Perry WJ, Kissinger HA, Nunn S., "A World Free of Nuclear Weapons", *The Wall Street Journal.* January 4, 2007:A15.
2. Auther? Institute of Medicine, Committee for the Study of Public Health. *The Future of Public Health* (Washington, DC: National Academy Press, 1988) pp.35–40. Levy B.S. Creating the future of public health: values, vision, and leadership. *Am J Public Health.* 1998, pp188–192.
3. Dunn, Lewis A., and Sharon A. Squassoni, Arms Control: What Next? (Boulder, Colorado?: West view Press, 1993).
4. Laird, Melvin R. "Why Scrap the ABM Treaty?" *Washington Post*, August 23, 2001, A25.
5. Sheehan, Michael, *Arms Control: Theory and Practice* (Oxford: Blackwell, 1988).
6. Peter Goodchild, J. Robert Oppenheimer: "*Shatterer of Worlds*" (London: BBC, 1980).
7. Leo Szilard: Biography. "Council for a Livable World" Web site. Available at: http://www.clw.org/about/szilard, accessed on June 20, 2007.
8. Schwartz SI. *Atomic Audit: The Costs and Consequences of US Nuclear Weapons Since 1940*(Washington, DC: Brookings Institute Press, 1998).
9. Rhodes R. *The Making of the Atomic Bomb.* (New York, : Simon and Schuster, 1986)pp.394–442.
10. Lamont L. *Day of Trinity.* (New York: Atheneum 1995).
11. Yokoro K, Kamada N. The public health effects of the use of nuclear weapons. In: Levy BS, Sidel VW, eds. *War and Public Health.* (Updated paperback edition)(Washington, DC: American Public Health Association, 2000), pp65–83.
12. Rhodes R. *Dark Sun: The Making of the Hydrogen Bomb* (New York : Simon and Schuster, 1995).
13. Author? Los Alamos National Laboratory, "The development of the hydrogen bomb", Available at: http://www.lanl.gov/history/postwar/development.shtml. accessed on June 30, 2006.

14. Witter LS. *Resisting the Bomb: A History of the World Nuclear Disarmament Movement, 1954–1970.*(Stanford, : Stanford University Press, 1997),p2.

15. "The Development and Proliferation of Nuclear Weapons" Nobel prize.org http://www.nobelprize.org/educational/peace/nuclear_weapons/readmore.html, accessed on September 20, 2014.

16. United Nations Secretary-General Ban Ki-moon, "Review Conference of the Parties to the Treaty on the Non-Proliferation of Nuclear Weapons", New York, May 3-29, 2010.

17. Address to the 2010 Review Conference of the States Parties to the Treaty on the Non-Proliferation of Nuclear Weapons, Secretary-General Ban Ki-moon, May 3, 2010.

18. "2010 Review Conference of the Parties to the Treaty on the Non-Proliferation of Nuclear Weapons (NPT) 3-28 May, 2010" http://www.un.org/en/conf/npt/2010/, accessed on May, 2010.

19. "Treaty on the Prohibition of the Emplacement of Nuclear Weapons and Other Weapons of Mass Destruction on the Sea-Bed and the Ocean Floor and in the Subsoil Thereof". United Nations Office for Disarmament Affairs.

20. Strategic Arms Reduction Treaty (START I): Executive Summary". The Office of Treaty Compliance, accessed on December 5, 2009.

21. Daryl Kimball "*START I at a Glance- Fact Sheet*", January 2009, ACA Arms Control Association.

22. http://www.un.org/disarmament/HomePage/ODAPublications/AdhocPublications/PDF/guide.pdf, accessed on12th August, 2011.

23. http://www.whitehouse.gov/sites/default/files/2010%20New%20START%20msg%20rel.pdf, accessed on September 20, 2010.

24. Letter of Transmittal: The Moscow Treaty 2002, at https://www.armscontrol.org/act/2002_07-08/docjul_aug02, accessed on January 6, 2016.

25. International Convention on the Suppression of Acts of Nuclear Terrorism, UN General Assembly Resolution 59/290, April 13, 2005

26. UN General Assembly Resolution 51/210, December 17, 1996, p. 5.

27. "President Obama Announces the New START Treaty , *The White House*", Whitehouse.gov. accessed on May 23, 2012.

28. "US and Russian leaders hail nuclear arms treaty". *BBC News*. 8 April 2012. Fred Weir. 5A.

29. "With Russian ratification of New START, what's next for US-Russia relations?" *CSMonitor. com.*,accessed on26 January, 2011.

30. "U.S.-Russia nuclear arms treaty finalized". *USA Today,* The Associated Press,. 5 February 2011.

31. David Holloway, Stalin and the Bomb: the Soviet Union and Atomic Energy 1939-1956 (New Haven: Yale University Press, 1994).

32. "The Iranian Nuclear Threat: Why it Matters" April 6, 2015, ADL, Anti-Defamation League,http://www.adl.org/israel-international/iran/c/the-iranian-nuclear-threat-why-it-matters.html?referrer=https://www.google.co.in/#.VyGP8TB97IU, accessed on January 6, 2016.

33. Warrick, Joby, "A North Korean H-bomb? Not likely, experts say," *Washington Post*, www.washingtonpost.com., accessed on January 6, 2016.

34. Sang-Hun, Chang, "North Korea Tests New Rocket Engine, State Media Says," *The New York Times,*, www.nytimes.com., accessed on March 24, 2016.

35. Payne, Keith B. "*Disarmament Danger: 'Nuclear Zero'* Would Make the United States and the World Less Safe." *National Review* (2010), p30. General One File. Gale. Web, accessed on January 18, 2011.

CHAPTER 8

International Terrorism: Non-State Actors and State Terrorism Post 9/11 Developments

Introduction

Globalisation has contributed to the growth of terrorism from a regional phenomenon into a global one. International terrorism has been explained in cultural, economic and religious terms linked to globalisation. Terrorism is characterised, first and foremost, by the use of violence. The idea of "terrorism" is a snare and delusion, a way of diverting the public's attention from the failings of western governments, the American and British ones especially. "International Terrorism" is a semantic technique employed by government, spokespersons to change the subject, a slick way of transforming the victims of injustice into its perpetrators. This tactic of violence takes many forms and often indiscriminately targets non-combatants.[1] Till the 1990s, the number of groups and their ability to engage in terrorism was limited. Acts of terrorism itself and their intensity and lethality were also limited in scale.

International terrorism is now in full-bloom around Afghanistan and Pakistan, a strategic centre of the Islamic World. Trained by CIA and ISI, there are now over 1lakh jihadists all over the Islamic world in Kashmir, Albania, Chechnya, Xinjiung (China), Central Asia and elsewhere.[2] The number of groups that resort to terrorism now has increased, and their abilities have also been enhanced. Acts of terrorism have become more widespread and their lethality has also increased in terms of the number of civilian and security personnel causalities and the high levels of physical destruction that they can cause. Suicide attacks are non-discriminatory with targets, including the old, the young, the wealthy, and the poor. These attacks impact all sectors of the civilian population and have been carried out in various types of crowded public venues, including transit stations, buses, restaurants, shopping malls, nightclubs, and outdoor markets. This method of attack is adaptable, can maximise casualties, is inexpensive and is far reaching by instilling fear in the general public. There are several factors that contribute to the effectiveness of this mode of attack: Today when we think about *"International terrorism"* we are more likely to associate it with the activities of private groups and organisations, described as *"non-state" actors*: Al Qaeda, *Jemaah Isalmiyah* (Indonesia), *Sendero Luminoso* (Peru), People's Revolutionary Armed forces (Colombia), *Al-Aqsa* Martyrs Brigades (Palestinian nationalists) PFLP, DFLP, PFLP-GC (Palestinian leftists), *Hezbollah*(Lebanon), *Mujahedeen-e-Khlq* (Iranian rebel),Chechnya-based Terrorists (Russia), ISIS etc.[3]International terrorism is, *"an anxiety-inspiring method of repeated violent action, employed by (semi) clandestine individual, group, or state actors, whereby the direct targets of the violence are not the main targets."* The immediate human victims of violence are generally chosen randomly (targets of opportunity) or selectively (representative or symbolic targets) from a target population, and serve as message generators.[4] The emerging trend in the pattern of terrorism since the end of the Cold War has arisen due to certain political, socio-economic, geo-political, and strategic factors.

One terrorist target could be of a nuclear nature. Terrorists might acquire a nuclear weapon or nuclear material to produce an improvised nuclear explosive device (IND) or obtain other radioactive material to produce a radioactive dispersal device (RDD). If used in a city, the consequences of an IND explosion would be devastating in terms of direct human loss, while if an RDD is used in a city, the prevailing damage might not only be in human terms due to relocation of the population, but also long-term decontamination, and possible long-term health effects. There are similar concerns regarding the risk of a sabotage of nuclear or other facilities or transport with radioactive material.

Meaning of International Terrorism

To begin, it seems appropriate to define the term *terrorism*. Within terrorism lies the word terror. Terror comes from the Latin *terrere*, which means "frighten" or "tremble." When coupled with the French suffix *isme* (referencing "to practice"), it becomes akin to "practicing the trembling" or "causing the frightening." Trembling and frightening here are synonyms for fear, panic, and anxiety—what we would naturally call terror. The word terror is over 2,100 years old. In ancient Rome, the *terror cimbricus* was a state of panic and emergency in response to the visit of the Cimbri tribe killers in 105 BCE. This description of terrorism as being rooted in terror is an example of etymology. *Etymology* is the study of the origin and evolution of words. From this standpoint, language is organic, changeable, fluctuating, depending on the needs of thinkers and speakers over time and place.[5]The word terrorism, in and of itself, was coined during the French Revolution's Reign of Terror (1793–1794). In the Reign of Terror (*Le Gouvernement de la Terreur*), a group of rebels, the Jacobins, used the term when self-reflexively portraying their own actions in—and explanations of—the French Revolution. The Reign of Terror was a campaign of large-scale violence by the French state; between 16,000 and 40,000 people were killed in a little over a year. It is not surprising, then, that the French National Convention proclaimed in September 1793 that "*terror is the order of the day.*" Maximilien Robespierre, a frontrunner in the French Revolution, declared in 1794 that "*terror is nothing other than justice, prompt, severe, inflexible.*"

Definitions of terrorism by some of the most distinguished scholars and institutions on the matter are as follows:

- **Walter Laqueur:** "Terrorism is the use or the threat of the use of violence, a method of combat, or a strategy to achieve certain targets... It aims to induce a state of fear in the victim that is ruthless and does not conform to humanitarian rules... Publicity is an essential factor in the terrorist strategy."[6]
- **Bruce Hoffman:** "Terrorism is ineluctably political in aims and motives, violent—or, equally important, threatens violence, designed to have far-reaching psychological repercussions beyond the immediate victim or target, conducted by an organisation with an identifiable chain of command or conspiratorial cell structure (whose members wear no uniform or identifying insignia), and perpetrated by a subnational group or non-state entity."[7]
- **Alex Schmid and Albert Jongman:** "Terrorism is an anxiety-inspiring method of repeated violent action, employed by (semi-)clandestine individual, group, or state actors, for idiosyncratic, criminal, or political reasons, whereby—in contrast to assassination—the direct targets of violence are not the main targets. The immediate human victims of violence are generally chosen randomly (targets of opportunity) or selectively (representative or symbolic targets) from a target population, and serve as message generators."[8]
- **David Rapoport:** terrorism is "the use of violence to provoke consciousness, to evoke certain feelings of sympathy and revulsion."[9]
- **Yonah Alexander:** terrorism is "the use of violence against random civilian targets in order to intimidate or to create generalised pervasive fear for the purpose of achieving political goals."[10]
- **Stephen Sloan:** "the definition of terrorism has evolved over time, but it's political, religious, and ideological goals have practically never changed".[11]
- **League of Nations Convention 1937:** terrorist acts are "all criminal acts directed against a State and intended or calculated to create a state of terror in

the minds of particular persons or a group of persons or the general public."[12]

- **U.S. Department of Defence:** terrorism refers to "the calculated use of unlawful violence or threat of unlawful violence to inculcate fear; intended to coerce or to intimidate governments or societies in the pursuit of goals that are generally political, religious, or ideological."[13]
- **Chomsky:** Terrorism is the use of coercive means aimed at populations in an effort to achieve political, religious, or other aims.[14]
- **Tilly** tell us that terrorism is "asymmetrical deployment of threats and violence against enemies using means that fall outside the forms of political struggle routinely operating within some current regime."[15]
- **Stern** defines terrorism as "an act or threat of violence against non-combatants, with the objective of intimidating or otherwise influencing an audience or audiences."[16]
- **Peter Chalk** offers a definition similar to the ones above when he conceptualises terrorism as the systematic use of illegitimate violence that is employed by sub-state actors as means of achieving specific political objectives, these goals differing according to the group concerned.[17]
- According to **Enders and Sandler** Terrorism is the premeditated use or threat of use of extra normal violence or brutality by subnational groups to obtain a political, religious, or ideological objective through intimidation of a huge audience, usually not directly involved with the policy making that the terrorists seek to influence.[18]

International Terrorism in Present Day Context

International terrorism did not begin in 2001 or in the 1990s for that matter. There is a long history behind the kind of violence that the mass media show us seemingly on a daily basis. The expression 'International Terrorism' came into current use in our language with attacks which took place on September 11, 2001. The attack on the twin towers and the Pentagon in USA was the first disturbing spectacle of its kind watched on the TV networks around the world. There are indeed a large number of terrorist groups scattered around the world, especially in weak states. Those who think that the terrorist threat is not so serious emphasise how the *Al-Qaeda* network is specifically connected to marginalised Muslim groups of *Mujahedin* (fighters for *Allah's* cause)who joined to fight against the Soviet occupation of Afghanistan and were able to use that country as a safe haven.[19] The London bomb attacks of 2005 demonstrated that Muslims with a relatively 'normal' background as citizens of the UK had been recruited for its activities is very large indeed; it is not merely confined to ex-Afghani *Mujahidin's*; it also comprises self-confessed members of local Muslim societies in the UK and other Western countries. Some commentators argue that the US-led war in Iraq leads to 'blowback terrorism' meaning that the war tends to increase, rather than decrease, the recruitment potential to international terrorism. There is the danger of international terrorists gaining access to and using weapons of mass destruction (WMD), that is, chemical, biological and nuclear weapons. It is clear that terrorist groups have incentives to use WMD; they would be able to create massive destruction and fear, and that would possibly elevate the groups to a new power position *vis-a–vis* their adversaries.[20]

International terrorism is a complex, multifaceted phenomenon that is social in nature and, in some instances, has a political aim. Terrorists attempt to exert political pressure on government leaders, attract world public attention to certain problems, demand the liberation of arrested supporters of extremist groups and the end of persecution of terrorist organisations and their leaders by law enforcement agencies, advance economic demands, and so forth. As a rule, global terrorists commit individual acts of an intentionally provocative nature, which may include threats of murder or the assassination of state and political figures, the seizure of hostages or potentially hazardous facilities, bombings, or the release of poisons, radioactive substances, or biologically active agents. International terrorist acts at potentially hazardous facilities—enterprises working with chemicals, radioactive materials, or explosives, hydro technical structures, unique tall buildings, subways, surface rail, and air transport facilities, and places where large numbers of people congregate, such as concert halls, stadiums, apartment buildings, and so forth (hereafter referred to as facilities)—present a great danger to personnel and the public and cause substantial economic damage. Terrorist acts at enterprises could be carried out by striking (destroying) a tank or pipeline holding catastrophically hazardous chemicals, a nuclear reactor, or a storage vessel containing highly flammable liquid. An explosion at a chemical-hazard facility could cause destruction over an area of up to 30 square kilometers, with the number of injured victims possibly reaching 60,000 and up to 5,000 fatalities. In places where large numbers of people gather, terrorists could use explosives, dangerous chemicals (including poisons), radioactive substances, and biologically active agents. The suddenness of a terrorist act, the rapid spread of the impact factors, the deaths of many people, the ensuing panic, and people's sense of being helpless create a powerful psychological blow to society. More than 50 countries have experienced the consequences of terrorist acts, including Iraq, India, Indonesia, Colombia, Pakistan, Afghanistan, Russia, Israel, Great Britain, France and Egypt. The number of acts carried out by suicide attackers has increased fivefold in the past 3 years. In 2006 alone, more than 15,000 terrorist acts were carried out worldwide, killing or injuring more than 90,000 people. This leads to the creation of a broader infrastructure for terrorist organisations and brings the ethno national factor to bear, which in turn creates a significant degree of uncertainty about the potential sources of the terrorist threat and forms and means of operation by terrorists. Primarily this refers to the aim of certain branches of Islam to create individuals who are psychologically prepared to commit violent acts *"in the name of Allah"* to achieve political goals, such as overthrowing unfavourable secular regimes and establishing a government according to Islamic doctrines.

The Islamic State of Iraq and the Levant (ISIS, also known as ISIL) used to be known as *Al-Qaeda* in Iraq. The Islamic State is not only a terrorist group but is also a political and military organisation that holds a radical interpretation of Islam as a political philosophy and seeks to impose that world view by force on Muslims and non-Muslims alike. The foundations of the ISIS were formed following the US-led invasion of Iraq in 2003. This group has been described as a "terrorist organisation" by the United Nations, European Union, the United States, Saudi Arabia, and many others. ISIS is already a threat to the United States. ISIS is not only dangerous in a regional context because it is overthrowing and obliterating modern state boundaries in ways that incur massive ethno-sectarian killing and cleansing. ISIS is also a global jihadist organisation that shares *al-Qaeda's* ideology, such that its progress drives towards a post-state and apocalyptic vision that involves the destruction of the modern state system. On November 13, 2015, a series of coordinated terrorist attacks took place in Paris and its northern suburb, Saint-Denis. The Islamic State of Iraq and the Levant (ISIL) claimed responsibility for the attacks.

Table-1

Jihad
Jihad is an Arabic word meaning "struggle." According to the *Qur'an* (where *jihad* appears forty-one times), Muslims have the duty of fighting enemies and invading non-Muslim territories to spread Islam. The belief is that the violent elimination of apostate regimes, the slaughter of the **People referred to in the Book** (monotheistic non-Muslims, mostly Jews and Christians), and the removal of *kafir* (those who disbelieve in *Allah*) are justified in the cause of *jihad*. This has driven non-state actors (e.g., *Al Qaeda*) to commit terrorism.[21] **The greater *jihad*** is the struggle a person has within him- or herself to fulfil what is right. On account of human pride, selfishness, and sinfulness, believers must continually wrestle with themselves and accomplish what is right and good. **The lesser *jihad*** refers to the external, physical effort to defend Islam (including terrorism) when the Muslim community is under attack.[22] The key characteristics of modern *jihad* ideology include (1) *hakimiyya* (true sovereignty of Allah over nation-states or civil laws), (2) Islamic society and upholding *hisba* (praising good, forbidding evil) by following the **sharia**(i.e., "Islamic law"; the required implementation of virtuous vs. materialistic, status-driven behaviour based on group interpretation), (3) the necessity for *jihad,* (4) occupation of Muslim lands (used as justification for *jihad* as individual duty), (5) **martyrdom** (i.e., "dying or suffering as a hero"; martyrdom is associated with *jihad* and praised through videos, poetry, songs, and web postings), and (6) *takfir*(i.e., "disbelief in *Allah*"; non-Muslim governments are viewed as infidels and unwilling to be subdued by Islamic law. Therefore, it is an object of *jihad).*[23] Jihadists have near enemies and far enemies. **Near enemies** are Muslim governments and forms of Islamic law that do not embrace the jihadist view. If non-Islamic powers or countries outside the jurisdiction of Islam (i.e., the West, the U.S., and Israel) do not embrace the jihadist view, they are referred to as the **far enemy**. [24]

Terrorists are creating a system of control with unified leading entities that plan their actions. Terrorist groups that are similar in their ideological, political, nationalistic, religious, and separatist positions are holding councils and meetings, bringing together the leaders of the largest groups. These regions where armed conflicts are prevalent include "Palestine- Israel," Iraq, and Afghanistan. Latin America is gradually becoming a promising source from which the Islamic fighters may augment their ranks. In addition to the Middle East and Western Europe, we should expect increased activity by *jihadists* in Bosnia, Kosovo, India, Bangladesh, Indonesia, Australia, Philippines, the Fergana Valley, and the Xinjiang Uighur Autonomous Region of the People's Republic of China. Continuous material and financial support for terrorism today comes through control of the drug trade, racketeering, prostitution, arms trade, contraband, gambling, and so forth. Terrorists are striving to gain access to weapons of mass destruction and their components. We must organise efforts to counter nuclear terrorism, cyber terrorism, eco terrorism, agro terrorism, and radiological terrorism. Terrorism in Pakistan has become a major and highly destructive phenomenon in recent years. The state and its Inter-Services Intelligence, in alliance with the CIA, encouraged the "*Mujahideen*" to fight a proxy war against Soviet forces present in Afghanistan. Majority of the *Mujahideen* were never disarmed after the war ended in Afghanistan and some of these groups were later utilised at the behest of Pakistan in the form of the *Lashkar-e-Taiba*, the *Harkat-ul-Mujahideen* and others like the *Tehrik-i-Taliban Pakistan* (TTP) to spread terror in its neighbouring countries. These groups are now taking on the state itself, making the biggest threat to it and the citizens of Pakistan through the politically motivated killing of civilians and police officials. On December 16, 2014, 7 gunmen affiliated with the *Tehrik-i-Taliban* (TTP) conducted a terrorist attack on the Army Public School in the north-western Pakistani city of Peshawar. They entered the school and opened fire on school staff and children, killing 141 people, including 132 school children between the age of 8 and 18 years. A rescue operation was launched by the Pakistan Army's Special Services Group (SSG) Special Forces, who killed all 7 terrorists and rescued 960 people. On January 2, 2016, a heavily armed group attacked the Pathankot Air Force Station, a part of the Western Air Command of the Indian Air Force. The attackers, who were wearing Indian Army fatigues, were suspected to belong to *Jaish-e-Mohammed*, an Islamist militant group designated as a terrorist organisation by India, the US, the UK and the UN.

Table-2

TOP TERRORIST GROUPS
1. Al-Qaeda
2. ISIS (Islamic State of Iraq and the Levant)
3. Taliban
4. Irish Republican Army
5. Liberation Tiger of Tamil Eelam
6. Hezbollah
7. Ku Klux Klan
8. Hamas
9. Boko Haram
10. Al-shabaab
11. Lashkar-E-Taiba
12. Tehrik-i-Taliban Pakistan

Non-State Actors and State Terrorism

The Non-state actors (NSAs) is described as any organised group that has a command structure, operating outside state and using forces to achieve politically or making an allegedly political approach. Some factors include 'rebel groups' and some anti-government factors which may or may not be recognised as a state. Conflicts in the world today often involve armed opposition groups who act autonomously from recognised government. Included in this category are rebel groups, irregular armed groups, insurgents, dissident armed forces, guerillas, liberation movements, freedom fighters and *de facto* territorial governing bodies. The Non-State Actors Working Group (NSAWG) believes that there are about 190 recognised non-state actors. This does not include farmers, drug cartels and many of the smaller loosely organised NSAs. Ideology, objectives, strategies, level of organisation, support base, legitimacy and degree of international recognition vary greatly. Terrorist groups can be defined as organisations that commit violent acts that seemingly have no purpose other than to inflict terror among the civilian population. The acts of violence are not directed at military troops or other military targets. They are not carried out for defending. The purpose of the acts of violence is to disrupt the social fabric by creating a high level of fear among the civilian population. A NSA may or may not be considered a terrorist group. The groups that fall under the NSA category can vary greatly. The Non-State Actors Working Group (NSAWG) defines them as "organisations with less than full international recognition as a government who employ a military strategy."[25]

Despite the spectacular high-tech nature of combat technology, most armed conflicts are fought on foot using low technology methods of guerilla warfare. Anti-personnel mines, manufactured by state and non-state parties are frequently used in counter insurgency warfare, a type of warfare that threatens the global landscape today. The combatants and non-combatants become victims of mines without discrimination. Landmines are inherently indiscriminate weapons, making them ideal to instill terror in a local community. This is especially significant in counterinsurgency warfare and the patrolling, ground-fighting, area denial and terror tactics are commonly used by Non-State Actors (NSAs) and terrorist groups. Landmines deny access to land and infrastructure, increase the difficulty of survival and impede post-war recovery and long-term development. By destroying the social fabric, landmines impede the peace process. The majority of wars fought in the latter half of the 20th century, and those currently being fought, involve non-state, anti-state or stateless actors outside the control of states or governments recognised by the United Nations.

In this era of globalisation the most significant threat to security and peace comes from self-sustained and strong network organisations such as the *Al Qaeda* and its followers. These stateless organisations can only be fought by neutralising each and every one of its members, since organisations like these are certain to annihilate everyone. As even big nations too cannot defeat the increasing power of non-state actors it is likely that at some point of time some small organisations will get their hands on nuclear weapons or material.[26]

State terrorism refers to acts of terrorism conducted by a state against foreign targets or against its own people.Terrorism is used by states internally and across state boundaries against their own population with the objective to maintain order and to overcome political opposition. This involves a wide range of actions including disappearances, illegal detention, torture, and assassinations. Terrorism was used in this manner, *inter-alia*, by the Latin American national security states during the Cold War. They targeted civilians at home to instil fear among a much wider population and they targeted their own citizens living abroad, in collaboration with other states, through programmes such as Operation Condor. This entailed intelligence gathering and sharing and the kidnap, interrogation, torture, and assassinations of nationals of one Condor state – Argentina, Brazil, Uruguay, Paraguay and Chile – by its own agents or agents of other Condor states.[27]

One of the most famous incidences of state terrorism, the Reign of Terror in the 18th century in France, involved the use of terrorist tactics by a nation on its own citizens. The French government, struggling for legitimacy in a chaotic nation, attempted to keep the populace subdued with draconian and violent policies. Many dictators use similar tactics to keep their citizens in check and to prevent protesting, although these activities may not always be viewed as terrorism. States also use terrorism outside its border in pursuit of specific foreign policy objectives, either by undertaking limited campaigns of terror against specific individuals or groups, often officials of that state, using acts such as assassinations and bombing campaigns or by engaging in much more generalised campaigns of terror which are intended to destabilise whole societies. More generalised state terrorism involves the following: acts of war that violate the Geneva Convention, including the torture and killing of enemy combatants that have been disarmed and the illegal targeting of civilians, hijackings, kidnappings, illegal detentions, torture and other degrading treatment. In both cases, there are varying degrees to which states are involved in terrorism. At times, they are the main perpetrators, deploying their own agents, such as armed forces or secret services, to engage in acts of terrorism.[28] Terrorism by the state (or non-state actors) involves deliberate coercion and violence (or the threat thereof) directed at some victim, with the intention of inducing extreme fear in some target observers who identify with that victim in such a way that they perceive themselves as potential future victims. In this way they are forced to consider altering their behaviour in some manner desired by the actor.[29]

State terrorism involves the following four key elements:

- *There must be a deliberate act of violence against individuals that the state has a duty to protect or a threat of such an act if a climate of fear has already been established through preceding acts of state violence;*
- *The act must be perpetrated by actors on behalf of or in conjunction with the state, including paramilitaries and private security agents;*
- *The act or threat of violence is intended to induce extreme fear in some target observers who identify with that victim; and*
- *The target audience is forced to consider changing their behaviour in some way.*

State terrorism refers to a state's politically motivated application of force inside its own borders. Military, law enforcement, and other security institutions are used to suppress perceived threats and can be supplemented by unofficial paramilitaries and death squads. The purpose of state terrorism is to demonstrate the supreme power of the government and to intimidate or eliminate the opposition. In environments where the central government perceives its authority to be seriously threatened, this force can be extreme. South Africa during the final years of apartheid, the system of racial separation, is a good example. When confronted by a combination of antiapartheid reformist agitation, mass unrest, and terrorist attacks, the South African government began a covert campaign to root out anti-apartheid leaders and supporters. This included government support for the Zulu based Inkatha Freedom Party in its violence against the multi-ethnic and multiracial African National Congress (ANC). The South African government also assigned security officers to command death squads called Askar, who assassinated ANC members both inside South Africa and in neighbouring countries.

The suppression of a rebellion by the Muslim Brotherhood in 1982 by the Syrian government is an apt case study. The Muslim Brotherhood is a transnational Sunni Islamic fundamentalist movement very active in several North African and Middle Eastern countries. Beginning in the early 1980s, it initiated a widespread terrorist campaign against the Syrian government. In 1981, the Syrian army and other security units moved in to crush the Muslim Brotherhood in Aleppo and the city of Hama, killing at least 200 people. Syrian President Hafez el-Assad increased security restrictions and made membership in the organisation an offence inviting capital punishment. In 1982, another Muslim Brotherhood revolt broke out in Hama. The Syrian regime sent in troops and tanks, backed by artillery, to put down the revolt; they killed approximately 25,000 civilians and destroyed large sections of the city.

Table-3

State Terrorism- Activity Profile			
Country	Incident	Target Group	Outcome
Rwanda	Rwandan President Habyarimana was assassinated.	Tutsis and Hutu moderates.	Genocidal violence; approximately 500,000 people killed by Rwandan army and Hutu militants.
Cambodia	Victory on the battlefield by the Khmer Rouge; imposition of a new regime.	City dwellers, educated people, upper class, Buddhists, fellow Khmer Rouge.	The Killing Fields; up to 2 million deaths.
Bosnia	The breakup of Yugoslavia and Serb resistance to the Declarations of Independence by Slovenia, Croatia, and Bosnia.	Muslims living in territory claimed by Serbs.	Ethnic cleansing assisted by Serbia, destruction of population, massacres, systematic rape, and cultural destruction.
Germany	Racially motivated genocide by the Nazi regime.	German Jews.	The Holocaust; deaths of most of Germany's Jewish population
United States	Conquering the frontier and 19th century frontier wars	Native Americans	Annihilation of some tribes; resettlement of others on reservations.

Source: Cited in Jessica Stern, *The Ultimate Terrorists* (Cambridge, MA: Harvard University Press, 1999).

State terrorist model adapted from one designed by Peter C. Sederberg.[30] It defines and differentiates broad categories of domestic state terrorism that are useful in critically analysing the motives and behaviours of terrorist regimes.
• Unofficial repression: vigilante domestic state terrorism.
• Repression as policy: overt and covert official state terrorism.
• Mass repression: genocidal state terrorism.

Vigilante terrorism is political violence perpetrated by nongovernmental groups and individuals. These groups can receive unofficial support from agents of the state. Vigilante violence committed on behalf of a regime is motivated by the perceived need to defend a demographic group or cultural establishment. The overall goal of vigilante state terrorism is to violently preserve the preferred order. In a classic terrorist rationalisation process, the end of an orderly society justifies the means of extreme violence. The vigilante terrorists, sometimes work along with members of the state security establishment, unofficially wage a violent suppression campaign against an adversarial group or movement. Non governmental vigilantes often organise themselves into paramilitaries and operate as death squads. Death squads have committed many documented massacres and atrocities, including assassinations, massacres, disappearances, and random terrorist attacks.

The goals of official state terrorism are to preserve an existing order and to maintain state authority through demonstration of state power. Regimes that officially selected violent repression as a choice of policy rationalised their behaviour as a legitimate method of protecting the state from an internal threat. Two manifestations of official state terrorism in the domestic domain must be distinguished: **overt** and **covert**.

- **Overt official state terrorism** refers to the visible application of state-sponsored political violence. A policy of unconcealed and explicit repression against a domestic enemy is common in totalitarian societies, such as Stalinist Russia, Nazi Germany, Khmer Rouge Cambodia, and Taliban Afghanistan.
- **Covert official state terrorism** refers to the secretive application of state-sponsored political violence. A policy of concealed and implicit repression against a domestic enemy, it is common in countries with extensive secret police services, such as President Hafez el-Assad's Syria, Saddam Hussein's Iraq, General Augusto Pinochet's Chile, and Argentina during the Dirty War.

Official state terrorism is not always directed against subversive elements. It is sometimes conducted to cleanse society of an undesirable social group. These groups are perceived as purveyors of a decadent lifestyle or immoral values, or as otherwise unproductive drains on society.

Table-4

Social Cleansing

Social cleansing refers to the elimination of undesirable social elements. These undesirable elements are considered to be blights on society and can include street children, prostitutes, drug addicts, criminals, homeless people, transvestites, and homosexuals. In Colombia, undesirable social elements are commonly referred to as disposables. Social cleansing has occurred in a number of countries. The term was probably coined in Latin America, where social cleansing took on the attributes of vigilante state domestic terrorism in Brazil, Guatemala, Colombia, and elsewhere. Participants in cleansing campaigns have included members of the police and death squads. In societies where social cleansing has occurred, the disposables have been killed, beaten, and violently intimidated.

Ethnic Cleansing

The term ethnic cleansing was coined during the war in Bosnia in the former Yugoslavia. It refers to the expulsion of an ethno-national group from a geographic region as a means to create an ethnically pure society. During the war in Bosnia, Serb soldiers and paramilitaries initiated a cycle of ethnic cleansing. They officially and systematically expelled, killed, raped, and otherwise intimidated Bosnian Muslims to create Serb-only districts. The most intensive campaigns occurred in 1992 and 1993. As the war progressed, Croats and Bosnians also engaged in ethnic cleansing, so that there were periods during the war in which all three groups cleansed areas populated by members of the other groups. Since the war in Bosnia, the term has become widely used to describe present and past campaigns to systematically and violently remove ethno-national groups from geographic regions.

Source: WalterLaqueur, *The Age of Terrorism* (Boston: Little, Brown, 1987), 66, quoted in Bruce Hoffman, Inside Terrorism (New York: Columbia University Press, 1998), p.24.

Genocidal state terrorism occurs, when the resources of a nation are mobilised to eliminate a targeted group. The group can be a cultural minority—such as a racial, religious, or ethnic population—or a designated segment of society—such as believers in a banned ideology or a socio economically unacceptable group. When ideological or socioeconomic groups are singled out, the resulting environment is one in which members of the same ethnic or religious group commit genocide against fellow members, a practice known as auto genocide (self-genocide). This occurred during the reign of the Khmer Rouge in Cambodia.[31]

Table-5

TEN WAYS USING WHICH THE ISLAMIC STATE IS MAKING MONEY
1. Sales of electricity and gas to the Syrian government through ISIS-controlled dams and gas fields.
2. Taxes on citizens of the Islamic State.
3. Customs revenue on import and export of goods in the caliphate.
4. Exporting goods such as fruits, vegetables, grains and fabrics.
5. Internet cafes.
6. Religious taxes – punishment for smokers, missing prayers and breaking sharia law.
7. Confiscating private lands and selling it on public auction.
8. Selling crude oil in the black market in Turkey.
9. Growing and selling drugs and black marketing of cigarettes and alcohol.
10. Looting museums and selling artefacts in the black market.

Source: *Raqqa Is Being Slaughtered Silently, The Syrian people's Campaign against #ISIS #Assad regime in #Raqqa - Raqqa.Slaughtered@gmail.com*

Post 9/11 Developments

Global War on Terrorism

The shocking incidents which happened on September 11, 2001 was a watershed in the manner in which the world acknowledged and responded to terrorism. The monstrosity of the multiple attacks which killed nearly 3,000 people in one planned strike brought universal condemnation of terror acts and the community of nations got together to formulate a collective response, in what came to be known as the '*Global War on Terrorism*' (GWOT). However, the principle aim of the GWOT was to wipe out *Al Qaeda* from its sanctuaries in Afghanistan, from where the 9/11 attacks had emanated. US President George W Bush saw the world divided into two camps - those who supported the war against terrorism and those who did not. In Afghanistan and Pakistan, over 1,200 *Al Qaeda* terrorists had been killed between 2004 and 2011, thereby greatly eroding the outfit's capacity to launch attacks on the US mainland. Thus, for the US, the broad goals of the GWOT had been achieved, considerably. Some of the important *Al Qaeda* leaders killed since 2001 include its leader, Osama bin Laden (2011), Atiyah Abdur al-Rahman (2011), Badar Mansur (2012), Aslam Awam (2012), Abu Ayyub al-Masri (2010), Abu Yazid (2010), Sheikh Fateh al Masri (2010) and Abu Zeid (2013).

International terrorism, after 2001 has become more diffused and widespread. The flame of Islamist terrorism has engulfed several countries in Africa and the

Middle East in addition to assuming monstrous proportions in Afghanistan and Pakistan. In Iraq the security situation has become far worse in recent years with a wave of suicide bombings targeted at Shias. The struggle of Sunni radical outfits to oust the Syrian government which is primarily led by Ahlawites is attracting Muslim fighters from across the globe, transforming Syria into a new symbol of the global jihad. The failure of the so-called Arab Spring has also given a new fillip to radicalisation and accentuated sectarian strife in the Muslim world. In the 45 months preceding 9/11, an average of 106 terrorist related incidents was recorded every month across the world. Terrorists inspired by *Al Qaeda* have expanded the theatre of attacks and are looking for opportunities to target westerners across the world. Bali bombings of 2002 and London tube bombings in 2005 were carried out by terror groups loosely affiliated with *Al Qaeda* or individuals inspired by its ideology. In November 2015, a series of coordinated terrorist attacks occurred in Paris and its northern suburb, Saint-Denis. The attacks were described by President Francois Hollande as an "*act of war*" organised by the Islamic State (IS) militant group. France had been on high alert since the January 2015 attacks on Charlie Hebdo offices and a Jewish supermarket in Paris.

Jihadi terrorism post 9/11 has become more integrated and complementary in nature as terror outfits across the globe have closely aligned under the broad *Al Qaeda* umbrella, willing to ideologically or logistically support each other for targeting their common enemies. For instance, the objectives of the *Laskhar-e-Taiba (LeT)*, which carried out the attacks in Mumbai in 2008 were ideologically similar to that of *Al Qaeda* and was in consonance with the latter's aim of targeting westerners anywhere in the world. Documents recovered from Bin Laden's Abbottabad hideout even indicate that the *Al Qaeda* Emir may have had some knowledge of the Mumbai plot. Additionally, the role played by members of the Pakistani state establishment in conceiving and facilitating the 26/11 attacks is well documented and underscores the deep linkages between Jihadists and the deep state in Pakistan.

As a consequence, the terrorist groups have not only become stronger and more ambitious in their objectives and the sanctuary provided by the state has given them more immunity from state action. Maintaining proxies to carry out calibrated attacks on rival countries, has become an extension of state policy for some countries. Proxies like the *LeT* in Pakistan have become institutions in themselves and have expanded to other domains to include education, charity and health. While the United States recognises Iran, Cuba, Sudan and Syria as state sponsors of terrorism, and has imposed a host of economic and military sanctions against them, dictates of geopolitics has allowed Pakistan to escape being designated as a rogue state. In fact, it was declared to be a frontline ally of the US in the Global War on Terrorism (GWOT) despite its continuance of overt support to anti-India terrorist groups and tacit backing of a few other groups active in Afghanistan. The countries which have borne the direct brunt of state sponsored terrorism include India where more than 50,000 people have lost their lives in the state of Jammu and Kashmir in violence directly perpetuated by Pakistan based terrorist groups since 1989. Acts of terrorism sponsored by Pakistan have claimed nearly 1,500 lives and injured more than 4,000 in the Indian hinterland since the serial blasts in Mumbai on March 12, 1993.The geographical expansion of terrorism into new theatres of Indonesia, Philippines and Thailand in South East Asia, Afghanistan, Pakistan, India, Gulf countries, Iraq and parts of Europe, North and East Africa, has also been accompanied by a shift in the pattern of attacks and tactics employed by terrorist groups.

Post 9/11, the international community, led by the US largely gave up this discriminatory approach and promised co-operation to present a strong and united front against terrorism. The principled position notwithstanding, in practice much was left to be desired. Yet, the horror and magnitude of the 9/11 attacks had created a universal wave and abhorrence to terrorism and its brutal methods. Since June 2014, the extremist terrorist group known as the *Islamic State of Iraq and the Levant* (*ISIL or ISIS*) has expanded quickly and seized significant territories in Iraq and Syria. It not only threatens the very existence of the Iraqi government, but also has changed the nature of the Syria conflict, and its influence is spilling over to outside the region. In 2014, the Islamic State expanded its militant forces from over 10,000 to more than 90,000 (over 50,000 in Syria, and over 30,000 in Iraq) in three months,[32] controlling an area of up to 260,000 square kilometers and selecting Raqqa as its temporary capital. As regards the composition of its militant forces, the backbone is the *al-Qaeda* branch of Iraq and the Chechnya Islamic militants. Later on about 3,000 jihadists, hailing from dozens of countries around the world, including second and third generation Muslims with American or European citizenship, dozens of Caucasians from Europe and the United States who converted to Islam, and dozens of ETIM terrorists also joined them. Since July 2013, the Islamic State overran several prisons demanding that prisoners become jihadists or be killed, save for those who can provide a special excuse under Islamic law.[33] The "Islamic State" appointed several thousand military and government officials from the former regime of Saddam Hussein and the rebel Syrian military personnel. On April 13, 2015 ISIS militants have released a sickening new video warning America of a new 9/11-style attack. The propaganda video called "We Will Burn America" warns that there is "no safety for any American on the globe".

The 11-minute long clip also calls on ISIS supporters to target America on its own soil.

ISIS makes intelligent use of the Internet, especially the social networks, to send messages to specific target audiences. Most important for ISIS are the Western countries and its Muslim communities. Intensive propaganda aimed at them is intended to deter the West from attacking ISIS, increase the image of the organisation's strength, frighten Western public opinion, spread ISIS's jihad ideology to the Muslim communities in the West and encourage foreign fighters in Western Muslim communities to enlist in the ranks of ISIS. Its propaganda activities include posting notices, videos, audio messages and pictures. So far its strategy has been very successful and it has positioned itself as the West's number one enemy and gained support from the Arab-Muslim street, jihadi organisations and Muslim communities in the West.

The social networks, especially Facebook and Twitter, play an important role in ISIS's propaganda activity in the West. According to a study carried out by Conflict Armament Research[34] the weapons captured by the Kurdish forces in Iraq and Syria indicated that ISIS uses captured American army weapons and ammunition. According to the study, ISIS operatives captured a significant quantity of light American arms including M16 rifles stamped "Property of U.S. Govt." The study also showed that antitank rockets used by the Syrian organisations were the same as the M79 90mm rockets delivered to the Free Syrian Army by Saudi Arabia in 2013.ISIS has light arms, various types of rockets (standard and locally produced), mortars, anti-tank missiles and launchers, and anti-aircraft weapons.

In January 2015, ISIS was also confirmed to have a military presence in Afghanistan[35] and in Yemen.[36] Additionally, in early February 2015, it was revealed that ISIS was smuggling fighters into the European Union, by disguising them as civilian refugees.[37]ISIS is the richest terrorist organisation in the world. It took over most of the oil and gas fields (6-8 oilfields) in Syria and several oilfields in Iraq. According to an American army estimate, ISIS sold refined oil from the refineries attacked by the Americans at the end of September 2014 for about US$2 million a day.[38] According to David S. Cohen, US Treasury Under Secretary for Terrorism and Financial Intelligence, ISIS earned close to US$1 million a day from selling petroleum products, as of mid-June 2014.

Amnesty International says it has new evidence that Islamic State militants are carrying out "a wave of ethnic cleansing" against minorities in northern Iraq. The human rights group said IS had turned the region into "*blood-soaked killing fields*".ISIS directs violence against Shia Muslims, indigenous Assyrian, Chaldean, Syriac and Armenian Christians, Yazidis, Druze, Shabaks and Mandeans in particular. The UN estimated that 5,000 Yazidis were killed by ISIS during the takeover of parts of northern Iraq in August, 2014.The UN reported that in June 2014 ISIS had killed a number of Sunni Islamic clerics who refused to pledge allegiance to it. ISIS has recruited Iraqi children as young as nine to its ranks, who can be seen with masks on their faces and guns in their hands patrolling the streets of Mosul. According to a report by the magazine Foreign Policy, children as young as six are recruited or kidnapped and sent to military and religious training camps, where they practise beheading with dolls and are indoctrinated with the religious views of ISIS. Children are used as human shields on front lines and to provide blood transfusions for Islamic State soldiers. In late 2014, ISIS[39] released a pamphlet that focused on the treatment of female slaves. It claims that the Quran allows fighters to have sex with captives, including adolescent girls, and to beat slaves to discipline them.[40] The pamphlet's guidelines also allow fighters to trade slaves, including for sex,[41] as long as they have not been impregnated by their owner. The Islamic state justifies sexual slavery by quoting Quran 23:5-6: It is permissible to have sexual intercourse with the female captive.

Countering International Terrorism

The United Nations (UN) is a primary focal point for conflict resolution and the establishment of universal legal norms and for the setting up of human rights standards. In the field of international terrorism, the UN system as a whole has taken a sustained interest in developing an effective multilateral legal response to acts of terrorism, as incidents and diverse forms of terrorism have gained prominence in the last four decades.[42]United Nations (UN) after the attacks which took place on September 11, 2001 attempted to improve the effectiveness and commitment of states to counter terrorism through the development of domestic legislation, policy and practice. The post-Cold War atmosphere provided an encouraging environment for the UN Security Council enabling it to adopt an *ad hoc* or case-by-case responses to acts of terrorism during the 1990s. Eighteen Universal Instruments (fourteen Instruments and four Amendments) against international terrorism have been elaborated within the framework of the United Nations. These instruments relate to specific terrorist activities. Member states, through the General Assembly, have been increasingly coordinating their counter-terrorism efforts and are continuing their legal norm-setting activities. The Security Council has also been playing an active role in countering terrorism through resolutions and by establishing several subsidiary bodies. At the same time a number of programmes, offices and agencies of the United Nations have been engaged in specific activities against terrorism further assisting member states in their counter-terrorism efforts.

- **Action taken by UN General Assembly to Counter Terrorism**

The UN General Assembly has identified terrorism as an international problem since 1972. In the 1970s and 1980s it addressed the problem through resolutions. During this period the General Assembly also adopted two counter-terrorism related conventions: the Convention on the Prevention and Punishment of Crimes against Internationally Protected Persons in 1973 and the International Convention against the Taking of Hostages in 1979. A supplement to this Declaration established an *Ad Hoc* Committee on Terrorism in 1996. Since 1997, member states have completed work on three specific counter-terrorism instruments, covering specific types of terrorist activities: the International Convention for the Suppression of Terrorist Bombings 1997, the International Convention for the Suppression of the Financing of Terrorism 1999 and the International Convention for the Suppression of Acts of Nuclear Terrorism 1999.

Member states held further reviews on the strategy to be adopted in September 2010 and in June 2012 and also to share their experiences and good practices in addressing the threat of terrorism. In the third biennial review of the Global Counter-Terrorism Strategy held on June 28-29, 2012, the General Assembly unanimously adopted a resolution renewing its unwavering commitment for strengthening international cooperation to prevent and combat all forms of terrorism.

- **Action taken by the Security Council to Counter Terrorism**

Since the early 1990s, the Security Council has been consistently dealing with terrorism issues. Its actions took the form of sanctions against states considered to have links to specific acts of terrorism such as Libya (1992), Sudan (1996) and the Taliban (1999). It was expanded to include *Al-Qaida* in 2000 by resolution 1333. A precursor to the intensification of its counter-terrorism work since 9/11, 2001 was the adoption of resolution 1269 in 1999, in which the Council urged countries to work together to prevent and suppress all terrorist acts. In the aftermath of 9/11, the Security Council established a Counter Terrorism Committee also comprising all members of the Security Council, under resolution 1373. Resolution 1373 (2001), which was adopted unanimously on September 28, 2001, calls upon member states to implement a number of measures intended to enhance their legal and institutional ability to counter terrorist activities, including taking steps to:

- *Criminalise the financing of terrorism.*
- *Freeze without delay any funds related to persons involved in acts of terrorism.*
- *Deny all forms of financial support for terrorist groups.*
- *Suppress the provision of safe haven, sustenance or support for terrorists.*
- *Share information with other governments on any groups practicing or planning terrorist acts.*
- *Cooperate with other governments in the investigation, detection, arrest, extradition and prosecution of those involved in such acts; and*
- *Criminalise active and passive assistance for terrorism in domestic law and bring violators to justice.*

The resolution wants member states to take a number of measures to prevent terrorist activities and to criminalise various forms of terrorist actions, as well as to take measures that would assist and promote cooperation among countries including adherence to international counter-terrorism instruments. Member states are also required to report regularly to the Counter Terrorism Committee on the measures they have taken to implement resolution 1373.

In 2004 the Council adopted resolution 1535, which called for the setting up of a Counter Terrorism Committee Executive Directorate (CTED) to monitor the implementation of resolution 1373 and to facilitate the provision of technical assistance to member states.

Through resolution 1540 (2004), the Council established an additional counter-terrorism - related body: the 1540 Committee - with the task of monitoring compliance of member states with resolution 1540, which calls on states to prevent non-state actors (including terrorist groups) from accessing weapons of mass destruction. Resolution 1566 (2004) established the 1566 Working Group made up of all members of the Security Council to recommend practical measures against such individuals and groups, as well as to explore the possibility of setting up a compensation fund for victims of terrorism. On the margins of the 2005 World Summit, the Security Council held a high-level meeting and adopted Resolution 1624 (2005) condemning all acts of terrorism irrespective of their motivation, as well as the incitement to such acts. It also called on member states to prohibit by law terrorist acts and incitement to commit them and to deny safe haven to anyone guilty of such conduct. United Nations Global Counter-Terrorism Strategy (*A/ RES/60/288*) and the related adoption of the General Assembly resolution *64/297*, the Security Council convened on September27, 2010 invited an open debate on the threats to international peace and security by terrorist acts.[43]

- **International Conventions Held to Discuss Measures to Counter Terrorism**
In 2005, the international community also introduced substantive changes to the three of the universal instruments to specifically account for the threat of terrorism.. The states adopted the Amendments to the Convention on the Physical Protection of Nuclear Material on July 8, 2005 and on October 14, 2005 they agreed to two Protocols, namely,the Convention for the Suppression of Unlawful Acts against the Safety of Maritime Navigation2005 and the Protocol for the Suppression of Unlawful Acts against the Safety of Fixed Platforms Located on the Continental Shelf 2005.

Two more legal instruments in this regard were added in 2010:

- the Convention on the Suppression of Unlawful Acts Relating to International Civil Aviation 2010 and
- the Protocol Supplementary to the Convention for the Suppression of Unlawful Seizure of Aircraft 2010.

These treaties further makes it criminal the act of using civil aircraft as a weapon and of using dangerous materials to attack aircraft or other targets on the ground. The unlawful transport of biological, chemical and nuclear weapons and their related material also becomes punishable under the treaties.

The major legal instruments and additional amendments dealing with terrorism are:-

- The Convention on Offences and Certain Other Acts Committed On Board Aircraft1963.
- The Convention for the Suppression of Unlawful Seizure of Aircraft(Unlawful Seizure Convention)1970.
- The Protocol Supplementary to the Convention for the Suppression of Unlawful Seizure of Aircraft 2010.
- The Convention for the Suppression of Unlawful Acts against the Safety of Civil Aviation 1971.
- The Convention on the Prevention and Punishment of Crimes Against Internationally Protected Persons 1973.
- The International Convention against the Taking of Hostages 1979.
- The Convention on the Physical Protection of Nuclear Material 1980.
- The Protocol for the Suppression of Unlawful Acts of Violence at Airports Serving International Civil Aviation, supplementary to the Convention for the Suppression of Unlawful Acts against the Safety of Civil Aviation (Extends and supplements the Montreal Convention on Air Safety) 1988.
- The Convention for the Suppression of Unlawful Acts against the Safety of Maritime Navigation 1988.

- The Protocol to the Convention for the Suppression of Unlawful Acts against the Safety of Maritime Navigation 2005.
- The Protocol for the Suppression of Unlawful Acts Against the Safety of Fixed Platforms Located on the Continental Shelf (Fixed Platform Protocol) 1988.
- The Convention on the Marking of Plastic Explosives for the Purpose of Detection 1991.
- The International Convention for the Suppression of Terrorist Bombings 1997.
- The International Convention for the Suppression of the Financing of Terrorism 1999.
- The International Convention for the Suppression of Acts of Nuclear Terrorism 2005.
- The Convention on the Suppression of Unlawful Acts Relating to International Civil Aviation 2010.[44]

Conclusion

International terrorism is a menace to the society that has threatened every fabric of it throughout history. "One man's terrorist is another man's freedom fighter,"[45]is not only a cliché but also one of the most difficult obstacles in coping with terrorism. This international threat has all but not a global solution as some countries are trying to present it. With regards to terrorism the world can share many things including intelligence, trafficking of money and information etc. but to deal with it can mostly be local. As a "language of communication" it calls for attention to certain grievances and is thus not a goal in itself but a means. "Think Globally and act locally"[46]would be an honest approach to deal with the menace of terrorism. There is no one accepted definition and there is no one solution to the problem. Sweeping generalisation and stereotyping brings in more resentment. An environment within the state and among the states needs to be created that do not breed terrorism.

Notes

1. Baylis, J. and Smith, S. (eds.), *"The Globalization of World Politics: An Introduction to International Relations"*. 5ᵗʰ Edition, (Oxford: Oxford University Press, 2011).
2. Dipak K. Gupta , "Exploring Roots of Terrorism" International Security and Conflict Resolution, (London: Routledge, 2004).
3. Jackson, R. and Sorenson, G. *"Introduction to International Relations: Theories and Approaches"*. (New York: Oxford University Press, 2008).
4. Walter Laqueur *"No End to War: Terrorism in the Twenty-First Century"* (New York: Bloomsbury Academic, 2003).
5. Burgess, Mark *A Brief History of Terrorism*,(Washington, D.C.: Center for Defence Information (CDI), 2003); Tuman, Joseph S.,*"Communicating Terror: The Rhetorical Dimensions of Terrorism"* (2nd ed.). Thousand Oaks, (California: Sage,2009).

6. Laqueur, Walter, The *Age of Terrorism* (2nd ed.). ,(Boston: Little & Brown, 1987), p.143.

7. Hoffman, Bruce, *Inside Terrorism* (2nd ed.).,(New York: Columbia University Press, 2006), p. 43.

8. Schmid, Alex, and Jongman, Albert, *Political Terrorism: A New Guide to Actors, Authors, Concepts, Data Bases, Theories, and Literature,*(Amsterdam: North Holland, Transaction Books, 1988), p. 28.

9. Rapoport, David C., "The Government Is Up in the Air over Combating Terrorism"*National Journal*, November 26, 1977, vol.9, pp.1853–1856.

10. Alexander, Yonah, *International Terrorism: National, Regional and Global Perspectives.*(New York: Praeger, 1976), p. xiv.

11. Sloan, Stephen, *Terrorism: The Present Threat in Context*(Oxford: Berg Publishers, 2006).

12. League Convention (1937). Convention for the Prevention and Punishment of Terrorism, Article 1(2).

13. Joint Chiefs of Staff DOD Department of Defence *Dictionary of Military and Associated Terms*, (Washington, D.C.: DOD, 2008).

14. Chomsky, Noam,*2001. 9-11*(New York: Seven Stories Press, 2001).

15. Tilly, Charles,.*Coercion, capital, and European states AD 990-1992*(Malden: Blackwell, 1990).

16. Stern, Jessica,*The Ultimate Terrorists*(Cambridge: Harvard University Press, 1999).

17. Chalk, Peter, "The Evolving Dynamic of Terrorism in the 1990s." *Australian Journal of International Affairs* (1999) no.53, pp151-167.

18. Enders, Walter and Todd Sandler, "Patterns of Transnational Terrorism, 1970–1999: Alternative TimeSeries Estimates." *International Studies Quarterly*(2002) no.46, pp145-165.

19. Ibid. no. 3.

20. Schmid, Alex Peter and A. J. Jongman,*Political Terrorism*(New York: Transaction Books, 1988).

21. Imre, Robert, Mooney, T. Brian, and Clarke, Benjamin,*Responding to Terrorism*(Farnham, England: Ashgate,2008).

22. Martin, Gus, Understanding *Terrorism: Challenges, Perspectives, and Issues.* Thousand Oaks, (California: Sage, 2010).

23. Ansari, Hamied,"The Islamic Militants in Egyptian Politics"*International Journal of Middle East Studies*no.16 (1984), pp136–140; Zeidan, David,"The Islamic Fundamentalist View of Life as a Perennial Battle"*Middle East Review of International Affairs,*(2001) 5(4), pp.10–21.

24. Gerges, Fawaz, *The Far Enemy: Why Jihad Went Global*(New York: Cambridge University Press, 2005).

25. "Non- State Actors and Their Significance" Margaret Busé, Editor, http://www.jmu.edu/cisr/journal/5.3/features/maggie_buse_nsa/maggie_buse.htm, accessed on Mach, 2001.

26. Anant Mishra,*Terrorism in the 21st Century: Battling Non State Actors*", 25 January , 2015, iDR, Indian Defence Review http://www.indiandefencereview.com/news/terrorism-in-the-21st-century-battling-non-state-actors/2/, accessed on 25 January , 2015.

27. Dinges, J.,*The Condor Years*(New York: The New Press, 2004).McClintock, M., The *United States and Operation Condor: Military Doctrine in an Unconventional War,* (Washington DC: Latin American Studies Association Conference, 2001);McSherry, J.P., 'Tracking the Origins of a State Terror Network: Operation Condor', *Latin American Perspectives*, 2002, no. 29 (1),pp38–60.

28. Stohl, M., 'The State as Terrorist: Insights and Implications', Democracy and Security, (New York: Greenwood Press, 2006).

29. Mitchell, C., Stohl, M., Carleton, D., Lopez, G. 'State Terrorism: Issues of Concept and Measurement', in Michael Stohl and George Lopez, ed.*Government Violence and Repression: An Agenda for Research*, (New York: Greenwood Press, 1986).

30. Hoffman, Bruce,*Inside Terrorism*(2nd ed.).(New York: Columbia University Press, 2006), p. 43.

31. William Shawcross, *Sideshow: Kissinger, Nixon, and the Destruction of Cambodia* (New York: Simon & Schuster, 1979).

32. "Islamic State 'Has 50,000 Fighters in Syria'," *Al Jazeera* August19, 2014, http://www.aljazeera. com/news/middleeast/2014/08/islamic-state-50000-fighters-syria-2014819184258421392. html., accessed on August 28, 2014.

33. "Iraq: Hundreds Escape from Abu Ghraib Jail," *Associated Press*, July22, 2013, http://www. theguardian.com/world/2013/jul/22/iraq-prison-attacks-kill-dozens, accessed on July 27, 2013.

34. A British organisation that identifies and tracks conventional weapons and ammunition in contemporary armed conflicts "Islamic State Weapons in Iraq and Syria," September 2014. Dispatch IS Iraq Syria Weapons.

35. "ISIS gaining ground in Yemen, competing with al Qaeda". CNNJanuary21, 2015.

36. Sohranas, "*Exclusive: 'It is not the end of fighting in Kobani' – expert fears IS could re*turn". Syrian Observatory for Human Rights, The Washington Post. Accessed on 2 August 2014.

37. Mike Giglio, Munzer al-Awad. "ISIS Operative: This Is How We Send Jihadis To Europe". Buzz Feed.(The Daily Beast, Accessed on June 19, 2014.)

38. "ISIS's Financial and Military Capabilities" Crethiplethi, September, 14, 2014.http://www. crethiplethi.com/isis-s-financial-and-military-capabilities/islamic-countries/syria-islamic-countries/2015/, accessed on August 2, 2014.

39. Amelia Smith, "ISIS Publish Pamphlet On How to Treat Female Slaves," *Newsweek*, September12, 2014.

40. AbulTaher, "Our faith condones raping underage slaves: ISIS publishes shocking guidebook telling fighters how to buy, sell and abuse captured women". *Daily Mail*, December 13, 2014.

41. Katharine Lackey, "Pamphlet provides Islamic State guidelines for sex slaves," *USA Today*, December13, 2014.

42. Grant Wardlaw*Political Terrorism: Theory, Tactics and Counter-Measures*(New York: Cambridge University Press, 1989).

43. "United Nations Action to Counter Terrorism", http://www.un.org/en/terrorism/ securitycouncil.shtml, *BBC* accessed on March 7, 2015.

44. "International Legal Instruments" http://www.un.org/en/terrorism/instruments.shtml, accessed on *The Guardian*, accessed on July 17, 2014.

45. KulwantKaur, "*Global Terrorism: Issues, Dimensions and Options*", (New Delhi: Kanishka, 2005).

46. Ibid., n. 2.

CHAPTER 9

Migration and Refugees

Introduction

Freedom of movement is a fundamental human right and is central to the functioning of the international refugee protection regime. The very ability to seek asylum depends on the ability to move in search of rights that have been denied in the country of origin. In a broader sense, it is now increasingly recognised that mobility of people provides an important means for people to improve their standard of living and to contribute to the economic and social life of their countries of origin and destination.[1] Every day, thousands of people embark on dangerous journeys to find a better life. Some are refugees fleeing conflict zones such as Syria, many others are in search of education for their children, jobs, better opportunities and freedom. All have aspirations and hopes for a better future.[2]UNHCR's changing attitude to mobility can be explained by a number of factors. There is a growing body of academic research indicating that the return of forced migrants to their home in most of the cases is neither possible nor desirable, and that transnational diasporic community networks can contribute positively to the *de facto* protection of refugees, asylum seekers, IDPs and other persons who are of concern to UNHCR.

The problem of the refugees of the world and that of internally displaced people is one of the most complicated issues before the world community today. A lot of discussions is taking place at the United Nations as it continues its search for more effective ways to protect and assist these particularly vulnerable groups. The authors who drafted the Charter of the United Nations had in mind the painful memories of generalised violence and mass sufferings, and called upon its signatories to save succeeding generations from the scourge of war. They wanted the United Nations to help achieve "international cooperation in solving international problems of an economic, social, cultural, or humanitarian character" and "to promote and encourage respect for human rights and for fundamental freedoms for all without distinction as to race, sex,language or religion".One of the first problems on the agenda of the United Nations which was to be tackled was the fate of refugees, displaced persons, stateless persons and "returnees," all uprooted by war and badly in need of assistance. The problem clearly have both international and humanitarian dimension.

Nearly 15 million people are currently identified as "refugees" by the United Nations High Commissioner for Refugees (UNHCR) and another 5 million are "of concern" to the world's oldest and largest refugee protection agency. An additional 20 million people have fled their homes, but as they have not crossed an international frontier, they are termed "Internally Displaced People" (IDPs).[3]The 40 million people so uprooted from their homes as refugees or IDPs constitute about 1 out of every 150 persons on earth. If we look at the worldwide situation it is observed that the refugee situation is getting worse on some fronts, while on other areas there are signs of hope. Because of the turmoil in Greek, Syria, Afghanistan and Iraq, hundreds of thousands of people have fled their countries or have become IDPs, although repatriation efforts are now underway. The Civil War has also recently uprooted over one quarter of a million people in Colombia, Liberia, Libya and one fears what the current escalation of tensions in the Middle East might result. The refugee problem in some cases such as those involving Somalis, Iranians, Iraqis, Burmese and Bhutanese is massive and remain unresolved even after a decade of efforts. On the other hand, nearly 1 million Eritreans have been able to return home now that a peace with Ethiopia seems to be in place.

The terms 'refugee' *and* 'migrant' is being used interchangeably in media and public discourse. But the two terms have distinct and different meanings, and confusing those leads to problems for both populations. Refugees are persons fleeing from areas of armed conflict or persecution. There were 19.5 million of them worldwide by the end of 2015. Their situation is often so perilous and intolerable that they cross national borders to seek safety in nearby countries, and thus become internationally recognised as 'refugees' with access to assistance from States, UNHCR, and other organisations. They are so recognised precisely because it is too dangerous for them to return home, and they need sanctuary elsewhere. These are people for whom denial of asylum has potentially deadly consequences. In February, 2016 the United Nations (UN) has identified 13.5 million Syrians requiring humanitarian assistance, of which 6.6 million are internally displaced within Syria, and over 4.8 million refugees are living outside Syria.[4] Turkey is the largest host country with over 2.7 million Syrian refugees.[5]The programme for assistance to internally displaced persons (IDPs) within Syria, and Syrian refugees in neighbouring countries, is coordinated largely through the United Nations High Commissioner for Refugees (UNHCR).

Meaning of migration and migrant

Migration is the movement of people from one place to another. Migration is defined broadly as a permanent or semi-permanent change of residence. No restriction is placed upon the distance of the move or upon the voluntary or involuntary nature of the act, and no distinction is made between external and internal migration. No matter how short or how long, how easy or how difficult, every act of migration involves an origin, a destination, and an intervening set of obstacles. Among the set of intervening obstacles, we include the distance of the move as one that is always present.

A migrant is someone who moves from one place to another in order to live in another country for more than a year. The International Organisation of Migration estimates that 232 million people become international migrants in a year and another 740 million move within their own countries. There are many reasons for people to become migrants but those who move to work or seek a better life are generally termed economic migrants. There are, also other categories of migrants such as international students, those who move for family reasons and those who migrate because they are fleeing war and persecution. An individual case can also be a mixture of all those things. It is, after all, possible for someone to flee from the war in Syria and seek a better life for your family. The United Nations defines a migrant as *'an individual who has resided in a foreign country for more than one year irrespective of the causes, voluntary or involuntary, and the means, regular or irregular, used to migrate'*.[6] This definition formally encompasses refugees, asylum-seekers and economic migrants.

Migrants choose to move not because of a direct threat of persecution or death, but mainly to improve their lives by finding work, or in some cases for education, family reunion, or for other reasons. Unlike refugees who cannot safely return home, migrants face no such impediment to return. If they choose to return home, they will continue to receive the protection of their government. For individual governments, this distinction is important. Countries deal with migrants under their own immigration laws and processes. Countries deal with refugees through norms for refugee protection and asylum that are defined in both national legislation and international law. All countries have specific responsibilities towards anyone seeking asylum in their territories or at its borders. The role of UNHCR is to helps countries deal with their asylum and refugee protection responsibilities.[7]

Migration can be international (movement between different countries) or intra-national (movement within a country, often from rural to urban areas). Migration has become a common trend and more people are migrating than at any other point of the history. People migrate in different ways and for different reasons. People move in order to improve their standard of living, to give their children better opportunities, or to escape from poverty, conflict and famine. Today, with modern transportation and communications, more people are motivated and able to move. *Intra-national* migration refers to a change of residence within national boundaries, such as between states, provinces, cities, or municipalities. An *internal migrant* is someone who moves to a different administrative territory. *International migration* refers to change of residence over national boundaries. An international migrant is someone who moves to a different country. International migrants are further classified as legal immigrants, illegal immigrants, and refugees. *Legal immigrants* are those who moved with the legal permission of the receiver nation, illegal immigrants are those who moved without legal permission, and refugees are those who crossed an international boundary to escape persecution. The majority of them stay for a while and then return home. They are migrants. Other kinds of migrants include contract workers engaged for a certain period of time, and professionals, usually working for transnational companies, who move from country to country. People migrate for numerous reasons: *economic, social, political or environmental.*

- *Economic motivation*: In search for work, better pay or to pursue a particular career path.
- *Social motivation*: Moving somewhere for a better quality of life or to be closer to family or friends.
- *Political motivation*: Moving to escape political, religious or ethnic persecution, or conflict.
- *Environmental motivation*: In order to escape natural disasters such as flooding or drought.

Table 1. Migrants, refugees, asylum seekers what do these words mean?

In the public debate, the terms *'asylum seeker'*, *'refugee'* and *'migrant'* are often used synonymously. However, it is important to distinguish the three terms. The term *'migrant'* corresponds to a generic term for anyone moving to another country with the intention to stay for a minimum period of time (i.e. it excludes tourists and business visitors). It includes both permanent and temporary migrants with a valid residence permit or visa, asylum seekers, and undocumented migrants who do not belong to any of the three mentioned groups. According to the UN definition, a long term migrant is a person who moves to a country other than that of his or her usual residence for a period of at least a year (12 months), so that the country of destination effectively becomes his or her new country of usual residence. OECD reports usually define permanent migrants as people who have a status that enables them to stay in the country under prevailing circumstances. Among this group one can distinguish between four broad categories: long-term migrants within a free mobility zone; labour migrants; family migrants; and humanitarian migrants. 'Asylum seekers' are persons who have formally submitted a request for asylum but have not yet completed the asylum procedure, i.e. whose request for asylum is pending. They are still candidates for humanitarian migrant status. In practice, only a minority of asylum seekers obtains some form of humanitarian migrant status and others have the obligation to leave the country. If people remain after being denied such status they become undocumented migrants. The term 'humanitarian migrant' refers to persons who have completed the asylum procedure with a positive outcome and have been granted some sort of protection (refugee status or another form of protection) or have been resettled through programmes outside the asylum procedure. For the sake of simplicity this brief considers all recipients of protection – whether refugee status, temporary protection, subsidiary protection, etc. – to be humanitarian migrants. In addition to migrants formally filing an asylum request, there are many people who have not filed an asylum request, either because they do not want to file it in the country through which they are transiting, or because there is a long wait to apply for asylum (either due to large inflows, as in Germany, or understaffed asylum systems), or because they know their prospects for obtaining humanitarian migrant status are slim. These people are also considered as undocumented migrants. The term migrant can, therefore, be used as a generic term to describe a situation where flows are mixed. Clearly not all people who currently enter the EU illegally will claim asylum and, among those who will do, only a fraction will be granted refugee status. This is why this brief uses the term migrant. However, it would not be entirely correct to refer to this crisis as a 'migration crisis'. Legal migration systems that enable people to enter with valid visa/permit are in place and tend to be adequately managed. What is currently observed would therefore be better described as a 'refugee' or 'asylum crisis' because it concerns specifically the European asylum system.

Source: "Is this humanitarian migration crisis different?" *Migration Policy Debates*, September 7, 2015,https://www.oecd.org/migration/Is-this-refugee-crisis-different.pdf, accessed on December 12, 2015.

Once migrants arrive in a country such as Britain there is little agreement over what the word covers. In the past "immigrant" has meant someone who intends to settle in a new country. "Migrant" has been increasingly adopted to cover those who come to work for a short period then return home. "The migrant population" is used to describe not only foreign national residents in a country, but also those who are foreign-born residents even if they have become citizens.[8]

Factors Relating to Migration
Human migration is due to social factors such as, racism, sexism and religion. The pushing factor from the social perspective is that people are being discriminated in their homeland. People in these countries are treated unfairly because of their differences and that they are small in numbers. The pulling factors come in the case of other countries, such as the United States, Brazil and Argentina. People often seek refuge status in such countries that are more open minded and accepts you for who you are disregarding race or religion. Furthermore, people migrate from their homeland as and when unfavourable political issues come up. The main reason behind their action of migrating is because they do not agree with the government's rule or policy. Instability in the government, war and oppression contribute towards the pushing factors of migration. Wars will result in the death of the innocents, and most people will try their best to escape from war. Moreover, people are migrating around the world due to pulling factors such as higher standard of living and better income while poverty and unemployment contribute to the pushing factors. People from the third world countries would choose to migrate from their homeland as there is no opportunity to grasp. These people would choose to take the risk and go with the objective of realising their dreams and hope to find the opportunities and fortune that they seek in life. In some cases the capability of people are also not properly used as their country is not able to make use of a certain profession or talent that would be more appreciated in some other places.[9]

Human beings are known to have migrated extensively throughout the period of prehistoric period and as also during the recorded history. The movement of populations in modern times has continued in the form of both voluntary migration within one's region, country, or beyond, and involuntary migration (which includes trafficking in human beings and ethnic cleansing). The people who migrate are called migrants, or, more specifically, emigrants, immigrants, or settlers, depending on historical setting, circumstance, and perspective. Between 1846 and 1940, mass migrations occurred worldwide. The size and speed of transnational migratory movements was unprecedented. About 55 million of migrants moved from Europe to America, and an additional 2.5 million moved from Asia to America. Of these transatlantic migrations, 65 percent went to the United States. Other major receiving countries were Argentina, Canada, Brazil, and Cuba.

During this period such a large number of people migrated across large distances within Asia. Southeastern Asia received 50 million migrants, mainly from India and south China. North Asia—Manchuria, Siberia, Central Asia, and Japan together—received another 50 million. Not much is known about exact numbers of the migrations from and within Africa during this period, but Africa had a small net immigration between 1850 and 1950, having a variety of origins. Transnational labour migration reached a peak of three million migrants per year in the early 20th century. Italy, Norway, Ireland, and the Quongdong region of China were the ones with especially high rates of emigration during these years. These large flow of migration influenced the process of formation of nation state in many ways. Restrictions on immigration as well as diaspora cultures and myths that reflect the importance of migration to the foundation of certain nations, like the American being the melting pot was observed. The rate of transnational migration of labour fell to a lower level from the 1930s to the 1960s and then a rebound in rate of migration was observed. The 20thcentury also experienced an increase in flow in migration caused by war and politics, with large number of refugees fleeing their homelands that had been taken over by factions hostile to their ethnicity or religion. Muslims moved from the Balkans to Turkey, while Christians moved the other way, during the collapse of the Ottoman Empire. Approximately 400,000 Jews moved to Palestine in the early 20thcentury. The Russian Civil War resulted in migration of about 3 million Russians, Poles, and Germans from the Soviet Union. The World War II and decolonisation in many places also caused migrations. People migrate for a number of reasons. These reasons can be classified into four categories: Environmental, Economic, Cultural and Socio-political. Within those, the reasons may also be 'push' or 'pull' factors.

Push Factors

Push factors are those that force the individual to move voluntarily, and in many cases, they are forced because the individuals are at risk if they continued to stay. Push factors may include conflict, drought, famine, or extreme religious views and activity to promote the same. Poor economic activity and lack of job opportunities are also strong push factors for migration. Other strong push factors include race and cultures discriminating people, political intolerance and persecution of people who question the status quo. Different types of push factors include:

- *Poor medical care.*
- *Not enough jobs.*
- *Few opportunities.*
- *Primitive conditions of living.*
- *Political reasons.*
- *Fear of torture and mistreatment.*
- *Not being able to practice religion.*
- *Loss of wealth.*
- *Natural disasters (including changes in climate).*

Pull Factors

Pull factors are those factors prevailing in one country which attract the individual or group to leave their home and migrate to another country in search of better opportunities. Those factors include utility of the place, which is in a better position to attract people and could utilise their skills. Better economic opportunities, more jobs and the promise of a better life often pull people into new locations. Sometimes individuals have ideas and perceptions about places that are not necessarily correct, but work as strong pull factors for that individual. Very often, people consider and prefer opportunities closer to their location than similar opportunities farther away. In the same vein, people often like to move to places with better cultural, political, climatic and general terrain in closer locations than locations farther away. It is rare to find people move across very long distances to settle in places that they have little knowledge. Different types of pull factors which can be observed include:

- *Chances of getting a job.*
- *Better living standards.*
- *Enjoyment.*
- *Education.*
- *Better medical care.*
- *Security.*
- *Family links.*

Migration Theories

- *Ravenstein's Laws of Migration*

The first attempt to spell out the 'laws of migration' was made by E.G. Ravenstein as early as in 1885.[10]ErnestRavenstein is widely regarded as the earliest migration theorist. Ravenstein, an English geographer, used census data from England and Wales to develop his *"laws of migration"* (1889). He concluded that migration was governed by a "push-pull" process that is, unfavorable conditions in one place (oppressive laws, heavy taxation, etc.) "push" people out, and favorable conditions in an external location "pull" them out. Using the data on place of birth, Ravenstein identified a set of generalisations, which he called as 'laws of migration' concerning inter-county migration in Britain in the 19th century. Most of these generalisations enumerated below hold good even today:

- There is an inverse relation between distance and volume of migration. Majority of migrants moves to short distance only. Migrants going long distance generally go by preference to the large centers of commerce and industry.
- Migration proceeds step by step. The inhabitants of countryside flock into the nearby rapidly growing town. The gap created by this out-migration in the countryside is filled up by in-migration from still remoter countryside. The inhabitants of the town then move to the nearby urban center up in the hierarchy.
- Every migration current produces a counter-current.
- The native of the rural areas are more mobile than their counterpart in the urban areas and the major direction of migration is from agricultural areas to the centers of industry and commerce.
- Females are more mobile than male in the country of birth, but male more frequently venture beyond.
- Migration is highly age selective where adults in the working age groups display a greater propensity to migrate.
- Volume of migration increases with the process of diversification of the economy, and improvement in transport facilities.
- Migration occurs mainly due to economic reasons.

- *Lee's Migration Theory*

Everett Lee (1966) reformulated Ravenstein's theory to give more emphasis to internal (or push) factors. Lee also outlined the impact that the intervening obstacles have on the migration process. He argued that variables such as distance, physical and political barriers, and having dependents can impede or even prevent migration. Lee pointed out that the migration process is selective because differentials such as age, gender, and social class affect how persons respond to push-pull factors, and these conditions also shape their ability to overcome intervening obstacles.[11]He begins his formulations with factors, which lead to spatial mobility of population in any area.These factors are:

- *Factors associated with the place of origin,*

- *Factors associated with the place of destination,*
- *Intervening obstacles, and*
- *Personal factors.*

According to Lee, each place possesses a set of positive and negative factors. While positive factors are the circumstances that act to hold people within it, or attract people from other areas, negative factors tend to repel them.[12] In addition to these, there are factors, which remain neutral, and to which people are essentially indifferent. While some of these factors affect most of the people in the area, others tend to have differential effects. Migration in any area is the net result of the interplay between these factors. Lee suggests that individuals involved in migration have near perfect assessment of factors in the place of origin due to their long association. However, the same is not necessarily true for that of the area of destination. There is always some element of ignorance and uncertainty with regard to reception of migrants in the new area.[13]

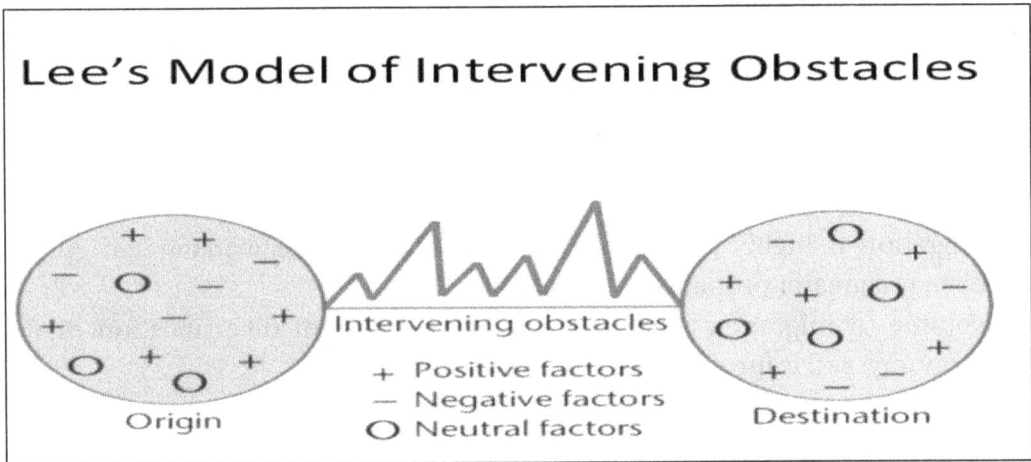

Source: *Evertt S. Lee in, "A Theory of Migration", from Demography, Vol., 3, No., pg. 50.*

Another important point is that the perceived difference between the areas of origin and destination is related to the stage of the lifecycle of an individual. A long association of an individual with a place may result in an over-evaluation of positive factors and under-evaluation of negative factors in the area of origin. At the same time, the perceived difficulties may lead to an inaccurate evaluation of positive and negative factors in the area of destination. The final decision to move does not depend merely upon the balance of positive and negative factors at the places of origin and destination. The balance in favour of the move must be enough to overcome the natural inertia and intervening obstacles. Distance separating the places of origin and destination has been more frequently referred to in this context by authors, but according to Lee, distance while omnipresent, is by no means the most important factor.[14] Furthermore, the effect of these intervening obstacles varies from individual to individual. Apart from the factors associated with places of origin and destination, and the intervening obstacles, there are many personal factors, which promote or retard migration in any area. Some of these are more or less constant throughout the life span of an individual, while others tend to vary in effect with the stages in life cycle. It may be noted that the real situation prevailing at the places of origin and destination are not as important in affecting migration as individual's perception of these factors. The process of perception depends, to a large extent, on the personal factors like awareness, intelligence, contacts and the cultural milieu of the individual.[15]The decision to migrate is the net result of the interplay among all these factors. Lee pointed out that the decision to migrate is, however, never completely rational. Also important to note here is the fact that not all persons who migrate do so on their own decision. Children and wives move with the family where their decisions are not necessarily involved. Lee outlined the following hypotheses relating to the characteristics of the migrants:

- *Migration is selective in nature. Due to differences in personal factors, the conditions at the places of origin and destination, and intervening obstacles are responded differently by different individuals. The selectivity could be both positive and negative. It is positive when there is selection of migrants of high quality, and negative when the selection is of low quality.*
- *Migrants responding to positive factors at destination tend to be positively selected.*
- *Migrants responding to negative factors at origin tend to be negatively selected.*
- *Taking all migrants together, selection tends to be bimodal.*
- *Degree of positive selection increases with the difficulty of intervening obstacles.*
- *The heightened propensity to migrate at certain stages of life cycle is important in the selection of migration.*

Several theories have been developed to treat international patterns of migration on their own terms, but these too are variants of push-pull theory. First, neoclassical economic theory[16] suggests that international migration is related to the global supply and demand for labour. Nations with scarce labour supply and high demand will have high wages that pull immigrants in from nations with a surplus of labour. Secondly, segmented labour-market theory[17] argues that First World economies are structured so as to require a certain level of immigration.

This theory suggests that developed economies are dualistic, they have a primary market of secure, well-remunerated work and a secondary market of low-wage work. Segmented labour-market theory argues that immigrants are recruited to fill these jobs that are necessary for the overall economy to function but are avoided by the native-born population because of the poor working conditions associated with the secondary labour market. Finally, world-systems theory[18] argues that international migration is a by-product of global capitalism. Contemporary patterns of international migration tend to be from the periphery (poor nations) to the core (rich nations) because factors associated with industrial development in the First World generated structural economic problems, and thus push factors, in the Third World.

Types of Migrants

- *Voluntary migrants* (migrant workers, elite migration, student migration) to whom most of the world´s estimated 185 million migrants belong. They are protected under general standards of international human rights law and under the UN International Convention on the Protection of the Rights of All Migrant Workers and Their Families (ICMW, 2003).
- *Forced migrants* to whom more than 10 million refugees and stateless persons worldwide belong and who suffer from severe human rights violations. Refugees are protected under the mandate of the UNHCR and the Geneva Convention, 1951, which ensures the right to claim asylum outside the country of origin and aims to provide protection and assistance to displaced persons.
- *Permanent settlers:* People who immigrate to a country to live there permanently, often with some family members already there. During the period from 1965 to 1989, the three major countries of immigration (Australia, Canada and the Unites States) received a total of 18.4 million permanent immigrants.
- *Guest workers:* Short-term, including seasonal, contract workers whose main motivation for seeking employment abroad is the wage differential. They are often unskilled or semi-skilled.
- *Cross-border commuters:* Sometimes referred to in migration literature as labour tourists or incomplete migrants, these are people who commute back and forth across international borders in search of employment, whether legally or otherwise. They work usually for just a few weeks at a time, but regularly.
- *Skilled transients:* Professionals who move from country to country, often within organised transfers of multinational companies. This category also

includes employees of international organisations, military personnel on peace-keeping missions, the clergy, academic researchers and students.

- *Migrants for family reunification:* Foreigners admitted to a country because of close family ties with other migrants who enjoy legal residence in that country or with nationals of the host country. Migration for family formation also comes within this category.

- *Irregular migrants:* A group also commonly referred to interchangeably as illegal, clandestine, undocumented and unauthorised migrants. They are present in the territory of a state without meeting the legal requirements of that state for entry, residence or participate in any economic or any other activity. According to some estimates, about 30 million migrants are believed to be staying illegally in a foreign country. The International Center for Migration Policy Development (ICMPD) estimates that between 400,000 and 500,000 irregular migrants are smuggled into the European Union each year.

Facts on migration

1. In 2013, there were 232 million international migrants globally; a number projected to exceed 250 million in 2015 (UNDESA).
2. Of the 59.9 million people forcibly displaced worldwide, 38.2 million are internally displaced persons (IDPs), 19.5 million are refugees and 1.8 million are asylum seekers.
3. The average period of displacement is 17 years. Many live in a stage of protracted displacement, or "second exile", caught between the inability to return home and the lack of durable and satisfactory solutions to their problems, elsewhere.

Source:"*Migration, refugees and displacement*",http://www.undp.org/content/undp/en/home/ourwork/sustainable-development/development-planning-and-inclusive-sustainable-growth/migration-refugees-and-displacement.html,accessed on December 21, 2015.

Status of Migration

The immediate post-Second World War period was marked by large transfer of population, in particular to Germany and Poland. The post-colonial period saw large repatriation movements to France in 1962 (almost one million people), to Portugal in the mid- 1970s (about 600 000 people in three years) and to a lesser extent to the United Kingdom and Belgium. All these movements of population were absorbed by these countries with very limited impact on their labour markets. Large migration movements based on ethnic migration were also recorded, for example, in Greece between the period from 1989 to 1993 (up to 160 000 Pontian Greeks from the Former Soviet Union) or in Germany between the late 1980s and the early 2000s (more than 3 million Aussiedler and Spät-Aussiedler). Outside Europe, Israel received about a million Jews from the former Soviet Union with their families during the decade following 1989. Inflows of economic migrants of comparable magnitude have occurred in recent years as well, notably in Spain, which has witnessed a tripling of its foreign-born population (above 4 million) between 2000 and 2010, in the United Kingdom where the EU-born population alone rose by 1 million since the enlargement of EU in 2004. Germany became, the second most important immigration country destination in the OECD after the United States, with more than 500 000 expecting permanent legal entries to that country in 2014. These waves of migration were not about refugees but also due to other large recent humanitarian crises such as the Bosnian conflict in 1992-95, which displaced about 1.2 million people, including about 800 000 to OECD countries and more than 300 000 to Germany alone. Also in 1992, more than 300 000 Albanians made attempts to resettle in Greece and Italy. The Kosovo war in 1998-99 resulted in large scale movements as well, mostly to neighbouring countries but also to several OECD countries. Germany, for example, recorded 78000 asylum applications, Switzerland 53 000, Belgium and the United Kingdom approximately 25 000 each, and Austria 15 000.

Migration take place due to large and unprecedented economic disparity across Europe. The situation at the southern Schengen border, in particular in Greece, is very difficult with high unemployment rates. By contrast, in Austria, Germany and Sweden – the three EU destination countries most affected by the recent increase in inflows apart from Hungary – unemployment is much lower than in the early 1990s, especially in Germany where the unemployment rate was 4.8 percent in the first quarter of 2015. In Germany, opinion polls suggest that the more favourable economic situation is also linked with a more favourable public opinion regarding the question of receiving refugees, although this has not prevented xenophobic attacks. Public opinion indicates that they are better prepared for immigration compared with the situation in the early 1990s.

In 2014, 630 000 requests for asylum were registered in EU member countries, a number which was reached during the conflict between Bosnia and Serbia in 1992. According to the most recent available data, up to 700 000 asylum applications have already been filed so far in 2014,[19]and the number could reach 1million by the end of the year. It is likely that between 350 000 and 450 000 people could be granted humanitarian protection in Europe in 2015 (refugee status, subsidiary protection status, or permission to stay for humanitarian reasons). In Europe, most people who seek asylum have entered through illegal border crossings. According to Frontex data for the first eight months of 2015, 500 000 illegal cases of border crossings were detected, as compared to 280 000 cases in 2014. More than 330 000 people have crossed the Mediterranean in 2014. According to UNHCR data, 15percent of them were children and more than 80percent of the adults were men.[20]The "Eastern Mediterranean and Western Balkan route", which is mainly used by asylum seekers from Syria, Iraq and Afghanistan, has been more frequently used, including by Pakistani and selected African migrant groups as well as by people leaving the Western Balkans territories themselves. In the first half of 2015, 66 000 people crossed the Mediterranean between Turkey and Greece and more than 137 000 people did so in July and August. Many of them headed to Hungary, where the number of illegal border entries consequently spiked.[21]This route is also largely used by families with children. This corridor may remain heavily used in the future unless Eastern border routes become a partly substitute. Not everyone arrives directly from their home country. About 2 million Syrians, mostly under temporary protection status, are estimated to be currently (2016) in Turkey. Another 3, 00,000 persons, mainly from Afghanistan, Iraq and Pakistan, are residing unlawfully in Turkey while waiting in transit to seek refuge in the EU. More than 1.1 million Syrians are currently in Lebanon where the situation is increasingly unstable. The arrival of large number of people is also recorded in Jordan (630 000) and Egypt (130 000). As time passess the difficulty of refugees currently living in the neighbouring countries of Syria to find employment, make a living through legal means, and to send their children to school- will increase and this is seen as one of the main factors for the rapid increase in migration to Europe.

The Definition of Refugee
Prior to the Second World War, refugees were defined on an *ad hoc* basis with reference to their national origin. Following the war, the United Nations General Assembly decided to adopt a "general" definition for refugee, which was included in UNHCR's 1950 Statute (annexed to Resolution 428 (V) of the United Nations General Assembly dated December 14, 1949) and shortly after in the Convention relating to the Status of Refugees 1951and its Protocol adopted in 1967. Nearly identical conditions were incorporated in both instruments. The definition of refugee in the 1950 Statute was subsequently extended by resolutions of the UN General Assembly and Economic and Social Council (ECOSOC). The definition of refugee are also contained in the regional refugee instruments and/or in national legislation of countries.

Refugees are persons who fear for their lives or safety in their home country, where the authorities of their home country are unable to provide them with effective protection. According to Article 1a (2) of the Refugee Convention 1951 as modified by Article I of the Protocol 1967, the term refugee shall apply to any person who " *owing to well-founded fear of being persecuted for reasons of race, religion, nationality, membership of a particular social group of political opinion, is outside the country of his nationality and is unable or, owing to such fear, is unwilling to avail himself of the protection of that country, or who, not having nationality, and being outside the country of his former habitual residence; is unable or, owing to such fear, is unwilling to return to it.*"[22]

The term 'refugee' shall also apply to every person who, owing to external aggression, occupation, foreign domination or events seriously disturbing public order, in either part or the whole of his country of origin or nationality, is compelled to leave his place of habitual residence in order to seek refuge in another place outside his country of origin or nationality.

"*A refugee is someone who was forced to flee outside his or her home country and is unable or unwilling to return due to fear of persecution.*"

The Cartagena Declaration considers as refugees those "persons who have fled their country because their lives, safety or freedom have been threatened by violence, foreign aggression, internal conflicts, massive violation of human rights or other circumstances which have seriously disturbed public order."

Table 2

Cartagena Declaration
• *Cartagena Declaration on Refugees adopted at a Colloquium held at Cartagena, Colombia in November, 1984, which relates to the 'refugee situation' in Central America.*
• *The prime purpose of the Cartagena Declaration was to promote the adoption of national laws to implement the Refugees Convention 1951 and Protocol 1967, 'thus fostering the necessary process of systematic paragraph III (1).*

The Organisation of African Unity (OAU), added to the definition found in the Convention 1951 to include a more objectively based consideration, namely-

"Any person compelled to leave his/her country *owing to external aggression, occupation, foreign domination or events seriously disturbing public order in either part or the whole of his country of origin or nationality.*"

The Convention relating to the Status of Refugees 1951

Article 1A, paragraph 1, of the Convention held in 1951 applies the term 'refugee', first, to any person considered a refugee under earlier international arrangements. The Convention also refers to the basic rights, which states should provide for refugees seeking asylum. There are 147 countries that have signed the UN Refugee Convention 1951 and/or its Protocol 1967. The Convention does not just say who is a refugee, however. It goes further and sets out when refugee status comes to an end (article 1C for example, in the case of voluntary return, acquisition of a new, effective nationality, or change of circumstances in the country of origin).[23] For a particular, political reasons, the Convention also puts Palestinian refugees outside its scope (at least while they continue to receive protection or assistance from other United Nations agencies (article 1D)), and excludes persons who are treated as nationals in their state of refuge (article 1E). Finally, the definition in the Convention categorically excludes from the benefits of refugee status to anyone against whom there are serious reasons to believe has committed a war crime, a serious non-political offence prior to admission, or acts contrary to the purposes and principles of the United Nations (article 1F).

The Convention proposes, as a minimum standard, that refugees should receive at least the treatment which is accorded to aliens generally. Refugees will have to be extended benefits of the most favoured nation. They will have the right to form association (article 15), and the right to engage in employment with wages to sustain himself and his family. (Article 17, paragraph 1). The latter is of major importance to the refugee who is in search of an effective solution to his problems. Most of the host nations, however, have expressed reservations on this provision. Many states have emphasised that the reference to most-favoured-nation shall not be interpreted as entitlement to refugees to the benefit of special or regional customs, or economic or political agreements. Other States have expressly rejected most-favoured-nation treatment, limiting their obligation to accord only that standard applicable to aliens in general while some view article 17 merely as a recommendation, or agree to apply it "so far as the law allows". The General Assembly identified a protection role for the High Commissioner with regard to and in particular, to international agreements on refugees. States who are party to the Convention 1951/ Protocol 1967 have accepted specific obligations in this regard, agreeing to cooperate with the Office and in particular to "facilitate its duty of supervising the application of the provisions" of the Convention and Protocol (article 35 of the Convention; article II of the Protocol).

The Protocol Relating to the Status of Refugees 1967

The Refugee Protocol 1967 is independent of, though at the same time integrally related to, the Convention 1951. This Protocol adopts the time and geographic limits laid down in the Convention's definition of refugee. The Refugee Convention and Protocol in total cover three main subjects:

- *The basic definition of refugee, along with terms for cessation of, and exclusion from, refugee status.*
- *The legal status of refugees in their country of asylum, their rights and obligations, including the right to be protected against forcible return or refoulement, to a territory where their lives or freedom would be threatened.*
- *Obligations of states, including cooperating with UNHCR in the exercise of its functions and facilitating its duty of supervising the application of the Convention.*

The Protocol is an independent instrument, not a revision within the meaning of article 45 of the Convention. State parties to the Protocol, which can be ratified or acceded to by a state without becoming a party to the Convention can simply agree to apply articles 2 to 34 of the Convention to refugees defined in article 1 thereof, as if the dateline were omitted (article I of the Protocol). As in August 2008, Cape Verde, Swaziland, the United States of America and Venezuela have acceded only to the Protocol, while Madagascar, Monaco, Namibia and St. Vincent and the Grenadines are party only to the Convention (and the Congo, Madagascar, Monaco, and Turkey have retained the geographical limitation).

UN Resolutions on Refugees

In the aftermath of the Second World War, problems of refugees and displaced persons were high on the international agenda. At its first session in 1946, the United Nations General Assembly recognised not only the urgency of the problem but also the cardinal principle that "no refugees or displaced persons who have finally and definitely ... expressed valid objections to returning to their countries of origin ... shall be compelled to return ..." (resolution 8 (I) of February 12, 1946). The first post-war response of United Nations was the setting up of a specialised agency, the International Refugee Organisation (IRO, 1946-1952), but notwithstanding its success in providing protection and assistance and facilitating solutions, it was expensive and also caught up in the politics of the Cold War. It was therefore decided to replace it with a temporary, initially non-operational agency, and to complement the new institution with revised treaty provisions on the status of refugees. The United Nations General Assembly established the Office of the United Nations High Commissioner for Refugees (UNHCR) on December 14, 1950, with goals pertaining to the protection of refugees and the resolution of refugee problems.[24]

Table 3

Four elements that characterise refugees
1. They are outside their country of origin;
2. They are unable or unwilling to seek or take advantage of the protection of that country, or to return there;
3. Such inability or unwillingness is attributable to a well-founded fear of being persecuted; and
4. The persecution feared is based on reasons of race, religion, nationality, membership of a particular social group, or political opinion.

Source: *Guy Goodwin-Gill and Jane McAdam, The Refugee in International Law (Oxford: OUP, 2007), p. 37.*

In December 1948, the General Assembly adopted the Universal Declaration of Human Rights,[25] article 14, paragraph 1, of which recognises that, "Everyone has the right to seek and to enjoy in other countries asylum from persecution", but the individual was only then beginning to be seen as the beneficiary of human rights in international law. After extensive discussions in its Third Committee, the General Assembly moved to replace the IRO with a subsidiary organ (under Article 22 of the Charter of the United Nations), and by resolution 428 (V) of December 14, 1950, it decided to set up the Office of the United Nations High Commissioner for Refugees with effect from January 1, 1951. Initially set up for three years, the High Commissioner's mandate was regularly renewed thereafter for five-year periods until 2003, when the General Assembly decided "to continue the Office until the refugee problem is solved" (resolution 58/153 of 22 December 2003, paragraph 9).

The primary responsibility of the High Commissioner as set out in paragraph 1 of the Statute annexed to resolution 428 (V), is to provide "international protection" to refugees and, by assisting governments, to seek "permanent solutions for the problem of refugees". Its functions with regard to protection specifically include "promoting the conclusion and ratification of international conventions for the protection of refugees, supervising their application and proposing amendments thereto" (paragraph 8 (a) of the Statute).

Earlier, in 1949, the United Nations Economic and Social Council appointed an *Ad Hoc* Committee to "consider the desirability of preparing a revised and consolidated convention relating to the international status of refugees and stateless persons and if they consider such a course desirable, prepare a draft the text of such a convention".[26] The *Ad Hoc* Committee decided to focus on the refugee (stateless persons were eventually included in a second convention, the Convention 1954 relating to the Status of Stateless Persons)[27], and duly submitted a draft convention. Its provisional draft drew on IRO practice under its Constitution, identified a number of categories of refugees, such as the victims of the Nazi or Falangist regimes and those recognised under previous international agreements and also adopted the general criteria of well-founded fear of persecution and lack of protection (See United Nations doc. E/AC.32/L.6, 2 January 23, 1950).

Table 4

Legal Foundations on Human Rights
• *1948 - The Universal Declaration of Human Rights.*
• *1949 - The Four Geneva Conventions on international humanitarian law.*
• *1951 - The Convention Relating to the Status of Refugees.*
• *1967 – The United Nations Declarations on Territorial Asylum.*
• *1968 - The Inter-American Convention on Human Rights.*
• *1969 - The Organisation for African Unity Convention Governing the Specific Aspects of Refugee Problems in Africa.*
• *1969 - The International Convention on the Elimination of All Forms of Racial Discrimination.*
• *1976 - The International Covenant on Civil and Political Rights.*
• *1976 - The International Covenant on Economic, Social and Cultural Rights.*
• *1984 - The Cartagena Declaration on Refugees.*
• 1985 - The Declaration on the Human Rights of Individuals Who Are Not Nationals of the Country in Which They Live.
• 1987 - The Convention against Torture and Other Cruel, Inhuman or Degrading Treatment of Punishment.
• 1990 - The International Convention on the Protection of the Rights of All Migrant Workers and Members of Their Families.
• The International Labour Organisation conventions.

The Role of UNHCR

In the aftermath of World War II, the United Nations General Assembly created the Office of the United Nations High Commissioner for Refugees (UNHCR). UNHCR is mandated to protect and find durable solutions for refugees. Its activities are based on a framework of international law and standards that includes the Universal Declaration of Human Rights 1948 and the four Geneva Conventions (1949) on international humanitarian law, as well as an array of international and regional treaties and declarations, both binding and non-binding,that specifically address the needs of refugees. At the international level, UNHCR promotes agreements on international refugee and monitors compliance of governments with international refugee law. UNHCR promotes refugee law among all people who are involved in protection of refugees including border guards, journalists, NGOs, lawyers, judges and senior government officials.

UNHCR's core mandate is defined in its Statute, but it has also been expanded further by General Assembly Resolutions and Ex-Commissioners' conclusions as well as decisions taken by the Secretary General. The Statute pertaining to the Office of the United Nations High Commissioner for Refugees was annexed to General Assembly Resolution 428 (V) of December 14, 1950. The mandate was subsequently broadened by resolutions adopted by the General Assembly and its Economic and Social Council (ECOSOC). According, to article 1of the Statute pertaining to the Office, the main task of the High Commissioner is to provide international protection to refugees and to seek durable solutions for refugees by assisting governments to facilitate the voluntary repatriation of refugees, or their integration within new national communities. The High Commissioner's function is qualified as "entirely non-political" and "humanitarian and social." In fulfilling its function for providing protection, the tasks of the High Commissioner as set out in the Statute, include:

- Promoting the conclusion and ratification of international conventions for the protection of refugees, supervising their application and proposing amendments;
- Promoting measures to improve the situation of refugees and to reduce the number requiring protection;
- Assisting efforts to promote voluntary repatriation or assimilation within new national communities;
- Promoting the admission of refugees to the territories of states;
- Facilitating the transfer of the assets of refugees, obtaining from governments information concerning the number and conditions of refugees in their territories, and the relevant laws and regulations;
- Keeping in close touch with governments and intergovernmental organisations;
- Establishing contact with private organisations dealing with refugee questions;
- Facilitating the coordination of private efforts.

UNHCR is one of the world's principal humanitarian agencies, with about 6,500 employees working from 267 offices in 116 countries.[28] During the period spreading more than half a century, the agency has provided assistance to well over 50 million people, earning two Nobel Peace Prizes in 1954 and 1981. The number of refugees who are the concern of UNHCR was 10.4 million refugees at the beginning of 2011. A further 4.7 million registered refugees are looked after in about 60 camps in the Middle East by United Nations Relief and Works Agency for Palestine Refugees in the Near East (UNRWA), which was set up in 1949 to deal with displaced Palestinians. The refugees of concern to UNHCR are spread around the world, with more than half in Asia and about 20percent in Africa. At the field level, staff of UNHCR work to protect refugees through a wide variety of activities, including responding to emergencies, relocating refugee camps away from border areas to improve safety, ensuring that refugee women have a say in food distribution and social services, reuniting separated families, providing information to refugees on conditions in their home country so they can make informed decisions about return, documenting a refugee's need for resettlement to a second country of asylum, visiting detention centres and giving advice to governments on draft refugee laws, policies and practices. UNHCR seeks long-term solutions to the plight of refugees by helping refugees repatriate to their home country, if conditions are conducive to return, integrate into their countries of asylum, or resettle in second countries of asylum.

Table 5

Persons of concern to UNHCR
"Persons of concern to UNHCR" are all persons whose protection and assistance needs are of interest to UNHCR. They include:
• *Refugees under the Refugee Convention.*
• *Persons fleeing conflict or serious disturbances of public order (i.e., refugees under the OAU Convention and Cartagena Declaration definitions).*
• *Returnees (i.e., former refugees).*
• *Stateless persons.*
• *Internally displaced persons (in some situations).*

UNHCR is funded almost entirely by voluntary contributions,principally from governments but also from intergovernmental organisations, corporations and individuals. It receives a limited subsidy of just over three percent of its funding from the United Nations regular budget, for administrative costs and accepts "in kind"contributions including relief items such as tents, medicines, trucks and air transport. UNHCR has expanded both the number and type of organisations it works with. United Nations sister agencies include the World Food Programme(WFP), the UN Children's Fund (UNICEF), the World Health Organisation(WHO), the UN Development Programme (UNDP), the Office forthe Coordination of Humanitarian Affairs (OCHA) and the UN High

Commissioner for Human Rights (OHCHR).Other organisations include the International Committee of the Red Cross (ICRC), the International Federation of Red Cross and Red Crescent Societies (IFRC), the International Organisation for Migration (IOM) and about 640 non-governmental organisations. UNHCR is engaged in a constant effort, alongwith states, to explain, clarify and strengthen the existing international law which was an offshoot of the Refugee Convention 1951.

At present, UNHCR is playing a more prominent role in countries where displacement is taking place. Its substantial involvement is reported to be in helping the returning refugees settle in their homes. Its increased activities also involve providing assistance to IDPs in countries such as Columbia, Sudan, Sri Lanka and Uganda. Keeping in view its particular expertise UNHCR was called upon to perform an even broader role. In the 1990s, for example, UNHCR conducted the world's longest eve air lift as part of its operation to assist besieged populations,as well as displaced ones, in Bosnia and Herzegovina. More recently– although it is not normally involved in natural disaster relief –UNHCR launched two major relief operations to help victims after the tsunami struck the Indian Ocean in 2004 and the earthquake in Pakistan in 2005. In both cases expertise of UNHCR in shelter and camp management,its two assistance specialities were at a premium and valuable assistance provided by UNHCR in these areas helped those providing relief to victims of disaster. In May 2008, UNHCR began helping victims of Cyclone Nargis in Myanmar. Later that month, the refugee agency provided thousands of tents for people left homeless by an earthquake in China's Sichuan province.

Table 6

Principle's of Non-refoulement

Article 33(1) of the Refugee Convention states:

1. "No contracting State shall expel or return ("refouler") a refugee in any manner whatsoever to the frontiers of territories where his life or freedom would be threatened on account of his race, religion, nationality, membership of a particular social group or political opinion."

    The principle of non-refoulement is the cornerstone of asylum and of international refugee law. Following from the right to seek and to enjoy in other countries asylum from persecution, as set forth in Article 14 of the Universal Declaration of Human Rights, this principle reflects the commitment of the international community to ensure to all persons the enjoyment of human rights, including the rights to life, to freedom from torture or cruel, inhuman or degrading treatment or punishment, and to liberty and security of person. These and other rights are threatened when a refugee is returned to persecution or danger.

2. Refoulement is also prohibited explicitly or through interpretation by the Convention against Torture and other Cruel, Inhuman or Degrading Treatment or Punishment (Article 3), the Fourth Geneva Convention of 1949 (Art. 45, para. 4), the International Covenant on Civil and Political Rights (Article 7), the Declaration on the Protection of All Persons from Enforced Disappearance (Article 8), and the Principles on the Effective Prevention and Investigation of Extra-Legal, Arbitrary and Summary Executions (Principle 5).

3. In addition, refoulement is prohibited explicitly or through interpretation in a number of regional human rights instruments, including the European Convention for the Protection of Human Rights and Fundamental Freedoms (Article 3), the American Convention on Human Rights (Article 22), the OAU Refugee Convention (Article II), and the Cairo Declaration on the Protection of Refugees and Displaced Persons in the Arab World (Article 2).

4. It is widely accepted that the prohibition of refoulement is part of customary international law. This means that even states which are not party to the Refugee Convention must respect the principle of non-refoulement.

5. States have an obligation under the Refugee Convention and under customary international law to respect the principle of non-refoulement. When this principle is violated or threatens to be, UNHCR respond by intervening with relevant authorities, and if it deems necessary, will inform the public. In some circumstances, persons facing refoulement may have recourse to relevant human rights mechanisms, such as the Committee against Torture.

UNHCR can at best provide effective legal protection if a person's basic needs– shelter, food, water, sanitation and medical care– are also met. The agency therefore coordinates the provision and delivery of such items, manages or helps manage individual camps or camp and has designed specific projects for vulnerable women, children and the elderly who comprise 80 percent of a "normal" refugee population. Education is a major priority once the dust has settled slightly. UNHCR also seeks ways to find durable solutions to refugees' plight, by helping them repatriate to their homeland if conditions warrant or by helping them to integrate in their countries of asylum or to resettle in third countries.

Regional Instruments

The Organisation of African Unity (OAU) Convention governing the specific aspects of refugee problems in Africa was adopted in 1969 by member states of the Organisation of African Unity[29] (OAU, now the African Union). It complements the Convention1951. It contains a broader definition of a refugee (Article I), an obligation to make the best efforts to grant asylum (Article II), provisions for durable solutions (Article V), and provisions on prohibiting subversive activities by refugees (Article III). According to this Convention, the term refugee "*shall also apply to every person who, owing to external aggression, occupation, foreign domination or events seriously disturbing public order in either part or the whole of his country of origin or nationality, is compelled to leave his place of habitual residence in order to seek refuge in another place outside his country of origin or nationality*". The Cartagena Declaration on Refugees was adopted in 1984[30] by government representatives, distinguished academics, and lawyers from the Latin America region. The Declaration established the legal foundations for the treatment of refugees in the region, including the principle of non-refoulement, the importance of integrating refugees, and the need to eradicate the causes of mass population movements. The definition of a refugee in the declaration is similar to that found in the OAU Convention.

The Cartagena Declaration is not binding on states. The Bangkok principles on the status and treatment of refugees were adopted by certain Asian, Middle Eastern, and African States in 1966. These principles, which were updated in 2001, are significant in that they reflect the views of many states that have had extensive experience in providing asylum, including some states that are not parties to the Convention1951 or its Protocol 1967.

Table 7

Facts on Refugees
Large numbers of people have been forced to abandon their homes and seek safety elsewhere in recent years. But many displaced people have also been able to go back to their own countries and communities.

- **Afghanistan:** *Since 1989, almost 2.6 million Afghan refugees have been assisted to return home from Pakistan and Iran.*
- **Africa's Great Lakes:** *Beginning in 1994 the UN provided humanitarian aid to over 1.7 million Rwandan refugees during the crisis in the Great Lakes region. In 1996 and 1997, most of these people returned home to Rwanda.*
- **Bosnia and Herzegovina:** *The airlift to Sarajevo was the longest-running humanitarian air operation in history. The airlift began in July 1992 and ended in January 1996. More than 2.7 million men, women and children were helped.*
- **Caucasus:** *In the newly independent states of Armenia, Azerbaijan and Georgia, about 450,000 refugees and asylum seekers and nearly 970,000 internally displaced persons were assisted.*
- **Guatemala, El Salvador, and Nicaragua:** *UNHCR and the UNDP assisted a total of 1.9 million internally displaced persons, to return home.*
- **Mali and Liberia:** *The UN is playing a vital role in peace and reconciliation through its reintegration programmes, over half a million refugees returned home.*
- **Mozambique:** *Nearly 400,000 refugees were assisted to return home to Mozambique, the organisation also spent an estimated US$100 million on development and reintegration programmes to help them restart their lives.*
- **Northern Iraq:** *In 1991, humanitarian assistance was provided to about 500,000 Iraqi Kurds displaced after the Persian Gulf War.*
- **Vietnam:** *Under UNHCR sponsorship 109,000 Vietnamese boat people returned to their country.*

International Human Rights Law (IHRL)

Under human rights instruments, rights are generally granted to all individuals, not only to nationals of states parties. Therefore, non-nationals usually also benefit from the rights guaranteed in human rights instruments- with limited exceptions, such as rights pertaining to political participation. Given the universality of these rights, [31] asylum seekers, refugees, and stateless persons must be granted all the rights and freedoms envisaged in human rights treaties without discrimination of any kind. Human rights norms are particularly relevant to refugee protection because:

- Some human rights instruments have been ratified by more countries than the Convention 1951 and its Protocol. For example, the Convention on the Rights of the Child[12] (CRC) has been ratified by 192 States. Therefore, in countries that are not states parties to the Convention 1951, Article 22 of the CRC, which addresses refugee children, may be used to provide protection to children who are refugees.

- Human rights instruments envisage a broader range of rights than that found in international refugee law instruments. Moreover, even when certain rights are protected under two branches of international law; those rights protected under human rights instruments are generally more widely applicable.
- Human rights instruments usually provide for the same treatment for nationals and non-nationals, including refugees, asylum seekers, and stateless persons.
- Human rights norms provide protection to everyone under the jurisdiction of a state party. Therefore, they are particularly relevant to those individuals, including refugees, who have not yet gained access to asylum procedures or who have not otherwise been regularised their stay and so might not yet meet the requirements of "lawfully staying in their territory"which is a precondition for many of the provisions of the Convention 1951.

International Humanitarian Law (IHL)

This branch of international law, which predates both human rights and refugee law, consists of rules that apply during armed conflict. These rules restrict the actions of the parties to a conflict by providing protection and humane treatment to persons who do not take part in the hostilities (civilians, medics, aid workers) and those who can no longer take part in the hostilities (wounded, sick, and shipwrecked troops, prisoners of war). IHL also regulates the means and methods of warfare. It does not, however,address the question of the legality of the armed conflict as such(commonly referred to as *jus in bellum*, i.e. whether the use of force is consistent with the provisions of Chapter VII of the UN Charter,including its Article 51 concerning the right to self-defence).The main instruments of international humanitarian law that are also relevant to international refugee protection are the four Geneva Conventions of 1949 and their two Additional Protocols, adopted in1977.IHL protects refugees only in situations of international or internal armed conflict. If a refugee flees armed conflict, but finds asylum in a country that is not involved in international or internal armed conflict,IHL no longer applies to that refugee. ICRC also plays an important role in protecting internally displaced persons who have been forced to flee their homes because of international or internal armed conflicts.

International Criminal Law (ICL)

Some developments in international criminal law are also relevant to the protection of refugees and other persons of concern to UNHCR. The Rome Statute of the International Criminal Court (ICC) established a Permanent International Criminal Court to adjudicate the cases of persons charged with some of the most serious crimes of international concern. The ICC Statute was adopted on July17, 1998 by a UN Diplomatic Conference and came into force on July 1, 2002.The jurisdiction of the ICC complements national criminal jurisdictions. The material jurisdiction of the Court is over four categories of crimes:

- Genocide,
- War crimes,
- Crimes against humanity, and
- Crimes against the administration of justice of the ICC.

The Rome Statute is guided by the interpretation of the refugee definition under the Convention 1951. It helps to determine which acts would attain the threshold of persecution and guides the delineation of excludable criminal acts under Article 1(F). For example, in the context of gender-based persecution, the Statute explicitly includes"rape, sexual slavery, enforced prostitution, forced pregnancy, enforced sterilisation, or any other form of sexual violence of comparable gravity."Such violations should be considered in the context of excludable crimes under Article 1F of the Convention 1951. Another significant development related to both criminal law and action taken at international level to combat human trafficking and smuggling. Increasing number of refugees are forced to rely on smugglers in their attempts to reach safety. In doing so, not only do they put their lives at risk, but they often also jeopardise the outcome of their claims for asylum in the destination state. The United Nations Protocol against Smuggling of Migrants by Land, Sea, and Air (2000), in force since January 2004, and the United Nations Protocol to Prevent, Suppress,and Punish the Trafficking of Persons (2000), in force since December2003, focus on the traffickers and smugglers, thus making it clear that the victims of trafficking and smuggling should not be punished solely for having been subject to these crimes. Both Protocols stipulate that nothing in their provisions affects the rights of individuals and the obligations of states under the Convention 1951/ Protocol 1967 or the principle of non-refoulement. These Protocols supplement the United Nations Convention against Transnational Organised Crime (2000) and provide for greater cooperation among governments in tackling cross border criminal activity.

Table 8

Refugee Law
• *Section IV B of the Final Act of the 1951 UN Conference of Plenipotentiaries on the Status of Refugee and Stateless Persons (on the principle of unity of the family).*
• *The UNHCR Handbook on Procedures and Criteria for Determining Refugee Status, Chapter VI.*
• *Ex Com Conclusions Nos. 9 (1977), 15 (1979), 24 (1981), 84 (1997), 85 (1998), 88 (1999), and 104 (2005.)*
• *The UNHCR Guidelines on Reunification of Refugee Families (1983).*
• *The UNHCR Refugee Children: Guidelines on Protection and Care (1994).*
• *The UNHCR Guidelines on Policies and Procedures in dealing with Unaccompanied Children Seeking Asylum (1997).*
• *The UNHCR Background Note: Family Reunification in the Context of Resettlement and Integration (2001).*
• *Council of Europe, Committee of Ministers, Recommendation No. R (99) 23 on family reunion for refugees and other person in need of international protection (1999).*
Instruments on Statelessness
• *Article 12 of the Convention relating to the Status of Refugees.*

In 2008, the High Commissioner for Refugees (HC) launched a Special Initiative on Protracted Refugee Situations (PRS) to promote durable solutions and improvements in the life of these refugees. The HC's initiative focused on five situations in different parts of the world, four of which have been selected for evaluation:

• the Croatian refugees in Serbia;
• the Rohingya refugees in Bangladesh;
• the Eritrean refugees in Eastern Sudan; and
• the Burundian refugees in Tanzania.

Challenges of Providing Support to Refugees

Conflicts, violence, human rights violations but also natural disasters are forcing millions of people to leave their homes and to flee from destruction and persecution. The majority of refugees and Internally Displaced Persons (IDPs) live in the developing world, which means that they find refuge in countries and among people who already struggle with poverty and hardship. Their survival usually depends on the availability of assistance which is provided by local communities and international organisations. There are over 59.5 million people in dire need of protection and assistance as a consequence of forced displacement. They include refugees, internally displaced persons and asylum-seekers. Globally, over 38.2 million people are internally displaced,[32] compared to more than 19.5 million refugees and 1.2 million asylum-seekers.[33] According to the latest UNHCR data, 51 percent of the global refugee populations are children, the highest proportion in over a decade. According to the UN, women and girls represent 50percent of the entire refugee population. In many societies, they face specific risks such as discrimination and are less likely than men and boys to have access to basic rights. When faced with displacement, these risks, particularly discrimination and sexual and gender-based violence, can be exacerbated. Unaccompanied women and girls, women heads of households and pregnant, disabled or older women may face particular challenges. Finding durable solutions for refugees is a challenge and includes voluntary repatriation to their home countries, which is the preferred long-term outcome for the majority of refugees. While some of the displaced populations are able to return home, the lack of political solutions in their home country prevents many from coming back and millions may stay in these protracted circumstances for several years and in some extreme cases for generations. Other solutions which are proposed are local integration or resettlement of refugees, either in the country where they live or in third countries where they can be permanently resettled. Sustainable solutions for settling the problems of IDPs can be: return to their place of origin, local integration in areas where they have taken refuge or integration in another part of the country. At present, Syria and Afghanistan remain the largest source of refugees, followed by Somalia, Sudan, South Sudan and the Democratic Republic of Congo (DRC). Around four-fifths of the world's refugees flee to neighbouring countries such as Pakistan, Iran, Lebanon, Jordan and Turkey. For the first time, Turkey became the largest refugee-hosting country worldwide, with 2.9 million refugees. Turkey was followed by Pakistan (1.5 million), Lebanon (1.1 million), the Islamic Republic of Iran (982,000), Ethiopia (659,500) and Jordan (654,100) (source: UNHCR Global Trends 2014). The most of IDPs currently live in Syria (over 6.5 million) and Columbia (over 6 million). Iraq and Sudan follow with 3.5 million and 2.1 million respectively. DRC, Pakistan, South-Sudan, Somalia, Nigeria and Turkey complete the list of the first 10 countries, which together account for 77percent of the world's all IDPs.[34] In the absence of durable solutions, those who remain internally displaced (IDPs) or in refugee camps face major challenges in terms of protection, access to shelter, food and other basic services such as health, nutrition, water, sanitation, hygiene and education. Refugees and IDPs who live in urban areas may encounter poverty, lack of psycho-social support and difficulties in normalising their status. Violence, abuse and exploitation against the most vulnerable often peak in the aftermath of emergencies, which underlines the importance of effective protection mechanisms to be put in place immediately.

Migration and forced displacement are long-term issues that require long-term solutions., UNDP has worked on issues relating to migration and displacement in different contexts forging partnerships with humanitarian and development agencies with a view to find durable solutions at the local and national level. Their efforts include preventing and mitigating conflicts, improving governance and access to justice, fighting poverty, providing jobs and opportunities, and implementing well managed migration policies, all in line with the new Sustainable Development Goals. UNDP also works in partnership with UNHCR and other humanitarian organisations on the refugee issue. While humanitarian agencies deal with the response towards displacement, for example setting up refugee camps and providing food and other services, UNDP works with the local and national authorities to help them deal with the increased population, support refugees on socioeconomic recovery and development, all closely in partnership with UNHCR.

The reception and integration of refugees presents major challenges that should not be underestimated. It is a difficult and costly task in the short term. In Europe, many countries have developed introduction programmes for refugees. Indeed, most introduction programmes tend to be explicitly or implicitly targeted at problems faced by migrants on humanitarian level, although other migrant groups such as family migrants may be eligible as well. The Scandinavian countries have experience in dealing with such programmes which generally last two to three years. The bulk of these programmes is generally related to language training, although recently the focus on labour market has been strengthened, given that integration with labour market is the most important determinant with regard to economic independence of migrants and a precondition for a positive economic impact of migration. The United States has devised programmes which help bring refugees from abroad for the purpose of resettlement. Such refugees are settled at different places in the country, in coordination with organisations which receive federal funding for providing work and services. The approach is proactive with the expectation that refugees will, where possible, rapidly enter the labour market. About one in four refugees opts for a six-month intensive support programme in lieu of cash support. Of these, three-quarters become self-sufficient by the end of this period. Most of the specific support tapers off after the first year, although some of the services are offered up to five years. Many refugees move from their destination of first settlement, towards communities or avail job opportunities. Overall their rates of employment are comparable to the national average or higher, although often they often work in low-wage jobs and at a greater risk of poverty. Canada, like the United States, has extensive experience in so-called "settlement services" for refugees, including provision of language training, labour market and social integration. The word "settlement services" implies that the recipients of these services are expected to remain in Canada and become part of the Canadian society.

Australia has a similar policy for the integration of migrants allowed into the country on humanitarian grounds. They are generally resettled as in Canada. It is based on intensive support programmes focussed on practical support early on arrival and continue throughout the initial period of settlement so as to help humanitarian migrants settle in the community (Humanitarian Settlement Services).Early access to language training is offered through flexible learning options to meet individual needs. The services offered vary widely depending on each individual migrant's circumstances and cover many aspects of economic and social integration (i.e. early practical support, English language courses, translating services, grant-based funding for projects to promote the integration of migrant groups etc.).[35]

UNDP has been a crucial partner in helping countries recover from crisis, whether natural or man-made, by balancing short-term humanitarian responses with long-term development needs. UNDP's work in Syria and neighbouring countries has impacted millions of people, providing temporary jobs to women and young people, increasing access to basic services, and working with other UN agencies to help those displaced by the ongoing conflict. The Syria Strategic Response Plan and the Regional Refugee and Resilience Plan represent important steps towards a more effective response to the crisis and plan for recovery.

UNDP has also helped host communities cope with the influx of refugees from neighbouring countries, as well as mitigate the effects of environmental degradation, another key driver of migration. These initiatives include women's cash-for-work projects in Jordan, an olive packaging and storage project in Turkey, installing a water network in Lebanon, social support and legal aid for women and girls in Iraq, and vocational training for youth in host communities in Egypt.[36]

In April, 2016 the European Commission, in association with the EEAS, adopted the Communication 'Lives in Dignity: from Aid-dependence to Self-reliance. Forced Displacement and Development', outlining a new development-led approach to forced displacement. The objective is to strengthen the resilience and self-reliance of both the displaced and their host communities, through a multi-action approach from the outset and to be continued throughout the displacement crises. The focus is on working with host governments, at the national and local level, towards gradual socio-economic inclusion of refugees and internally displaced persons. The framework aims to harness the productive capacities of refugees and IDPs by helping them to access education, housing, land, productive assets, livelihoods and services, and by supporting interaction between them and their host communities. The Communication was adopted following consultation with a broad range of stakeholders. The European Commission gave more than €1.064 million or about 72 percent of its annual humanitarian aid budget in the financial year 2015 to projects helping refugees and IDPs. Humanitarian aid for refugees delivered by the European Commission helps to:

- Meet the most pressing needs of refugees,
- Protect and support refugees during their displacement and when returning to their place of origin,
- Increase the self-reliance of refugees and reduce their dependency on aid.

About 45percent of the world's refugees and IDPs are currently trapped in protracted circumstances. The European Commission's Humanitarian Aid and Civil protection department (ECHO) invests heavily in assisting displaced people and is currently responding to crises such as Syrian refugees in Jordan, Lebanon, Turkey, Iraq and Greece, Afghan refugees in Iran and Pakistan, Somali refugees in Kenya and Yemen, Congolese refugees in the Great Lake region, Colombian refugees in Ecuador and Venezuela, Myanmar refugees in Thailand, Rohingya refugees in Bangladesh and Sahrawi refugees in Algeria.

Refugees and Humanitarian Assistance

- The humanitarian consequences of the crisis in Syria have reached an unprecedented scale. Due to the ongoing civil war around 12.2 million Syrians are internally displaced or are living as refugees in Lebanon, Jordan, Turkey, Iraq, Egypt and North Africa. Many of those who were able to reach the neighbouring countries are now living in hardship struggling to find shelter and food for their families and schooling for their children. To support the Syrian refugees and their host-communities, the European Commission and its member states have since the beginning of the crisis allocated over €3.6 million. EU humanitarian assistance channeled through the European Commission's Humanitarian Aid and Civil Protection Department (ECHO) primarily supports life-saving medical emergency responses, the provision of essential drugs, food and nutritional items, safe water, sanitation and hygiene (WASH), shelter, distribution of basic non-food items and protection programmes. This funding is channeled through UN agencies and accredited international humanitarian organisations to meet the needs of the most vulnerable people.

- *Afghanistan* is still the country of origin for the second largest number of refugees in the world (after Syria). A major part of this population arrived in Iran and Pakistan during the Communist regime and the period when *Mujahidin* and *Taliban* were in charge (1979 to 2001). Pakistan continues to host the largest number of Afghan refugees (around 1.6 million registered refugees), and Iran hosts over 850 000 Afghan refugees. In addition, 4 million refugees have returned from Pakistan and Iran between 1992 and 1997 and more than 5.7 million individuals have voluntarily repatriated to Afghanistan in the last 10 years. The European Commission is providing funds to UNHCR and other partners to support the voluntary and sustainable repatriation of Afghan refugees and for working out other durable solutions where conditions are not conducive to return. This is done through dissemination of information and providing education, shelters, water and sanitation, health and protection services, livelihood initiatives via vocational training and cash-based programmes, and more broadly by sustaining and providing protection to asylum space in hosting communities.
- At the beginning of 2014, the small towns of Kentzou, Garoua-Boulai and Ngaoui in eastern Cameroon faced a refugee problem when they received a flow of people escaping the conflict. Tens of thousands have been left to fend for themselves. Following ECHO's assessment mission in early February 2014, the European Commission decided to support the partners with a view to provide support to improve the conditions of refugees and organise their re-settlement to more appropriate sites. The refugees are, therefore, being provided with emergency shelter, non-food items, health care, food, water and education. Thousands of children who suffer from severe and acute malnutrition are receiving appropriate care in the five health districts of the Far North region covered by the International Medical Corps (IMC), an ECHO supported project. However, access to the health facilities is still difficult for populations living far from the urban centers. To overcome this challenge, community volunteers have been trained to screen and refer undernourished children to the closest centers. The persons who care for children needing specialised healthcare are provided with money for both transportation and food during their stay at the hospital's stabilisation center.
- Colombia is the second country with more internally displaced people after Syria, with over 6 million. According to the UN refugee agency, UNHCR, almost 397 000 Colombians are in need of international protection in neighbouring Ecuador and Venezuela. There is thousands of pending asylum cases awaiting resolution. The conflict continues to inflict forced recruitment,

sexual violence, murder, disappearances and restriction of movements and lack of access to healthcare upon civilians. The European Commission's contribution for the year 2015 to people affected by the conflict and natural hazards totalled €13.4 million, with aid focused on providing protection, food aid, health care, water and sanitation. Funding also includes improving access to education and protection for children and adolescents affected by armed conflict in Colombia, Venezuela and Ecuador and disaster preparedness activities. ECHO aid targets the areas most affected by the conflict, where there is limited government presence.[37]

• Refugees from Myanmar have lived for almost three decades in nine camps along the border with Thailand, making it one of the world's longest protracted crises. Currently the population in the camp is around 110,000. The European Union has been an important donor to these camps since 1995, channeling €118.4 million through ECHO. Its support has focused on basic humanitarian aid, i.e. food assistance, primary health care and protection. The EU promotes durable solutions, for instance, through a recent project with UNHCR, profiling of the camp population has been carried out in preparation of future voluntary return to Myanmar, when conditions allow it.

Conclusion

A peaceful and prosperous world is one in which people can feel safe and secure in their homes, with their families and in their communities. Boundaries between nation-states are undermined as the globalisation of labour increasingly connects countries of varying levels of economic development. Migrants also move because they are looking for better educational opportunities for themselves and their offspring. Still others are forced migrants because of political unrest, war, polluted environments or natural disasters in their places of origin, yet they nevertheless have an impact on the labour market. The geographic patterns formed by these migration flows have changed over time with the advent of new communication technologies and faster transportation systems around the world. The accompanying case studies illustrate the dynamics of migration in several international contexts.

It is a world in which they can feel confident in their country, their culture and in the family of nations and peoples on our common planet. In the process, UNHCR made it possible for 2.8 million refugees and IDPs to return home. It also actively served the needs of some 2.9 million stateless persons and 800,000 asylum-seekers and others of concern. A total of 31.7 million people were provided the basic safety and security needed to live productive and meaningful lives.

Unfortunately, conflict and natural disasters continue to take their toll on such persons. But their plight is much more better than it might have been, thanks to the commitment of the UN family to help them return to their homes, and to protect and sustain them until their return becomes possible.

UN bodies actively involved in this cluster approach include the Food and Agriculture Organisation of the United Nations (FAO), the United Nations Development Programme (UNDP), the United Nations Children's Fund (UNICEF), the Office for the Coordination of Humanitarian Affairs (OCHA), the World Food Programme (WFP), the World Health Organisation (WHO), and the Office of the High Commissioner for Human Rights (OHCHR).The Office of the UN High Commissioner for Refugees has twice been the recipient of the Nobel Peace Prize in 1954 and 1981. In addition, the United Nations Relief and Works Agency for Palestine Refugees in the Near East (UNRWA), established in 1949, is the main provider of basic services— education, health, relief and social services —to more than 4.5 million registered Palestine refugees in the Middle East. That includes 1.3 million living in 58 refugee camps in Jordan, Lebanon, Syria and the occupied Palestinian territory, comprising the Gaza Strip and the West Bank. UNRWA provides emergency humanitarian assistance to mitigate the effects of the on-going crisis on the most vulnerable refugees in Gaza and the West Bank and was among the first to respond to the emergency needs of conflict-affected refugees in Lebanon after the fighting there from July-August 2006.

Notes

1. *The truth about asylum - Who's who: Refugee, Asylum Seeker, Refused asylum seeker, Economic migrant*, (London, England: Refugee Council), September 7, 2015.
2. "Global migration: from crisis to opportunity", February10, 2016, Shaping policy for developmenthttps://www.odi.org/events/4332-global-migration-crises-opportunity, accessed on 12ʰFebruary, 2016.
3. IDPs are defined as "persons or groups of persons who have been forced to flee or leave their homes or places of habitual residence as a result of armed conflicts, internal strife or systematic violations of human rights, and who have not crossed and internationally recognised state border." Luke T. Lee, The Refugee Convention and Internally Displaced Persons, 13 *InternationalJournal of Refugee Law (2001)*p.363.
4. UN Head Office, UN Office for the Coordination of Humanitarian Affairs, series no.16/34(New York; General Assembly and Conference Management, February 16, 2016).
5. "Syrian Refugees Take Arctic Route to Europe". *The Wall Street Journal*. September 3, 2015.
6. https://www.iom.int/key-migration-terms.,Glossary on Migration, International Migration Law Series No. accessed on March 25, 2011.
7. Author,"UNHCR viewpoint: 'Refugee' August 27, 2015)"Migrants, refugees and asylum seekers: what's the difference?" http://www.theguardian.com/world/2015/aug/28/migrants-refugees-and-asylum-seekers-whats-the-difference, accessed on August 27, 2015.

8. Daniel Goh, "*What are the causes of human migration and the effect on the sending and/or host country?*" https://www.academia.edu/5025685/What_are_the_causes_of_human_migration_and_the_effect_on_the_sending_and_or_host_country, accessed on January 16, 2016.

9. Ravenstein, "The Laws of Migration," *Journal of the Royal Statistical Society*, LII (June, 1889),p288.

10. Everett S. Lee,"A theory of Migration", Demography, Vol. 3, No. 1. (1966),pp.47-57. http://www.students.uni-mainz.de/jkissel/Skripte/Lee.pdf, accessed on 12th February, 2015.

11. Ibid.

12. Ibid.

13. Ibid.

14. MitaliVerma,"4 General Theories of Migration – Explained!",Your Article Library, http://www.yourarticlelibrary.com/population-geography/4-general-theories-of-migration-explained/43257/, accessed on December 21, 2015.

15. Sjaastad, L, "The costs and returns of human migration",*Journal of Political Economy*, Vol.?70, 1962, pp.80–93:Todaro, M, "A model of labour migration and urban unemployment in less developedcountries", *American Economic Review*, Vol.?59, 1969,pp.138–148.

16. Piore, M.J, *Birds of Passage: Migrant Labour Industrial Societies*(New York: Cambridge University Press, 1979).

17. Sassen, Saskia,*The Mobility of Capital and Labour: A Study in International Investment and Labour Flow* (Cambridge: Cambridge University Press, 1988).

18. Data refer to January to early September and include pre-registration in Germany.

19. http://data.unhcr.org/mediterranean/regional.php, accessed on June 18, 2016.

20. Between January and mid-September 2015, the Hungarian authorities have recorded as many as 190 000 illegal entries.

21. UNHCR, International Legal Instruments on Refugee in Africa, (Geneva: UN Media Centre,1979), pp. 26-28.

22. UN Media Centre, Geneva, publisher in each case, Handbook on Procedures and Criteria for Determining Refugee Status under the 1951 Convention and the 1967 Protocol relating to the Status of Refugees HCR/IP/4/Eng/REV.1Reedited, Geneva, January 1992, UNHCR 1979.(See also the website of the Office of the United Nations High Commissioner for Refugees for other handbooks and guidelines: http://www.unhcr.org. accessed on December 21, 2015).

23. Statute of the Office of the United Nations High Commissioner for Refugees. General Assembly resolution 428 (v) of UNHCRCommunicationsand PublicInformation Service, Switzerland, 1950.

24. Universal Declaration of Human Rights, General Assembly resolution 217 (III) of December10, 1948, United Nations information centre, New York, 1948.

25. Report of the Ad Hoc Committee on Statelessness and Related Problems, Provisional draft of parts of the definition article of the preliminary draft convention relating to the status of refugees, prepared by the Working Group on this article (E/AC.32/L.6 and Corr. 1 and Rev.1, January23, 1950).Guy S. Goodwin-Gill,United Nations Audiovisual Library of International Law, 2008.

26. Ad Hoc Committee on Statelessness and Related Problems, First Session, E/AC.32/SR.20, (1950), 11-12, paras. 54-55.UN Economic and Social Council, UN Ad Hoc Committee on Refugees and Stateless Persons, New York, February 10, 1950.

27. Refugee situations numbering 25,000 or more persons by the end of 2003 which have been in existence for five or more years. Industrialised countries are not included. Source: 2003 UNHCR Annual Statistical Report. Author, place, publisher(Numbers rounded to two significant figures. Totals may not add up due to rounding.)

28. OAU/AU Convention Governing the Specific Aspects of Refugee Problems in Africa, Addis Ababa, September 10, 1969, United Nations, Treaty Series, vol. 1001, p. 45.

29. Cartagena Declaration on Refugees, Adopted by the Colloquium on the International Protection of Refugees in Central America, Mexico and Panama, Cartagena de Indias, Colombia, November 22, 1984.

30. "International Covenant on Civil and Political Rights", New York, December16, 1966, United Nations, Treaty Series, vol. 999, p. 171.

31. "IDMC 2015 Global Overview- People internally displaced by conflict and violence", May 2015, http://www.internal-displacement.org/assets/library/Media/201505-Global-Overview-2015/20150506-global-overview-2015-en.pdf, accessed on May 18, 2015.

32. "UNHCR Global Trends 2014-Forced Displacement in 2014", http://unhcr.org/556725e69.htmlaccessed on 22 January, 2014.

33. Ibid.

34. OECD-EU, "Indicators of Immigrant Integration 2015: Settling In"(Paris: OECD Publishing, 2015), "Labour Market Integration of Immigrants and their Children: Developing, Activating and Using Skills", in *International Migration Outlook 2014*(Paris: OECD Publishing, 2014).

35. "Migration, refugees and displacement", http://www.undp.org/content/undp/en/home/ourwork/sustainable-development/development-planning-and-inclusive-sustainable-growth/migration-refugees-and-displacement.html, accessed on June 16, 2016.

36. "Examples of the Projects on Refugees and IDPs" bit.ly/echo-fs ECHO Factsheet – April 2016 "Refugees and IDPs"http://ec.europa.eu/echo/files/aid/countries/factsheets/thematic/refugees_en.pdf, accessed on June, 16, 2016.

CHAPTER 10

Feminist Perspective in the Contemporary International Relations

Introduction

Feminist perspective on international relations draws upon a variety of literatures and from multiple fields of study so that it has always been an interdisciplinary undertaking. Feminist international relations have tended to flourish as a subfield of the main field of international relations, without much impact on the field as a whole. In broad terms, feminist international relations has expanded and built on, the work of feminist political and economic theory to examine the masculinist framing of politics and economics and associated institutions, including notably the state and its key military and governmental components, as well as the discourses through which these institutions operate and are reproduced over time. Feminist theory is the extension of feminism into theoretical or philosophical discourse. It aims to understand the nature of gender inequality. It examines women's social roles, experience, interests, and feminist politics in a variety of fields, such as anthropology and sociology, communication, psychoanalysis, economics, literature, education, philosophy, and even linguistics. By the early 2000s it became widely known as *'feminist IR'* or *'gender and IR'*. "Feminist IR scholarship is not simply about women, it is about the interdependence of masculine and feminine as socially constructed categories that shape how we know and experience the world". IR feminism is "the study of gender (rather than women) and the differences that gender makes to world politics". IR feminists *"share the post-positivist commitment to questioning what we take for granted and to problematising what is given as truth or knowledge".*

Feminist international relations has identified male stream international relations theory as one of the discourse that help perpetuate a distorted and partial world view that reflects the disproportionate power of control and influence that men hold, rather than the full social reality of the lives of women, children and men. Thus this theory is more reflective and expressive of historically established male power than it is an open and comprehensive exploration of the political and economic process in which all members of societies are engaged. It is more a discourse about the powerful than one that seeks to examine deeply how power works, including its gendered, radicalised and socio-economic dimensions, or to situate individuals and groups differently in terms of contrasting levels of capacity, control, and influence and freedom.

Feminism is basically a western concept. In the second half of the 20[th]century, feminism emerged as the most powerful movement that almost swept the literary world. It has been articulated differently in different parts of the world including India, by different people especially women depending upon their class, background and level of consciousness. The term 'Feminism' was first used by the French dramatist Alexander Dumas in 1872 in a pamphlet L. Homme femme' to designate the then emerging women's movement for rights. Feminism stands for the struggle or protest by women against their continuing low status at work, in society and in the culture of the country. Initially, in western countries, women revolted to fight for emancipation and liberation from all forms of oppression by the state, by society and by men. According to the World Book, "Feminism is a belief that women should have economic, political and social equality with men".[1] In the same book we find that feminism also refers to a, "*Political movement that works to gain such equality as economic, political and social. This movement is sometimes called Women's Movement or Women's Rights Movement*".[2] Thus, feminism is a socio-cultural movement to secure complete equality of women with men in enjoyment of all rights, moral, religious, social, political, education, legal, economic and so on.

In the 1840s the women's rights movement had started to emerge in the United States with the Seneca Falls Convention of 1848 and the resultant Declaration of Sentiments, which claimed for women the principles of liberty and equality expounded in the American Declaration of Independence. This was followed by Elizabeth Cady Stanton and Susan B. Anthony's founding of the National Woman Suffrage Association. In Britain, too, the period from 1840s onwards saw the emergence of women's suffrage movements. But even before the emergence of organised suffrage movements, women had been writing about the inequalities and injustices in women's social condition and campaigning to change it. Mary Wollstonecraft had published a book, *A Vindication of the Rights of Women,* in 1792 and at the same time in France a few women, for example Olympe de Gouges and The roigne de Mericourt, were fighting for the extension of the rights promised by the French Revolution to women. Therefore, although we can trace the development of women's rights movements from the mid-19th century, this was not the starting point for women's concern about their social and political condition. Feminism is thus a term that emerged long after women started questioning their inferior status and demanding an amelioration in their social position. Even after the word feminism was coined, it was still not adopted as a term of identification by many of those who campaigned for women's rights.

Gender in International Relations

Masculinity and politics have a long and close association. Characteristics associated with "manliness," such as toughness, courage, power, independence, and even physical strength, have, throughout history, been those most valued in the conduct of politics, particularly international politics. Frequently, manliness has also been associated with violence and the use of force, a type of behaviour that, when conducted in the international arena has been valourised and applauded in the name of defending one's country. This celebration of male power, particularly the glorification of the male warrior, produces more of a gender dichotomy than exists in reality for, as R. W. Connell points out, this stereotypical image of masculinity does not fit most men. Connell suggests that what he calls "*hegemonic masculinity*," a type of culturally dominant masculinity that he distinguishes from other subordinated masculinities, is a socially constructed cultural ideal that, while it does not correspond to the actual personality of the majority of men, sustains patriarchal authority and legitimises a patriarchal political and social order.[3]

Hegemonic masculinity is sustained through its opposition to various subordinated and devalued masculinities, such as homosexuality, and, more important, through its relation to various devalued femininities. Socially constructed gender differences are based on socially sanctioned, unequal relationships between men and women that reinforce compliance with men's stated superiority. Nowhere in the public realm are these stereotypical gender images more apparent than in the realm of international politics, where the characteristics associated with hegemonic masculinity are projected to the behaviour of states whose success as international actors is measured in terms of their capabilities with power and capacity for self-help and autonomy. Connell's definition of hegemonic masculinity depends on its opposition to and unequal relationship with various subordinated femininities. Many contemporary feminists draw on similarly socially constructed, or engendered, relationships in their definition of gender difference. Historically, differences between men and women have usually been ascribed to biology. But when feminists use the term gender today, they are not generally referring to biological differences between males and females, but to a set of culturally shaped and defined characteristics associated with masculinity and femininity. These characteristics can and do vary across time and place. In this view, biology may constrain behaviour, but it should not be used "deterministically" or "naturally" to justify practices, institutions, or choices that could be other than they are. While what it means to be a man or a woman varies across cultures and history, in most cultures gender differences signify relationships of inequality and the domination of women by men. Joan Scott similarly characterises gender as "*a constitutive element of social relationships based on perceived differences between the sexes, and... a primary way of signifying relationships of power.*"[4]

Early work in feminist international relations in the 1980s had to address this problem directly by peeling back the masculinist surface of world politics to reveal its more complex gendered dynamics. Key scholars such as Cynthia Enloe focused on core international relations issues of war, militarism and security, highlighting the dependence of these concepts on gender structures-e.g. dominant forms of masculine subject as protector/conqueror/exploiter of the feminine object/other-and thus the fundamental importance of subjecting them to gender analysis. In a series of works, including the early *Bananas, beaches and bases,Making feminist sense of international politics* (1989), Enloe has addressed different aspects of the most overtly masculine realms of international relations, conflict and defence, to reveal their deeper gendered realities.[5] This work has launched a powerful critique of the taboo that made women and gender most invisible, in theory and practice, where masculinity had its most extreme, defining and violent expression. Enloe's research has provided one of the most comprehensive quantum of evidence for the logical revisionism required from mainstream international relations, especially in relation to its core concerns. When Enloe claimed that '*gender makes the world go round,*'[6] she was in fact turning the abstract logic of male stream international relations inside out. The abstract logic saw little need to take theoretical and analytical account of gender as a social force because in practical terms only one gender, the male, appeared to define international relations. Ann Tickner has recently offered the reminder that this situation persist: "During the 1990s, women were admitted to most combat positions in the U.S. military, and the U. S. President appointed the first female Secretary of State, but occupations in Foreign and military policymaking bodies in most states remain overwhelmingly male, and usually elite male.[7]Nearly a decade earlier, in her ground-breaking work *Gender in International Relations: feminist perspectives on achieving global security,*[8] she had asked the kinds of questions that laid the foundation for early feminist international relations: 'Why is the subject matter of my discipline so distant from women's live experiences? Why have women been conspicuous only by their absence in the world of diplomacy and military and foreign policy-making?'

Indeed one could characterise most contemporary feminist scholarship in terms of the dual beliefs that gender difference has played an important and essential role in the structuring of social inequalities in much of human history and that the resulting differences in self-identifications, human understandings, social status, and power relationships are unjustified. Scott claims that the way in which our understanding of gender signifies relationships of power is through a set of normative concepts that set forth interpretations of the meanings of symbols. In Western culture, these concepts take the form of fixed binary oppositions that categorically assert the meaning of masculine and feminine and hence legitimise a set of unequal social relationships.[9]Scott and many other contemporary feminists assert that, through our use of language, we come to perceive the world through these binary oppositions. Our Western understanding of gender is based on a set of culturally determined binary distinctions, such as public versus private, objective versus subjective, self-versus other, reason versus emotion, autonomy versus relatedness, and culture versus nature; the first of each pair of characteristics is typically associated with masculinity, the second with femininity.[10]Scott claims that the hierarchical construction of these distinctions can take on a fixed and permanent quality that perpetuates women's oppression. It is, therefore,necessary that those must be challenged. To do so we must analyse the way these binary oppositions operate in different contexts and, rather than accepting them as fixed, seek to displace their hierarchical construction.[11] When many of these differences between women and men are no longer assumed to be natural or fixed, we can examine how relations of gender inequality are constructed and sustained in various arenas of public and private life. In committing itself to gender as a category of analysis, contemporary feminism also commits itself to gender equality as a social goal. Extending Scott's challenge to the field of international relations, we can immediately detect a similar set of hierarchical binary oppositions. But in spite of the seemingly obvious association of international politics with the masculine characteristics described above, the field of international relations is one of the last of the social sciences to be touched by gender analysis and feminist perspectives.[12]

Feminists also apply the terms 'gender' and 'patriarchy' when analysing how situations have been shaped to exclude women from the international political arena. As with many theories, "feminist theory" reflects a wide range of perspectives generating many internal debates concerning how it should be represented. As Diana Thorburn notes, "there can never be a truly singular voice of feminist foreign policy simply because of the diversity of views within feminism itself." However, a brief look at some relevant facets of the discipline can be seen through Lorraine Codes' summary of two salient areas within feminist IR theory, standpoint feminism and radical feminism.[13]

J. Ann Tickner's view on feminism

J. Ann Tickner (born c. 1937) is a feminist international relations (IR) theorist. Her books include *Gendering World Politics: Issues and Approaches in the Post-Cold War Era* (Columbia University Press, 2001), *Gender in International Relations: Feminist Perspectives on Achieving International Security* (Columbia University Press, 1992), and *Self-Reliance Versus Power Politics: American and Indian Experiences in Building Nation-States* (Columbia University Press, 1987).One of Tickner's most famous journal articles was the piece "*You Just Don't Understand*" (International Studies Quarterly, 1997), which critiqued mainstream international relations theorists for the omission of gender from their theory and practice. Tickner argued against this assertion, claiming that it misunderstood one of the premises of feminist IR. Most feminist IR theory takes a strongly de-constructivist approach to knowledge, arguing that theories reflect the gendered social positioning of their authors and they, therefore, questioned positivist ("scientific") methods for obscuring the gendered politics of knowledge construction. She favours a social, "*bottom-up*" method of analysis that makes the role of women in IR visible, as opposed to the usual scientific methodologies that are "top-down" and focus on traditionally masculinist subjects, including men, money, and war.

Sovereignty is a core concept in international relations because it defines the pre-eminent role of states as political actors, and by implications also defines political identity in state-centred term, binding '*authentic politics exclusively within territorially-bound communities*'.[14]For feminist international relations there are ways in which sovereignty can be regarded as a foundational problem in the masculinist distortions of the nature of politics and political agency.

"*Masculinist dominance is institutionalised by the 'sovereignty contract' and the 'sexual contract' of modern European state-making, which is simultaneously-and not coincidentally-the making of rational man, the sovereign subject and political agency. In this historical context, politics-as concept and action-is rendered definitely masculine and political identity is gendered both conceptually (in term of how we think about political agency, subjectivity and subjective relations) and empirically (in terms of how we organise political activities, structures and objective relations).*[15]

Radical thinkers such as John Hoffman argue for the reconstruction of the political concept of sovereignty as 'emancipatory, for sovereignty beyond the state'. States are an expression of patriarchal power. "Empirically, states are run by men, defended by men and advance the interests of men... Logically, state sovereignty is gendered by its assertion that leadership is monolithic, hierarchical and violent. These principles are all *"masculinist"* in character since the idea of concentrating power so that the few rules by force over the many is associated with the domination of men."[16] This characteristic of the state and issues of violence associated with it is central to the concept of security in international relations. Feminists have examined extensively the degree to which mainstream concepts of security in the fields have been traditionally constrained by masculinist blinkers, failing to take account of security issues women confront daily that are associated with their unequal or oppressed conditions of existence in relation to men, for example domestic violence. One of the most powerful, and perhaps controversial, aims of different kinds of feminist analysis in these areas is the opening up of consideration that different kinds of oppression, including in extreme forms as violence, may be interconnected. As J. Ann Tickner has explained:

"Whereas conventional security studies has tended to look at causes and consequences of wars from a top-down, or structural, perspective, feminists have generally taken a bottom-up approach, analysing the impact of war at the micro level. By so doing, as well as adopting gender as a category of analysis, feminists believe they can tell us something new about the cause of war that is missing from both conventional and critical perspectives. By crossing what many feminists believe to be mutually constitutive levels of analysis, we get a better understanding of the interrelationship between all forms of violence and the extent to which unjust social relations, including gender hierarchies, contribute to insecurity, broadly defined."[17]

Tickner's book, in particular, presents an early feminist critique of the realist tradition and the first step to evaluating prevalent notions of security from a gender-sensitive perspective. With its military focus, IR security studies had become, according to Tickner, a "dysfunctional" response to the challenges of human and environmental security. As Tickner explains, realism stresses rationality, strength, power, autonomy, and independence, qualities as associated with foreign policy and military affairs as they are with masculinity.[18] She challenges as well the erogeneity of domestic affairs in the realist account and shows how ostensibly objective realist national security studies attempt to explain the causes of war through a discourse that privileges a view based on hegemonic masculinity. While realists take power as the coercive means by which states obtain security at the expense of other states, Tickner suggests instead that an ethos of "mutual enablement rather than domination" could underlie a positive-sum notion of security inspired by peace activism.[19] Like Elshtain, Tickner challenges the realist aversion to morality in IR, questioning the adaptation of a set of public (and thus international) values as a basis for security so wildly at odds with the values we "espouse at home".[20] Applying gender as a category of analysis to show the possibility of a more comprehensive notion of security, Tickner traces the linkage between the system of international relations (and its theorisation) and multileveled, gendered insecurities. Against realism's assumption of autonomous states and its prescription of self-help in a hostile anarchical environment, Tickner argues that the threats of the nuclear age, cross-border environmental degradation, and evidence of increasing international cooperation demand that interdependence be taken seriously.[21] For Tickner, the assumption that there is order within and anarchy beyond the bounds of the community affects a divide between international and domestic politics that mirrors the public-private split that feminist theorists argue perpetuates domestic violence. Tickner rejects the analytic separation of explanations for war into distinct levels and the identification of security with state borders, arguing that violence at the international, national, and family levels is interrelated, ironically taking place in domestic and international spaces beyond the reaches of law.[22]

J. Ann Tickner's Reformulation of Hans Morgenthau's Principles of Political Realism

J. Ann Tickner targets Morgenthau's 6 principles of political realism as exemplary of the school of thought as a whole. She starts by arguing that "diplomacy, military service, and the science of international politics have been largely male domains"and within the upper tier of international decision making process, men have consistently controlled those decisions. Even though more women are breaking through barriers of entry, they typically do not advance to the highest levels, and when they do, they find themselves feeling like "a mouse in a man's world" as Jeane Kirkpatrick did. For Tickner, the lack of women advancing through international relations is a result of not only discrimination, but also "through a process of self-selection which begins with the way in which we are taught about international relations". In other words, the very framework through which scholars analyse international politics (realism in this case) is structured in a way that precludes women's success.

Tickner's largest critique of Morgenthau is his assumption of a *"rational (and unemotional) theory of international politics based on objective laws that have their roots in human nature"*.[23] Drawing on the work of Evelyn Fox Keller, Ticker argues that this assumption places Morgenthau squarely against feminist thought, since "most share the belief that knowledge is socially constructed: since it is language that transmits knowledge, the use of language and its claims of objectivity must continually be questioned".[24] Objectivity itself is linked with masculinity as being impermeable and absolute, in contrast, subjectivity is linked with femininity for being irrational and non-scientific. This is because "women are socialised into a mode of thinking which is contextual and narrative rather than formal and abstract."[25] Ticker points out that thinking contextually is absolutely essential, since the prescriptions of Morgenthau's time are not infinitely and temporally viable. For example, "given that any war between the major powers is likely to be nuclear, increasing security by increasing power could be suicidal," thus challenging one of the key ideas coming from Morgenthau.Moreover, in order to create his rational theory of international politics, Morgenthau fashions a theory of "political man," who is a "beast completely lacking in moral restraints". In Tickner's reading of Morgenthau, politics is an amoral business, since real men cannot live up to abstract universal moral codes. On the international level, that translates into Morgenthau's tolerance of Hobbesian competition for power maximisation and survival between states. However, feminist scholars would reject the distinction between politics and morals. For Tickner, Morgenthau's reconstruction of human nature is fundamentally lacking: "one might well ask where the women were in Hobbes' state of nature; presumably they must have been involved in reproduction and childrearing, rather than warfare, if life was to go on for more than one generation".[26] Additionally, focusing on conflicts within international relations underplays the role of cooperation and regeneration that have continuously played a role in sustaining international politics and human life itself.Like Hannah Arendt, who theorised power as a deliberative, collective and cooperative action, Tickner finds that a feminist reformulation of security studies would fundamentally alter the field, especially "since women have had less access to the instruments of coercion, women have been more apt to rely on power as persuasion." For Tickner, this reformulation would lead to an analysis of security in terms of north-south instead of east-west and about human security instead of national security, and would even tie in the environment as a site of mutual cooperation. At the end of her article, Tickner notes that she does not deny the validity of Morgenthau's work; rather, "*adding a feminist perspective to the epistemology of international relations... is a state through which we must pass if we are to being to think about constructing an engendered or human science of international politics which is sensitive to, but goes beyond, both masculine and feminine perspectives."*[27]

- A feminist perspective believes that objectivity, as it is culturally defined is associated with masculinity. Therefore supposedly 'objective' laws of human nature are based as a partial masculine view of human nature. Human nature is both masculine and feminine and it contains elements of social reproduction and development as well as political domination. Dynamic objectivity offers us a more connected view of objectivity with less potential for domination.

- A feminist perspective believes that the national interest is multi-dimensional and contextually contingent. Therefore it cannot be defined solely in terms of power. In the contemporary world the national interest demands co-operative rather than zero sum solution to set of interdependent global problems, which include nuclear war, economic well-being and environmental degradation.

- Power cannot be infused with meaning that is universally valid. Power as domination and control privileges masculinity and ignores the possibility of collective empowerment another aspect of power often associated with femininity.

- A feminist perspective rejects the possibility of separating moral command from political action. All political action has moral significance. The realist agenda for maximising order through power and control prioritises the moral command of order over those of justice and the satisfaction of basic needs necessary to ensure social reproduction.

- While recognising that the moral aspirations of particular nations cannot be equated with universal moral principles, a feminist perspective seeks to find common moral elements in humans aspirations which could become the basis for de-escalating international conflict and building international community.

- A feminist perspective denies the validity of the autonomy of the political culture. Since autonomy is associated with masculinity in Western culture, disciplinary efforts to construct a world view which does not rest on a pluralistic conception of human nature are partial and masculine. Building boundaries around a narrowly defined political realm defines political culture in a way that excludes the concerns and contributions of women[28].

Standpoint theory considers how "the gendered construction of knowledge helps to understand traditional topics in international relations" and is "alerting us to the idea that gender may be structuring how we think in the international context."[29] Author Martin Griffiths classifies feminist scholar J. Ann Tickner as a standpoint feminist.[30]Before even addressing existing IR theory, Griffiths first argues that the purpose and definition of 'theory' is in itself male centered, because it is "oppressing normative rather than conjectural and analytic."[31] Simply put the processes of forming and learning theory is constructed around an automatically accepted idea of what is standard and normal, rather than first challenging the 'norm' and questioning if the 'standard' is objective enough. In this case, 'theory' lacks female perspective because it is not objectively sought at the onset of formulating ideas. Tickner argues that IR is gendered to *"marginalise women's voices,"* and stresses *"that woman has knowledge, perspectives and experiences that should be brought to bear on the study of international relations."* For example, Tickner would argue that security, a main topic in IR, should not only be understood as "defending the state from attack," but should also consider that security for women "might be different because women are more likely to be attacked by men they know, rather than strangers from other states."[32] In other words, in contrast to traditional IR views that view security as protecting the state from other states, feminists argue the topic of security should address acts of rape and violence, not only from foreign perpetrators, but from their own fellow citizens as well. Feminists would also add that occurrences of rape increase during times of war, and is even used as a method of ethnic cleansing among the rivalries within their state,[33] yet would never enter into typical IR discussions that focus solely on state-to-state interaction, simply because IR discussions traditionally remain focused on states as the key actors. Thus, the topic of security shows how gender consideration, excluded from the very beginning of the discussion, results in policymaking that would be subsequently exclusive of and likely to be detrimental to women. In addition to standpoint feminism, Griffiths also presents an explanation of radical feminist theory. "The radical feminist focuses on the lives and experiences of women...showing how women's activities are made invisible on the international scene."[34] She describes the writings of feminist Cynthia Enloe, who is famous for the question "where are the women?" One of Enloe's main arguments is that feminists should not only seek to include themselves in the higher realms of policymaking and leadership, but should search where women have already fulfilled their roles to ensure that the international system works smoothly and efficiently such as the work done by diplomatic wives and military prostitutes.[35]

Tickner's Three Key Dichotomies

J. Ann Tickner has elaborated the three dichotomies in the study of feminist perspective in international relations.[36]

1. Problem-Solving Theory vs. Critical Theory Dichotomy

Misunderstandings between IR scholars and feminists arise from their different methodological approaches to IR theory. IR scholars favour traditional "*problem-solving*" methods and regard recent critical approaches as irrelevant to understanding international relations. Tickner claims that this unwillingness to acknowledge the legitimacy of new approaches to IR is a great cause of silence which feminist approaches have received by mainstream scholars of international relations. "Problem-solving" methods were traditionally favoured by leading IR scholars such as Morgenthau who, in countering German fascism in the 1930s, claimed that theories must have a purpose. IR scholars continue to uphold this view and argue that building of theory must be based on the possibility to control and predict events in the future, so as to understand solid tangible outcomes. Feminists, on the other hand, challenge this fundamental assumption that theories must have a purpose and are able to "solve" problems.[37]While "problem-solving" IR scholars implicitly accept "laws of nature" which help them understand and govern international politics, feminists deny the prevailing order of the world and instead ask "how" that order came about. This is a method of "truth-seeking" that attempts to question the validity of the IR theorists' understanding of a neutral, value-free world.[38] Adding to this, feminists also claim that the IR scholars' belief in an objective, deterministic world is largely shaped by "naturalised" female subjugation and takes the weaker, vulnerable roles of women as granted. Not only is the IR scholars' claim to objective "problem-solving" invalid, but also reproachable for including female subjugation as part of their objective world views.

2. Positivist vs. Post-Positivist Dichotomy

- *Positivism:* A philosophy which holds that the only authentic knowledge is that based on actual sense experience. Such knowledge can come only from affirmation of theories through strict scientific method.
- *Post-positivism:* A school of thought which values qualitative over quantitative research, questions the possibility of objectivity, and draws upon the methods of deconstructionism. Many IR scholars also posit that scientific observations of the world can help people understand causes of events and hence diminish the likelihood of war in the future.[39] Also called positivists, these IR scholars argue that scientific approach to international relations is possible based on the objective truth they see in the laws governing world politics. Feminists, as post-positivists, reject objective view of world politics and prefer epistemological pluralism that pays attention to historical, humanistic and

philosophical traditions of international relations.[40] According to feminists, there can be no impartial, value-neutral Archimedean perspective evidenced in mainstream IR.[41]Instead, events in world politics are "socially constructed" and "variable across time, place and cultures," a view that fundamentally challenges IR scholars' theories based on natural sciences.

3. Asocial vs. Social Dichotomy

Feminists are deeply concerned with social relations, especially in terms of the causes and consequences of the unequally structured relationships between men and women. They believe that international relations has been socially constructed on the basis of misguided associations of power, autonomy, rationality, and the public sphere with masculinity and weakness, dependence and the private sphere with femininity. They argue that IR scholars' asocial approach greatly overlooks these problems.

Much of contemporary feminism has emancipatory goals, particularly to achieve equality for women by eliminating unequal gender relations embedded in the structure of international relations.[42] Theories in the realist paradigm are a great hindrance to achieving this goal given that they deny epistemological pluralities and critical approaches to international relations. Even liberalism, while it is committed to emancipatory goals of justice and peace, is still "constructed out of a definition of human nature that excludes or diminishes women."[43] The purpose of feminist IR theory is to essentially challenge the unequally gendered structural relations in contemporary world politics and seek to bring about change that would better the lives of individuals and particularly women.

While IR scholars claim that feminism is irrelevant to understanding international politics, feminists claim that this is a clear "misunderstanding," because feminism ultimately differs in the epistemological and ontological approaches to international relations. It is crucial that feminists' critical approaches to IR theory are legitimised, even if this means departing from the traditional analysis of international relations on the basis of scientific, falsifiable theories. Essentially, IR theories should move "beyond knowledge frameworks" currently established in world politics which hinder the participation of women and perpetuate "inequalities between men and women in the world of international politics."[44] IR scholars must accept the fact that feminist's challenge the "core assumptions, concepts and ontological presuppositions" based on gender bias, and with this in mind, seek to further their dialogues with feminist IR scholars.

Three Waves of Feminism

The history of western feminist movement or feminism and the efforts to overturn gender inequality have been divided into three major periods which the Feminist scholars termed as *"Three Waves."* Feminism, as it stands today, has evolved through three distinct phases. The *First Wave* Feminism which began in about 1800 and lasted until the 1930s was largely concerned with demanding equal rights for women and men. The *Second Wave* Feminism that began in the late 1960s continued the fight for equality but also developed a range of theories and approaches that stressed the difference between women and men and also draw attention to the specific needs. The final and third wave known as the *Third Wave Feminism*, began in the mid-90 and was influenced by post-colonial and post-modern thinking. In this phase many conceptions have been weakened, including the ideas of *"universal womanhood,"* body, gender, and sexuality.

- **First Wave Feminism**

The first wave of feminism known as the Suffrage Movement, took place in the late 19th and early 20th centuries, emerging out of an atmosphere of urban industrialism and liberal, socialist, and politics. The goal for most of the first wave feminists was largely to get white middle and upper class women inside the public and cultural world from which they were excluded. In keeping with liberal tenets, they argued that women were rational, differences between men and women were largely social rather than natural in origin and therefore education and training could make women citizens in the same way men were. The goal was equality. The general themes of this early movement were virtue, equality, rationality and nature over nature. The first wave of feminism in the United States was linked with other reform movements, such as abolition and temperance, and primarily closely involved women of the working classes. However, it was also supported by black women abolitionists, such as Maria Stewart, Sojourner Truth, and Frances E. W. Harper, who agitated for the rights of women of colour. There were many people during this time who were considered to be feminists, Mary Wollstonecraft, Susan B. Anthony, Lucy Stone, Olympia Brown, and Helen Pitts and countless more. Mary Wollstonecraft's *Vindication of the Rights of Women* (1792), was an early first-wave feminists agenda which was liberal and naturalistic and her pressing socio-political agenda was suffrage for women. They were primarily concerned with establishing a policy which recognises that women are human beings in their own right and not the property of men. They campaigned for women's suffrage and, as was the case for subsequent second-wave feminism, they fought against the subordination and exploitation of women.

The early feminists such as Aphra Ben and Mary Stell in the later part of the 18th century and in the beginning of the 19th century advocated women's welfare and the importance given to the notion of natural human worth, individual value, equality, equal rights, reason, education, free opportunity, privilege, heredity, wealth and power. Elizabeth Candy Stanton, the 19th century American Suffragist showed a clear sense of women's role and responsibilities and argued that because man and woman complement one another, we need women's thought in national affairs to make safe and stable government. Margaret Fuller and Lucretia are some of the other feminists who were concerned with securing legal rights for women in marriage, education and employment.

Feminists in France argued that the values of liberty, equality, and fraternity of the Revolution should apply to all, while women activists in America called for an extension of the principles of the American Declaration of Independence to women, including rights to citizenship and property. Mary Wollstonecraft demanded equality and better education for women, and made the first sustained critique of the social system which relegated women to an inferior position. In the early 19th century, a small group of middle-class women in the United Kingdom began to call for better education, improved legal rights (especially within marriage), employment opportunities, and the right to vote. The Equal rights feminism was given theoretical justification by John Stuart Mill, who wrote "The Subjection of Women" (1869), which was partly influenced by his wife Harriet Taylor. From the 1850s onward, the campaign for equal rights for women became focused on winning the right to vote (women's suffrage), and suffragist movements appeared in New Zealand, Germany, Poland, Austria, and Sweden. Towards the end of the 19[th]century, another strand of feminist thinking appeared which questioned social attitudes towards women, including cultural and literary representations and social prescriptions for women's behaviour. By the 1920s, feminists began to turn their attention from questions of equality between women and men to issues which mainly concerned women, for example, calling for improved welfare provision for mothers and children. These factors would become stronger in the second wave of feminism.

- **Second Wave Feminism**

The second wave of Feminism started during the 1960s when Women's Liberation Movements gathered strength as wide-spread radical protests by students, workers, blacks and women took place especially in the USA and France. Betty Frieden's "The Feminine Mystique" brought it to life in 1963. Women formed their own groups and raised their voice against the secondary role of women. "In their groups, class and race had little importance and sisterhood was the only one motivating force."[45]Eminent feminists who had played an important role in women's liberation movement were *Simone de Beauvoir* (The Second Sex, 1949), *Betty Friendan* (The Feminine Mystique, 1963), *Kate Millet* (Sexual Politics, 1969) and *Germaine Greer (*The Female Eunuch, 1970). After the 1970s, there came a sudden change in the feminist movement. During 1970-80 different groups of women were fragmented and fission of women's movement had started after the recognition of the complexities of experience of women. The *'universalist'* claims of the 1960s have been challenged by the women of working class, third world and black women. Thus, second wave feminism dealt with inequality of laws, gender as well as cultural inequalities. From the year 1980 onwards, further changes were seen in political and critical realms in the feminists' point of view. In the Anglo-American tradition there was a growth of *"Radical Binarism"* (Radicals distinguished from Liberal or social feminism).[46]

Secondwave feminists challenged the prevailing notions of the women's role in the family, workplace, and society. They highlighted the sexual division of labour and were instrumental in promoting women's equality in the labour market. Secondwave feminists sought to address diverse issues, relating to *inter alia* access to childcare, equal pay, employment and education opportunities, reproductive rights, and women and children's safety. There was a focus on structural change and a critique of psychoanalytic theory and the psycho dynamic approach in social work *'on the grounds that it is biologically essentialist.'*[47] In the early stages of second-wave feminism, issues of race and class were of secondary concern to gender, women's wellbeing was prioritised, and gender binaries prevailed: 'there are two sorts of people in the world, the superior and inferior, or in terms of power relations, the dominant and the subordinate. We are all equal irrespective of our gender. Social relations that obliterate this fact must, therefore, be transformed and recreated in ways that reflect equality in terms of gender." [48] Hence second wave feminists were mainly concerned with the elimination of gender inequality. Second wave liberal feminists continued the work of their predecessors by fighting for women's liberation through rights and recognition in freedom of expression and choice, and equal rights, treatment, and opportunities for women. They sought to break through, what they termed 'the glass ceiling', that is, the barriers preventing women from obtaining high-ranking positions in government, business and industry. Liberal feminists were reformists who sought to work via juridical means for the introduction of women-friendly legislation. They lobbied for legal and civil reforms through affirmative action and anti-discrimination campaigns. Their strategies were democratic engagement, reasoned argument and peaceful campaigning so as not to upset the capitalist *status quo*. They argued that women were 'oppressed' before capitalism, [49] thus ignoring non-white, middle-class, heterosexual women. Liberal feminists sought to promote women's interests and protect them from exploitation, abuse, and sexual harassment. They believed in women's autonomy and right to self-determination and assumed the right of women to participate in the economy even though many were not in a position to do so. Few social workers were at odds with liberal feminism though some were more aligned with critical second-wave feminism.

The original impetus for the "*Second Wave*" of feminism came from socialist and civil rights movements which emerged in the 1960s in North and Central America, Europe, and Australasia. The women's liberation movement, which started in the United States, combined liberal, rights-based concerns for equality between women and men with demands for a woman's right to determine her own identity and sexuality. These two strands of ideology were represented in the seven demands of the movement, established between 1970 and 1978. These were equal pay, equal education and equal opportunities in work, financial and legal independence, free 24-hour nurseries, free contraception and abortion on demand, a woman's right to define her own sexuality and an end to discrimination against lesbians, and more significantly, freedom from violence and sexual coercion. This stage refers to the resurgence of feminist activity in the late 1960s and 1970s, when protest again focussed around women's inequality, although this time not only in terms of women's lack of equal political rights but in the areas of family, sexuality and work.[50] Central to second-wave feminism is the notion that the personal is political that is, individual women do not suffer oppression in isolation but as the result of wider social and political systems. In *The Second Sex* (1949) de Beauvoir argued that Western culture regarded men as normal and women as an aberration and she called for the recognition of the special nature of women. Kate Millett, in *Sexual Politics* (1970)[51], drew attention to the ubiquity of patriarchy and to the ways in which it reproduced itself through the family and culture, notably in literature. Second-wave feminism emphasised the physical and psychological differences between women and men. Some feminists criticised traditional psychoanalysis, notably the work of Sigmund Freud, for assuming that all people are, or should be, like men. They became concerned with ways in which women's perceptions were determined by the particular nature of the female body and the female roles in reproduction and childbearing. This strand of feminism, which became known as cultural or radical feminism, focused on differences between women and men that they believed make women superior to men, and advocated female forms of culture.

The Three Waves of the Feminist Movement

1. *First Wave 1848-mid-1930s ("Declaration of Sentiments and Resolutions")*
- *Suffrage.*
- *Creation of social and child-labour laws.*
- *Start of campaign for legalised birth control.*
- *Equal Rights Amendment (1923) is drafted.*
2. *Second Wave rises out of anti-war and civil-rights movements (The Feminine Mystique, Betty Friedan 1963)*
- *predominately white, middle class Americanbased, educated women; eventually moves into the*
- *academy (National Women's Studies Association).*
- *organisation of women's liberation groups in major US cities.*
- *activist activities: consciousness-raising (CR) groups and speak-outs occur in major cities across the US.*
- *women step into male dominated political arenas.*
- *successful passing of Title IV (equal funding for boys and girls activities in educational settings that are federally funded).*
- *women's health issues are recognised: Our Bodies, Ourselves, 1971.*
- *legal and social recognition of: domestic violence, sexual harassment, sexual assault, child sexual abuse, women in the workplace, women in the military, women's reproductive rights, rape, pornography, homophobia.*
3. *Third Wave late 1980s to the present*
- broader inclusion of recognition: women of colour, sexual diversity, age (recognition of young girls and older women), and men.
- inclusion becomes more trans global; activist activities becomes a fight for all women everywhere, beyond US borders (Transnational/Global Feminism).
- volunteerism is new force for activist activities.
- CR groups form through new texts: the 'zine movement gives way to the use of writing, new technologies (Internet, filmmaking, music).
- women begin stepping into male-dominated cultural arenas.
- women's health issues are recognised through activist activities: reproductive health rights marches on DC in 1989, 1992 and 2004.
- legal and social recognition of date: rape, sexual identity issues (custody battles, gender reassignment, marriage rights), reclamation of language (cunt, bitch, slut), objectification (body image is major issue).
- shifting of Second Wave ideals on "proper" feminism: marriage, pornography.
- voter registration among women becomes driving force for many activist activities.

Source: "The Three Waves of the Feminist Movement" *http://www.michelepolak.com/ WMST100fall10/Media_Page_files/ThreeWaves.pdf*, accessed on month, date and year.

• **Third Wave Feminism**

The Third wave feminism began in the mid-90s and was informed by post-colonial and post-modern thinking. In this phase many conceptions have been weakened, including the ideas of "universal womanhood," body, gender, and sexuality. Third wave feminism manifests itself in "girl" rhetoric, which seeks to overcome the theoretical question of equity or difference and the political question of evolution or revolution, while it challenges the notion of "universal womanhood" and embraces ambiguity, diversity, and multiplicity in transversal theory and politics.[52]Thirdwave feminists often focus on "micro-politics" and challenge the second wave's paradigm as to what is, or is not, good for women, and tend to use a post-structuralist interpretation of gender and sexuality. The third wave is sustained by the confidence of having more opportunities and less sexism. Third wave feminism is characterised by an interest in various groups of women, including women of colour, lesbian, bisexual, and transgendered women and low income women. Rebecca Walker argued that motherhood was a form of servitude, first coined the term 'third-wave feminism' in a 1992 essay. She typifies the third-wave feminist who has been brought up within competing feminist structures. Most typically, third wave feminists accept contradiction, pluralism, and hybridity as given,[53] since no account of oppression is true for all women in all situations all of the time. Though Gamble (2001) believes that it takes a number of different forms – some more dominant than others – and it achieves change in diverse ways, for the most part third-wave feminism is a product of the popular media and academic cultural studies programmes.[54]

Third wave feminism seeks to challenge or avoid second-wave "essentialist" definitions of femininity, which over-emphasised the experiences of white, upper middle class women. A post-structuralist interpretation of gender and sexuality, or an understanding of gender as outside binary maleness and femaleness, is central too much of the third wave's ideology. Proponents of third wave feminism claim that it allows women to define feminism for them by incorporating their own identities into the belief system of what feminism is, what it encompasses, and what it can become through one's own perspective. For third wave feminists, therefore, "sexual liberation," a major goal of second wave feminism, was expanded to mean a process of first becoming conscious of the ways one's gender identity and sexuality have been shaped by society and then intentionally constructing (and becoming free to express) one's authentic gender identity. Third wavers inherited a foothold of institutional power created by second wavers, including women's studies programs at universities, long-standing feminist organisations, and well-established publishing outlets such as *Ms. Magazine* and several academic journals. These outlets became a less important part of the culture of the third wave than they had been for the second wave. Third-wave theory usually incorporates elements of queer theory, anti-racism and women of colour consciousness, womanism, girl power, post-colonial theory, post modernism, trans-nationalism, cyberfeminism, ecofeminism, individualist feminism, new feminist theory, transgender politics, and a rejection of the gender binary.[55]The third wave feminism challenges previously accepted definitions of beauty and femininity, and continues to fight for equal rights. Through the development of the PC, third wave feminists are more able to keep tabs on important political and social issues debasing their gender worldwide. This particular wave is defined as the feminist activity and study from the 1990s to present times.[56]

Theories of Feminism
• Liberal feminism
Liberal feminists hold that the exercise of personal autonomy depends on certain enabling conditions that are insufficiently present in women's lives, or that social arrangements often fail to respect women's personal autonomy and other elements of women's advancement. They also hold that women's needs and interests are insufficiently reflected in the basic conditions under which they live, and that those conditions lack legitimacy because women are inadequately represented in the processes of democratic self-determination. Liberal feminists hold that autonomy deficits like these are due to the "*gender system,*"[57] or the patriarchal nature of inherited traditions and institutions, and that the women's movement should work to identify and remedy them. As the protection and promotion of citizens' autonomy is the appropriate role of the state on the liberal view, liberal feminists hold that the state can and should be the women's movement's ally in promoting women's autonomy. There is disagreement among liberal feminists, however, about the role of personal autonomy in the good life, the appropriate role of the state, and how liberal feminism is to be justified.

Some liberal feminists, inspired by John Rawls' contractualist liberal theory of justice,[58] argue that the state should ensure that the basic structure of society distributes the benefits and burdens of social cooperation fairly, that is, in a manner that women as well as men could endorse.[59] They argue that the basic structure currently distributes benefits and burdens unfairly, in part due to the gender system, or the patriarchal nature of inherited traditions and institutions.

> *Liberal Feminism- equality type of feminism*
> - *Liberal feminism is a form of feminism that argues that equality for women can be achieved through legal means and social reform.*
> - *Liberal feminism leans towards an equality or sameness argument with men.*
> - *Liberal feminism conceives of politics in individualistic terms and looks to reform present practices in society, rather than advocating for a revolutionary change. Feminist writers associated with this tradition include early feminist Mary Wollstonecraft and second-wave feminist Betty Friedan.*

Liberal feminists were reformists who sought to work via juridical means for the introduction of women-friendly legislation. They lobbied for legal and civil reforms through affirmative action and anti-discrimination campaigns. Their strategies were democratic engagement, reasoned argument and peaceful campaigning so as not to upset the capitalist status quo. They argued that women were 'oppressed' before capitalism,[60] thus ignoring non-white, middle-class, heterosexual women. Liberal feminists sought to promote women's interests and protect them from exploitation, abuse, and sexual harassment. They believed in women's autonomy and right to self-determination and assumed the right of women to participate in the economy even though many were not in a position to do so.

All that the term liberal means in the context of feminism is that it starts from the notion that the key units of society are individuals and that these individuals have rights. Therefore, liberal feminists argue that the same rights should be granted to women as have traditionally been granted to men. Thus, to ask 'where there is a radical political act, precisely because they were not written about in the main texts, and thus appeared invisible.' Then writers such as Cynthia Enloe, through her writings published in 1989, 1993, 2000,[61] began to show just how involved were women in world politics. In her first two books on this subject (1989, 1993) she looked at the roles women actually occupied in world politics. It was not that they were not there but they in fact played central roles, either as cheap factory labour, as prostitutes around military bases, or as the wives of diplomats. Enloe was intent on showing just how critically important were the activities of women to the functioning of the international economic and political systems and how much power it took for international politics to keep functioning as it has done. Accordingly, liberal feminists look at the ways in which women are excluded from power and from playing a full part in political activity and they were being restricted instead to roles critically important for the functioning of things, but that are not usually deemed to be important for theories or world politics. Fundamentally, liberal feminists want the same rights and opportunities which are available to men, extended to women, although using Enloe as an example of a liberal feminist writer is problematic because she also has socialist and even standpoint leadings.

- **Radical Feminism**

Radical feminism is a movement that believes sexism is so deeply rooted in society that the only cure is to eliminate the concept of gender completely. Radical feminists suggest changes, such as finding technology that will allow babies to be grown outside of a woman's body, to promote more equality between men and women. This will allow women to avoid missing work for maternity leave, which radical feminists argue is one reason women aren't promoted as quickly as men. In fact, radical feminists would argue that the entire traditional family system is sexist. Men are expected to work outside the home while women are expected to care for children and clean the house. Radical feminists note that this traditional dichotomy maintains men as economically in power over women, and therefore, the traditional family structure should be rejected.

Radical feminists made inroads in promoting women's health, and taking a stand against pornography and sexual violence. Radical feminists seek to abolish patriarchy by challenging existing social norms and institutions, rather than through a purely political process. This includes challenging the notion of traditional gender roles, opposing the sexual objectification of women, and raising public awareness about such issues as rape and violence against women. They favoured a cultural focus on women's personal lives, personal stories and narratives, 'using writing as a vehicle to communicate their own narratives of pain'.[62] European radical feminists, such as Irigaray, Kristeva, and Cixous, were critical of Western thought's dualism of man/woman that resulted in unequal relationships. 'The superiority of the male half of the equation is predicated upon the subordination of the female half, which is thus exiled from the value paradigm'.[63] As a result, radical feminists sought to develop their own totalising discourse as a way of supplanting the dominant male discourse[64] and thus they re-enforced gender binaries. They created separate structures and services for women, such as domestic violence and sexual assault counselling services. Their anti-pornography stance tended to essentialise men as aggressive and women as passive victims. All men were seen as complicit in subordinating women whether or not they were active agents of abuse. Thus, radical feminist social workers historically viewed men with suspicion and their work with men was focused on getting them to see 'the "true" reason for their behaviour'.[65] They made the matter personal and political by 'questioning notions that a woman's place is primarily at home, that women should take the main responsibility for child-rearing and that women are naturally suited to low-paid and low-status caring work'.[66] They saw this patriarchal order of social relations as the means by which women were oppressed by men. However, the separatist interests and essentialist arguments of some radical feminists and social workers were seen as anti-men, leading to connections between radical and lesbian feminism and criticisms that women were recast as passive victims of men's biological impulses. While radical feminism has been central to social work practices in the UK, Australia, and Canada, it has also been heavily critiqued by those who believe that transformation requires that we recognise that men can take a pro-feminist standpoint,[67] partner with men to find solutions to men's violence, and acknowledge men's contribution. Further, Molyneux (in the year 2000) has highlighted how women's activism in Latin America has, unlike feminism in the USA and Europe, never fully embraced equality feminism, but has sought rather to examine 'how citizenship can be reformulated to encompass gender difference without at the same time signifying inequality'.

Radical feminists proposed that the experience of women had been ignored, except where they have been unfavourably compared to male experience. The aim then is to re-describe reality according to a female view. In the work of influential feminist theorists such as Sandra Harding (in the year 1986), this approach is taken further towards standpoint feminism, which is an attempt to develop a female version of the world. Standpoint feminists want to improve on that understanding by incorporating a female perspective. This is a controversial move in feminism since it assumes that there is such a thing as a feminist view of the world (as distinct from a variety of female views) according to their social, economic, cultural, sexual locations. It also runs the risk of essentialsing and fixing the views and nature of women, by saying that this is how women see the world. Nonetheless despite these dangers of standpoint feminism, it has been very influential in showing just how male dominated are the main theories of world politics.

Radical Feminism

- *Radical feminism is a branch of feminism that views women's oppression (which radical feminists refer to as "patriarchy") as a basic system of power upon which human relationships in society are arranged.*
- *Radical feminism considers the male-controlled capitalist hierarchy as the defining feature of women's oppression and the total uprooting and reconstruction of society as necessary.*
- *It seeks to challenge this arrangement by rejecting standard gender roles and male oppression.*
- *Radical feminists locate the root cause of women's oppression in patriarchal gender relations, as opposed to legal systems (liberal feminism) or class conflict (like socialist or Marxist feminism).*
- *Radical feminism views patriarchy as dividing rights, privileges and power primarily by gender, and as a result oppressing women and privileging men.*

- **Cultural Feminism**

Cultural feminism is a movement that points out how modern society is hurt by encouraging masculine behaviour, but society would benefit by encouraging feminine behaviour instead. Cultural feminism, which views women's ways as different to men's, may be seen as a variant of radical feminism divested of its redistributive aspirations and replaced with a desire for recognition of women's innate difference while, at the same time, seeking to destabilise the *'binary model inscribed in the masculine/feminine'*.[69] Simone de Beauvoir in the Second Sex (in the year 1949) highlighted the patriarchal tendency to position women as different and lesser, or as other juxtaposed against the male claim to self. She viewed the explanations of biologists, Freudian psychoanalysts and Marxists as unacceptably deterministic casting women as subordinate to the masculine norm. Betty Friedan called 'for a drastic reshaping of the cultural image of femininity'.[69] European feminists, such as Irigaray, Kristeva, and Cixous, drew attention to the way in which women develop distinctive feminine and feminist cultures and discourses[70] but, being anti-essentialists, they 'do not refer to the female body in biological terms, but only in so far as it is enveloped, produced and made meaningful by language'. Drawing on Derrida, European feminists challenged the 'binary opposition which situates the male as the legitimating principle and the standard against which truth and value are measured: a process he labels phallocentric'.[71] Thus arose 'the complex and multifaceted theoretical debates springing from postmodernism, post structuralism and psychoanalysis'. Hence cultural feminists are sometimes positioned as postmodernists.

Cultural Feminism

- *Cultural feminism believes that a female nature or female essence is essential to society.*
- *It's the theory that there is fundamental personality and psychological differences between men and women, and that woman's differences are not only unique, but superior.*
- *This theory of feminism takes note of the biological differences between men and women-such as menstruation inherent "women's culture". For example, the belief that "women are kinder and gentler than men, "prompts cultural feminists call for an infusion of women's culture into the male-dominated world, which would presumably result in less violence and fewer wars.*
- *Cultural feminism seeks to improve the relationship between the sexes and often cultures at large by celebrating women's special qualities, ways, and experiences, often believing that the "woman's way" is the better way, or that the culture discussed is overly masculine and requires balance from feminine perspectives.*

- **Socialist/Marxist Feminism**

Socialist feminism is a movement that calls for an end to capitalism through a socialist reformation of our economy. Basically, socialist feminism argues that capitalism strengthens and supports the sexist status quo because men are the ones who currently have power and money. Those men are more willing to share their power and money with other men, which mean that women are continually given fewer opportunities and resources. This keeps women under the control of men. As the name implies the influence here is Marxism, with its insistence of the role of material, primarily economic, force in determining the lives of women. For Marxist feminism, the cause of women's inequality is to be found in the capitalist system and overthrowing capitalism is the necessary route for the achievement of the equal treatment of women. Socialist feminism, noted that the oppression of women occurred in pre-capitalist societies, and continues in socialist women's unequal treatment, namely the patriarchal system of male dominance. Capitalism is the primary oppressor for socialist feminists it is capitalism plus patriarchy. For Marxist feminists, then, the focus of a theory of world politics would be on the patterns by which the world capitalist system and the patriarchal system of power lead to women being systematically disadvantaged as compared to men. This approach is especially insightful when it comes to looking at the nature of the world economy and the differential advantages and disadvantages of it that apply to women. Socialist feminists assert that women are unable to be free due to their financial dependence on males in society. Women are subjects to the male dominance in capitalism due to an uneven balance in wealth. They see economic dependence as the driving force of women's subjugation to men.

Socialist Feminism

- *Socialist feminism focuses upon both the public and private spheres of a women's life.*
- *Argues that liberation can only be achieved by working to end both the economic and cultural sources of women's oppression.*
- *Incorporates radical feminism's theory of the role of gender and the patriarchy.*
- *"Socialist feminism confronts the common root of sexism, racism and classism: the determination of a life of oppression or privilege based on accidents of birth or circumstances. Socialist feminism is an inclusive way of creating social change.*

Marxist Feminism

- Connects the oppression of women to Marxist ideas about exploitation, oppression and labour.
- Marxist feminism's argument is that capitalism is the source of all women's oppression.
- Unequal standing in workplace and the domestic sphere holds women down.
- Prostitution, domestic work, childcare and marriage as ways in which women are exploited by a patriarchal system that devalues women.
- Oppression of women as a part of a larger pattern that affect everyone involved in the capitalist system.

Marxist-oriented socialist feminists focused on the political economy, particularly social inequalities resulting from capitalism. They sought to revolutionise consciousness by critiquing the '*ideological frameworks of contemporary social formations*',[72] especially capitalism, and were centrally concerned with redistribution.[73] Unlike the stance of positive, affirmative action of liberal feminism, its negative view -first of male and then all forms of oppression-led to social work, towards demanding anti-oppressive and anti-discriminatory practice. In time, feminists attacked all 'isms', starting with sexism and racism[74] and extending to ethnocentrism in its postmodern reincarnation. A product of left-wing radicalism in the UK, socialist and Marxist feminists distanced themselves from male-dominated Left-wing Marxism. They organised decentralised and localised women's groups whose major goal was raising consciousness to help women realise the extent to which they were subordinate to and oppressed by men in capitalistic societies. This caused problems for women who did not perceive their situation in this way and were perceived to have false consciousness or to, in some way, werecomplicit in their own oppression. Socialist feminists, with their focus on the political economy, sought to highlight how reproduction and unpaid work within the family was a key factor in the exploitation of women, benefiting both men and capitalism. They sought to expose domestic women's work as work: 'Socialist feminists persuasively argued that capitalism requires ... hidden unwaged labour [mostly that of women] in order to function'.[75] Feminist social workers highlighted how this patriarchal view of family accepted in welfare policy overlooked women's interests and, as a consequence, care was undervalued. Thus they sought to socialise domestic labour by removing it from its naturalised association with women's work in the house .[76] As an increasing number of women entered the job market, care became a shrinking commodity, forcing governments to turn to the market for provision of care.[77] The legacy of socialist feminism is its perspective that class concerns can also be part of women's oppression. However, the socialist focus on class interests and exploitation, which gives rise to arguments for redistribution, shifted to a focus on cultural domination in cultural feminism, with recognition being the main remedy against injustice.

According to Engels, women are the proletariat, and men the bourgeoisie in the family. Therefore, entering into the heterosexual relationship necessarily leads to the exploitation of woman by man. According to Marxism, there was no sexual discrimination in a primitive maternal communal society. However, with the increase of productive forces, inequality in the distribution of wealth and private property were brought in. Then, with the collapse of the maternal society women became domestic slaves under patriarchal domination. The proponent of Marxist feminist theory is Christine Delphi. According to Marxist feminism, it is not true that the myths of the female and the male sexes existed in the beginning, and later the modern patriarchy was established. The patriarchy of the middle class fabricated such myths and naturalised and universalised them in order to maintain the capitalist system.[78]As a matter of fact, Marxist feminism declared the fight against the capitalist exploitation system where women are exploited.

- **Postmodern Feminism**

Post-modernity offered a widely endorsed critique of the great synthesising theories of the 19th century and proposed (Foucault) that the way to interpret life in the late 20th century was through participation within, and engagement with, a series of over-lapping discourses and identities. This approach to the social and emotional world, made perfect sense to many feminists as it allowed differences in gender and sexual identity, and gave theoretical space to the multi-faceted lives of women.[79]Three writers have been instrumental in the establishment of Postmodern feminism as a philosophy: *Helene Cixous, Luce Irigaray, and Julia Kristeva.* Postmodern Feminists have built on the ideas of Foucault, de Beauvoir, as well as Derrida and Lacan. While there is much variation in postmodern feminism, there is also some common ground. Postmodern Feminists accept the male/female binary as a main categorising force in our society. As the name implies this is a series of theoretical works that bring together post-modern work on identity with a focus on gender. Here, the difference with other variants of feminism,is the concern with gender, and not women. Gender refers to the social construction of differences between men and women, and for postmodern feminism the key issue is what kind of social roles are assigned for men and women by the structures and processes of world politics. In other words, what kinds of 'men' are required to serve in the armies. There was a recent fierce debate about women, homosexual and transgender serving in the armed forces. In other words how has world politics led to certain kind of 'men' and women' being produced. Following Simone de Beauvoir, they see female as having being cast into the role of the other. They criticise the structure of the society and the dominant order, especially in its patriarchal aspects. Many Postmodern feminists, however, reject the feminist label, because anything that ends with an "ism" reflects an essentialist conception. Postmodern feminism is the ultimate acceptor of diversity. Multiple truths, multiple roles, multiple realities are part of its focus. There is a rejection of an essential nature of women, of only one-way to be a woman. Helene Cixous is a writer of prose who built on Derrida's works to criticise the very nature of writing. According to Cixous, man's writing is filled with binary oppositions but woman's writing is scribbling, jotting down, interrupted by life's demands. She also relates feminine writing to female sexuality and women's body concepts. Her idea is that development of this kind of writing will change the rules that currently govern language and ultimately the thinking processes and the structure of society. Luce Irigaray is a psychoanalyst whose primary focus is to liberate women from philosophies of men's writing,even though she is making use of the observations of some writers including the ones of Derrida and Lacan.

Postmodern Feminism
- *Postmodern feminism is an approach to feminist theory that incorporates postmodern and post-structuralist theory. The largest departure from other branches of feminism is the argument that gender is constructed through language.*
- *It is the view that "one is not born women, but become one" and thus here the focus is on the social and cultural construction of women by the system.*
- *Feminism has been seen by some as having a special affinity for the postmodern through a shared interest in social practices and multiple voices.*
- *Postmodern feminist provide a model for critiquing both traditional and feminist approaches.*

Julia Kristeva rejects the idea that the biological man and the biological woman are identified with the "masculine" and "feminine" respectively. To insist that people are different because of their anatomy is to force both men and women into a repressive structure. Kristeva openly accepts the label of feminist, but refuses to say there is a "woman's perspective".Kristeva sees the problems of women as other similar to the problems of other groups excluded from the dominant: Jews, homosexuals, racial and ethnic minorities. Like other postmodern feminists, she viewed the use of language as crucial. In her view, linear, logical "normal" writing was repressed, and writing that emphasised rhythm and sound and was syntaxically illogical was not repressed.

Feminist postmodern IR theorists challenge the hierarchical dichotomies of order-anarchy, dependency-sovereignty, domestic-international, and subject-object which have traditionally defined the theory and methods of IR. Jean Elshtain[80] in her book, *"Women and War"* (1987) and Christine Sylvester[81] in her article *"Some Danger in merging Feminist and Peace Projects"* (1990) refuse to include women in IR on the basis of their dichotomous conflation with peace, co-operation, concrete subjectivity and domesticated politics, that mirrors men's conflation with war, competition, abstract objectivity and anarchical politics. Instead, they have problematised the defining dichotomies of the field that are reinforced through their association with the masculine-feminine gender dichotomy. They question how gender hierarchies are constructed, legitimated, resisted and reproduced and how they serve to naturalise other forms of super ordination in world politics. From this perspective, gender or sexual difference is not just about the relations between male-masculine and female-feminine but about the politics of knowledge, how and from what position we can know and signifying human relationship of power more generally.

Conclusion

Feminist perspectives, bring renewed theoretical and political insight to the field of IR by revealing the gendered nature of its foundational assumptions-the masculine identity of the core actors, structures, defining concepts, modes and purposes of social enquiry-that are premised on the exclusion of women, femininity and feminism and on the pervasive presence of global gender hierarchies. Women and gender are both important, for separate but related reasons. Where women have been largely absent from mainstream international relations, it has become essential to develop increasing quantum of theoretical and substantive research related to them. The concept of gender keeps to the fore the relational nature of categorisations of male and female, and signals the importance of not taking either as given or necessarily natural. Both women and gender have, therefore, been identified by feminist analyses as problematically absent from mainstream approaches and which was essential for the proper understanding international relations.

Feminist IR research exposes the male-dominance of international political-economic institutions and policy-making, the militaristic construction of masculinity in sovereign states and the dependency of men-masculinity on women and feminized others, who 'run', even if they do not 'rule' the world. The future for feminist international relations looks especially bright as gender analysis is extended to new and existing areas of international studies. What is now the 'sub-field' of feminist IR is growing in interest and research at a rapid rate. The persistent challenge, however, is to develop 'empathetic co-operation' between non-feminist and feminist international relations. Thus, it would be beneficial for mainstream IR scholars to engage with feminist IR approaches that have analysed the reproduction of the material on states and international systems and the symbolic exercise of power with authority within the family-household and community. Under such a background gendered identities get reproduced and gendered divisions of power and labour is treated as natural. This needs to be challenged.

Feminism deals with challenging rather than accommodating to what individuals are told by society is the right or wrong way. It is standing up for yourselves and individuals taking pride in what they do. The women and men should be seen and understood their relation to the world rather to just go along with what they thought was wrong. Feminism is a movement away from historically conventional norms to a more exposed and equal way of living. Feminism movement which has been incredibly important to the success and failures has been a necessary journey for the women around the globe so that they can discover and create their own unique place in society.

Notes

1. *The World Book Encyclopedia*, Vol. 7, 1992 ed., London Sydney p. 49.
2. Ibid, p.49.
3. Connell, *Gender and Power*, Characteristics that Connell associates with hegemonic Gender in International Politics: Chapter 1 http://www.ciaonet.org/book/tickner/tickner12.html (13 of 16), Journal of American College Health; May 2000; 48, 6; Health & Medical Complete, pg. 247 accessed on March 24, 2000.
4. Scott, "Gender: A Useful Category of Historical Analysis" in*Gender and the Politics of History*, My analysis of gender draws, was originally published in the *American Historical Review* (December 1986), 91(5)
5. Cynthia Enloe, *Does khaki become you? The militarisation of Women's lives* (London: Pandora, 1988; first publ. 1983*); Bananas, beaches and bases: making feminist sense of international politics* (London: Pandara, 1989); *The morning after: sexual politics at the end of the Cold War* (Berkeley: University of California Press, 1993); *Maneuvers: the international politics of militarising women's' lives* (Berkeley: University of California Press 2000). Judith Stiehm's work in this area includes *Women's and men wars* (Oxford: Pergamon, 1983) and *Arms and the enlisted women* (Philadelphia: Temple University Press, 1989).

6. Enloe, *Bananas, beaches and bases*, p.1. On debates in feminist theory and international theory see e.g. Christine Sylvester, *Feminist theory and International Relations in a postmodern era* (Cambridge: Cambridge University Press, 1994); Jill Steans, *Gender and International Relations: an introduction* (Cambridge: Policy, 1997); Christine Sylvester, *Feminist International Relations: an unfinished journey* (Cambridge: Cambridge University Press, 2001).

7. J. Ann Tickner, *Gendering world politics: issues and approaches in the post-Cold War era* (New York: Columbia University Press, 2001), pp.1-2.

8. J. Ann Tickner, *Gender in International Relations: feminist perspectives on achieving global security* (New York: Columbia university Press, 1997).

9. Ibid.,no. 4, p. 43.

10. Broverman et al., *Sex-Role Stereotypes: A Current Appraisal* Although the original study was published in 1972, replication of this research in the 1980s confirmed that these perceptions still held in the United States, Journal of Social Issues, Wiley Online Library, April 1972.

11. Scott, n.4., p. 43.

12. As of 1986, a study showed that no major American international relations journal had published any articles that used gender as a category of analysis. Steuernagel and Quinn, "Is Anyone Listening?" Apart from a special issue of the *British international relations journal Millennium* (Winter 1988), 17(3), on women and international relations, very little attention has been paid to gender in any major international relations journal.

13. Lorraine Code. *"Encyclopedia of Feminist Theories"* (London; New York: Routledge, 2002), 273, Netlibrary/eBook Collection, accessed on November29, 2003.

14. Tickner, J. Ann. "A Feminist Critique of Political Realism"in *Women, Gender, and World Politics: Perspectives, Policies, and Prospects*, edited by Peter R. Beckman and Francine D'Amico. Westport, (New York: Palgrave1994).

15. Ibid.

16. Tickner, J. Ann. "International Relations: Post-Positivist and Feminist Perspectives," in *A New Handbook of Political Science*, edited by Robert E. Goodin and Hans-dieter Klingemann(New York: Oxford University Press, 1996).

17. Tickner, J. Ann. "Feminist Perspectives on International Relations," in *Handbook of International Relations*. (2002): pp.275-291.

18. J. Ann Tickner,*Gender in International Relations Feminist Perspectives on Achieving Global Security* (New York, Columbia University Press, 1992), p.3.

19. Ibid, p.65.

20. Ibid, p.138.

21. Ibid.

22. Ibid, p.58, p. 193.

23. Connell, n.3.

24. Tickner, n.7, p 432.

25. Ibid.

26. Tickner, (1988), *"Hans Morgenthau's principles of political realism: a feminist reformulation"*, *Millennium – Journal of International Studies*,(New York: Knopf)1988, pp.429-440.

27. Ibid.

28. Ibid.

29. Scott,n.4.

30. Ibid., p. 43.

31. n.10.

32. Scott, n.4, p. 43.

33. Eric M. Blanchard. *"Gender, International Relations, and the Development of Feminist Security Theory."* Signs v28, i4 (Summer 2003): 1289. Expanded Academic ASAP, Infotrac,accessed on November 15, 2003).

34. Lorraine Code. *Encyclopaedia of Feminist Theories.* (London; New York: Routledge, 2002), 273, Net library/eBook Collection, accessed on November29, 2003.

35. Ibid.

36. Tickner, n.18.

37. Tickner, "You just don't understand: Troubled engagements between Feminists and IR Theorists", *International Studies Quarterly*, 1997, 41, pp. 611-632.

38. Ibid., p. 629.

39. Ibid., p. 618.

40. Ibid.,p. 619.

41. Ibid,.p. 622.

42. Ibid,.p. 616.

43. Ibid., p. 617.

44. Lee, Yoke-Lian, *The Politics of Gender-A Survey"*, (New York: Routledge,2010) .

45. R.K. Dhawan, *"Feminism and Recent Indian Literature"*,(New Delhi:Prestige, 2008) p.9

46. 'http:/wikipedia.org/wiki/"radical feminism"accessed on June, 2008.

47. Phoca, S., Wright, R.,*Introducing post feminism*(Cambridge: Icon,1999), p. 11.

48. Dominelli, L.,*Anti-racist social work: A challenge for white practitioners and educators*(Basingstoke: MacMillan, 1988),p. 1.

49. Rowbotham, S.,*Woman's consciousness, man's world.* (Harmondsworth: Penguin, 1973).

50. Jane Freedman, *Feminism* (New Delhi: Viva Books Private Limited, 2002), p.4.

51. Millett, K.,*Sexual politics*(London: Virago, 1971).

52. Freeman, Jo. *"From Suffrage to Women's Liberation: Feminism in Twentieth Century America."* Women: A Feminist Perspective, no. 5 (1995):pp.509-528.

53. Gamble, S.,*The Routledge companion to feminism and post feminism*(London: Routledge, 2001).

54. Genz, S., Third Wave,.*Feminist Theory*, 2006, 7(3), 333-353.

55. Butler, Judith,*Gender trouble: feminism and the subversion of identity*(New York: Routledge, 2006).

56. Ruthsdotter, Mary. "Living the Legacy: The Women's Rights Movement." Legacy 98. 1997. http://www.legacy98.org/move-hist.html, accessed on 13th June, 1998.

57. Okin, Susan, *Justice, Gender and the Family*(New York: Basic Books, 1989).

58. Rawls, John, *Political Liberalism*(New York: Columbia University Press, 1993).

59. Alstott, Linda, *No Exit: What Parents Owe Their Children and What Society Owes Parents*(New York: Oxford University Press,2004); Bojer, Hilde 'Women and the Rawlsian Social Contract.' *Social Justice Research*(2002) 15 pp.393–407;Lloyd, S.A., 'Toward a Liberal Theory of Sexual Equality.' *Journal of Contemporary Legal Issues* 1988, 9,pp.203–224.McClain, Linda (2006). *The Place of Families: Fostering Capacity, Equality and Responsibility*. Cambridge: Harvard University Press.

60. RowBotham, S. *Woman's consciousness, man's world.* (Harmondsworth: Penguin, 1973)

61. Enloe, n.5.

62. Whelehan, I.,*Modern feminist thought: From the second wave to 'post-feminism'*(Edinburgh: Edinburgh University Press,1995); Roche, S. E., and Goldberg Wood, G., A narrative principle for feminist social work with survivors of male violence. *Affilia*,2005, 20(4), pp.465-475.

63. Gamble, S.n.53.

64. Millett, K.,n.51.

65. Featherstone, B.,*Where to for feminist social work?* Critical social work, 2001, 2(1).

66. Reynolds, J.,*Feminist theory and strategy in social work.* In J. Walmsley, Reynolds, J., Shakespeare, P., &Woolfe, R. (Eds). Health, welfare and practice (London: Sage, 1997).

67. Pease, B. Developing pro-feminist practice with men in social work. Critical Social Work, 2001,2(1), pp.1-8.

68. Phoca, n.47.

69. Ibid no. 63.

70. Agger, B.,*Critical social theories: An introduction. Boulder,*(Colorado: Westview Press, 1998);Phoca, n.47.

71. Ibid no. 63, p. 215.

72. Whelehan, I., *Modern feminist thought: From the second wave to 'post-feminism.*(Edinburgh: Edinburgh University Press, 1995),p. 61.

73. *"Recognition or redistribution?* A critical reading of Iris young's justice and the politics of difference", Nancy Fraser, *Journal of Political Philosophy*1995, 3 (2)pp.166–180.

74. Baines, D.,. *Feminist social work in the inner city: The challenges of race, class, and gender.*Affilia, 1997, 12(3), pp.297-317, Dominelli, L., Anti-*racist social work: A challenge for white practitioners and educators*(Basingstoke: MacMillan, 1988); Featherstone, B.,*Where to for feminist social work?* Critical social work, 2001,2(1).

75. Agger, B., Critical *social theories: An introduction. (Boulder, Colorado*: Westview Press, 1998), p.112.

76. Daly, M., & Lewis, J., The concept of social care and the analysis of contemporary welfare *Journal of Sociology*, 2003, 51(2), pp.281-298.

77. Ibid.

78. Kazuko Takemura, *Feminism* (in Japanese) (Tokyo: Iwanami Shoten, 2000), p.17.

79. Mary Evans, *Introducing Contemporary Feminist Thought* (Cambridge, UK: Polity Press, 1997), pp.20-21.

80. J.B. Elshtain, J.B. *Women and War* (New York, 1987), p41.

81. C. Sylvester, *Feminist Theory and International Relations in a Postmodern Era* (Cambridge, 1994a), p.102.

Global Shifts: Power, Governance and Processes

CHAPTER 11

Global Shifts: Power and Governance, Emerging Multi-Polarity (BRICS, EU, Japan, India, China and Russia)

Power can be defined as the ability to influence the outcome of events. In global politics this includes the ability of a country to conduct its own affairs, without the interference of other countries. The Realist school of international relations, represented by Hans Morgenthau, emphasised on military strength and preparedness as main calculations of national power. However the Liberal school led by scholars like Joseph Nye emphasise on soft power as the basis for growing interdependence and increasing cooperation between countries today. The distribution of powers between the states, and amongst states and other key actors giving rise to patters of relationship and behaviour, generally constitutes the "World Order". With the end of the cold war in 1991, the phrase "new world order" or "post-cold war world order" has gained currency in the literature and research work on international relations. While the cold war confrontation between the USA and the erstwhile USSR was termed "Bipolar Politics", the collapse of the Soviet Union led scholars to analyse the post-1991 world as "Unipolar", with America as the sole super power on the world stage. A structural power, in command and control of the most advanced economic and military resources, the US was hence regarded as the "Hegemony country". But the world has been a witness to numerous changessince 1991. During this period of more than two decades a number of upheavals have taken place in the world, numerous events of strategic importance have occurred, significant geo-economic centres have evolved and new norms of global conduct have emerged.

The relationship of major and rising powers are a central feature of international politics today. Far-reaching structural changes taking place at different parts of the world are affecting the distribution of wealth and power among nations, reflecting in the talk about 'rising' and 'emerging' powers, the prospects of an American decline, and a return to economic and political multi-polarity.[1] But what qualifies a state to be called as a major or rising power? What do rising powers want, and whatinfluence will they have on world order? What worldviews underpin the foreign policies of new and aspiring powers? And how will this affect the institutional structures of world order?[2] These are some significant but perplexing questions being raised today. In the first decade of the new millennium, the international system embarked on a grand process of transformation from the short-lived and unipolar post-Cold War regime to an unprecedented and heterogeneous configuration of international relationships and a global political economy. This significant transition is perceived to emerge from a multifaceted shift from Western political, economic, and cultural predominance to a more diverse and sophisticated system in which emerging/resurgent powers increasingly assert their respective interests, distinctive values and worldviews. The wider redistribution of political and economic power as well as deepening interdependence among the established and new actors, are the fundamental ingredients of the emerging global order which render issues of global governance increasingly vital.[3] On the side of the global political economy, the main driving forces of the emerging order have been the accelerated trends of global integration through transnational production networks, and strenuous flows of trade, finance, information and services. Mature industrial economies, conceptualised through the widespread notion of the 'Triad' – made up of the U.S., Western Europe and Japan – have become increasingly integrated and interdependent with several groups of emerging economic powers, led by China, India and Brazil, over the course of this transformation[4].In the emerging system of multi-polarity, major players such as China and Russia are cautiously using their economic influence over Western politico-economic interests as a diplomatic tool to accelerate the transformation of global governance structures toward a more balanced *status quo*. The major revisionist bloc in the world economy includes China, Russia, India, Brazil and South Africa (BRICS)[5]. As the transformation of the modern global political economy has been predominantly driven by the emergence of rapidly growing economic actors, it is becoming necessary to construct a new paradigm that reflects the complexity of this new order. The diffusion of economic power resources progresses along with global economic integration and widening channels of finance, trade, information and services and thereby offering opportunities for further empowerment of newly emerging powers. Due to this diffusion of power, formerly hegemonic actors in the global political economy are increasingly facing diminished ability to effectively shape and influence the preferences of other actors. Therefore, exerting leadership on issues of general concern and matters of global governance has become more difficult and requires search of intensive multilateral consensus-seeking.

Multipolarity and Multilateralism

Multipolarity is a system of power distribution in which several countries have very substantial influence.

Our deepest challenge," US National Security Advisor Henry Kissinger wrote in 1969, will be "to base order on political multipolarity even though overwhelming military strength will remain with the two superpowers."

"Global politics," Samuel Huntington argued after the Soviet Union ceased to exist, "is now passing through one or two uni-multipolar decades before it enters a truly multipolar order by 21st century."

US Secretary of State **Hillary Clinton** said in 2009 that, "We will lead by inducing greater cooperation among a greater number of actors and reducing competition, tilting the balance away from a multipolar world and toward a multi partner world."

Multilateralism happens when several countries start working together. Inevitably, the more powerful countries wield greater influence, but the vision adopted is of countries seeking win-win solutions, and not playing zero sum games, which is implicit in a multipolar system. The basis of multilateralism is interdependence. Multilateralism supposes the existence of institutions to facilitate this and set of principles and norms. Example: WTO.

The emergence of truly global problems such as climate change, proliferation of weapons of mass destruction and many others have indeed led to an increasing paradox of governance.

As such the building blocks of multilateralism, the states, seem to be less and less capable of dealing with the challenges of globalisation. The new paradigm is one of collaboration between governments at different levels (including sub-national governments) and between governments with all other relevant actors in society.

Source: https://crossick.blogactiv.eu/2010/05/22/multpolarity-vs-multilateralism/,accessed on May,10,2016.

With its foundation being threatened the post Second World War order seems to be under relentless pressure, with its foundation being threatened. Analysts of this contemporary world order tend to fall into two camps. While scholars like Samuel Huntington have talked about the inevitability of clashing of autonomous entities, Robert Kaplan announced a "coming anarchy" of ethnic conflict and crime, Richard Barnett and John Cavanagh have suggested a future dominated by global corporations in which states are of declining importance, while James

Rosenau has talked about a sense of insecurities in a "turbulent world". On the other end of the spectrum are those who see a "less turbulent future". John Ikenberry is of the opinion that the liberal democratic order is here to stay and that capitalist democracies with their rules, institution and networks provide easy avenues for any new comers to join and accommodate. Where both these view point converge is the fact that presently the United States holds all the commanding (power) variables still in its hands and is still holding together the multi-lateral world order together. One major theme cutting across all these views is the analysis relating to the rise of China, and its potential to challenge the US hegemony, making the US a "hegemony country"

Declining Hegemony and Power Transition

Situating the US and China
International systems in transition are predictably defined by competition among the established and emerging powers.[6] Late comers, whose international prestige lags behind their newly augmented and still improving actual power, typically seek to extend their control and influence over more territory, other states, the world economy, and the set of rules and rights that govern interactions among states (e.g., international norms and regimes, the nature of diplomacy, and property rights on a global scale). This is the classic story of hegemonic war and international change[7]. Periods of crisis have been common in history; some have been resolved peacefully, others have not. It is likely that many factors explain why some shifts in power lead to bloody contests over global norms while others don't. One important reason, is how the established powers respond to the demands of emerging powers.[8]

The crisis can only be resolved peacefully if and when there is recognition and general consent among the established powers of the irrevocable breakdown of the specific conditions that made the prior order possible. That is to say, whether a late comer decides to challenge the order is not simply a matter of its innate character or identity. What the established countries agree to do or not to do also has a measurable effect on the decisions of late comers to promote a disruptive agenda of change or support revisions within the established order. The current trend of "global power diffusion" has witnessed traditionally poor states experiencing historically unprecedented surges of upward mobility. Quite naturally, they seek greater representation and voice at international bargaining tables commensurate with their new found power; they talk about making the international system more democratic, about the evils of one state dominating global affairs, and about the benefits of multipolarity.

The main thrust of the Power Transition Theory is the emergence of a rising challenger one dissatisfied not only with its place in the established order but with the legitimacy of the order itself. The insatiable revisionism of the rising challenger triggers persistent crises that eventually ignite a hegemonic war. It is not obvious, why the emerging power or powers would seek to spoil the established order and why they would choose an enormously costly global war of uncertain outcome to overthrow an order that has demonstrably worked for them, only to replace it with an untested one that they (and no one else) must pay the costs to start up and manage. What are they so dissatisfied about that they are willing to risk all the gains that they have made to this point and will make in the future? The answer given by the theory is that an ever widening disjuncture between actual power and prestige causes rising powers to become increasingly dissatisfied with the *status quo* order. As a counter to this idea there are arguments about rising powers, who may not be "dissatisfied", who may be" "benefitting" from the existing rules of economic governance and who may not be interested in "toppling the hegemony country ".

Dismissing the idea of a clash between USA and China, David Shambaugh writes, "most rising powers are not complete powers but rather, "partial powers." They simply do not have the full complement of power capabilities (both hard and soft power) needed to mount a serious global challenge to the existing hegemon. As transitioning countries, rising powers typically do not have a fixed identity especially one with universal appeal. Thus, China's reach, while undeniably global, is almost universally shallow as can be seen from the following actions. Despite being a member of every major IGO, China neither seeks nor accepts leadership in any major international project. Its foreign policy is truculent, reactionary, and driven almost exclusively by domestic politics. Its non resource related economic activities abroad are very limited and have mostly foundered. Its *'sui generis'* culture is a mystery to outsiders and the Communist Party's attempts to explain it to the world have been almost insurmountably inept.It is true that it has hard but no soft power. It commands powerful awe but no deep admiration. It has plentiful of collaborators but no true friends. Indeed, China's diplomatic relations everywhere in the world are mixed and currently deteriorating. More recently, political scientist G. John Ikenberry has insisted that the Western liberal world order laid down in 1945, and which emerged victorious during the Cold War era, is here to stay. This "Liberal Leviathan" has powerful advantages: First, capitalist democracies still hold a majority of global power. Second, today's "sprawling landscape of rules, institutions and networks" easily accommodate newcomers, making it both "easy to join and hard to overturn." Third, rising powers will never align into a cohesive, counter-hegemonic bloc, given their distinct histories, identities, and interests. Finally, all major powers, rising and established alike, have a *status quo* orientation. Far from revolutionary, emerging powers are only mildly revisionist: they seek not to overhaul existing regimes, but to attain greater voice and weight within them.

There are numerous interpretations of the distribution of power in the post-cold war world order, but for a group of scholars the principal narrative currently revolves around the US–Chinese relationship. This simplistic perspective does not sufficiently take into consideration other regional actors such as Japan and India, new instruments of leverage in the world in the form of the non-state actors, new powerhouses like the BRICS, new regional groupings like the EU, or the extent and complexity of changing relationships across the globe. In oversimplifying the situation, some scholars and observers in the Asia-Pacific countries and the United States risk narrowing the aperture through which they evaluate policy choices regarding regional challenges. At the same time, the bipolar perspective, potentially invoking Cold War-type mentalities, could exacerbate tensions rather than relieve them. Seeing US–Chinese competition as the main variable in the region could become a self-fulfilling prophecy. While the trajectory of the rising powers is uncertain, their present influence is now a fact of geopolitics. That raises questions about the relationship between U.S. power and the changing international order. Already the problems of the financial crisis, the Copenhagen climate negotiations and the sanctions against Iran have illustrated the potential, the pitfalls, and above all the centrality of the relationship between American power and the influence of the rising actors. The emerging powers cannot dictate the shape of the coming era, but they can block and complicate U.S. initiative. Nearly a decade ago, Joseph Nye identified "the paradox of American power." While the United States has unique military strength, it is constrained by the dynamics of the global economy and the need for international institutions to manage an interdependent world. Today, after two wars and an economic crisis that have tested the limits of American power, American leadership is far from overturned, but it is constrained. The question is thus posed: can the United States still lead the international system? Will the rising actors acquiesce to U.S. leadership and cooperate with it? Or are they contending to challenge if not the system itself—from which they profit—but the U.S. leadership of it? An overarching picture which emerges is that America's dominance has diminished but its influence is sustained. From its new position, the United States confronts not a rigid bloc of emerging powers, but a complex and shifting coalitions of various interests. The greatest risk to U.S. lies not in a single peer competitor but in the erosion of systems and institutions vital to U.S. interests and a stable order. U.S. power is indispensable for the international order, but not sufficient.[9]Expanding the horizons of analysis, but not at the same time ignoring the fact of China's rise, one can locate five major approaches[10] to understand the contemporary world order:

- **The rise of China:** This presumes that the rise of China has been the main reason for change in the world. This view take into account the competition between the United States and China that is likely to become more virulent as the latter continues to rise.
- **Global flux:** This argues that the main shifts in power distribution are between the developed West and the emerging economies (particularly those in the Asia-Pacific).
- **Power diffusion:** This suggests that regional changes are fostering multiple centres of power in the Asia-Pacific, with none dominant.
- **Asia for the Asians:** This describes an Asia that is defined and managed within the region, with little role for outsiders, including the United States.
- **Norms and values-based polarity:** This presumes that regional dynamics are led by partnerships based on common values.

Emerging Multipolarity

The New Power Centres

Multilateral relations between states are not a game where all players have equal rights and duties. There are also differences in power equations between states. Examination of multilateralism cannot be done without referring to the world order and understanding the way international relations are organised in terms of power. The world order, sometimes also called 'international order' has been defined by as 'a pattern of activity that sustains the elementary or primary goals of the society of states, or international society'. Within this framework one can picture 'poles' (sometimes also labelled as 'powers') as states endowed with the resources, political will and institutional ability to project their interests at the global level. Since 2001 there are numerous signs and developments that testify that the unipolar moment of the US has come to an end. This does not necessarily implies a weakening of the US. As noted by Fareed Zakaria, the current shift to multipolarity can be seen as largely due to 'the rise of the rest': the unprecedented economic growth over the past decades in countries all over the world. Others speak of a 'non-polar' world: "a world dominated not by one or two or several states but rather by dozens of actors" possessing and exercising various kinds of power. The Economists even mention the birth of a 'neo-polar' world. While it is certainly true that the position of the US has weakened in recent years, this does not mean however that we can now picture the world order as one where several (super) powers compete with each other for dominance. Reality is that there is still only one state with a global predominance, the US. The other poles are (still?) more regional than global (Brazil, India, China and Russia). When we look at today's power transitions, two things stand out. The first is the sheer number of emerging powers. Never before have we seen the simultaneous rise of multiple regional (and potentially even global) powers—led by China, of course, but also including India, Brazil, and—though smaller in economic size and political clout—South Korea, Turkey, Mexico, Indonesia, and South Africa. Building the world order is more complicated today, owing to an ongoing diffusion of global power, diversity on issues among major players, and the sheer complexity of the international agenda. The new world order promises to be the product of ongoing negotiations and compromise among established Western and rising non-Western powers, as to how best to reform old and create new institutions—and how to allocate burdens and privileges within them. What follows, is a detailed analysis of the emerging power centres in the world today.

BRICS

Transforming Global Economy
The BRICS acronym, a concept floated for the first time in 2001, represents the loose grouping of Brazil, Russia, India and China. The idea was coined by economist Jim O'Neill of Goldman Sachs in a paper as part of an economic modelling exercise to forecast global economic trends over the next half-century. The main finding was that the BRICS would play an increasingly important role in the global economy. Taking forward this main finding, another paper by Goldman Sachs prepared in 2003 described the evolving dynamics of the world economy over the next 50 years. The findings of the paper were startling and perhaps unexpected for the larger global community. It was predicted that over the next 50 years, the BRICS economies could become a major force in the world economy. In less than 40 years, the BRICS economies taken together could be larger than that of the Group of Six (G-6) in US dollar terms. By 2025 their size could be over half the size of the G-6. The study also predicted that by 2050, only the US and Japan of the current industrialised countries could remain among the six-largest economies in US dollar terms. The emerging dynamics over the last decade tend to support the predictions. Starting with a share of a little over 10 percent in world gross domestic product (GDP) and less than 4 percent in world trade in 1990,

BRICS (with the recent inclusion of South Africa to the forum) now constitutes about 23.6 percent of world GDP and 15 percent of world trade.

Share of World GDP, 2013

Share of World GDP by G-7 and BRICS, 2013

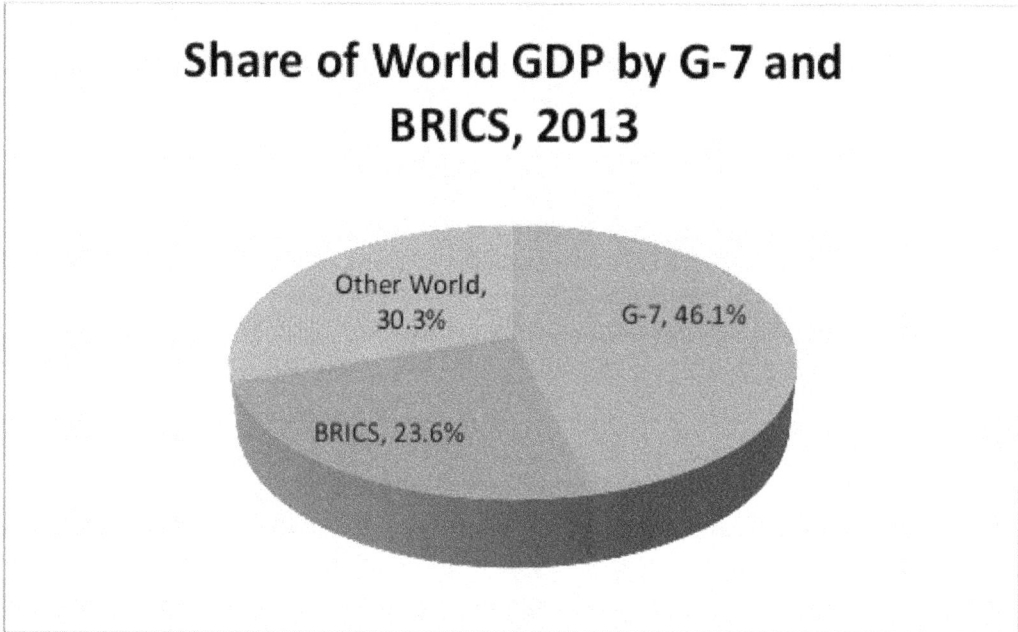

Source: World Bank, January 2015

The increase in GDP implies that the economic size of BRICS in terms of its share in world GDP has expanded by 150percent in the past two decades. In addition, all the BRICS countries are now members of major international and multilateral institutions, such as the World Trade Organisation, the UN,the Group of 20 (G-20) and the UN Framework Convention on Climate Change, and are very active participants in those organisations. There are various other indicators, such as trends in inflows and outflows of foreign direct investment, opening of trade and removal of trade barriers, current account balance, forex reserves and economically active labour forces that could make BRICS a formidable forceto reckon with in future.

BRICS is the acronym for an association of **five major emerging national economies**:

Brazil	Russia	India	China	South Africa

B R I C S

History:

➤ Originally BRIC before inclusion of South Africa in 2010
➤ BRIC was coined by Jim O Neill, then chairman of Goldman Sachs in 2001.
➤ Foreign ministers of BRIC met in Sept, 2006 beginning a series of high level meetings, followed by a full scale diplomatic meeting in June, 2009
➤ In 2010, South Africa began efforts to join BRIC and the group was then renamed as BRICS.

For the next few years after the term was coined (2001–06), the idea of an institutionalised BRICs was floated but there was no specific move to formalise the group. The BRIC countries gaining strength through their economic reform processes, buoyed by a newly emerging confidence, reached a few milestones during 2001–08. Some of the most important milestones achieved by these nations during this period include China joining the World Trade Organisation (WTO) (2001) and opening up a process of modernisation of its industries and services (2001), Brazil kick-starting a period of unprecedented economic prosperity (2003),China overtaking Germany as the third-largest economy (2007), and Brazil joining China and the Persian Gulf states by becoming a global creditor for the first time, as well as introducing a sovereign wealth fund to invest excess capital (2008).As far as formalisation of the group is concerned, a first move in this direction was made in September 2006 when the first meeting of the BRIC Foreign Ministers took place, as a side event to the 61st UN General Assembly in New York. This was followed by several other meetings. At the third meeting of Foreign Ministers, it was decided to boost co-operation between the four countries on several fronts in various ways. The broad objective was the building of a more democratic international system founded on the rule of law and multilateral diplomacy. The BRIC countries also resolved to work together and with other countries in order to strengthen international security and stability.

An Engine of Growth

In 2006, the four countries initiated a regular informal diplomatic coordination, with annual meetings of Foreign Ministers on the General Debate of the UN General Assembly. This successful interaction led to the decision that the dialogue has to be carried out at the level of Heads of State and at Government level every year. In the First Summit, held in Yekaterinburg in 2009, the depth and scope of the dialogue among the Members of BRICs – which became BRICS in 2011 with the inclusion of South Africa – was further enhanced. More than an acronym that identified countries emerging in the international economic order, BRICS became a new and promising political-diplomatic entity, far beyond the original concept tailored for the financial markets.

After the Yekaterinburg Summit, five annual Summits were held (Brasilia, 2010; Sanya, 2011; New Delhi, 2012; Durban, 2013; and Fortaleza, 2014 and Russia, 2015). During this period, BRICS has evolved progressively strengthening its two main pillars: (i) coordination in multilateral fora, with a focus on economic and political governance; and (ii) cooperation between members. The efforts towards reforming the structures of global governance, especially in the economic and financial fields – G-20, International Monetary Fund, World Bank – have been receiving special emphasis over the years, along with the reforms of political institutions, such as the United Nations. Intra-BRICS cooperation has also been gaining strength and a broad agenda has been developed, comprising areas such as finance, agriculture, economy and trade, combating transnational crime, science and technology, health, education, corporate and academic dialogue and security, among others. [11]The fifth BRICS Summit was held in Durban on March 27, 2013 with the theme: "BRICS and Africa: Partnership for Development, Integration and Industrialisation.," It completed the first cycle of BRICS Summits and it was for the first time that the Summit was hosted in the African continent. The BRICS Leaders agreed for the establishment of a New Development Bank and indicated that the initial capital contribution to the bank should be substantial and sufficient for the bank to be effective in financing infrastructure. In addition, the Leaders also agreed on the establishment of the Contingent Reserve Arrangement (CRA) with an initial size of US$100 billion. The CRA would help BRICS countries forestall short-term liquidity pressures and further strengthen financial stability. It would also contribute to strengthening the global financial safety net and complement existing international arrangements as an additional line of defence.

BRICS INITIATIVES: NDB AND CRA

- The BRICS proposals establish two separate institutions, the *Contingency Reserve Arrangement* (CRA) and the *New Development Bank* (NDB)
- The CRA is a virtual institution whereas the NDB will be an institution that will be established
- The NDB will have its headquarters in Shanghai and a regional office in Johannesburg
- What is the context of these proposals?
  - Major gap in development finance to fund long-term infrastructure and sustainable development
  - The departure by US from expansionary fiscal policy led to large outflows from emerging economies and significant decline in exchange rates
  - This experience indicated potential vulnerability of emerging economies to shocks emanating from developed countries

Another outcome of the Summit was the establishment of the BRICS "Think Tanks Council" and the BRICS "Business Council". The BRICS "Think Tanks Council" will link respective Think Tanks into a network to develop policy options such as the evaluation and future long-term strategy for BRICS. The BRICS "Business Council" will bring together business associations from each of the BRICS countries and help the engagement between the business communities on an on-going basis. These two new BRICS structures that were initiated under the South African chairpersonship, will strengthen intra-BRICS cooperation to develop new paradigms for sustainable and inclusive growth models, as well as new learning and knowledge paradigms to deal with our contemporary growth and development challenges. Two Agreements were concluded under auspices of the BRICS Interbank Cooperation Mechanism. The BRICS Multilateral Infrastructure Co-Financing Agreement for Africa paves the way for the establishment of co-financing arrangements for infrastructure projects across the African continent. The BRICS Multilateral Cooperation and Co-Financing Agreement for Sustainable Development sets out to explore the establishment of bilateral agreements aimed at establishing cooperation and co-financing arrangements, specifically around sustainable development and green economy. The outcome of the Summit known as the eThekwini Declaration and Action Plan were adopted at the conclusion of the Summit.

The establishment of the Bank and the CRA conveyed a strong message on the willingness of BRICS members to deepen and consolidate their partnership in the economic-financial area. New Development Bank (NDB) will have a President (an Indian for the first six years), a Board of Governors Chair (a Russian), a Board of Directors Chair (a Brazilian), and a headquarters (in Shanghai). The NDB has been allocated US$50 billion as initial capital. As with similar initiatives in other regions, the BRICS bank appears to work on an equal-share voting basis, with each of the five signatories contributing US$10 billion. The capital base is to be used to finance infrastructure and "sustainable development" projects in BRICS countries initially, but other low and middle income countries will be able to join and apply for funding. BRICS countries have also created a US$100 billion Contingency Reserve Arrangement (CRA), meant to provide additional liquidity protection to member countries when faced with balance of payments problems. The CRA—unlike the pool of contributed capital to the BRICS bank, which is equally shared—is being funded 41 percent by China, 18 percent from Brazil, India, and Russia, and 5 percent from South Africa. Long-standing dissatisfaction with Bretton-Woods institutions has pushed BRICS towards creation of a developing-country alternative to global development finance. Developing nations hope that BRICS bank/CRA may eventually challenge World Bank-IMF hegemony over matters such as: funding for basic services, emergency assistance, policy lending, and funding to conflict-affected states. The World Bank's own estimates point to a US$1 trillion infrastructure investment "gap" in developing countries. Existing multilateral development banks are able to fill approximately 40 percent of that gap. So, the fact that a BRICS bank aims to make electricity, transport, telecommunications, and water/sewage a priority is important. The demand for funds for infrastructure development is expected to grow sharply as more countries are trying to move out from low-income status. In terms of scale, it has been suggested that—after a couple of decades, should membership be expanded, and should co-financing by governments and private investors be mobilised—the quantum of loans from BRICS Bank could surpass that of World Bank.

The Fortaleza Summit launched a new phase for the BRICS. The focus of that meeting was social inclusion and sustainable development. It gave visibility to policies implemented by member countries, and to the contribution of the BRICS towards economic growth and reduction in poverty. The theme "inclusive growth, sustainable solutions" is not only in line with the social policies of member countries, but also highlights the need to tackle challenges in the social, economic and environmental fields, and create new opportunities for the BRICS in different areas, including the negotiations on the post-2015 development agenda.

The BRICS

Problems and Prospects

Liberal scholarship has focused on international regimes defined as the principles, norms, rules, and decision-making procedures around which expectations of actors converge in a given issue or area. According to this,stand taken by states on issues such as the World Trade Regime or the climate regime, matter in global governance because they affect the behaviour of the states. The conventional belief is that states create regimes which are expected to improve their welfare. Determined to end the hegemony of rich Western nations in shaping Global economic policies, two agreements- the major agreement on extending credit facilities in local currencies and, BRICS multilateral letter of credit confirmation facility agreement was signed- by the Development Banks from BRICS countries. Such intra-BRICS initiatives are being perceived as a step towards replacing the dollar as the main unit of trade between BRICS countries. According to officials this will not only contribute to enhanced trade and investment among the BRICS countries but would also facilitate economic growth in difficult economic times. In this context it is no surprise that the rise of the BRICS has had a marked impact on international affairs and global governance. Nowhere is this clearer than with the rise of G20 (grouping of developing nations) which by including the BRICS has superseded the G8 as the premier forum on international economic cooperation and increasingly on non-economic issues as well. On the other hand rising power of the BRICS has been viewed as a challenge to the existing international order and a fundamental threat to the west. The move by the BRICS to challenge the power of the US dollar and push for a more diversified reserved currency, is a case in point.

BRICS – SWOT ANALYSIS

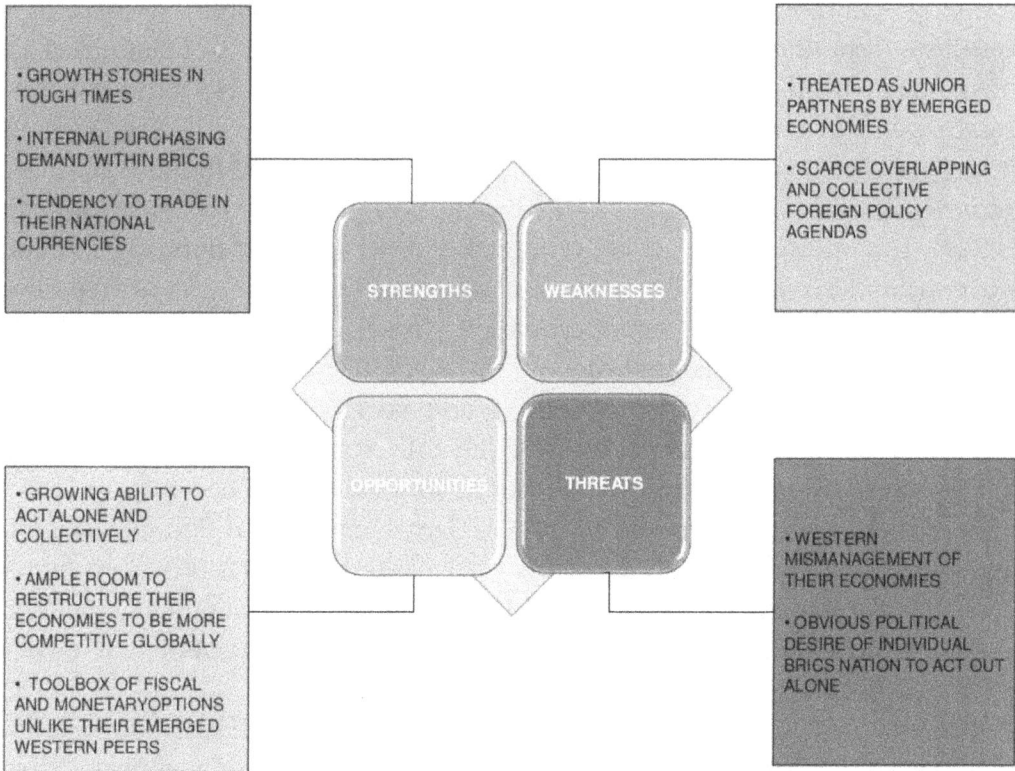

• GROWTH STORIES IN TOUGH TIMES

• INTERNAL PURCHASING DEMAND WITHIN BRICS

• TENDENCY TO TRADE IN THEIR NATIONAL CURRENCIES

• TREATED AS JUNIOR PARTNERS BY EMERGED ECONOMIES

• SCARCE OVERLAPPING AND COLLECTIVE FOREIGN POLICY AGENDAS

STRENGTHS

WEAKNESSES

OPPORTUNITIES

THREATS

• GROWING ABILITY TO ACT ALONE AND COLLECTIVELY

• AMPLE ROOM TO RESTRUCTURE THEIR ECONOMIES TO BE MORE COMPETITIVE GLOBALLY

• TOOLBOX OF FISCAL AND MONETARYOPTIONS UNLIKE THEIR EMERGED WESTERN PEERS

• WESTERN MISMANAGEMENT OF THEIR ECONOMIES

• OBVIOUS POLITICAL DESIRE OF INDIVIDUAL BRICS NATION TO ACT OUT ALONE

Source: http://www.slideshare.net/IamSwatiTyagi/brics-monetarypolicypresentation,accessed on June 8,2016.

The critics tend to highlight the limits of BRICS cooperation and coordination, by highlighting the political and economic differences and historical distrust within the grouping. The political differences are most glaring, because whereas Brazil and India are two of the largest democracies in the world, there are autocracies like Russia and China. Likewise China's economic power is such that its economy is larger than those of the other BRICS members combined. Their trading interest and preferences also diverge. Russia and Brazil are commodity exporters while China is a commodity importer. Historical distrust and foreign policy tensions especially within Asia also raises significant question about the capacity of the grouping as a coordinated coalition.[12] As liberals would argue, states will only form a grouping and establish or reform institutions if they see utility in doing so. It is true that the group does not fit into the conventional definition of a regional(i.e. EU) or international organisation (i.e. OPEC), and that the still-hesitant attitude of group members to determine common political positions on major international issues prevails. However, this unorthodox grouping of emerging economic powers is created on the basis of certain features which constitute a common denominator among member states: BRICS countries are substantial in terms of their populations and dominate their respective regions – and the globe for some– in terms of vast demographic potential. When combined, these countries constitute the largest economic bloc outside the industrialised countries in the Organisation of Economic Cooperation and Development (OECD) with impressive figures of economic growth and large domestic markets with considerable capacity for expansion. Yet, at the same time, they are regarded as developing countries in international comparisons, due to their substantial developmental needs, regional income disparities, informal economic sectors and poverty alleviation necessities. When it comes to their principal geo-strategic alignments and security constellations, the BRICS group comprises countries that generally adopt autonomous positions and stay distanced from politico-military frameworks considered to be NATO-type or Western dominated while also avoiding special security relations with Western powers. BRICS countries seem convinced that pushing implicitly toward a multipolar global political economy and inter-state system through 'soft actions' would better serve their fundamental long-term interests.[13]

However, in spite of these similarities some observers still maintain that the BRICS group lacks internal coherence and that the notion of BRICS as an analytical set is a 'mirage' enforced superficially for specific political agendas. They point out that BRICS countries are dissimilar national units with radically different political/geo-strategic interests and that these countries do not constitute a natural trading bloc. In fact, a careful evaluation of the individual BRICS members would reveal radical differences in terms of domestic political structures, economic capacities, regional environments and links to major global powers, while each taking advantage of the benefits of global economic integration and striving to accelerate the evolution of the global political economy toward a multipolar configuration. In this context, BRICSis generally cited as one of the main institutional instruments employed by the Beijing administration to spearhead a multi-pronged strategy of instigating transformations in the global order without directly challenging the U.S. Vladimir Putin, is trying to command a prevalent role on the world stage by supplementing their diminished military/geo-strategic capacity inherited from the Cold War era with the economic, technological and demographic potential of China. Russia's diplomacy toward the institutionalisation of the BRICS and the development of a widespread awareness within the global public opinion concerning the idea of a multipolar global economic and increasingly, political order could be considered one of Moscow's most successful international initiatives in recent decades. It earned BRICS major status in global platforms of economic diplomacy – such as the G-20 and the WTO – by stubbornly defending the interests of the global South. The vibrant interest shown by India's political establishment in the BRICS initiative should be interpreted in this wider context of seeking a more effective and honourable position in the evolving international system by becoming one of the major global representatives of the developing world.[14]However, as opposed to their Russian and Chinese counterparts, the mainstream political elites in India are extremely reluctant to place their diplomatic pro-activism on an anti-American ideological footing. This is also true of Brazil, as Brazil carefully avoids raising anti-western foreign policy stance. Both the size and dynamism of its economic structure are not comparable to other BRICS members. Its industrial infrastructure and entrepreneurial environment are fragile and economic growth is lack lustre. There are increasing grounds for scepticism about the quality of economic management architecture. There have been various question marks surrounding the material basis of South Africa's BRICS membership in view of structural barriers to sustainable growth stemming from social, political and economic fields.

Irrespective of some visible differences, it is however clear that the BRICS countries will become an increasingly significant group in the coming years. Their emergence might require the establishment of a new world economic and political order and might lead to enhanced engagement with other groups such as the Organisation for Economic Co-operation and Development (OECD) for advancing mutually beneficial discussions. This will also be needed for improving economic environments and to ensure a global level playing field for business. Because of their economic importance, the BRICS countries could be the main focus of the OECD. This could be achieved, economists believe, by working together, and carving out the future economic order. At the sectoral level, it is being argued that whereas China will dominate in manufactured goods, India will control services, and Russia and Brazil supplies of raw materials. South Africa, on the other hand, could emerge as a very important supplier of minerals within and outside BRICS. With a view to occupying controlling positions of the world economy,the BRICS need to stabilise the international environment and prevent encirclement. It has to exchange ideas and experiences. It should coordinate common positions and improve their bargaining positions with Western countries. It has to help other developing countries and strengthen their identity as developing countries. It has to restrain American hegemony and revisionism and minimise dependence on the U.S. by exploring other options.

The European Union (EU)

Since the 1990s, the European Union (EU) presents itself as a leading actor in international trade and climate change negotiations. According to the homepage of the Trade General Directorate (Commission 2005), the Union is 'one of the key players in the World Trade Organisation … and is one of the driving forces behind the current round of multilateral trade negotiations'. In the current post-Kyoto climate negotiations, it is portrayed as 'leading global action to 2020 and beyond' (Commission 2009) and as having 'been at the forefront of efforts to combat climate change' (Commission 2008). The description of the EU as a key actor with leadership capabilities has been widely echoed by scholars. In the emerging new complex world order as exemplified by the Doha Round trade negotiations and the post-Kyoto negotiations in Copenhagen, roles of traditional great power are obviously challenged. In multilateral negotiations concerning issues of global interdependence, the role of military might now minimal. It is true that in the overall dynamics of the altered power relations of a new world order, the EU might face a number of strategic challenges in the years to come. Probing the possibility of a more or less encompassing transatlantic alliance in key areas would be one potential avenue for success.[15]

Formation, Structures and Policies

The European Union (EU) is an economic and political federation consisting of twenty-seven member countries that make common policy in several areas. The EU was created in 1993 with the signing of the Treaty on European Union, commonly referred to as the Maastricht Treaty, but it was preceded by various European organisations that contributed to the development of the EU. The EU represents the latest and most successful in a series of efforts to unify Europe, including many attempts to achieve unity through force of arms. It makes its own policies concerning the area of economies, societies, laws and to some extent security of member states. The EU is considered as the best way to meet challenges smaller nations might face – such as sustaining economic growth or negotiations with larger nations and they consider it is worth surrendering some sovereignty to achieve these objectives. The end of the Second World War left Europe divided between the Communist, Soviet dominated, Eastern Bloc, and the largely democratic Western nations. There were fears as to what direction a rebuilt Germany would take, and in the western thoughts of a federal European Union re-emerged, hoping to bind Germany into pan-European democratic institutions to the extent that it, and any other allied European nation, both wouldn't be able to start a new war, and would resist the expansion of the Communist east. Efforts began to forge a political union through increasing economic interdependence. In 1951 the European Coal and Steel Community (ECSC) was formed to coordinate the production and trading of coal and steel within Europe. In 1957 the member states of the ECSC ratified two treaties creating the European Atomic Energy Community (EURATOM) for the collaborative development of commercial nuclear power and the European Economic Community (EEC), an international trade body whose role was to gradually eliminate national tariffs and other barriers to international trade involving member countries. Initially the EEC, or, as it was more frequently referred to at that time, the Common Market, for the institution of a common external tariff among its members for a period of twelve- to fifteen-years., The timetable was accelerated and a common tariff was instituted in 1967. Despite this initial success, participation in the EEC was limited to Belgium, France, Germany, Italy, Luxembourg, and the Netherlands. Immediately following the creation of the EEC a rival trade confederation known as the European Free Trade Association (EFTA) was created by Austria, Britain, Denmark, Finland, Norway, Portugal, Sweden, and Switzerland. Although its goals were less comprehensive than those of the EEC, the existence of the EFTA delayed European economic and political unity.[16]

By 1961 the United Kingdom indicated its willingness to join the Common Market if allowed to retain certain tariff structures which favoured trade between Britain and its Commonwealth. Negotiations between the EEC and the United Kingdom began, but as insurmountable differences arose and Britain was denied access to the Common Market in 1963. Following this setback, however, the Common Market countries worked to strengthen the ties between themselves, culminating in the merger of the ECSC, EEC, and Euratom to form the European Community (EC) in 1967. In the meanwhile the importance of the Commonwealth to the British economy waned considerably and by 1973 Britain, Denmark, and the Republic of Ireland had joined the EC. Greece followed suit in 1981, followed by Portugal and Spain in 1986 and Austria, Finland, and Sweden in 1995. Like the ECSC, the EEC created several supranational bodiessuch as a Council of Ministers to make decisions, a Common Assembly (called the European Parliament from 1962) to give advice, a court which could overrule member states and a commission to put the policy into effect. The Brussels Treaty 1965 merged the commissions of the EEC, ECSC and Euratom to create a joint and permanent civil service. The EC took its largest step to date toward true economic integration among its members with the 1992 ratification of the Maastricht Treaty, after which the EC changed its name to the European Union (EU). Following the advent of the European Union (EU) in 1993, the treaty that had established the EEC remained one of the EU's core documents, though the EEC itself was renamed the European Community (EC). EC was formally eliminated with the signing of the Lisbon Treaty in 2009 and the Treaty of Rome that had established EU was formally renamed the Treaty on the Functioning of the European Union.

Even as it expanded, the EC worked to strengthen the economic integration of its membership, establishing a European Monetary System (EMS) featuring the European Currency Unit (ECU, later known as the Euro) in 1979. The EC then passed the Single European Act, which strengthened the EC's ability to regulate the economic, social, and foreign policies of its members, in 1987. One of the goals of the EU is economic integration and a common European currency. EU leaders expect great benefits from the adoption of a single currency. International trade with a single currency will be greatly facilitated by the establishment of what amounts to a single market, complete with uniform pricing and regulation, substituting separate national markets. The creation of a single market is also expected to spur increased competition and the development of more niche products and ease the acquisition of corporate financing, particularly in what would formerly have been international trade among members of the single currency area. The creation of a single European economic area based on a common market was the fundamental objective of the Treaty of Rome. Article 2 of that Treaty set out that objective as follows: "The Community shall have as its task, by establishing a common market and progressively approximating the economic policies of member states, to promote throughout the Community a harmonious development of economic activities, a continuous and balanced expansion, an increase in stability, an accelerated raising of the standard of living and closer relations between the States belonging to it". It is obvious that the common market was not an end in itself, but a means to achieve economic and political goals.

It took nearly a quarter of a century after the removal of customs duties and quantitative restrictions between member states to complete *in tandem* customs union and common market. However delayed, the achievement of a single market is a great step forward in the process of European integration. To create this single market, hundreds of technical, legal and bureaucratic barriers to free trade and free movement between the EU's member countries have been abolished. As a result, companies have expanded their operations. The competition has brought prices down and given consumers more choice: Phone calls in Europe cost a fraction of what they did 10 years ago and air fares have fallen significantly and new routes have opened up. Many homes and businesses can now choose their electricity and gas suppliers.

At the same time, with the help of Europe's various competition and regulatory authorities, the EU works to ensure that these greater freedoms don't undermine fairness, consumer protection or environmental sustainability. European businesses in the EU have unrestricted access to nearly 500 million consumers, helping them to stay competitive. The single market is also attractive to foreign investors. Economic integration can also be a great advantage in times of recession, allowing EU countries to continue trading with one another, rather than resorting to protectionist measures that would worsen the crisis. Free movement reduces the manufacturing and transport costs of goods, facilitates exports and the realisation of potential of important economies. The reduction of administrative and financial costs of intra-European trade and the realisation of potential of economies of this scale tend to provide i the dynamism and creativity of European businesses and gave them a solid base enabling them to tackle international competition from other regions. . In a global economy characterised by fierce competition, particularly between multinational companies, the economies and the position of companies of small and medium European countries would certainly have been much worse than they are today, if it was not for the large internal market, which is their safe haven and springboard for utilisation of opportunities in external markets. This is the reason for business interest groups back the multinational integration process. On its part, the European Union helps businesses and particularly SMEs striving to adapt to the conditions of the single market. The common market has also boosted the welfare of the citizens of the member states. European consumers, previously confined to their respective national markets, now enjoy a huge choice of high quality goods and services at prices dictated by free competition. The free movement of workers, freedom to provide services and freedom of establishment for self-employed persons constitute fundamental rights, guaranteeing the citizens of the EU the right to pursue an occupation in any member state. The citizen of a member state, be he or she worker, businessman or tourist, can no longer be regarded as an alien in another member state, but as an EU citizen, and no discrimination against him or her is permitted.

EU and Great Britain

The 28 countries within the European Union include Austria, Belgium, Bulgaria, Croatia, the Republic of Cyprus, Czech Republic, Denmark, Estonia, Finland, France, Germany, Greece, Hungary, Ireland, Italy, Latvia, Lithuania, Luxembourg, Malta, the Netherlands, Poland, Portugal, Romania, Slovakia, Slovenia, Spain and Sweden.

The European Economic Area (EEA) includes EU countries and also Iceland, Liechtenstein and Norway. It allows them to be part of the EU's single market.

Switzerland is neither an EU or EEA member but is part of the single market. This means Swiss nationals have the same rights to live and work in the UK as well as other EEA nationals.

Though Great Britain became a member of the European Union in 1973 it faced resistance to its entry. With rows over contributions to monetary policy disputes and threats to leave, Britain has had a bumpy ride within the European Union. On June 23, 2016, in a nationwide referendum (BREXIT), Britain has decided to exit from the EU.

EU and the Multilateral Order

National Intelligence Council, a Washington-based think-tank in a report titled "Mapping the Global Future," points out that the EU has the potential to become a major world player, but only if it undertakes radical reforms to boost economic growth and stem population losses. In raw statistical terms, the EU is already a fledgling superpower. With 458 million citizens, its current population dwarfs that of the United States and is third only to India and China. It is also the world's largest and most powerful economic bloc, with a bigger gross domestic product than America, China or Japan. "By most of the criteria which measures whether it is the market size, advantages of a single currency, availability of highly skilled work force, stable democratic governments, unified trade bloc, and GDP, an enlarged Europe will have the ability to increase its pull on the international scene," says the NIC report. Clearly, Europe is in no position to rival the military might of the United States, but its use of "soft power," the EU is the world's largest aid donor, is attractive to such emerging world players such as China and India. "Europe's strength may be in providing, through its commitment to multilateralism, a model of global and regional governance to the rising powers, particularly if they are searching for a "Western" alternative to strong reliance on the United States," says the NIC study.

Being or becoming a global power is indeed not determined by an internal and voluntary policy of that actor. It also depends on a number of external factors. Two developments taking place in the world together are weakening the position of the EU to be an aspiring global power. These have been highlighted as follows: the first trend is a shift in economic gravity from the East to the West, the second is the demographic decline in Europe. Both these trends make it increasingly challenging the position of the EU to be a global power. It has to be noted that the US is still the most powerful economy in the world and the EU is second in size in terms of economy, but the fact that the BRICs are also gaining economic strength is already an unmistakable trend. And, more specifically, China and India are becoming economic giants that account for a huge share in growth of the world's GIP. It is reported that by 2050, the parts of the shares of EU and the US in the world economic output are going to further decrease dramatically. The same study predicts that the exports of the EU would account for 32 percent of the world volume in 2025 while the share of Asia will be 35 percent. The EU will then no longer be occupying the first position as exporter in the world. At the same time, Europe (and the US) is losing its scientific and technological supremacy and advantage. This will prove to be benefitial to Asia. The Eurocentric world would be a thing of the past, and so would be the transatlantic predominance of the West. It is predicted that, by 2030, 75 percent of all people on the planet will live in Asia and Africa, and the population of the EU will account for only 6.5 percent of the world population. This will have effect on multilateralism as membership and voting rights in multilateral organisations will need to adapt to that reality. These economic and demographic challenges affect the EU's efforts to become a global power. Europe is struggling to promote itself in a legitimate role within the global order. This is not to say though, that Europe is being left behind. In fact, it is working to create bilateral ties with the rising powers. This is perhaps not out of choice though. Faced with the Eurozone crisis,[17] EU is forced to enter into cooperative dealings. Given the Eurozone crisis and its global implications, it is perhaps easy to denounce Europe's successes in the field of foreign policy. Coupled with impending defence and development aid budget cuts, Europe's prestige in international affairs may not recover for some time.

However, it is important not to dismiss the European Union as an international actor simply because of the Euro zone crisis. The continent was widely praised for leading the military action in Libya. Together with the US, the EU is working with China in stopping nuclear proliferation in Iran and North Korea. This approach has largely been collective, which would suggest that there is still room for convergence in European security policy. The fact that the efforts are being led by France, the UK and Germany would suggest again though, that following up on some policies are becoming somewhat in national interest – with Germany abstaining on the UN Resolution regarding Libya but getting involved in other security matters it appears to be becoming a situation in which member states instead of safeguarding the interest of EU in totality simply opt for their national interests. Consistency in policy on external affairs can be difficult for the EU, mainly because of the great spread of the interest in external relations of EU members with the rest of the world and its resultant activities. We can still observe a divide between the 'old' and 'new' Europe in terms of ideology – those member states reluctant to match leading countries in terms of military and defence capabilities. Several policies in recent years have fallen victim to this lack of consistency and coherence, including the "inability to give a decisive reaction to Kosovo's declaration of independence from Serbia in mid-2008." It is to be noted that the bigger member states, i.e. Germany and France, have worked more towards achieving the objective of fulfilling their national interest as individual nations rather than following the most effective policies for the EU as a whole. Even in what was seen as Europe's big success, the response to the Libya uprising, there was disagreement from Germany, who abstained from voting on the UN Resolution. Also, many would also argue that although Europe led the invasion, they depended heavily on US military equipment and assets. It would be unfair though, to claim that the EU has been completely ineffective due to a lack of collective action. Member states even acknowledge that this is a growing problem and have worked to create institutions and processes for the Common Foreign and Security Policy (CFSP) and the Common Security and Defence Policy (CSDP). This shows that efforts are being made in these areas and that it is high on the agenda.

The Lisbon Treaty now having came into force, it is time for the EU to get back to work and more specifically to focus on its foreign policy. In a world that is increasingly complex and multipolar, the EU must act strategically. To avoid becoming an irrelevant international actor, Brussels needs to (1) develop a grand strategy to define the true purpose of its foreign policy; (2) forge solid strategic partnerships with key global players; and (3) contribute to the building of a new effective multilateral system which takes into account the new global structure of power The action to be taken by EU in these areas is described as follows:

- A Need for a Grand Strategy: The kind of power the EU chooses to be is in part conditioned by the international environment. Marked by inter-polarity, defined as "multipolarity in the age of interdependence", that environment is very challenging, but at the same time presents the EU with an opportunity to pursue a distinctive grand strategy. This strategy is distinctive in the sense that the emphasis is on a holistic approach, putting to use the full range of instruments, through partnerships and multilateral institutions, for a permanent policy of prevention and stabilisation.
- A Need for Truly Strategic Partnerships: In a world that is increasingly

multipolar and interdependent this is to say interpolar the EU cannot continue to approach emerging global powers without a clear strategy. The EU has or is negotiating seven strategic partnerships with other States (Brazil, China, India, Japan, Mexico, Russia, and South Africa), and one with an international organisation (the African Union). It seems quite obvious that not each one of these parties is equally strategic or relevant. Most of these countries undeniably exercise regional leadership or are a significant player for one specific global issue. This makes them strategic as regards one region, or one issue.

- A Need for a Reformed Multilateralism: The preference of EU is a cooperative form of multipolarity is well-known as it constantly promotes an international order based on systemic and rule-based multilateralism referred to in Brussels jargon as "effective multilateralism". This preference inscribes itself in a long-term strategy for promoting peace and multilateral cooperation, based on a strong historical conviction that multilateralism is the best path towards peace, stability and prosperity.

The dynamics and tensions created by the developments described above, mirroring the altered power relations of a new world order, confront the EU with a number of strategic challenges. It is increasingly clear that a weak, *status quo* oriented bargaining position resulting from internal division will not allow for a continued leading role. It is still possible for the EU to act as an example, either unilaterally or together with selected allies. It is for the European Union to identify such number of developments with regard to multilateralism that provide opportunities for the EU to increase its influence as a global player.

China and the New World Order

James Hoge Jr., in his recent article in the prestigious Foreign Affairs magazine pointed out, "the transfer of power from West to East is gathering pace and soon will dramatically change the context for dealing with international challenges – as well as the challenges themselves. Many in the West are already aware of Asia's growing strength." Similar thoughts have been echoing in the writings of numerous defence and strategic analysts as they try to unravel the emerging global landscape. What echoes in each of these analysis is the fact that the locus of power is witnessing a strategic shift to Asia, and this unstoppable rise is being led by China. Over the past 35 years China has undergone major social and economic transformations that have had a huge domestic impact and redefined its relationship with the rest of the world. The 1980s saw the first phase of 'reform and opening up'. In the 1990s the pace of global economic integration increased. These economic transformations entered a new and more substantial phase of global integration following China's accession to the World Trade Organisation (WTO) in 2001. In the 2000s the size of China's economy became a dominant feature of any narratives of global change, symbolised by its overtaking of Japan to become the world's second-largest economy by aggregate GDP in 2010.Chinese leaders' insistence on a different political system and the Chinese polity as a distinct and valid alternative to liberal democracy, as well as their ability to maintain this position in the face of external pressure and Western efforts to promote Western values in Asia,heightens the sense of challenge felt by many in the West as a result of China's rise. 'Inevitably China has become for the United States the symbol of a future in which its control is diminished.' This is often presented as a story about changes in global power distribution, with China depicted as the only country with the potential to challenge the United States in military and economic terms. There are many, however, who are somewhat sceptical of China completely overtaking the US, or even scheming to do so. David Shambaugh, for example, has argued that the consequences of China's rise so far have been more at the regional than at the global level. Others, by contrast, have stressed a more deliberate, sustained and zero-sum effort by the Chinese leadership to eclipse the United States as the world's most powerful country. There is a debate too over the nature of this regional power, from qualified visions of China emerging as the most powerful of a number of strong regional players, to more alarming scenarios that see it as the new regional hegemony promoting its own version of the Monroe Doctrine that obliges the United States to retreat from the region as China establishes its own Asian sphere of influence.

China is well on its way to becoming a formidable global power. The size of its economy has quadrupled since the launch of market reforms in the late 1970s and, by some estimates, will double again over the next decade. It has become one of the world's major manufacturing centres and consumes roughly a third of the global supply of iron, steel, and coal. It has accumulated massive foreign exchange reserves, worth more than US$1 trillion at the end of 2006. China's military spending has increased at an inflation-adjusted rate of over 18 percent a year, and its diplomacy has extended its reach not just in Asia but also in Africa, Latin America, and the Middle East. Indeed, whereas the Soviet Union rivalled the United States as a military competitor only, China is emerging as both a military and an economic rival heralding a profound shift in the distribution of global power. In order to examine this dramatic rise of china, and its impact on the emerging multi-polarity, it is imperative to divide the study into the following:

- China's economic might.
- Geo-strategic implications of a rising China, for Asia.
- How much of a challenge does the Chinese threat pose for the United States.

China: An Economic Superpower

The International Monetary Fund (IMF), the most prestigious international financial institution in the world, has rated China's ranking to number one economic superpower in the world surpassing the United States based upon the purchasing power parity of GDP indicator (gross domestic product).[18] IMF has asserted that China produced 17 percent of the world gross domestic product (GDP) in 2014 exceeding USA's share of World GDP at 16 percent.

Catching up and overtaking

China's GDP as a % of US GDP (at purchasing power parity)

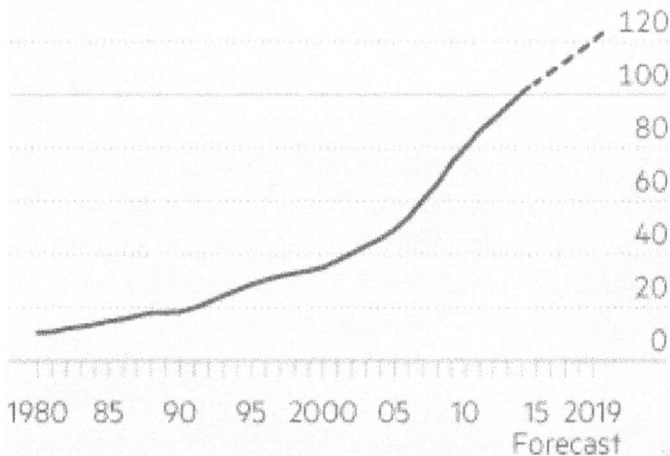

1980 85   90   95 2000 05   10   15 2019
                                       Forecast

Source: IMF

The Chinese economy experienced astonishing growth in the last few decades that catapulted the country to become the world's second largest economy. In 1978—when China started the programme of economic reforms—the country was ranked ninth in national gross domestic product (GDP) with US$ 214 billion, 35 years later it jumped up to second place with a nominal GDP of US$ 9.2 trillion. Since the introduction of the economic reforms in 1978, China has become the world's manufacturing hub, where the secondary sector (comprising industry and construction) represented the largest share of GDP. However, in recent years, China's modernisation propelled the tertiary sector and, in 2013, it became the largest category with a share of 46.1 percent of GDP, while the secondary sector still accounted for a sizeable 45.0 percent of the country's total output. China weathered the global economic crisis better than most other countries. In November 2008, the State Council unveiled a CNY 4.0 trillion (US$ 585 billion) stimulus package in an attempt to shield the country from the worst effects of the financial crisis.

In a report in 2011, Goldman Sachs had predicted that China will overtake the US as the world's largest economy in 2026.China has just dethroned Japan as the world's second largest economy, a title the latter has held for much of the last four decades. On August 16, 2010, Japan announced that its nominal gross domestic product (GDP) was valued at about US$1.28 trillion for the second quarter, less than China's US$1.33 trillion. The slow pace of Japan's economic growth indicates that China's economy (growing atan annual rate of 11.1 percent in the quarter) will race ahead of Japan's for the full year. The speed of China's rise to today's economic status is spectacular. Just 32 years ago in 1978, China was ranked 11[th]in the world by economic size, equivalent to less than eight percent of the then US economy. Now its GDP is more than 31 percent of the US economy at market prices and 60 percent of the latter by purchasing power parity (PPP). In terms of PPP and GDP, China has already been the world's second largest economy since 2002.China's overtaking of Japan has rekindled speculation about the time when its economy will become the world's largest. Forecast scenarios that China will overtake the US by total economic size in the 2020s itself have increasingly become an important reference point for assessment of international geopolitics. With such rate of growth, the size of the economy doubles every 7.3 years. China thus has increased its total GDP more than 17 times in just 30 years. With a 12-fold rise in just 30 years, China's per capita income has increased from merely one tenth of the world average to about one third of the latter in the past 30 years. By 2008, China lifted itself from the status of low-income country to the rank of middle income countries. Meanwhile China has also become a global manufacturing hub, the largest exporter in the world market and the largest consumer of energy in the world. In total economic size, China has quickly caught up with other large economies. It surpassed Italy to be the world's sixth largest economy in 2000 and then Britain and France by 2005 to become the fourth largest economy. In 2008, it overtook Germany to be the third largest economy. By that time, it was widely expected that China would pass Japan to be the second largest in 2009.

The economic innovation in China started in the early eighties during the rule of Deng Xiaoping and continued throughout the regime of Hu Jintao implementing innovative economic policies which lifted China's sluggish economy by introducing private ownership, market driven economy, and less governmental control contributing to robust economic performance. The innovative economic policies took advantage of globalisation and export orientation, attracting foreign investment, and maintaining a sound monetary and fiscal policy. China became a member of the World Trade Organisation (WTO). Beginning in early 1980s, China shifted its economic strategy from self-sufficiency to export orientation. The shift proved to be pivotal to the spectacular rate of growth of China's GNP. Concurrently, China is building its domestic consumer sector so that in the future it will have a strong and well-developed domestic market. The multi-billion dollar natural gas contract with Russia signed in May 2014 will give a major advantage while meeting the demand for energy of China. China's drive for the development of non-fossil fuel under its twelfth five-year plan could make it a world leader in energy exports and offer unmatchable prices on alternative energy in the world market contributing to convergence of per capita income of the silk route countries.

The global economic crisis which began in 2008 greatly affected China's economy. As a result China's exports, imports, and flow of foreign direct investment (FDI) declined, GDP growth slowed, and millions of Chinese workers reportedly lost their jobs. The Chinese government responded to the crisis by implementing a US$586 billion economic stimulus package and loosening its monetary policies to increase lending from banks. Such policies enabled China to effectively weather the effects of the sharp global fall in the demand of Chinese products. However, the Chinese economy has slowed down in recent years, due partly to sharp slowdowns in the growth rates of export and fixed investment. The rate of growth of real GDP fell from 10.4 percent in 2010 to 7.8 percent in 2012and again to 7.3 percent in 2014. The IMF estimates that China's real growth of GDP will slow down to 6.8 percent in 2015 and to 6.3 percent in 2016. The ability of China to maintain a rapidly growing economy in the long run will depend largely on the ability of the Chinese government to implement more comprehensive economic reforms that would quickly hasten China's transition to a free market economy, rebalance the Chinese economy by generating consumer demand, rather than exporting and fixed investment, boosting productivity and innovation, addressing growing income disparities and enhancing environmental protection. The ability of the Chinese government to implement such reforms is likely to determine whether China can continue to maintain relatively rapid economic growth rates, or will instead begin to experience significantly lower rates of growth. China's growing economic power has led it to become increasingly involved in global economic policies and initiatives, especially aimed at financing infrastructure development abroad, including the recent creation of two new investment banks by China.

China's growing economic influence globally has raised a number of questions, and in some cases, concerns, as to how China's rise will affect US economic interests and influence the global economic policies. China's economic rise has become a factor in congressional debate over various aspects of US trade policy.

China: An Asian Giant

The 21st century is often referred to as the Asian or Pacific century, indicating a shift of economic and political power from the United States (US) and Europe towards the emerging economies of Asia. While the financial crisis in 2008 hit the US and Europe hard, the rates of growth in Asia was barely affected. Through this period, the world witnessed a new phase in the process of globalisation marking the end of the hegemony of the old triad: the US, Europe, and Japan.[19]

The Asian continent as a whole is moving to the central stage of international politics. Key players, most notably China and India, are starting to pull more weight in a nascent multi-polar world order. The region's rise over the past 30 years has been nothing short of miraculous, and will define the dynamics of the emerging multipolar world. Asia is already an engine of global economics, accounting for 33 percent of the world economy in 2000 (compared to 21 percent and 23 percent for the United States and Western Europe, respectively).[20] Asian countries are also becoming global political and military actors, playing decisive roles on issues such as climate change, non-proliferation, and countering piracy. This rise has led several adroit strategic observers to opine that the 21st century will be Asian. Moreover, the ongoing shifts in geopolitical power from West to East have made the Asia-Pacific region increasingly important to US interests. The rise of Asia's economic powers has gradually enabled the emergence of new Asian military powers, some of whom will become pivotal states – states with a significant degree of influence over the security of commons. The emergence of these pivotal states within the global commons will simultaneously drive two countervailing trends: cooperation and competition.[21]Pivotal states wielding newfound military capabilities within the global commons, it is believed, will signal the end of long-standing US dominance in the Asia-Pacific.

These changes in the strategic equations are viewed by scholars as pointing to the emergence of a strategic triangle in the Asian region, with the three corners being China, the US and India respectively. As the confrontational atmosphere of the Cold War has largely receded, the strategic interactions between these three countries have become the subject of intense analysis by interested observers. There are two defining characteristics of the security environment in the Asia-Pacific region after the end of Cold War. First, the United States has become the only superpower in the world today. It is also the most important external power in Asia, and plays a key role in Asian security. Secondly, old rivals, China and India have emerged as strong regional powers, as evidenced by impressive economic growth, the development of nuclear arsenals, and demonstrated ambitions for exercising influence in the Pacific and South Asian regions. While China's role as an economic and geo-strategic player is more widely recognised, India is slowly emerging as a regional competitor to be taken seriously. The events of September 11, 2001 and their aftermath have further succeeded in providing new incentive to bring these two countries together to share common security concerns. Further with the unprecedented US military presence in South Asia due to the war against terrorism, a third player, the world's remaining superpower, is now more closely involved in the historic Sino-Indian rivalry.

In the first two decades since the end of the Cold War, Chinese analysts have been continuously assessing (or reassessing) their country's external security environment and debating over the necessity to make appropriate adjustments. Crucial to these debates are issues such as:

- The structure of the international system after the Cold War (multipolarity or unipolarity).
- Whether America's role in global affairs is in decline?
- China's role in the international system and a proper grand strategy (i.e., the distinctive combination of political, economic, and military means to ensure the state's national interests or to achieve the objectives of the regime).
- The best ways to deal with the United States, and
- Relations with other great powers (Japan, Russia, and India in particular).

Chinese security analysts have come to visualise major threats to China in the form of four rings.[22] In the first ring, the entire territory that China administers or claims is believed to be threatened by foreign actors and forces. A second ring of security involves China's relations with 14 adjacent countries. These include the five countries with which China has fought wars in the past 70 years (India, Japan, Russia, South Korea, and Vietnam) and a number of states ruled by unstable regimes. None of China's neighbours perceives its core national interests as congruent with Beijing's. The third ring of Chinese security concerns consists of the politics of the six distinct geopolitical regions that surround China: Northeast Asia, Oceania, continental Southeast Asia, maritime Southeast Asia, South Asia, and Central Asia. Each of these areas presents complex regional diplomatic and security problems. Finally, there is the fourth ring: the world far beyond China's immediate neighbourhood. China has truly entered this farthest circle only since the late 1990s and so far only for limited purposes such as to secure sources of commodities, such as petroleum, to gain access to markets and investments, to get diplomatic support on Taiwan and Tibet and to recruit allies for China's positions on international norms and legal regimes. In each of China's four security rings, the United States is omnipresent.

The major Asian players need to accept that this is not a region where only a single power or even a group of powers can decide the affairs. They also need to intensify their own cooperation efforts and stop a revival of a cold war mentality that further destabilises the region. The rise of China and India is inevitable and should be accepted as such. However, a peaceful rise can also be assured, which would not unnecessarily disrupt the current power configurations. Improvements in relationship of states, however incremental, will go a long way in assuring a stressed region that peace and stability are indeed shared goals. Since it is the two comparatively longer sides of the triangle (China and US) that matter, these two sides could have "a cooperative relationship." But cooperation would depend on certain conditions. China should calm what is generally termed as called a "cauldron of anxiety" in the United States about its rise.[23] It should "explain its defence spending, intentions, doctrine, and military exercises,"reduce its trade surplus with the United States and cooperate with Washington on Iran and North Korea. In September 2009, James Steinberg, the then Deputy Secretary of State, introduced the idea of "strategic reassurance." Steinberg defined the principle in the following way: "Just as we and our allies must make clear that we are prepared to welcome China's arrival … as a prosperous and successful power, China must reassure the rest of the world that its development and growing global role will not come at the expense of the security and well-being of others." China would need to "reassure others that this build-up does not present a threat"; it would need to "increase its military transparency in order to reassure all the countries in the rest of Asia and globally about its intentions" and demonstrate that it "respects the rule of law and universal norms".

China may be Asia's economic powerhouse but it won't become the region's dominant power, according to a new report. In examining the factors that go towards the development of Chinese national power-and its ability to use it to achieve national objectives-predictions about a Chinese superpower with the ability to dominate Asia would be premature, if not improbable. The defence sector receives the lion's share of government finances, nearly 15 percent of the 2014 budget, but as per the report China will not become a military superpower until it's capable of taking decisive action on a global scale. "Although China has developed potent military capabilities to make it hazardous for U.S. forces to operate in the approaches to China, the fact remains that Beijing could not enforce a full military blockade of Taiwan or attempt a full-scale amphibious invasion of that island,"Moreover, as a result of territorial disputes with Japan and the majority of Southeast Asia, China has few friends in Asia.[24]

China: A Threat to US Preponderance

China's development, as well as that of the rest of Asia, as per the observers of the Chinese rise, will necessarily alter the preeminent geopolitical position that the United States has enjoyed since the end of the Cold War, and that Western nations have enjoyed since the 19th century. According to a study by the Pew Research Centre, almost half of respondents across all regions believe that China has overtaken the US as the world's leading superpower, or will eventually.

In 1956 the Russians politely informed Westerners that "history is on our side. We will bury you." In the 1980s history seemed to side instead with Japan. Now it appears to be taking China's part. Arvind Subramanian of the Peterson Institute for International Economics argues that China's economic might will overshadow America's sooner than people think. He denies that his prophecy is self-denying. Even if America heeds its warning, there is precious little it can do about it. Three forces will dictate China's rise, Mr Subramanian argues: demography, convergence and "gravity". Since China has over four times America's population, it only has to produce a quarter of America's output per head to exceed America's total output. Indeed, Mr Subramanian thinks that China is already the world's biggest economy, when due account is taken of the low prices charged for many local Chinese goods and services outside its cities. Though it is big, China's economy is also somewhat "backward". That gives it plenty of scope to enjoy catch-up growth, unlike Japan's economy, which was still far smaller than America's when it reached the technological frontier. Buoyed by these two forces, China will account for over 23 percent of world GDP by 2030, measured at PPP, Mr Subramanian calculates. America will account for less than 12percent. China will be equally dominant in trade, accounting for twice of America's share of imports and exports. That projection relies on the "gravity" model of trade, which assumes that commerce between countries depends on their economic weight and the distance between them. China's trade will outpace America's both because its own economy will expand faster and also because its neighbours will grow faster than those in America's backyard. Mr Subramanian combines each country's share of world GDP, trade and foreign investment into an index of economic "dominance". By 2030 China's share of global economic power will match America's in the 1970s and Britain's a century before. The US trade deficit with China was US$365.7 billion in 2015and the trade deficit exists because US exports to China were only US$116.2 billion while imports from China hit a new record of US$481.9 billion. The deficit keeps growing because imports are rising faster than exports. The United States imports consumer electronics, clothing and machinery from China. A lot of the imports are from US-based companies that send raw materials to China for cheap assembly. When they are shipped back to the US, they are called imports even though they are profiting from American-owned companies. Quite simply, China is able to produce goods that Americans want at the lowest cost. How does China keep prices so low? Most economists agree that China's competitive pricing is a result of two factors. A lower standard of living which allows companies in China to pay lower wages to workers, and an exchange rate that is partially set to be always priced lower than the dollar.

US

GROWTH RATE
average annual growth rate, 1990-2008

2.8 percent

Projection for 2009: **−2.7** percent

NATIONAL DEBT
Projection for 2009

$**12.9** trillion

of which foreign debt comprises
$**3.4** trillion (as of June 30, 2009)

FOREIGN TRADE
Exports to China, 2008

$**69.7** billion

Trade deficit with China:
$**268** billion

CHINA

GROWTH RATE
average annual growth rate, 1990-2008

9.6 percent

Projection for 2009: **8.5** percent

FOREIGN CURRENCY RESERVES
September 2009

$**2.3** trillion

FOREIGN TRADE
Exports to the US, 2008

$**337.8** billion

Source: Census, IMF, US government, SAFE

DER SPIEGEL

When a state occupies a commanding position in the international system, neither it nor any weaker states have an incentive to change the existing order. But when the power of a challenger state grows and the power of the leading state weakens, a strategic rivalry ensues, and conflict, perhaps leading to war,is likely. Many Neo-realists and power transition theorists see this dynamics emerging in U.S.-Chinese relations. According to John Mearsheimer, "If China continues its impressive economic growth over the next few decades, the United States and China are likely to engage in an intense security competition with considerable potential for war."

Scholars like Joseph Nye and Michael Cox however feel that the rise of China does not have to trigger a wrenching hegemonic transition. The U.S.-Chinese power transition can be very different from those of the past because China faces an international order that is fundamentally different from those that rising states confronted in the past. China does not just face the United States, it faces a Western-centred system that is open, integrated, and rule-based, with wide and deep political foundations. The nuclear revolution, meanwhile, has made war among great powers unlikely eliminating the major tool that rising powers have used to overturn international systems defended by declining hegemonic states. Today's Western order, in short, is hard to overturn and easy to join. Across history, international orders have varied widely in terms of whether the material benefits that are generated accrue disproportionately to the leading state or are widely shared. In the Western system, the barriers to economic participation are low, and the potential benefits are high. China has already discovered that the massive economic returns that are possible by operating within this open-market system. The most farsighted Chinese leaders understand that globalisation has changed the game and that China accordingly needs strong, prosperous partners around the world. From the United States' perspective, a healthy Chinese economy is vital to the United States and the rest of the world.[25] Technology and the global economic revolution have created a logic of economic relations that is different from the past making the political and institutional logic of the current order all the more powerful.

China is of critical importance to the US for all sorts of reasons, ranging from the U S need for China to keep buying U S debt, to China's unique diplomatic position vis a vis two of the three "axes of evil," North Korea and Iran. As Harvard celebrity historian Niall Ferguson has emphasised, it is the symbiotic relationship of "Chimerica" on which the global economy now depends. From stabilising the Middle East, to neutralising Islamist radicalism or countering nuclear proliferation, China and the West have shared common interest. A China whose emergence as a diplomatic and military power is only just beginning to match its economic might, could become a vital partner for protecting peace and stability. China's "future and destiny has never been more closely connected with those of the international community," says the country's 2010 Defence White Paper. The rise of China, and in its wake India, Brazil and, maybe, even a resurgent Europe, will create a multi-polar world where no one holds a hegemonic position. Constrained by checks and balances and needing to work together in the face of threats from terrorism, energy insecurity or climate change, the new great powers will develop into what Hillary Clinton calls "a multi-partner world." Now is the time to rethink America's policy toward China. The United States can benefit economically from China's rise, strengthen Chinese advocates of human rights and democracy, and avoid a new Cold War.

Increased tensions with China could have dire consequences. They could lead to a military conflict over Taiwan's political status, over whether Japan or China holds sovereignty to a group of uninhabitable islands and offshore energy resources in the East China Sea or over the ownership of small islands and energy resources in the South China Sea. In a worst case scenario, those conflicts could escalate, by accident or by design, to a nuclear exchange. It is essential to remember that China's rise strengthens America's economy and future prosperity. Today, China is the largest growth market in the world for US goods and services. Trade with China, America's third-largest export market and the leading market for US agricultural products, has helped America's recovery from the global financial crisis. From 2000 to 2011, U.S. exports to China increased by approximately 640 percent, from about US$16 billion to US$104 billion. During this period, American exports to China grew seven times faster than US exports to all other countries in the world.

US still sells China $100 of goods

Balance of Trade:
US: - $500
China: + $500

China now sells US $600 of goods

(c) 2015 BackpackInvesting.com

Looking to the future, the US stands to benefit from billions of dollars of Chinese investment that will reduce production costs for American companies and prices for American consumers, enhance consumer welfare, spur the development of innovative products and, most importantly, result in "in sourcing"—the creation of hundreds of thousands more American jobs. By successfully negotiating a bilateral US-China free trade agreement and supporting China's membership in the Trans-Pacific Partnership, the regional free trade area of the Asian Pacific, the US will stimulate unprecedented levels of international trade and investment. These agreements will eliminate tariff and non-tariff trade barriers to American goods and services, achieve far greater transparency in China's regulatory practices, and enable the United States to benefit from the economic dynamism of Asia—the new "engine" of global growth.

India: An Emerging (Economic) Superpower

The discussion on the emerging global power centres will remain incomplete without a discussion of India's progress and the various predictions made by scholars about the likelihood of India becoming a major global power. The latest World Investment Report released by UNCTAD clearly indicates that India possesses a great potential to challenge China economically in the very near future. Foreign investors are very much ready to grab Indian markets. In fact the country is among the top ten hottest destinations for foreign investors. Investments by foreign institutional investors (FIIs) as early as 2003 crossed the US$7 billion mark-more than double the previous high of US$3 billion recorded in 1995. Statements from Britain that, "The two Asian giants, India and China, would take away more UK services and manufacturing jobs if Britons remained poor-skilled and under-educated" speaks volumes about the rising international stature of India. India is also the centre of cutting-edge research, the global original equipment manufacturers of auto ancillaries and the preferred supplier of goods for erection of infrastructure combined by construction skills. Advancement in Science and Technology is racing ahead, discovering new avenues. Implementations and improvisations are being carried out in India on regular basis improving the living standards and finding new solutions for problems, which were never thought to emerge in the near future. Specilised skills in genetic engineering has led to invaluable depth of knowledge in all walks of life. The 21st century is going to reap the fruits of these developments.

In terms of geographical area, population and economic power, India far outstrips its South Asian neighbours, given its high economic growth that has touched 8 percent in recent years. It is also preparing to close in and reduce the gap now existing with the present world's economic powers. Experts from the media, investment banks and research institutes agree that there is another China in the making, an economic and political powerhouse that will soon overtake Germany and Japan. India then would have fulfilled the economic conditions required to be a leading political power that plays a role in moulding international relations. Of late there has been no global report that does not predict an impressive future for India. From Goldman Sachs, JP Morgan to Deutsche Bank and others and think tanks, all see India emerging as a global economic super power in the next 25 years. The background for such optimism stems from the steady growth in GDP of 5 percent alongwith the availability of a young, empowered working population every year over the next couple of decades. Economists and Researchers at Harvard University have projected 7 percent annual growth rate for India which would continue through 2024which would put it ahead of China, making India the fastest growing economy in the world. Over the years, the Indian economy has gone through phases of remarkable transformation. The Indian economy got its first "big push" with the first phase of economic reforms in 1980s. The economy recorded annual average growth of around 5.6 percent during that decade, with significant decline in population below the poverty line from more than 50 percent in late 1970s to below 40 percent in late 1980s. The second major push came post 1991, following liberalisation of the economy, which helped it to move on to a sustainable higher growth trajectory.

Chart 1.2: India to become a US$ 5 trillion (current market price) economy by 2020

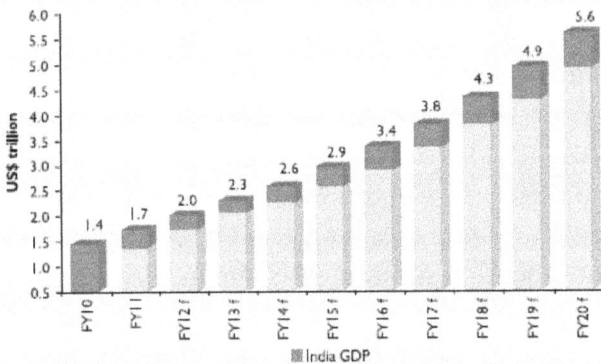

According to D&B's estimates, India is expected to be more than US$ 5 trillion economy by FY20, equivalent to Japan (in terms of GDP in US$) as of 2010.

Note: GDP figures are at MP Current Prices; GDP figures from FY12 are D&B forecasts
Source: CSO, RBI and D&B India

India has increasingly been looked at as an engine that will drive global growth in future. This is enough reason to look at the economic progress of India over the current decade. Forecasts indicate that the likelihood of India sustaining a 9.0 percent growth during the current decade is very high. According to Dunn and Bradstreet's estimate, in this process during the current decade as India traverses a high growth path, it would eventually surpass Japan's GDP level by 2020. The concomitant rise in levels of income coupled with increasing young working-age population will help towards increasing the share of discretionary spending in private final consumption expenditure and raising the savings rate. Growth of urban population will be one of the most important demographic shifts that we will witness during the current decade. Infrastructure will be both a cause and a consequence of economic growth during the current decade. The rising incomes and urbanisation will boost demand for investment in infrastructure in sectors such as electricity, roads, telecom etc. Massive infrastructure investment by the Government along with increased investment activity by the private sector will accelerate overall investment during the current decade. Government of India's thrust on infrastructure development in recent years and the structural policy changes is expected to provide the third "big push" to the Indian economy, enabling it to achieve inclusive growth during the current decade.

While economic statistics form a greater part and form the basis for such predictions, it is not giving the complete picture, which rising India presents. India's growing military might, its significant memberships of regional and multilateral groupings and recent strategic posturing on global issues, also add on to the rising clout of India. India is gradually playing an important role in shaping multilateral agreements. In the World Trade Organisation (WTO) negotiations it increasingly acts as the mouthpiece for developing countries. It is recognised that India's cooperation on global environmental policy is essential, as it will be one of the largest energy consumers in the 21st century. The country's future defence policy is crucial to the non-proliferation of weapons of mass destruction and for the future of the moratorium on nuclear testing. This is owing to the fact that India is a nuclear weapon power, with the third largest military in the world. The west already ranks it as one of India's most important trading partners. As long as the economic upsurge in the country continues, India offers a growing market for global products. This is especially true in respect of the machines and equipment required to develop infrastructure and allow the country to further industrialise and manufacture. The energy sector, particularly alternative energy, offers scope for cooperation, as do education, research and technology. While devising a global strategy based on peace and democracy, it is important that India also be integrated into the dialogue process on global security policy.[26] There is still a danger of an uncontrolled arms race among the nuclear powers, China, India, and Pakistan. Political conflicts in neighbouring countries like Bangladesh, Nepal, Pakistan and Sri Lanka also underline the importance of winning over India as a partner for an Asian security policy.

The rise of India has been highlighted by analysts and scholars for over a decade. Dietmar Rothermund's *India the rise of an Asian giant*, Mira Kamdar's *Planet India*, Edward Luce's *In spite of the gods: the strange rise of modern India*, Arvind Pangariya's *India the emerging giant*, Robyn Meredith's *The elephant and the dragon* and Brahma Chellaney's *The Asian giants: China, India and Japan* are some prominent examples amongst the recent literature on India's global ascent. Most hail India's rise as a positive and constructive phenomenon for global politics. And there are good reasons to think that. Globally, India remains committed to multilateralism, the democratisation of international organisations and cooperative regional frameworks such as SAARC, ASEAN, IBSA, BRICS or BIMSTEC, to promote regional security and cooperation. Such constructive and cooperative foreign policy orientation has won enormous goodwill for India globally. Berlin and Brussels have acknowledged India's importance. Since 2000, annual summits have been held between India and the EU, accompanied by Parliamentarian and civil society dialogue forums. At the fifth summit in Hague in 2004, a "strategic partnership"was agreed upon between India and the EU with a focus on multilateral, economic and development cooperation, cultural and scientific exchange and better institutional parameters for Indo-European relations. The United States qualifies India as the largest democracy in the world and as an important ally. At the same time India insists on its "strategic" autonomy in global affairs. As a regional power, India is already playing a decisive role in South Asia and beyond for example, in Afghanistan.

Rising and Shining

India has the potential to serve as a leading example of how to combine rapid economic growth with fairness and inclusion of those at the bottom rungs of the ladder.

By 2025, India is likely to emerge as one of the world's least corrupt developing economies. While widespread corruption is a reality in almost all developing economies (as well as some of the developed ones), India is one of the very few developing economies with a free press that continues to be vigilant and merciless in exposing corruption.

India is likely to emerge as one of the world's leaders in leveraging information technology (IT) to boost the effectiveness and efficiency of its institutions - the corporations, the government and as well as civil society organisations.

India will almost certainly become a leading example of efficient utilisation of ,resources especially in energy sector. The industries, government and consumers in India will respond vigorously to the imperative necessity for even greater efficient utilisation and the development of renewable energy sources.

India is likely to emerge as one of the world's leaders in market-driven innovation.

By 2025India is likely to emerge as one of the world's most entrepreneurial societies. Entrepreneurs will not only serve as the engines for the country's rapid economic growth but will also benefit from the vast new opportunities that a larger economy will open up for them domestically within India as well as globally.

Source: http://articles.economictimes.indiatimes.com/2011-01-09/news/29382860_1_third-largest-economy-superpower-india-s-gdp, accessed on April 4,2016,

In the words of the political theorist Sunil Khilnani, "India has been 'a substantial bridgehead of effervescent liberty on the Asian continent'. As such, it inspires hope that the largely poor, still divided, and formerly colonised countries of Africa and the Middle East can likewise move towards a more democratic political system. Meanwhile, through its collective co-existence of different faiths, languages, cultures, and cuisines, India is a better model for world governance than more homogeneous countries such as China, Japan, or the United States. Once, the heterogeneity of India was seen as its greatest flaw, now, on the other hand it may justly be celebrated as its greatest strength. India was not expected to survive as a democracy nor hold together as a single nation but it has. These manifest successes, achieved against the odds and against the logic of human history, have compelled worldwide admiration. If calls are now being heard that India must be made a Permanent Member of the Security Council of the United Nations, then these demands are not just legitimate, but also overdue."[27]It is

India's long-term record as a stable, multicultural democracy that lies behind its claims for a place at the High Table of Global Affairs.

Challenges and Complexities on the Road to Great Power Status
Superficially, India seems to have travelled a long way since independence in 1947. It is clear that India is and will be a single country, whose leaders shall be chosen by (and also replaced by) its people. Indians no longer fear their existence as a sovereign nation or as a functioning democracy. Every Indian hopes for a gradual enhancement of material and political powers, and the acknowledgement of Indian nation as one of the most powerful and respected on earth. But as Amy Chua points out that India still faces many problems such as "pervasive rural poverty, entrenched corruption, and high inequality just to name a few". Lant Pritchett, reviewing the book In Spite of the Gods: The Strange Rise of Modern India, writes that, while India has had impressive growth and has some world-class institutions, several other indicators are puzzlingly poor. The malnutrition and the coverage of immunisation programmes are at levels similar or worse than in much sub-Saharan African nations. In the Demographic and Health Surveys, India's child malnutrition was the worst of the 42 nations with comparable and recent data. Adult illiteracy is 61 percent. Caste politics in India remains an important force. Manjari Chatterjee Miller of the Boston University writes, "India is a "would-be" great power but "resists its own rise".Three factors contribute to this stagnation. First, foreign policy decisions are highly individualistic. This autonomy, in turn, means that New Delhi does very little collective thinking about its long-term foreign policy goals, since most of the strategic planning that takes place within the government happens on an individual level. Second, a dearth of think tanks helps insulate Indian foreign policymakers from outside influences. US foreign policymakers, by contrast, can expect strategic guidance from a broad spectrum of organisations that supplement the long-term planning that happens within the government itself. Third, many of India's political elites believe that the country's inevitable rise is a Western construct that has placed unrealistic expectations on India's economic growth forecasts and its international commitments. By contrast, Chinese political leaders pay very close attention to the international hype surrounding their country's growing stature. India's inability to develop top-down, long-term strategies means that it cannot systematically consider the implications of its growing power. So long as this remains the case, the country will not play the role in global affairs that many expect.[28]

According to the critics India does suffer from infrastructural deficiencies. The country's two biggest weaknesses are inadequate educational and physical infrastructure. Only 65 percent of the adult population is literate i.e. able to write in a vernacular language. While 20 percent can understand English, 0.03 percent uses it as a first language. Considering that the country's economic growth in the last 20 years has been services-driven, this lack of international exposure raises doubts about India's further growth potential. Government estimates suggest the country's young demographic profile could lead to difficulties within another 10 years, if the number of higher education institutes is not increased by at least 150percent . Only 12.4 percent of Indian students currently enter university, where the quality of education provided is below international standards. The few institutes with a reputation for excellence are confined to three fields: information technology, biotechnology, and space research. It is their alumni who have gone on to build up the country's image as an economic superpower with a highly skilled workforce. This image obscures the fact that 60 percent of Indian workers are still engaged in agricultural labour. While there are significant pointers to internal constraints, external threats are also increasingly being highlighted. Apart from the threats from the Western front including from jihadist terrorists , India also faces encirclement by China. As part of its military build-up, China is emerging as a major naval power in the Indian Ocean. Its construction of ports in Kyauk Phyu in Burma, Hambantota in Sri Lanka and Gwadar in Pakistan could be converted into Chinese naval bases. The string of Naxalite rebellions through eastern India provide troubled waters with enough co-ideologists for the Chinese to fish if they seek to create an internal dagger into the heart of India. To counter these possible future threats, India needs urgently to expand its Navy. India can no longer depend on the US to provide a unilateral naval shield. It is in its interest to see that China remains a peaceful and not a threatening expansionist power in the emerging new geostrategic order. As natural importers of resources,,China and India share an interest with the US and Japan to keep vital shipping lanes safe and open. With Australia's growing export of resources to China and its projected naval expansion,a five-power formal naval agreement to police the Asian seas maybe feasible. But, for India to meet all these geopolitical challenges, rapid economic growth and increasing military strength remains essential.[29] Closer economic relations with China may not materialise, as sections of the Indian business class are apprehensive of low-priced Chinese goods flooding the Indian market. With the delineation of the Sino-Indian border still a contested issue and border incidents continuing to occur, the scope for cooperation remains limited. Considering that China remains Pakistan's closest military ally, it is also hard for New Delhi to ignore the adverse implications of Sino-Pakistani strategic collaboration for its own security. While the United States and India have no conflict of interests, doubts persist as to whether there is scope for closer defence cooperation. India is unwilling to give up its strategic autonomy, believing that doing so would reduce its status.[30]

INDIA : ECONOMY & MONETARY POLICY

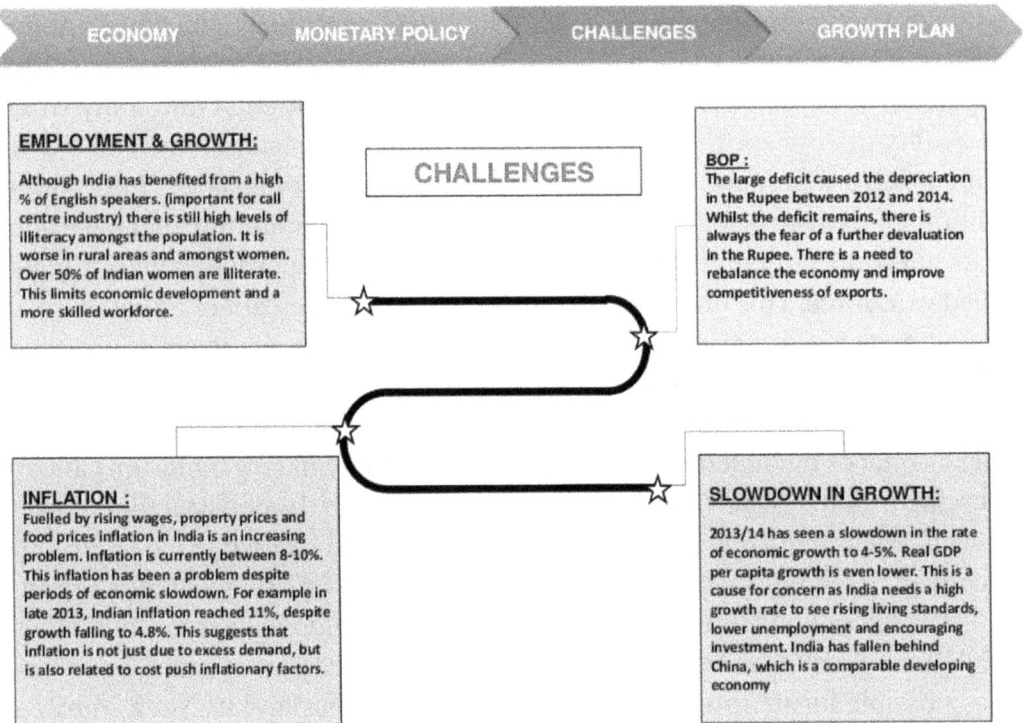

| ECONOMY | MONETARY POLICY | CHALLENGES | GROWTH PLAN |

EMPLOYMENT & GROWTH:

Although India has benefited from a high % of English speakers. (important for call centre industry) there is still high levels of illiteracy amongst the population. It is worse in rural areas and amongst women. Over 50% of Indian women are illiterate. This limits economic development and a more skilled workforce.

CHALLENGES

BOP :
The large deficit caused the depreciation in the Rupee between 2012 and 2014. Whilst the deficit remains, there is always the fear of a further devaluation in the Rupee. There is a need to rebalance the economy and improve competitiveness of exports.

INFLATION :
Fuelled by rising wages, property prices and food prices inflation in India is an increasing problem. Inflation is currently between 8-10%. This inflation has been a problem despite periods of economic slowdown. For example in late 2013, Indian inflation reached 11%, despite growth falling to 4.8%. This suggests that inflation is not just due to excess demand, but is also related to cost push inflationary factors.

SLOWDOWN IN GROWTH:
2013/14 has seen a slowdown in the rate of economic growth to 4-5%. Real GDP per capita growth is even lower. This is a cause for concern as India needs a high growth rate to see rising living standards, lower unemployment and encouraging investment. India has fallen behind China, which is a comparable developing economy

It can be highlighted that India's political scenario, economic strengths, expected living conditions in 2020 and the nature of its role in international relations, all depend on a variety of external and internal factors all of which will have a bearing on India's rise to power. In this connection it may be pointed out that:

• Even today India has no option but to import almost 75 per cent of the oil it needs. As indigenous energy reserves dwindle while the country's oil consumption rises due to sustained economic growth, India will become increasingly vulnerable to rising oil prices.

• Indian companies competing with foreign firms for a market share are directly affected by changes in the exchange rate. In the second quarter of 2007 alone, the Indian currency appreciated by 7 per cent against the US dollar. This was the rupee's strongest appreciation in a quarter in the last 30 years. A further pronounced fall in the value of the US dollar (likely, given the current high deficit of both the state budget and the trade balance in the USA) would cause Indian companies to suffer corresponding losses to revenue and profit. Crises in the international financial markets also affect the financial markets in India. A global stock market crash would cause stock quotations in India to plummet and disrupt the investment and consumption patterns of the middle and upper classes.

- Relations between India and Pakistan could deteriorate. The two countries that have waged three wars against each other since independence enjoy relatively peaceful relations today. However, peace efforts may falter yet again, either because of increasing conflict between the government and opposition in Pakistan and/or because violent attacks by terrorist groups trigger internal turmoil in India.

To quote Ashley Tellis, "whether India becomes a great power depends on its ability to achieve multidimensional success in terms of improving its economic performance and wider regional integration, acquiring effective military capabilities for power projection coupled with wise policies for their use, and sustaining its democracy successfully by accommodating the diverse ambitions of its peoples." Although contemporary projections of global growth by 2050 suggest that India will become a true pole by then, they also conclude that it will remain the weakest of the principal entities—China, the United States, the European Union, and India—dominating the international system at that time. A detailed analysis from 2012 suggested that India, representing only 7 percent of the global product in 2050, will remain well behind China at 20 percent and the United States and the European Union at 17 percent each, though it will be somewhat ahead of Japan at 5 percent and comfortably lead Russia and Brazil at 3 and 2 percent, respectively. The way forward would, therefore, have to involve small and non-controversial policy changes. For example, in the field of energy security, increased reliance could be placed on solar and wind energy. This would reduce dependence on energy imports and could partially meet demands for rural electrification, thus ameliorating societal discontent within poorer regions. For economic diversification, India could expand trade relations with continental Europe and thereby create a stronger foundation for economic growth. Increased cultural exchanges with Europe would also promote international exposure among the Indian workforce and make it more competitive, thus increasing the likelihood of further economic reforms.[31]Fareed Zakaria, points out that India's young population coupled with the second largest English speaking population in the world could give India an advantage over China.[32] He also believes that while other industrial countries will face a youth gap, India will have lots of young people, or in other words, workers, and by 2050, its per capita income will rise by twenty times its current level. According to Zakaria, another strength that India has is that its democratic government has lasted for 60 years, providing for long-term stability.[33] It is hence clear, that on the road to leading power status, India needs to complete the structural reforms necessary to create efficient products and factor markets as well as create an effective state to leverage India's capacity to build its national power.

Japan

The rise of Japan to a world power during the past 70 years is the greatest miracle in world history. The mighty empires of antiquity, the major political institutions of the Middle Ages and the early modern era, the Spanish Empire, the British Empire, all needed centuries to achieve their full strength. Japan's rise has been meteoric. After only 70 years, it is one of the few great powers that today contribute towards determining the fate of the world. History recalls Japan as the worst victim of the devastating atomic bombs which destroyed Hiroshima and Nagasaki, the two Japanese cities in 1945. In September 1945, Japan had nearly 3 million dead in the war and the lost a quarter of its national wealth. How did Japan become the second largest economy in the world in the 1980s? Post Second World War Japanese economic take-off has been due to a variety of factors, mainly relating to American policies towards Japan, the favourable international market, social mobilisation, existent industrial capacities and experience, and government policies and expertise, among other things. It is increasingly being argued in the global strategic circles that among the Asian giants as well as among the rising power centres of the world, Japan is all set to play one of the leading roles.

History and Evolution

The characters that make up Japan's name mean "sun-origin," which is why Japan is sometimes called the "Land of the Rising Sun". The first written records of Japan appear in Chinese history texts from the first century. Ancient Japan had extensive cultural exchanges with the neighbouring countries such as China and Korea. Japan's cultural development has been characterised by foreign influences, developed in a uniquely Japanese way. While sharing a similar Far Eastern culture based upon Confucianism and Buddhism with China and Korea, Japan actively adopted elements of Western culture after it abandoned its long-time policy of seclusion in 1854. Japan's process of modernisation utilised Western technology and methods of political and social organisation. Japan can be regarded as the country that pioneered the path to economic growth and prosperity in Asia.[34] During the period of European imperialism, the leaders of Japan carried out a concerted modernisation effort, Meijie rare forms transformed the Empire of Japan into an industrialised world power that embarked on a number of military conflicts to increase its access to natural resources. After victories in the First Sino-Japanese War (1894–1895) and the Russo-Japanese War (1904–1905), Japan gained control of Korea, Taiwan, and the southern half of Sakhalin. In 1910, Japan annexed Korea. Following the Russo-Japanese war, Japan maintained a military presence in Manchuria. In 1937, Japan invaded other parts of China, precipitating the Second Sino-Japanese War(1937–1945) and resulted in an oil embargo on Japan by the United States.[35] On December 7, 1941, Japan attacked the United States naval base in Pearl Harbour and declared war on the United States, the United Kingdom, and the Netherlands.

The Japanese nation and its military, which controlled the government by the 1930s, felt that it then could, and should, control all of East Asia by military force. Japan's invasion of other Asian countries, however, brought resistance from not only the European colonial powers, but also the Asian people themselves, and finally, the United States. The Japanese regime tried to convince the Japanese people that complete loyalty and obedience would make Japan invincible. Japan's early victories seemed to prove this, but the victory of US in the conflict at Midway Island in June 1942 led to the steady encirclement of the Japanese islands, cutting them off from needed supplies of raw materials. The Japanese navy was also destroyed. This was followed by massive bombardment from the air and the final blow was the dropping of the atomic bombs on Hiroshima and Nagasaki. The Japanese invincibility was proved to be a myth. At the end of the war, the Japanese nation was not only starving and devastated by the bombing, but bewildered and shocked by the defeat. Nationalism and the desire to catch up with the West persisted after World War II, but now the efforts were focused on achieving economic and industrial goals. The great devastation of the Japanese economy during the war and the need to rebuild it from scratch often led to the introduction of new technology and new management styles, which gave these companies a chance to update and upgrade themselves. These changes were met with a friendly international environment of free trade, cheap technology and cheap raw materials. During the Cold War period , Japan was the client and friend of the advanced U.S. economy and Japanese markets were allowed to be closed while the American market was open to Japanese goods. After the war was over, many of the wartime companies and much of the technology used during the war were converted to peaceful economic development. Japanese private companies expanded quickly and fearlessly.

Japan capitalised on reconstruction efforts by exploiting 'two key opportunities of backwardness' as Angus Maddison describes it, the low base which provided for mass employment in reconstruction efforts and the revival of the suspended Meiji Restoration to catch up with the west once again. The main reasons which spurred Japan's growth are debated a lot on their marginal effectiveness but the most common ones, according to Maddison were: (i) Socio political stability: It is culturally a homogeneous society with no stalled internal rebellions (ii) Demilitarisation: Complete demilitarisation helped release a lot of economic surplus that was directly put for nation building (iii) Extremely high labour productivity: Military personnel and people employed by the military provided Japan with one of the most disciplined workforces ever created(iv)Demographic Dividend: the timing of Japan's demographic dividend was impeccable. The demographic transition allowed it to have a very high population of workers and historically lowest dependency ratio. (v)High Savings Rate: The high savings rate led to rapid capital accumulation in Japan compared to other war torn countries and gave the government an extraordinary ability to spend on infrastructure projects.[36]Japan had excellent industrial basis, sound industrial system, great amount of sophisticated engineers and scholars, and high average level of education remained from the time before World War II, even though the material factories, facilities had all been damaged during the war, their immaterial property, the brainpower and manpower remained. After World War II, the United States established a significant presence in Japan to slow the expansion of Soviet influence in the Pacific. The United States was also concerned with the growth of the economy of Japan because there was a risk after World War II that an unhappy and poor Japanese population would turn to Communism and by doing so ensure that the Soviet Union would control the Pacific.

The distinguishing characteristics of the Japanese economy during the "economic miracle" years included: the cooperation of manufacturers, suppliers, distributors, and banks in closely knit groups called keiretsu; the powerful enterprise unions and shuntō; good relations with government bureaucrats, and the guarantee of lifetime employment (Shūshinkoyō) in big corporations and highly unionised blue-collar factories. This economic miracle was spurred mainly by Japanese economic policy, in particular through the Ministry of International Trade and Industry. The period of rapid economic growth between 1955 and 1961 paved the way for the "Golden Sixties," the second decade that is generally associated with the Japanese economic miracle. In 1965, Japan's nominal GDP was estimated at just over US$91 billion. Fifteen years later, in 1980, the nominal

GDP had soared to a record US$1.065 trillion. The export-driven economy that Japan consequently developed also benefited enormously from an international market of low tariffs (by joining the GATT, forerunner of WTO), low prices of oil and other raw materials needed for industrial development.

Because Article 9 of the Japanese constitution forbids Japan from rearmament, Japan has lived under the umbrella of U.S. military protection, spending only 1 per cent of their GNP on the military's defencive abilities (which is a huge sum of money as the Japanese economy grew to be the second largest in the world), which, percentage wise, helped save the Japanese much money if they were to militarise on their own.

Economic Miracle and the Developmental State

Developmental state is a term used by international political economy scholars to refer to the phenomenon of state-led macroeconomic planning in East Asia in the late 20th century. In this model of capitalism (sometimes referred to as *state development capitalism*), the state has more independent, or autonomous, political power, as well as more control over the economy. A developmental state is characterised by having strong state intervention, as well as extensive regulation and planning.[37]The United States is a good example of a state in which the regulatory orientation predominates, whereas Japan is a good example of a state in which the developmental orientation predominates. As in the case of Japan, there is little government ownership of industry, but the private sector is rigidly guided and restricted by bureaucratic government elites. These bureaucratic government elites are not elected officials and are thus less subject to influence by either the corporate-class or working-class through the political process. The argument from this perspective is that a government Ministry can have the freedom to plan the economy and look for long-term national interests without having their economic policies disrupted by either corporate-class or working-class short-term or narrow interests. In Japan, a welfare society rather than welfare state exists, characterised by total employment, including cartels of small and medium sized companies to prevent them from bankruptcy in order to maintain total employment. The welfare society and total employment enabled the Japanese state to devote much of the money it would have spent on welfare to industrial development, in the form of bank loans. Japan became the second largest economy in the world after the United States in 1968,experiencing an average growth of up to 9 percent per year between 1955 and 1973.

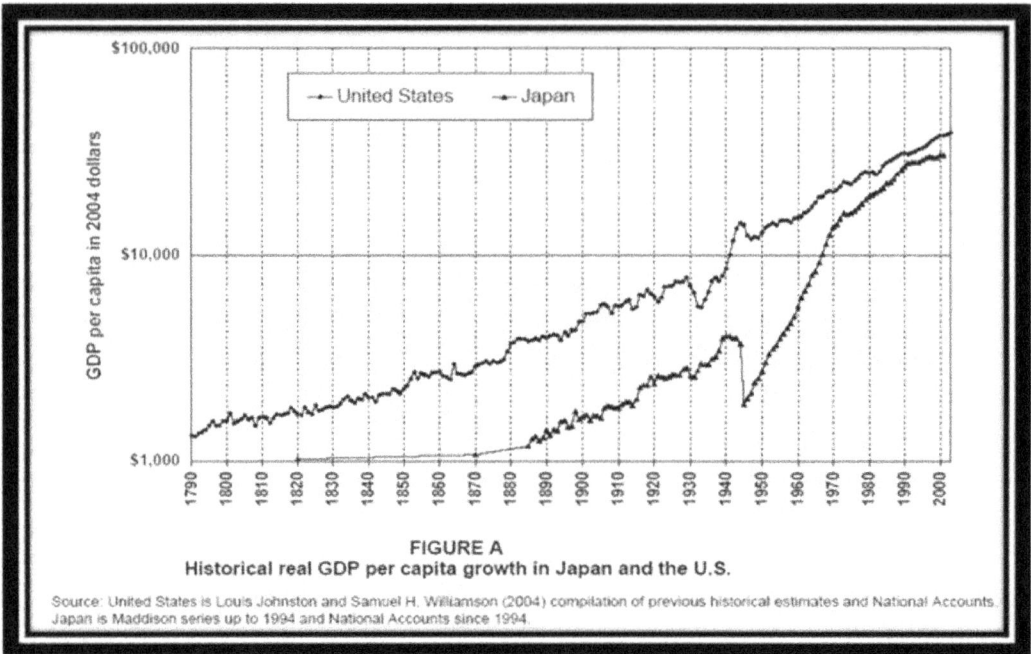

FIGURE A
Historical real GDP per capita growth in Japan and the U.S.

Source: United States is Louis Johnston and Samuel H. Williamson (2004) compilation of previous historical estimates and National Accounts. Japan is Maddison series up to 1994 and National Accounts since 1994.

In Japan the economic turnaround was driven by firms with strong employee loyalty gained by the promise of rising wages and jobs for life, as well as innovative products that were exported worldwide. Whether they were pre-war conglomerates such as Mitsubishi or Sumitomo, smaller pre-war companies like automaker Toyota or new firms representing now-familiar brands — such as consumer electronics giant Sony and car manufacturer Honda — Japanese firms were rigidly hierarchical institutions that closely resembled a family or religious institution, according to experts. Japanese business leaders saw that however closely Japanese business groups and industries coordinated and cooperated, the possibilities for continued growth were limited as long as participation was confined to Japanese businesses. Japan's major "trading companies", found that their extensive domestic organisations were of very little use when it came to competing and expanding overseas. It soon became clear that in the new global economy, the key to growth was transnational capability. With this in mind, many of the Japanese corporate groups that drove domestic growth in the past have sought to generate value addition by linking up with other business groups around the world. Banking, insurance, real estate, retailing, transportation, and telecommunications are all major industries today. Japan has a large industrial capacity and is home to some of the largest and most technologically advanced producers of motor vehicles, electronic equipment, machine tools, steel, and nonferrous metals, ships, chemicals, textiles, and processed foods. It is home to leading multinational corporations and commercial brands in technology and machinery. Japan is a leading nation in the fields of scientific research, technology, machinery, and medical research. Nearly 700,000 researchers share a US$130 billion research and development budget, the third largest in the world. Some of Japan's more important technological contributions are found in the fields of electronics, machinery, industrial robotics, optics, chemicals, semiconductors and metals. Japan leads the world in robotics, possessing more than half (402,200 of 742,500) of the world's industrial robots used for manufacturing. Close cooperation between government and industry, a strong work ethic, mastery of high technology, and a comparatively small defence allocation have helped Japan become the second largest economy in the world, after the United States, with around US$4.5 trillion in terms of nominal GDP and third after the United States and China in terms of purchasing power parity. Tight coordination by the powerful industry Ministry helped drive economic growth till the beginning of the new millennium, though Japan fell behind China in annual GDP terms in 2010, to its current third place globally.

Economic Position of Japan in the World Ranking (189 countries)

Population (million, share%, 2013)

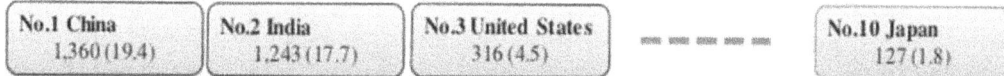

No.1 China	No.2 India	No.3 United States		No.10 Japan
1,360 (19.4)	1,243 (17.7)	316 (4.5)		127 (1.8)

GDP per capita (US$, 2013)

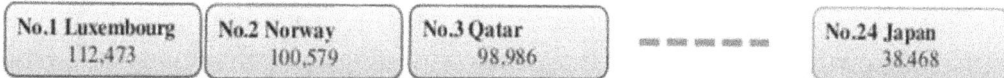

No.1 Luxembourg	No.2 Norway	No.3 Qatar		No.24 Japan
112,473	100,579	98,986		38,468

GDP (trillion US$, share%, 2013)

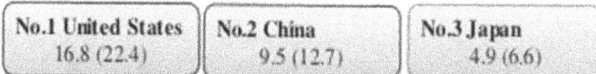

No.1 United States	No.2 China	No.3 Japan
16.8 (22.4)	9.5 (12.7)	4.9 (6.6)

IMF World Economic Outlook Database, October 2014

Challenges Ahead

A sharp downturn in business investment and global demand for Japan's exports in late 2008 pushed Japan into recession. Government stimulus spending helped the economy recover in late 2009 and 2010, but the economy contracted again in 2011 as the massive 9.0 magnitude earthquake and the ensuing tsunami disrupted manufacturing. The economy has largely recovered in the years since the disaster, but reconstruction in the Tohoku region has been uneven. The present Prime Minister Shinzo Abe has declared the revamping of the economy to be his government's top priority and he has overturned plan of his predecessor plan to permanently close nuclear power plants and is pursuing an economic revitalisation agenda of fiscal stimulus, monetary easing, and structural reform. Japan joined the "Trans Pacific Partnership" negotiations in 2013, a pact that would open Japan's economy to increased foreign competition and create new export opportunities for Japanese businesses. Measured on a purchasing power parity (PPP) basis that adjusts for price differences, Japan in 2013 stood as the fourth-largest economy in the world after second-placed China, which surpassed Japan in 2001, and third-placed India, which edged out Japan in 2012. To help raise government revenue and reduce public debt, Japan decided in 2013 to gradually increase the consumption tax to a total of 10 percent by the year 2015. Japan is making progress on ending deflation due to a weaker yen and higher energy costs, but reliance on exports to drive growth and an aging, shrinking population pose other major long-term challenges for the economy.

Over the past 20 years, the belief that Japanese industry can prevail merely by virtue of its domestic vertical and horizontal linkages has been slowly but surely discredited. During a particular period in Japanese history, government investment in industrial structure to support key "growth industries" was regarded as a pillar of economic growth. But with each progressive economic downturn over the past 20 years, it has become more and more evident that reliance on public works as an engine of growth is no longer practical, and continuing along that road has led only to massive fiscal deficits. While some measure of spending will always be needed to repair or upgrade aging infrastructure, it should now be evident to anyone that once the industrial infrastructure has reached a certain level, additional spending will not fuel another round of rapid economic growth. Japanese flare for miniaturisation, which made possible the development and manufacture of even more compact and function-packed consumer electronics once helped Japan dominate the consumer electronics industry, but the rise of the emerging markets as the prime engines of global growth in recent years has not been accompanied by a commensurate jump in global demand for Japanese electronics.

Japan needs to lay a new foundation for economic growth in the 21st century. And there can be no doubt that an economic globalisation must be a primary consideration in this process. At the level of government policy, this means making the most of such multilateral frameworks as free-trade agreements and economic partnerships, including the Trans-Pacific Partnership. One reason such frameworks are vital to Japan is that globalisation has given rise to an international division of labour within industries, making companies increasingly reliant on parts and materials from overseas.[38] This is becoming the rule even within Japan's largest corporate groups. And this is now an important means for an industry to display its own uniqueness. In the East Asian context, for example, Japanese businesses will need to decide what part of the industrial pyramid they propose to occupy in a rapidly industrialising region and identify new business areas accordingly. From this perspective, membership in the TPP is vital if Japanese industry is to effectively identify and nurture the seeds of future economic growth.

The Trans-Pacific Partnership (TPP) is the most important trade agreement in world history in both economic and geopolitical terms. It incorporates 40 percent of the global economy, including its largest and third largest countries. It will increase the income of the participating countries by almost US$300 billion (in 2007 dollars, so much more in current dollars when it is fully implemented in a few years). It sets the stage for eventual expansion to a comprehensive Free Trade Area of the Asia Pacific (FTAAP) that will include virtually every country in the region. The TPP includes 12 countries but is largely a free trade agreement between the United States and Japan. These two countries account for about 60 percent of its economic benefits. Japan will clearly be the largest national beneficiary of the TPP. Japan's percentage gains will be two and half to five times those of the United States. Prime Minister Abe has rightly seized on the TPP as a promising catalyst for the kinds of changes that the country desperately needs, and the agreement indeed offers a major opportunity for Japan. Japan's investment climate will significantly improve as will its ability to participate in global supply chains.

Source: https://piie.com/commentary/op-eds/trans-pacific-partnership-and-japan

The structural shift in the world order to multipolarity offers Japan a clear choice. Will it expand and strengthen its security contributions to the US alliance in order to buttress American primacy in East Asia, or will it seek to carve out a more independent regional and global role for itself, which takes into account the declining American power? Option for Japan in the transition from a US-dominated world order to multipolarisation is to 'stand as a pole'.Standing as a pole presents Japan with several feasible options that are not necessarily mutually exclusive. In military affairs, it might entail Japan developing a greater capacity to defend itself through an enhanced deterrence capability beyond so-called threshold deterrence and mobilisation. The primary thrust of such a strategy would be to reduce Japan's reliance on the United States in crucial areas of national defence, such as improving Japan's satellite intelligence-gathering capability and developing greater sea and airpower to defend its maritime territory.

In the triangular relationship with the United States and China, Japan might seek a more balanced or equidistant position between the United States and China that matches the measured but perceptible tilt in the US orientation towards China. Such a stance would anticipate one of Japan's greatest alliance tests over the next decade: how to deal with a United States that was increasingly preoccupied with engaging China at the same time as managing China's emergence as a great power and rival hegemonic influence in Asia. Adjusting to the reordering of America's Asian priorities might involve a Japanese reassessment of its dependence on the alliance to provide backing for its own dealings with China and as a guarantee to its importance to the United States. In terms of alliance management, standing as a pole might require Japan to build a new model of US-Japan bilateral cooperation on the basis of independent Japanese or shared bilateral initiative in the pursuit of jointly formulated economic, financial, trade and security goals. In terms of Japan's regional affairs, standing as a pole might entail the pursuit of more independent minilateral and/or multilateral approaches.[39] A new minilateralism might grow up around coordinated Japan-US-China action on international policy issues, or coordinated security cooperation with friendly states such as Australia and India. Japan might also lead the creation of new or expanded regional frameworks based on a more durable multilateralism in areas such as trade, finance, diplomacy and security.

Russia

According to Stephen Cohen, in the view of most Western commentators the Soviet breakup was an unambiguously positive turning point in Russian and world history. Most specialists no longer asked, even in the light of the human tragedies that followed in the 1990s, if a reforming Soviet Union might have been the best hope for the post-Communist future of Russia. Nor have mainstream commentators asked if its survival would have been better for world affairs. On the contrary, they concluded that everything Soviet had to be discarded by "the razing of the entire edifice of political and economic relations". Similarly, a growing number of Russian intellectuals have come to believe that with the disintegration, something essential was lost, a historic opportunity to democratise and modernise Russia by methods more gradualist, consensual and less traumatic, and thus more fruitful and less costly, than those adopted after 1991.[40] According to Pete Glatter, "a few years ago post -Communist Russia was commonly dismissed as a basket case, but today fear of a resurgent Russia is driving a new agenda. Just how democratic is post-Communist Russia? Why does Russia feel the need to dominate many of its neighbours? And how is Russia positioned in relation to the main imperialist powers? There are all questions that have a habit of recurring."[41]

The Disintegration and After

In the year 1990, when the Declaration of Sovereignty of the Russian Soviet Federative Socialist Republic was adopted, it was a period in which the Soviet Union's rapidly progressing decline had become patently clear. The processes that were to lead to the country's disintegration in December 1991 were already at work. The USSR was disturbed by mass rallies whose participants demanded radical economic and political reforms. The protesters insisted on the abolition of the Communist Party's monopoly of power and eventually succeeded. The U.S.S.R. legally ceased to exist on December 31, 1991. The new state, called the Russian Federation, set off on the road to democracy and a market economy without any clear conception of how to complete such a transformation in the world's largest country. Like most of the other former Soviet Republics, it gained independence in a state of serious disorder and economic chaos. In 1991 the Democratic Party and its leader, Boris Yeltsin, was left in control of Russia after replacing the Communist party. The democrats had a major problem on their hands: in order to completely get rid of Communism, they would have to do a great deal of damage to everything Communism had sustained in the country. This included Russia's economy and political structure. The democrats had not expected to come into power as suddenly as they had, and as a result President Yeltsin had no clear plans regarding the transition that had to be made.

On October 28, 1991 Yeltsin finally announced several drastic changes that would begin the transition. Prices of common products, which had been controlled by the government up until now, would be set free by the end of the year, and privatisation would begin. This plan was known as "shock therapy." Privatisation was the individual purchase of almost everything that had once been controlled by the state, including land, retail stores, and factories. The "shock therapy" plan also opened Russia to foreign investments. The Russian people were not ready for this sudden economic freedom, and a number of problems arose. Inflation caused prices to go up three hundred percent in the first month, and 2,591 percent by the end of 1992 (Freeze 414). This resulted in devaluation of savings, salaries and pensions, and left the economy in a terrible state. While the prices of most products were made independent of the government, the costs of energy and transportation were still set, and both were made about four times as expensive. Many factories were forced to shut down because the government no longer supported them financially in return for their goods.

In the first five years after the collapse, the Russian economy contracted to approximately half its former size. Problems of economic transition were exacerbated by the disruption of trading links to neighbouring newly independent states. As unemployment and underemployment grew, the rouble's value collapsed, destroying people's savings. While the Soviet system had always provided a basically adequate standard of living for most of its citizens, the post-Soviet economic transition, currency collapse, mass unemployment and disintegration of the social safety net took away the population's economic security. The consequent hopelessness and frustration were evident in rapidly declining birth rates and life expectancy, particularly among males. Overall, Russia's population declined from 148.3 million in 1990 to 142.3 million in 2003. In short, Russia was experiencing a profound crisis in its economy, politics, legal system, society, health, demographics, foreign policy and identity, creating an equally profound demoralisation among its citizens. When Vladimir Putin assumed the presidency in 1999, the agenda was reasonably clear: stabilising and enhancing his own hold on power; regenerating the reasserting central control over Russia's regional authorities and, in particular, preventing the loss of further territory or the spread of insurgency in Chechnya and the North Caucasus more broadly. As one prominent commentator observed, "On March 26, 2000, Vladimir Putin inherited a weak, corrupt and paralysed country on the verge of disintegration ... Putin's strategic goal was to get Russia back on its feet." In other words, the starting-point of contemporary Russian foreign policy was a reasonably clear-headed recognition of Russia's weakness, both internally and in comparison with the other great powers, notably the United States. In this respect, the Russian case contrasts starkly with the situation of at least two of the other 'emerging powers' (China and India), both of which combine dynamic growth with increasing assertiveness in foreign affairs. The Foreign Policy Concept of the Russian Federation 2000 identified the systemic tendency towards unipolarity and American unilateralism as significant threats to Russia and declared that 'Russia shall seek to achieve a multi-polar system of international relations'. These sentiments were echoed in the National Security Concept of the Russian Federation, adopted earlier the same year, which went on to define the eastward enlargement of NATO as a threat to the Russian Federation. In particular, Russia seeks enhanced access to international markets for its exporters, equal treatment on such issues as anti-dumping measures, an end to what is perceived to be discrimination against Russian exports, and a greater role in the management of international economic relations. In this area, too, there was significant (and, from a Russian perspective, positive) change in Russian–American relations after 9/11. In early 2002 the United States recognised Russia's status as a market economy, and embarked on a dialogue about energy with the Russian leadership. In addition, in May 2002 President Bush acknowledged that Russian accession to the WTO was a matter of national interest for the United States. In the meantime, the Russian Federation completed its accession to full membership of the G8 at Kananask is in 2002,and Moscow was spoken of as a favoured location for the 2006 G8 Summit. Here too, there was evidence of significant pay off from the choice of partnership. Russia has seen some discussion regarding its potential of re-emerging as a superpower, while others have made the assertion that it is already a superpower. In 2009, Hugo Chavez, late President of Venezuela whose government was noted to have enjoyed warm relations with the Kremlin, stated that "Russia is a superpower", citing waning American influence in global affairs, and suggested the roublebe elevated to a global currency. Israeli Prime Minister Benjamin Netanyahu called Russia an important superpower, praising its effectiveness as an ally of Israel and foe of Iran. In his publication entitled *Russia in the 21st Century: The Prodigal Superpower*,Steven Rosefielde, predicted that Russia would emerge as a superpower before 2010 and augur another arms race.

Russia

The Emerging Energy Superpower

The petroleum industry in Russia is one of the largest in the world. Russia has the largest reserves, and is the largest exporter, of natural gas. It has the second largest coal reserves, the eighth largest oil reserves, and is the largest producer of oil. It is the third largest energy user. Russia produced an average of 10.83 million barrels (1,722,000 m³) of oil per day in December 2015.[1] It produces 12percent of the world's oil and has a similar share of global oil exports. In June 2006, Russian crude oil and condensate production reached the post-Soviet maximum of 9.7 million barrels (1,540,000 m³) per day. Russia is by far the world's largest natural gas exporter. Most, but not all, authorities believe that Russia has the world's largest proven reserves of natural gas. Sources that consider that Russia has by far the largest proven reserves include the US CIA (47.6 trillion cubic meters), the US Energy Information Administration (47.8 tcm). In addition to having the world's largest proved reserves of natural gas, according to US Geological Survey estimations, Russia is also likely to have the world's largest volume of still-undiscovered natural gas: a mean probable volume of 6.7 trillion cubic meters. The Russian oil industry claims to be in need of huge investment. Strong growth in the Russian economy means that local demand for energy of all types (oil, gas, nuclear, coal, hydro, electricity) is continuing to grow.

Gas and oil have been the mainstay of the Soviet and now Russian economy for decades. Energy accounts for about half of Russian export earnings. According to Brookings economist Clifford Gaddy, "Every dollar's increase in the price of a barrel of petroleum translates into roughly US$1.5-$2.0 billion of additional yearly export revenues." During 1999-2000, energy exports accounted for about 90 percent of Russia's growth in GDP. Thanks to high oil prices, at the end of 2001 the economy had enjoyed its best three-year performance since 1966-69. Russia's August 1998 financial crisis, the devaluation of the rouble, and the subsequent—although entirely unrelated—rise in oil prices revived the industry. The devaluation drastically lowered input costs for Russian energy producers, while sharply higher oil prices boosted revenues even without new investments or increase in production. In 2001, oil companies boosted production and expanded their international reach. Russian companies are drilling for oil in Algeria, Sudan, and Libya. In 2000, Lukoil acquired a chain of gas stations along a stretch of the American East Coast and planned to strengthen its position in the United States by refining crude oil. In Eastern Europe, Lukoil acquired refineries in Ukraine, Romania, and Bulgaria. New regulatory instruments and fixed tax rates implemented by the Putin government in 2001 greatly improved the investment climate for international operators. By the end of 2001, Russia was becoming a real international energy player.[42] New stretches of export pipelines had been completed, and a new Russian oil terminal was operating on the Gulf of Finland. Russia concluded an ambitious agreement with the European Union on long-term energy cooperation that would increase oil exports to its neighbour. The European Union already buys more than half of Russia's total oil exports, accounting for about 16 percent of its oil consumption.

The heightened media attention has raised the possibility that Russia could take on OPEC and help shift global oil supply away from the Middle East and Persian Gulf. Could Russia be poised to become an energy superpower in the 21st century? The short answer is yes, but not in the near future—and not in oil. Russia may well break into some global energy markets as an alternative supplier to unstable states in the Persian Gulf. But Russia's energy future is in natural gas. As the next decade unfolds, continued crises in the Middle East and growing concern about pollution and global climate change will inevitably focus attention on Russia's vast reserves of cheaper, cleaner natural gas. Russia's success in international gas markets, however, is not a given situation. It will depend on major increases in production, serious investments—both foreign and domestic—in infrastructure, and the development of fully functioning gas markets in Asia. But for all its recent success, Russia will never displace OPEC in the world of oil markets. Over the long term, it cannot match OPEC's oil reserves. In oil production, Russia ranks third behind Saudi Arabia and the United States, at just over 7 mbd. In exports, it ranks second, at about 4 mbd, behind Saudi Arabia with close to 7 mbd. But it ranks seventh in proven oil reserves, with only 5 percent—as against the OPEC countries' collective 77 percent. Because of OPEC's huge reserve base the International Energy Agency predicts that increases in world production during 2010-20 will primarily be from Middle East OPEC countries.

Will Russia fare any better with natural gas? Many in Russia's energy complex think so, and many Russian oil companies are expanding their activities in the gas sector. Russia's gas reserves far exceed those of any other country. Indeed, Russia is to natural gas what Saudi Arabia is to oil. With 32 percent of proven world reserves, Russia far outranks Iran (15 percent), Qatar (7 percent), Saudi Arabia and the UAE (4 percent), and the United States and Algeria (3 percent). Single-handedly, Gazprom, Russia's giant gas company, holds a quarter of all world gas reserves, controls 90 percent of Russian output, and is Russia's largest earner of hard currency. Its tax payments account for around 25 percent of total federal government tax revenues. Gas accounts for 22 percent of EU energy consumption and Russia has long been Europe's dominant supplier. The EU buys 62 percent of Russia's total gas exports, which in turn account for 20 percent of the EU's overall gas consumption. Since 1997, Russia has also been Turkey's major supplier, accounting for around 70 percent of its gas imports. The Russian government wants to increase exports to Turkey and to double exports to Europe over the next 20 years.

World's Largest Conventional Natural Gas Reserves (Trillion Cubic Metres)

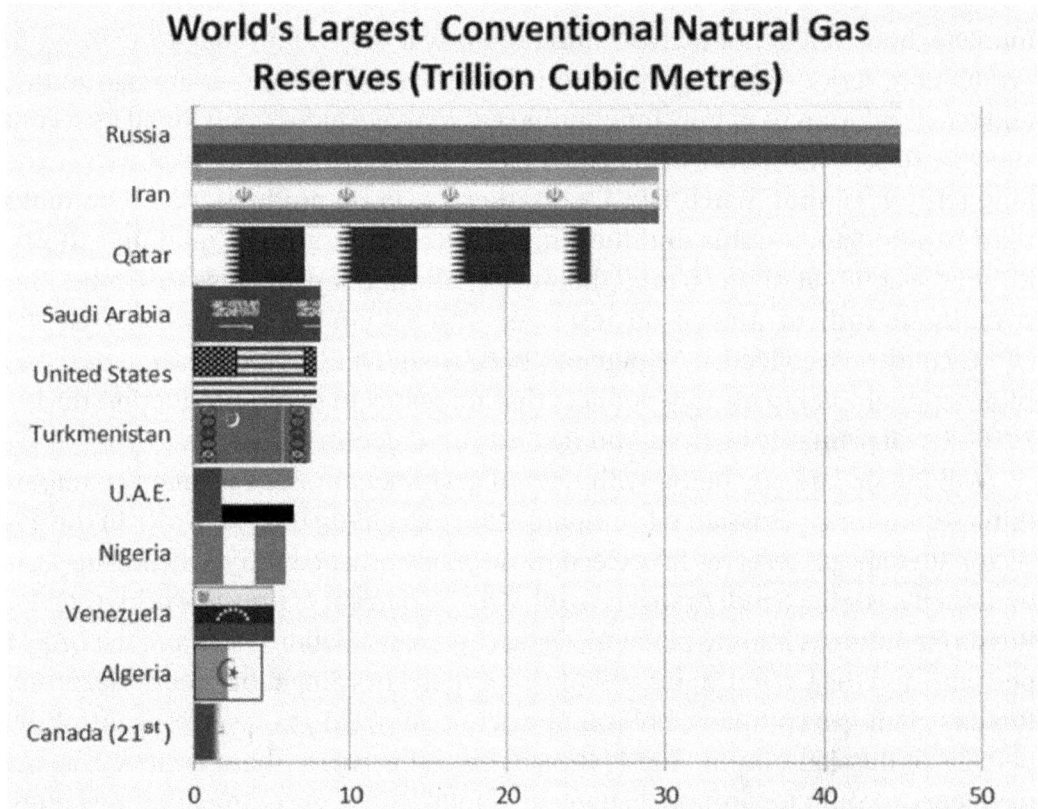

Source: CIA World Fact book

Although geopolitics seems to be working in Russia's favour in world gas markets, the economic picture is less rosy. The country's infrastructure, building and manufacturing stock all suffer from extreme energy inefficiency. A recent World Bank study found that improvements in efficiency in Russia could cut its energy consumption by 45percent , an amount equal to France's total annual energy consumption. Income inequality is a similarly profound obstacle to progress in Russia, with some reports suggesting that Russia's disparity in wealth between the rich and poor is the worst in the world. In particular, a report from Credit Suisse found that just 110 Russian citizens hold 35 percent of the nation's household wealth. Then there are Russia's environmental problems: in the Russian Federation, fossil fuels are king. Not only do oil, gas and coal produce 90 percent of the country's energy, they are also responsible for more than half of the federal government's budget. As regards energy from hydroelectric and nuclear power, Russia's non-fossil fuel energy resources are fledgling, almost to the point of nonexistence. In the wake of the Chernobyl nuclear accident the country enshrined strong environmental protection principles in its constitution could not provide appropriate relief. The challenge, of course, is whether those protections will be enforced. The sanctions levied against Russia by the European Union, the US and others in the wake of the Ukraine crisis have further created challenges for the state and its global aspirations. In 2014, Russia made several military incursions into Ukrainian territory. Beginning with Crimea, took control of strategic positions and infrastructure within the Ukrainian territory of Crimea, which Russia annexed after a disputed referendum. The majority of members of the international community and organisations such as Amnesty International condemned Russia for its actions in post-revolutionary Ukraine, accusing it of breaking international law and violating Ukrainian sovereignty. This led to the implementation of economic sanctions by many countries   against Russia. In July 2014, sanctions were enacted in a coordinated manner by the European Union, the United States, Canada, and other Allies and partners. These sanctions were further strengthened in September 2014. There are three types of economic sanctions. The first restricts access to Western financial markets and services for designated Russian state-owned enterprises in the banking, energy, and defence sectors. The second places an embargo on exports to Russia of designated high-technology oil exploration and production equipment. And lastly, it imposes an embargo on exports to Russia of designated military and dual-use goods.

The justification for these Western sanctions is internationally well-understood. But to muddy the waters, Russia imposed a ban on food imports from Western nations in August 2014. That ban remains in place. The sanctions are generally estimated to have exacerbated the macroeconomic challenges Russia was already facing, notably the rapid and pronounced fall in oil prices that started in the last months of 2014.Furthermore, the combined effect of these sanctions and of the fall in oil prices caused significant downward pressure on the value of the Rouble.

Russia and the International Political Architecture
It has been two decades years since the iron curtain of Cold War has come down. Today Russia is making an endeavour to influence the contemporary global events. With this prowess, Russia is on the way to shake the power triad of USA which she had been enjoying since the end of cold war. The tension has been increasing throughout the years and was most significantly noticed during the conflicts in the Middle East, and during the Arab Spring conflict. These sparks of unrest are very similar to the ones during the period of Cold War. One could even classify the current Iran nuclear crisis and crisis in Syria as proxy wars between

Russia and the United States. Proxy wars are defined as conflicts between third parties who are fighting on behalf of much more powerful nations. The Cold War was filled with proxy wars in which the majority of the fighting took place in foreign lands. This is not much different from the wars in the Middle East. It seems that the civil war in Ukraine is yet another one of the proxy wars of today. As Western countries issue sanctions against Russia, these can be seen as attempts being made by Western countries to shape public opinion against the Russian population. As similar action was done during the Cold War, this has caused many people to worry that the Ukraine crisis has re-sparked the instability. However, now as the Ukraine crisis continues to boil, it is important to consider that the Cold War may never have officially ended. Russian re-emergence is probably going to instigate a power rivalry which would shake the US dominance and lead them both towards a new cold war era.

Where nuclear weapons were the security foundation of the Soviet Unions, they have now moved to a secondary role. Natural gas is the foundation on which Russia intends to maintain its role as a superpower. This can be seen in the way that the EU and USA have responded to the annexation of Crimea. While sanctions have been put in place, they are not aimed at the natural gas industry of Russia, and it is concluded that this shows that Russia have attained a strong position using their natural gas. The relationship between Russia and the Central Asian nations have not changed greatly since the Soviet era. These nations remain closely tied to Russia through economic ties such as Russia being the largest importer of the natural gas extracted in the region. Second, Russia has through acquisitions gained a foothold in the energy sectors of nations in the Central Asian nations. Russia have found a new identity, but that this is not a completely new identity. It is one that is based on a combination of existing ideas ingrained in Russian society, and new ideas formalised which are derived from adapting to the changes following the dissolution of the Soviet Union. When the cold war ended, Russia found themselves in a situation where they could allegorically be called the loser of the ideological struggle that was the cold war. Faced with a world that was changing and a nation that was also changing, Russia had to reinvent themselves in order to find their place in this new world order. Russia could still be considered one of the most powerful countries in the world, but this power was measured by military might. Russia has the world's second most powerful military, according to the annual ranking made by Global Firepower, an analytical website exploring the military power of different countries. The United States headed the list, while China was ranked third in the rating, which does not include nuclear weapons, only conventional ones. And while this might still counts, the world has changed where interdependence and cooperation have taken the front seat instead of getting things done through the threat or use of military power.

From the Russian point of view, the new international order should be based on multipolarity, not unilateral U.S domination, and with Russia as a leading centre of global international relations. During the first Presidency of Vladimir Putin the major doctrinal statement of Putin administration recognised that there is "enhanced possibilities for interstate cooperation in the post-Cold War era" and "significant concern over the global distribution of power." [43]It has been two decades since the iron curtain of Cold War fell down .Today Russia is making an endeavour to influence the contemporary global events.[44]Russia in 2011 and 2012 used its veto-power in the United Nations Security Council against resolutions promoted by Western and Arab countries, to prevent possible sanctions or military intervention against the Syrian government, and Russia continued supplying large amounts of arms that Syria had earlier contracted to buy.[45] On September 30, 2015, Russia started a military intervention in the Syrian Civil War in support of the Al-Assad government, consisting of air strikes against militant groups opposed to the government.

The **Russian military intervention in the Syrian Civil War** began in September 2015 after an official request by the Syrian government for military help against rebel and jihadist groups. The intervention consisted of air strikes primarily in north-western Syria against militant groups opposed to the Syrian government, including Syrian National Coalition, the Islamic State of Iraq and the Levant (ISIL), al-Nusra Front (al-Qaeda in the Levant) and the Army of Conquest. Prior to these operations, Russian involvement in the Syrian Civil War had mainly consisted of supplying the Syrian Army. [84] Russian officials have said that their objective is to help the Syrian government retake territory from various opposition groups, including ISIL, but also groups backed and armed by the United States. Moscow's strategy is born of its historic relationship with the Assad regime and its priorities for the future of a fast-changing Middle East.

Source: https://en.wikipedia.org/wiki/Russian_military_intervention_in_the_Syrian_Civil_War, accessed on June 11,2016.

Moscow's interest and acceptance of membership in the economic groupings like the BRICS is a compulsion due to several geo and economic reasons. Like other emerging economies Russia was (and is) discontent with the global economic and financial system which, the Kremlin believed, was established for the benefit of the 'club' of highly developed countries. It is not incidental that BRICS has institutionally consolidated itself in the context of the global financial crisis of

2008-2010: its member states strongly believed that the West should be blamed for a 'short-sighted' and 'reckless' financial policies that led to the crisis and that they should act together in this critical situation. Their decision to establish a US$100 billion bank to finance infrastructure projects and a US$100 billion reserve fund to steady their currency markets is aimed at creating safeguards against new global crises and making them less dependent on economic and financial rules imposed on the world by the wealthiest nations. Moreover, as Russia believes, the BRICS countries share common economic and financial problems as well as the need for a large-scale modernisation".

Moscow believes that the BRICS countries have an immense potential not only to solve existing problems but also to ensure their sustainable and prosperous socio-economic development. In the aftermath of the September 2013 G20 summit in St. Petersburg (where the BRICS countries had a meeting on the margins) Vladimir Putin announced that "BRICS is the world's biggest market and accounts for 40percent of the world's population – 2.9 billion people," thereby indicating that whenever BRICS speaks, the world really should listen. Overall the Russian policies towards BRICS represent a combination of ideational and material motives. On the one hand, BRICS is important for the Kremlin in terms of status it provides : it believes that by joining forces with other major states it will be easier for Russia to return and maintain its status of a great power, to shape the future world order and to make the West (particularly the United States) abide by the rules of that order.

Rising Clout of India and China

Emerging Challenges

The rise of China and India as major world powers promises to test the established global order in the coming decades. As the two powers grow, they are bound to change the current international system—with profound implications for themselves, the United States, and the world. And whether they could agree on the changes to be made, especially when it comes to their relationship with the West, will influence the system's future character.[46] A close examination of Chinese and Indian perspectives on the fundamentals of the emerging international order reveals that Sino-Indian differences on many issues of both bilateral and global significance are stark:[47]

- Global Order: China and India tend to agree on the importance of state sovereignty and the need to reform global governance institutions to reflect the new balance of power. They also share a strong commitment to the open economic order that has allowed both powers to flourish in the global marketplace. But the two diverge on many details of the international system, such as the future viability of the Non-Proliferation Treaty and the role of state-owned enterprises in fostering globalisation.

- Regional Security: Both China and India want a stable Asia-Pacific that will allow them to sustain their economic prosperity, but they perceive threats very differently and have divergent priorities. Importantly, India seeks a resolute American presence in the region to hedge against possible Chinese excesses, while China sees the United States as significantly complicating its pursuit of its regional goals and worries about American containment attempts.

Security in the Global Commons

- Beijing and New Delhi rely heavily on open sea lines of communication, and as a result, they both support the current maritime security regime. However, their interpretations as to its provisions have occasionally diverged. In space, China enjoys significant advantages over India and has emphasised the military dimensions of its programme, while New Delhi has only recently begun developing space-based military technology. Both countries are just beginning to wrestle with the difficult task of forming cybersecurity policies, but they have already acted to limit objectionable or illegal activities online.
- Non-traditional Security: Chinese and Indian approaches to both energy and the environment broadly converge. Because India and China face a rising domestic demand for energy, they heavily rely on foreign suppliers of energy resources. This has prompted both governments to seek more efficient power sources and to secure their presence in overseas energy markets. On environmental policy, the two countries focus on primarily local and short-term concerns that must be balanced with the need for economic growth.

Due to both their size and the enormous pace of their growth, China and India constitute a "class of their own" among the group of anchor countries, forcefully altering the basic patterns of world politics and the world economy and with them the relationship between the industrialised and developing worlds. A research paper by the German development institute lists the challenges that rising China and India pose. According to the paper, the gradual rise of India and China will lastingly alter the system of global governance in the following ways: the growth of their economic power is also increasingly finding expression in Chinese and Indian interventions in various areas of world politics. Because of their huge demand for energy and natural resources, both countries are pursuing active strategies to secure sources of raw materials in Africa, Latin America, and the Caucasus, and in the process competing with theUS and also with Europe. How will the fact that China and India, two developing countries, becoming important actors of global governance affect the ability of the industrialised countries to respond in a timely fashion to the process of change ahead of them? Western decision makers underestimate the future power of the two drivers of global change, which are at the same time home to roughly 50percent of the world's poor. And will India and China continue to play the role of "advocates"of the interests of the developing countries, possibly risking the emergence of new "North-South tensions,"or will they look primarily to look after their own interests, which need not at all coincide with the interests of the world's other developing economies. What implications will this have for the legitimacy of global governance processes, which of course depend not least on the legitimacy of the relevant actors involved in shaping them? Will binding worldwide human rights, social, and environmental standards prove even more difficult to implement and establish in the altered context of global governance? The significance of an Asia-driven shift in the global balance of power was underlined in a far-reaching exercise that was undertaken by the National Intelligence Council (NIC) of the US Central Intelligence Agency in 2004. Looking ahead to the world in 2020, the report of the NIC's "2020 Project" summed up its findings as follows: In the same way that commentators refer to the 1900s as the "American Century," the 21st century may be seen as the time when Asia, led by China and India, comes into its own. A combination of sustained high economic growth, expanding military capabilities, and large populations will be at the root of the expected rapid rise in economic and political power for both countries. Most forecasts indicate that by 2020 China's gross national product (GNP) will exceed that of individual Western economic powers except for the United States. India's GNP would have overtaken or be on the threshold of overtaking European economies. Because of the sheer size of China's and India's populations – projected by the US Census Bureau to be 1.4 billion and almost 1.3 billion respectively by 2020– their standard of living need not approach Western levels for these countries to become important economic powers. Barring an abrupt reversal of the process of globalisation or any major upheavals in these countries, the rise of these new powers is a virtual certainty. Yet how China and India exercise their growing power and whether they relate cooperatively or competitively to other powers in the international system are key uncertainties. Under such scenarios their foreign policies will, therefore, be watched intensely in future international policy calculations.

International Restructuring

Challenges of Global Governance

Although the concept of governance is not uniformly defined in the social sciences, its Latin origins suggest that governance pertains to the process of "steering" society and is most often used to describe authority, institutions, interests and actors within the state, wherein, rather than independently ruling a country, the role of the state would be to steer society by brokering competing interests and interacting with private and social actors. According to Rosenau, the concept of governance is more inclusive than government as it embraces "governmental institutions and informal, non-government mechanisms whereby needs and wants are fulfilled." For him, governance is a system of rules accepted by the majority. The key components of governance are rules, roles, responsibilities and accountabilities and processes.[48]

As an emerging concept in international relations (IR) theory global governance is a global political project that has challenged the capacity of the social sciences to generate theoretical insights and practical tools to explain contemporary transformations in the global order. Indeed, in the absence of an overarching political authority in the anarchic international realm, academics have sought to make sense of the new world order – global governance is an example of this attempt. The discourse around global governance has followed a series of developments: initially it focused on the emergence of international governance regimes and norm setting within regimes and then pertained to the growth in the number of international regimes in the 1980s and 1990s and research on the influence of the regimes on policies pursued by nation states. Though the theoretical dimensions of global governance relate majorly to the architecture of the world order and the distribution of power, the practical or functional part of the same has come to be associated with the cooperative endeavours of nation-states to cooperatively manage the common interests, issues or problems. In an era where the gap between the demand for and the supply of global governance is growing, it is increasingly urgent that established and emerging democracies find common ground on norms and delivery of global public good, especially on democracy and human rights issues. There is cause for optimism: Rising democracies like India, Brazil, South Africa, Indonesia, and Turkey are embracing democracy and human rights at home and to varying degrees promoting them in their neighbourhoods. But they are not yet stepping up to address the gap on these and other issues in global governance internationally. Simultaneously, the rules-based system under which international relations take place is influx, providing an opportunity to reshape and redirect the global order. Emerging powers emphasise the importance of democratisation both domestically, where they are grappling with their own internal processes of reform, and multilaterally, where they question whether actions of established powers are commensurate with their principles, argue for universal application of rules and norms, and insist on a greater voice at the decision-making table. They have the opportunity to shape the future of global governance as leaders and are proving themselves important players in global affairs, but this shift has been more marked at the level of regions. The results of multipolarity in the global sphere have been more ambiguous and it remains to be seen whether the liberal world order persists or a new framework emerges with rising powers at the helm of a more elastic set of norms.

- In the modern era, peace generally reigns amongst democracies. Democracies also perform better than non-democracies in economic development, and democracy, economic development, and regional integration work hand-in-hand to promote peace and stability. Non-democracies are more likely to be failed states spawning internal or external conflict. It would be expected, therefore, that democracies would identify the spread of democracy as in their national interests and would partner on certain issues, such as support for democratic transitions, human rights and rule of law.

- It is clear that a fundamental shift has taken place regarding humanitarian intervention and that more and more states embrace the broad values expressed by R2P. For example, most of the 118 states that mentioned Syria at the UN General Assembly in 2012 expressed concern about the population, up from less than a third who invoked Kosovo and East Timor in 1999. In addition, the IBSA Dialogue Forum sent a delegation to Syria, as did Turkey, a new rallying of emerging powers to address threats to human rights both inside and outside their own neighbourhoods. This level of attention and the unprecedented advocacy of a policy of intervention by rising powers can be attributed at least in part to the improved quality of democracy in the rising democracies.

- For any country to retain credibility in international cooperation on human rights and democracy, a strong human rights record at home is a vital requisite. Otherwise, the rules-based system that governs behaviour is weakened by the perception that great powers write the rules but are not necessarily committed to following them. In this respect, emerging powers emphasise the importance of addressing human rights challenges domestically.

Today's salient question is whether the post-1945 Western liberal order can survive the fastest redistribution of global economics in world history, a process likely to upset at least the membership if not the existence of many of these global institutions. Some of the significant rules of the world order and how they stand challenged today can be enumerated as follows:[49]

- Sovereignty and Non-Intervention: Although the post-1945 order was founded on state sovereignty and non-intervention, emerging security threats and competing normative claims have weakened this presumption. According to the Responsibility to Protect (R2P) norm, endorsed unanimously at the 2005 UN High Level Summit, a state may forfeit its presumption against external intervention if it makes war on its people or fails to protect them from atrocities.

- No Altering Borders by Force: Resurgent great power imperialism is also testing norms of territorial integrity. Russia's seizure of Crimea and intervention by proxy in eastern Ukraine represents the clearest violation of national sovereignty since Saddam Hussein's 1990 conquest of Kuwait.

- No Use of Force without Security Council Approval: the UN Charter prohibits military force in the absence of UNSC authorisation (except for self-defence). Over the past two decades, the norm has suffered major blows. This includes the NATO intervention in Kosovo in 1999 (launched without the prior approval of the UNSC) and, even more damaging, the invasion of Iraq by a U.S.-led coalition invasion in 2003.

- Non-proliferation of Weapons of Mass Destruction: Today, world order depends more than ever on agreement among world powers to control Weapons of Mass Destruction (WMD). Nevertheless, pressing challenges remain; making sufficient progress on the disarmament obligations of recognised nuclear powers under Article 6 of the NPT ratification of the Comprehensive Test-Ban Treaty (CTBT)—in which states agree to ban all nuclear explosions in all environments.

- An Obligation to Combat Terrorism: Since 9/11, UN member states has made uneven progress in multilateral efforts to combat transnational terrorism. One bright spot is UNSC Resolution 1373, passed in September 2001 in the aftermath of the terrorist attacks on the United States. It established a UN Counter Terrorism Committee (CTC), which requires all states to crack down on terrorist groups.

- Maintaining an Open, Non-Discriminatory World Economy: Major players disagree over the governance reforms needed in IFIs; the dollar's role as the world's reserve currency; the appropriate ambition and scope of regional trade agreements; the right standards that should govern development cooperation;

the wisdom of capital market controls; and the proper role of the state in the market.

• Mitigating—and Adapting to—Climate Change: For nearly two decades after negotiating the Kyoto Protocol (1997), the parties to the UN Framework Convention on Climate Change were deadlocked by normative as well as interest based disputes over the relative burden of adjustment that should be assumed by developed versus developing countries, including how to translate the principle of "common but differentiated responsibilities" into concrete action.

• Promoting Human Rights and Democracy: Since 1945, international treaties such as the International Covenant on Civil and Political Rights (1976) have recognised that individuals have fundamental rights under international law. However, many of the major rights abusers of the world routinely win election to the UN Human Rights Council.

• Safeguarding Access to the Open Global Commons: A major challenge to contemporary world order is preserving the stability of and open access to the global commons—domains that are not under sovereign control but upon which all nations depend for security, prosperity, and welfare—as these become "congested, contested, and competitive." The four most important global commons are the maritime, air space, outer space, and cyberspace domains.

• Technological Innovation and the Frontiers of Global Governance:- Several recent technological breakthroughs cry out for regulation. The controversial use of unmanned aerial vehicles (UAVs) by the United States for "targeted killings"(assassinations) of suspected terrorists, coupled with the global proliferation of drone technologies in both public and private hands, underscores the need for international regulation and some legal agreement on their appropriate use as instruments of war.

The multi-polar world that we face is vastly different from the bipolar power struggle of the Cold War. Not only are there multiple states exerting significant global influence, but also a number of non-state actors. States are being challenged from above, by regional and global organisations; from below, by militias; and from the side, by a variety of nongovernmental organisations (NGOs) and corporations. Power is now found in many hands and in many places. As the world inevitably moves toward multipolarity, countries should prepare for future challenges to benefit most from this long-awaited gift from globalisation, to give balance to the globe, limit the abuses of some powers and empower those they abuse. Universal issues previously ignored, for the of lack of international coordination or lack of powers, evasion of responsibility and procrastination, will require more world attention. Nuclear threats, climate change, deforestation, illegal migration, economic monopoly, or interfering in the sovereignty of other nations are no more a business of a single country. Fewer states can no longer act on their own on critical issues affecting the entire planet.

Notes

1. Stephen, Mathew D, "States, Norms and Power", RL: http://mil.sagepub.com/content/42/3/888. short, accessed on April 10, 2016.
2. Ibid.
3. Unay, Sadik, "Reality or Mirage? BRICS and the Making of Multipolarity in the Global Political Economy", *Insight Turkey,* Vol. 15, no. 3, 2013, p.77.
4. Ibid.
5. Ibid.
6. The Hegemonic Stability Theory has been used to explain international change. This theory indicates that the international system is more likely to remain stable when a single nation-state is the dominant world power, or hegemony. Thus, the fall of an existing hegemon or the state of no hegemon diminishes the stability of the international system. When a hegemon exercises leadership, either through diplomacy, coercion, or persuasion, it is actually deploying its "preponderance of power."
7. Schweller, Randell, "Rising Powers and Revisionism in Emerging International Orders," URL: http://eng.globalaffairs.ru/valday/Rising-Powers-and-Revisionism-in-Emerging-International-Orders-17730, accessed on April 6, 2016.
8. Given the law of uneven growth among states, a gap emerges over time between the actual distribution of power in the system and its distribution of prestige (or reputation for power), throwing the system into disequilibrium and causing persistent instability. To peacefully restore system equilibrium, the waning hegemony must cede influence to the rising challenger to the point where the latter's prestige matches its actual power.
9. Jones, Bruce, "The Changing Balance of Influence and US Strategy," URL: http://www.brookings.edu/research/papers/2011/03/global-order-jones, accessed on May 6, 2016.
10. Wickett, Xenia, "The Asia Pacific Power Balance: Beyond the US-China Narrative", Chatham House, September, 2015, p.14.
11. Singh, Suresh P., "BRICS and the World Order: A Beginners Guide", May 2014, p.19.
12. Downie, Christian, "Global Energy Governance: Do the BRICS Have the Energy to Drive Reform?" *International Affairs,* vol.91, no.4, 2015, p.805.
13. Unay, Sadik, n.3, p.84.
14. Downie, n.12, p.806.
15. Elgström, Ole, "Eu Leadership in an Emerging New World Order", URL: http://www.jhubc.it/ecpr-porto/virtualpaperroom/015.pdf, accessed June 9, 2016.
16. "European Union", URL: http://www.encyclopedia.com/topic/European_Union.aspx, accessed May 9, 2016.
17. The European debt Crisis is a multi-year debt crisis that has been taking place in the European Union since the end of 2009.

18. Kamrany, Nake M China's Rise to Global Economic Superpower" URL:http://www.huffingtonpost.com/nake-m-kamrany/chinas-rise-to-global-eco_b_6544924.html,accessed on June 9, 2016.
19. "Contours of Conflict in the21ˢᵗ Century", HCSS Report,March, 2011, URL: http://www.strategyandchange.nl/rapporten/contouren-van-conflict-in-de-21-ste-eeuw/113/, accessed on July 2, 2016.
20. Abraham M., "Security and the Global Commons", The National Bureau of Asian Research, Denmark, 2010.
21. Ibid.
22. Nathan, Andrew JandAndrew Scobell, "How China Sees America", *Foreign Affairs*, September-October 2012, pp.34-40.
23. Ibid.
24. Bower, Ernerst Z "Decoding China's Emerging Great Power Strategy in Asia"https://csisprod.s3.amazonaws.com/s3fspublic/legacy_files/files/publication/140603_Johnson_DecodingChinasEmerging_WEB.pdf, accessed on June 23, 2016.
25. Morrison, Wayne M,"China's Economic Rise: History, Trends, Challenges, and Implications for the United States",October, 2015, accessed on May,14,2016.
26. Peter Gey, Matthias Jobelius and Renate Tenbusch, "India: Challenges On The Road To Becoming A World Power",Stifting Paper, September,2007,.http://library.fes.de/pdf-files/iez/05251.pdf, accessed on June 10,2016.
27. Ramachandra Guha,"Will India Become a Superpower?" http://www.lse.ac.uk/IDEAS/publications/reports/pdf/SR010/guha.pdf,accessed on May 16, 2016.
28. Dwiwedi, Ratnesh, "Potential Superpowers",https://www.linkedin.com/pulse/potential-super-powers-1brazil-india-ratnesh-dwivedi, accessed on June 4, 2016.
29. Lal, Deepak, "Tasks for an Emerging Superpower"http://www.econ.ucla.edu/lal/busta/busta0509.pdf accessed on May 31, 2016.
30. Mishra, Ashutosh "India a Rising Power", http://www.aspistrategist.org.au/india-a-rising-power/accessed on May 31, 2016.
31. Tellis, Ashley J," India as a Leading Power"http://carnegieendowment.org/2016/04/04/india-as-leading-power-pub-63185,accessed on May 31, 2016.
32. Zakaria, Fareed, "India Rising"URL: http://www.newsweek.com/india-rising-106259,accessed on July 2, 2016.
33. Ibid.
34. "Japan", URL http://www.newworldencyclopedia.org/entry/Japan,accessed on May 5, 2016.
35. Ibid.
36. Angus, Madison,*Contours of the world economy 1-2030 AD: Essays in macro-economic history.* (Oxford: Oxford University Press, 2007).
37. "Japanese Economic Miracle" https://en.wikipedia.org/wiki/Japanese_economic_miracle., accessed on June 9, 2016.
38. Naoki, Tanaka, "Beyond the Myth of the Economic Superpower", http://www.nippon.com/en/in-depth/a00901/, accessed on July 4, 2016.
39. Mulgan, Aurelia George, "Japan's Choices in a Multipolar World" URL http://www.eastasiaforum.org/2009/02/06/japans-choices-in-a-multipolar-world/, accessed on July 2, 2016.
40. Glatter, Pete, "Russia: Rising from the East", URL: https://www.theguardian.com/commentisfree/2006/dec/13/comment.russiahttp://socialistreview.org.uk/313/russia-rising-east,accessed on June 1, 2016.
41. Ibid.

42. Hill, Fiona, Russia: The 21st Century's Energy Superpower, URL: http://www.brookings.edu/research/articles/2002/03/spring-russia-hill,accessed on July 3, 2016.

43. "Russia's National Security Concepts and Military Doctrines: Continuity and Change", URL: http://www.idsa-india.org/an-oct-00-5.html, accessed on July 4, 2016.

44. Wolfgang Seiffert, "Russia's Role in the NewWorld Order", *Current Concerns*, No. 14, 2007.

45. Gady, Franz Stefan , "How the West Underestimated Russia's Military power", October 17, 2015, *The Diplomat*, URL: http://thediplomat.com/2015/10/how-the-west-underestimated-russias-military-power/ Accessed on May 7,2016.

46. Tellis, Ashley J and SeanMirski, *Crux of Asia: China, India, and the Emerging Global Order*, URL: http://carnegieendowment.org/2013/01/10/crux-of-asia-china-india-and-emerging-global-order, accessed on July 5, 2016.

47. Ibid.

48. Lennox, Victoria, "Global Governance" URL: http://www.e-ir.info/2008/10/03/conceptualising-global-governance-in-international-relations, accessed on July 5, 2016.

49. Patrick, Stewart, "World Oder: What, Exactly, are the Rules?" May 3, 2016, *Council on Foreign Relations*, URL:http://blogs.cfr.org/patrick/2016/05/03/world-order-what-exactly-are-the-rules/, accessed on July 5, 2016.

CHAPTER 12

Revisiting Security: The Human Security Dimension

The global political architecture has undergone vast changes and challenges since the last few decades. Devastating environmental shocks of climate change, its impact on food, water and energy resources impacting economy of nations, problems relating to migration, threat of pandemic diseases cutting across political boundaries, transnational crimes and global financial crises are being increasingly recognised as critical issues having repercussions on national, regional and international security. Challenges to the very survival and well-being of people, groups and states have taken place. As a result, security merely seen as protection against war and preparation for war seems to be an inadequate and incomplete analysis.[1] The study of security has always been a central concern in the academic discipline of international relations (IR). This relates to the birth of the discipline in a background which was rot with the shocking violence of World War I, and also relates to the concern of nations to engage in a systematic study of war and potential foundations of lasting peace. The concept of security hence dominated the intellectual preoccupations of the students of international relations, well into the Second World War and through nearly half century of the Cold War.

Compared with the period of the Cold War, international security ceased to be a central theme during the decade between the dismantling of the Soviet State and the destruction of the World Trade Centre. 9/11 saw the questions relating to security/insecurity once again rising to the top of agenda. However, this time various issues and new threats generated by globalisation and fed by the war on terrorism have come to inform the scholarly concerns with the ever engaging question of security.[2] It is however important to point out that thinking of the security until the 1980s had predefined answers to predefined questions, the subject as well as the subject matter has been an area of contestation since the end of the Cold War. The 'rethinking security' debate has taken on a new urgency with the world's most significant power declaring its global war on terrorism after September 11, 2001. The entire world is traumatised, though in different ways and for different reasons, by clouds of destruction, terror or terrorism. At the same time, huge disparities in access to human well-being across the globe, demands urgent attention.

Globalising processes are accelerating and yet localising processes remain powerful. Many nation states are weakening and yet others are undiminished. Wealth is expanding and yet poverty is omnipresent. New technologies are adding to the comforts of daily life and yet ubiquitous regions are unifying yet others are mired in conflict and war. Scholars like James Rosenau point to the fact that the essential quagmire which is emerging in the contemporary world characterised by globalisation, relates to concepts which are challenged, theories which are being revisited and a world order which is turbulent.[3] The widespread lack of clarity about the emerging international order directly connects to the ongoing debate in security studies. While national security had some basic geopolitical precepts that stand is challenged today. All of this suggests uncertainty about the future and the likely shape of dangers in the future.

From defining security in the purely militaristic terms, to examining security as being related to poverty, human rights, development, environment and terrorism, the subject has travelled a long distance. Those who argue that militaristic or traditional notions are insufficient to explain security today, put forth their ideas of non-military threats to contemporary security. This discourse claims to be more holistic and comprehensive and rests its analysis on the theme of individual as the focus of study. Hence, human security is how security is discussed, debated and conceptualised today. In order to have a clear understanding of the evolving meaning of security and the paradigmatic change the concept has undergone, the chapter would be divided into:

• Conceptualising security.
• The widening and deepening debate.
• The non-military dimension.
• Themes and challenges in human security.

Conceptualising Security

The Definitional Parameters
Security is an elusive term. Just like the concepts of justice, peace and honour, the term security also denotes a quality of relationship which resists definition. There are two images which come to mind when we think of the word 'security'. As a noun, security evokes the picture of a solid object in the form of an alarm or

weapon used to protect or defend against intrusion or attack. On the other hand, as an activity, the portrayal of security also displays vulnerability and makes us feel unsafe.[4] In terms of states' perception of the intentions of its rivals, security becomes a negative freedom, that is, the absence of threats. Hans Morgenthau believes that national security must be defined as integrity of the national territory and its institutions, and emphasises that survival of a political unit constitutes the necessary element of its interest *vis-à-vis* other units. According to Arnold Wolfers, "security in an objective sense measures the absence of threats to acquired values, in a subjective sense, the absence of fear that such values will be attacked". Montesquieu understood security in relation to political freedom: political freedom consists in security, or at least in the opinion which one has of one's security. Adam Smith referred to the freedom from the prospect of violent attack on the person or the person's property as relating to the security of the individuals.[5] Emma Rothschild locates the meaning of security as a concept relating to individuals and groups, as well as states, and maintaining that the object of the state is common security.

Security can thus be understood as a human value overlapping the values of freedom, order, and solidarity. It is not an exaggeration to point out that security is a complex and contested notion, heavily laden with emotion and deeply held values. Most people would agree that a security problem arises when a group or an individual threatens another's life. Many others would extend the meaning of security to other values and interests. They would apply the term to environmental damage caused by global warming or to the struggle for subsistence by billions of people, or to protection of human rights from torture and genocide. Edward Kolodzieg raises some pertinent questions here. Where do we draw the line in studying security? What should be included or excluded? If a broad and inclusive understanding of security is accepted, then will it be correct that almost every human value and interest is a security issue. Conversely, if a narrow conception of security was adopted, identifying solely with force and coercive threats, we may fall into the danger of excluding important actors and factors bearing crucially on security. In the historical debate about how best to achieve national security realist writers like Hobbes, Machiavelli and Rousseau tended to paint a rather pessimistic picture of the implications of state sovereignty. The international system was viewed as a rather brutal arena in which state would seek to achieve their security at the expensive the neighbours. Interstate relations were seen as a struggle for power, as states constantly attempted to take advantage of each other. According to the new Neorealists, state claiming sovereignty will inevitably develop military capabilities to defend themselves and extend their power.

According to this view, national security or insecurity is largely the result of the structure of the international system, which is characterized by anarchy.[6]

Security and State Centrism
In the state-centric notions of security, the security specialists have tended to assert the primacy of military security over other goals. The logic is that in anarchy, security is the highest end. Only if survival is assured can states safely seek such other goals as tranquillity, profit and power. In this notion of security, governments almost invariably commit as many resources as they feel necessary to preserve their national security. This is because a state can have no higher goal than survival since profits matter little when enemy is occupying your country and slaughtering your citizens.

Source: Buzan, Barry and Lene Hansen, *International Security* (London: Sage, 2007), p.106.

Hence, in the traditional sense, the security of states was deemed to be threatened by any change that might threaten the monopoly of violence, whether through external invasion or internal rebellion. From the late 1940s to the late 1980s, national security focused on the military dimension of the Cold War confrontation of the major world powers. These Cold War security studies focused on deterrence and the finer points of preventing nuclear war. Four broad themes are said to have dominated the entire literature of security studies during this period. First, security was viewed not as the primary goal of states but rather as one among several values, the relative importance of which varied from one state to another. Security was at times defined as a 'derivative value', being meaningful only in so far as it promotes and maintains other values which have been or are being realised. This view focused attention on trade-offs between military security and other values such as economic welfare, economic stability and individual freedom. Second, national security was viewed as a goal to be pursued by both non-military and military techniques of state craft. Third, awareness of the security dilemma led to emphasis on caution with respect to military policy and fourth, much attention was paid to the relationship between security and domestic affairs such as economy and domestic political processes.[7]

The Cold War affected both the level of activity and the substantive focus of research on security. It focused attention on nuclear weaponry and strategies, and military instruments of statecraft became the central concern of security specialists. In the words of Barry Buzan and Lene Hansen, "The Cold War had been the meta-event upon which the international security studies had been founded and great power politics and technology had been the two most significant forces shaping the evolution inside that framework. Post-Cold War traditional international security studies were compelled to answer two fundamental questions: why did the Cold War end? And would traditional military state-centric approaches be of much use with bipolarity gone?".[8] The pre-occupation with technology, primarily nuclear technology had been enormous. With the end of the Cold War, the link between technology development and rivalry was broken. However, the material reality of nuclear technology was still to be dealt with. Security studies were hence forced to locate answers to challenging questions like the role which remained for strategic studies and the military side of peace research in the emerging scenario. The end of bipolarity was one thing, but the manner in which it had come about, peacefully and voluntarily rather through military confrontation formed a challenge of its own. Realism along with its emphasis on state, security and military preparedness was under scanner. The understanding of security as concerned primarily with external threats, stood challenged. The need to shift from external threats to internal ones was apparent as evidenced by the upsurge in the so-called ethnic or civil conflicts and the upsurge of humanitarian crisis in different parts of the world. This was indicative of the need to widen the analysis on security.

Beyond the State

The Widening and Deepening of Security

The inadequacy of thinking about security as purely in militaristic terms, was apparent to some theorists and political leaders even when the Cold War was at its most intensive stage. The effect on developing countries of low-intensity proxy wars between the super powers and the heightened tension caused by the nuclear forces was already placing a question on the adequacy that such policies purported to serve. However, it was the fall of the Berlin war and the disintegration of the Soviet Union which provided the major shock to the theoretical system from which international security had been born as a concept, and security studies as its appropriate academic discipline. A narrow, state-centred and military-focused definition of security was no longer appealing and feasible. According to David Baldwin, the most significant question was what should post-Cold War security studies be about? Baldwin himself points out to three options. The first option was to do nothing. This option is based on the assumption that the international system was still as competitive, dangerous and war-prone as ever: states still have to focus primarily on the problems of military security. The second option was modest reform. Baldwin was of the opinion, for most of the scholars' attention started shifting to the challenges of conflict elsewhere in the world. This agenda pointed to regional security problems, especially, civil wars.

The third option put forth by Baldwin was proper radical reform. This required scholars to expand the notion of security threat to include such matters as human rights, the environment, economics, epidemics, crime and social injustice. This agenda involved both widening security studies to cover non-military threats and deepening security studies to cover threats at multiple levels below and above the state (i.e. threats to people, communities, states, regions and the world).

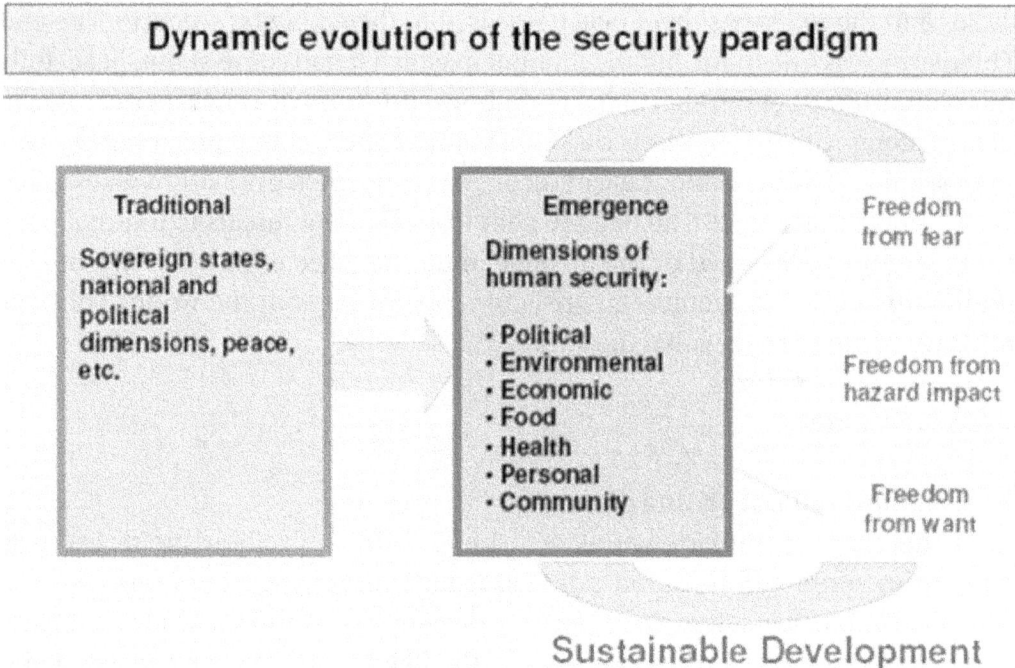

Dynamic evolution of the security paradigm

Traditional

Sovereign states, national and political dimensions, peace, etc.

Emergence

Dimensions of human security:

- Political
- Environmental
- Economic
- Food
- Health
- Personal
- Community

Freedom from fear

Freedom from hazard impact

Freedom from want

Sustainable Development

Source: http://pubs.sciepub.com/jephh/2/5/2/

A detailed framework for widening security was provided by Barry Buzan in his most celebrated work "People, States and Fear". Buzan proposed five sectors where security maybe threatened: military, political, economic, societal and environmental. Military security is the traditional core of strategic studies. Political security concerns the capacities and stabilities of state institutions. Economic security is about sufficient access to resources, finance and markets. Societal security concerns the sustainability of cultural, ethnic and religious identity. Finally, environmental security covers the protection of the local and global biospheres. Writers like Richard Ullman talked about the fact that excessive military focus of security studies would not accurately reflect the security challenges facing states. Ullman proposed that security policy should give more attention to non-military events and trends that threaten to greatly reduce national policy options or drastically degrade the quality of life for a nation. Thus, the post-1990 security analysis has appeared in an 'extended sense'. According to Emma Rothschild,[9] the extension takes four main forms. In the first, the concept of security is extended from the security of nations to the security of groups and individuals: it is extended downwards from nations to individuals. In the second, it is extended from security of nations to the security of international system, or of a supra-national physical environment: it is extended upwards, from the nation to the biosphere. In the third operation, the concept of security is extended horizontally, or to the sorts of security that are in question. The concept of security is extended, therefore, from military to political, economic, social, environmental, human security. In a fourth operation, the political responsibility for ensuring security is itself extended: it is diffused in all directions from nation-states, including upward to international institutions, downwards to regional or local government, and sideways to non-governmental organisations, to public opinion and the press.

The Concept of Securitisation

One of the contemporary approaches in the international relations theories relates to social constructivism. The central concept in constructivism is that of 'norms', which are beliefs shared by a community about who they are, what the world is like, and how they can and should act in given situations. Norms are institutionalised and reproduced through community discourse, doctrines, policies and practices. Constructivists have produced studies of how norms prescribe or should prescribe security practices. One of the most influential attempt of incorporating the methods and methodology of constructivism for security studies is the concept of securitisation. The peace studies in Denmark, especially Ole Weaver took forward the widening agenda of Barry Buzan and highlighted the concept of securitisation. The focus here is to analyse the multiple and complex ways in which security threats are generated and constructed. Weaver adapted the concept of the 'Speech Act' and applied it to the discourse on security. He argued that when something is identified as a security issue, this constitutes a particular 'Speech Act' involving a process of securitisation, whereby an issue is presented as posing an existential threat to a designated referent object. Barry Buzan has refined this definition to the exertion of an existential threat which requires exceptional measures and/or emergency action to deal with it, which means that it is removed from the realm of politics to the realm of security. The securitisation approach is closely linked to the wider post-Cold War security agenda and has focused on the ways in which, after the end of the Cold War, non-traditional security threats such as the environment, migration or transnational organised crime has been securitised.

Source: Buzan, Barry and Lene Hansen, *International Security* (London: Sage, 2007), p.151.

Such ideas of extended security were hardly new in the 1990s. In fact, similar ideas were expressed, as early as 1982 in the report of the Palme Commission. The report stated, states can no longer seek security at each other's expense; it can be attained only through cooperative undertakings. Security should be thought of in terms of economic and political as well as military objectives. Military security is a means, while the economic security of individuals, or the social security of the citizens to chart futures in a manner of their own choosing, or the political system that follows when the international system is capable of peaceful and orderly change, were ends in themselves. The second point made in the report was that lasting security should be founded on an effective system of international order. A third conception was that security is a process as much as a condition, and one in which participants are individuals and their groups as well as popular opinion. Analysts of the changing dimensions of security point out that though the end of Cold War was the loss of a meta-event and led to the marginalisation of military-political agenda, the traditional wing of security studies has continued to evolve their adaptation to the new realities of the post-Cold War era is visible in their emphasis on nuclear proliferation, ballistic missile defence and the latest revolution in military affairs. However, though the post-Cold War traditionalists are still holding on to their beliefs, the raging debate on widening and deepening the security agenda clearly emerges victorious. This debate has come to manifest itself in the discussion on non-traditional or non-military security threats and has broadened into the over-arching concept of human security.

Non-Traditional Security (NTS)

The Human Dimension

The international system has changed dramatically since 1945. Not only has the disappearance of the Soviet Union marked this change, but there have also been substantial changes that have accumulated overtime and are expressed with particular strength in this era. Contemporary global politics has witnessed the emergence of a plethora of actors on the world stage. There are sovereign states as significant actors, no doubt, but the stage has also come to be occupied by numerous other actors; inter-governmental organisations, international non-governmental organisations, multinational corporations, international regimes and even the presence of violent non-state actors including terrorist outfits. These actors are not just international agencies capable of changing their surroundings, but a series of transnational forces expressed with particular strength in the world today. Their emergence has meant that state is now enjoying comparatively less power. In other words, the state has seized to enjoy monopolistic control in six basic areas:[10]

- *Communications* are no longer under the complete control of the state, the internet being one of the examples.
- *Technological development* depending more on the private sector than the state.
- *Financial transactions* freely flowing with little capacity for intervention by the state.
- *International migration* and the ability to control the movement of the people has diminished.
- *Trade* has increasingly opened up and states are compelled to lower controls and restrictions.

All of the above has implications in threat perceptions that are different from the traditional ones, and hence the mechanisms of actions to cope with them. Coordinating policies, establishing regulations and generating international regimes based on shared values are some of the themes that are therefore gaining salience. New types of instabilities have led to the challenge of the notion of traditional security by such concepts as cooperative, comprehensive, societal, collective, international, and human security. Although these concepts moved away from the focus on interstate relations, human security takes the most dramatic step by making the reference point not the state, society, or community, but the individual.[11] This shift is meant to direct research and policy towards the actual issues threatening people's lives.

Challenge of balancing Human Security and State Security

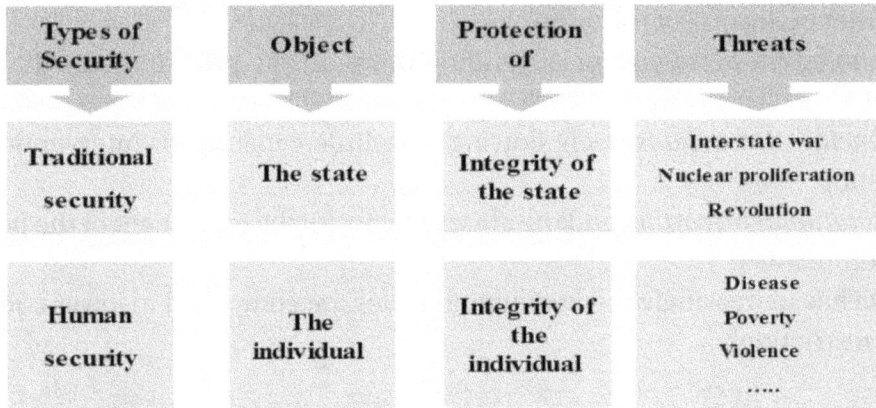

Types of Security	Object	Protection of	Threats
Traditional security	The state	Integrity of the state	Interstate war Nuclear proliferation Revolution
Human security	The individual	Integrity of the individual	Disease Poverty Violence ......

Source: Challenge of balancing Human Security and State Security, at http://slideplayer.com/slide/6068262/ accessed May 6, 2016.

This movement has led to what many may term as 'Paradigmatic Shift' in the conceptual understanding of security from military to non-military or from traditional to non-traditional threats. Therefore, the core scheme of security today can be extended in various directions by combination of the following attributes:

- Reference object – state, region, alliance, society, various social groups – minorities, ethnic groups, individuals, global system.
- Areas in which existential disturbances (threats) are emerging (sectors) – political, military, economic, ecological, societal.
- Methods of prediction (identification) of disruptions – beginning from the search for objective threats and ending with subjectively perceived threats, also resulting from social discourse (securitisation).[12]

It is clear that the new globalised world order begets new challenges. The list of these non-traditional challenges to security is exhausting and includes energy security, food security, water security, environmental security, terrorism and transnational crime, illegal migration, pandemics, natural disasters and last but not the least human security. Non-traditional security challenges have taken as their reference point the concept of human security in order to promote a focus on the individual *per se*, as such, this inquiry into 'threats to the lives of people', thereby, makes a clear distinction between traditional and human security. The concept of human security rose into prominence in the debate following the 1994

United Nations Development Program (UNDP) report. Starting from the premise that the end of Cold War gave an impetus to re-thinking the concept of security, the UNDP proposed that the focus of states should shift from nuclear security to human security.

With the dark shadows of the cold war receding, one can now see that many conflicts are within nations rather than between them. For most people, a feeling of insecurity arises more from worries about daily life than from the dread of a cataclysmic world event. Will they and their families have enough to eat? Will they lose their jobs? Will their streets and neighbourhoods be safe from crime? Will they be tortured by a repressive state? Will they become a victim of violence because of their gender? Will their religion or ethnic origin target them for persecution? In the final analyses, human security is a child who did not die, a disease that did not spread, a job that was not cut, an ethnic tension that did not explode in violence, a dissident who was not silenced. Human security is not a concern with weapons – it is a concern with human life and dignity.[13]

Four Features of Human Security

The UNDP report notes four main features of the concept of human security:

- It is a universal concern, relevant to people everywhere because the threats are common to all.
- Its components are interdependent. Since the threats to human security do not stay within national borders.
- It is easier to achieve through early rather than later intervention, and
- It is people-centred, in that it is concerned with how people live and breathe in society.

Source: Booth, Ken in,*Critical Security Studies and World Politics*, (Boulder and London: Lynne Rienner,2005)p. 52.

Human Security: New Agenda for a New Age

The concept of human security forms a core component of the contemporary security studies. This concept has questioned the dominant state-centric approach to security, which makes the state the referent object or the entity to be made secure. By contrast, human security by shifting the focus to the individual, and making people the referent object, places increasing attention on people suffering insecurities inside states. The idea that people need to be secure in their daily lives is not a new one. In fact, the political philosophy of liberalism placed people at its epicentre by providing them necessary conditions such as freedom and equality. By emphasising on the adoption of universal human rights, liberalism also sought to invest in the discipline of international relations with a broad normative vision. However, these instances of philosophical and political human centric traditions have now acquired the formal garb of 'human security'. The UNDP report, 1994, talks about giving relief to people from all the traumas that besiege human development. The emphasis is on providing safety from chronic threats such as hunger and disease and protection from sudden disruptions in the patterns of daily life.

The UNDP report outlines seven areas which deal with human security. Since the annual report in 1994, though the UNDP refined its concept and in 1997 introduced a distinction between income poverty and human poverty (the former refers to an income of US$1 a day and less, and the latter two factors such as life expectancy and illiteracy), the major thrust areas remain the same and can be highlighted as:

- Economic security: poverty; vulnerability to global economic change.
- Food security: hunger and famine, vulnerability to extreme climate events and agricultural changes.
- Health security: injury and disease, vulnerability to disease and infection.
- Environmental security: resource depletion, vulnerability to pollution and environmental degradation.
- Personal security: violence, vulnerability to conflicts, natural hazards, and "creeping" disasters.
- Community security: violations of the integrity of cultures; vulnerability to cultural globalisation.
- Political security: political repression, vulnerability to conflicts and warfare.[14]

Scholars have highlighted the various purposes that the concept of human security serves. The focus that the concept puts on the nexus between conflict and development is very useful and important. Since the 1990s conflicts are seen as occurring or frequently surrounding disrupted states. An analysis of conflicts and the related human suffering not only brings to the fore an understanding of state failure, but also its dire local, regional and global effects. From a normative perspective, human security and its concern serve to highlight the importance of global norms. One can see this in the fact that discussions on human security have been the underlying motivation for the Universal Declaration of Human Rights, the UN Charter, the Geneva Conventions, the Ottawa Treaty, and the International Criminal Court. Human security often serves as an umbrella norm for various treaties and conventions aiming to protect the vulnerable. Some scholars have linked the study of conflict and security to economic development. Caroline Thomas maintains that material sufficiency is at the core of human security. According to her, 'human security describes a condition of existence in which basic human needs are met, and in which human dignity, including meaningful participation in the life of the community can be realised'. In the words of Amitav Acharya, 'we have three different conceptions of human security today: one focusing on the human costs of violent conflict, another stressing human needs in the path to sustainable development and a third emphasising human rights.[15]

Schools of Thought on Human Security

▸ **Freedom from Fear:**
  ▹ Protecting individuals from violent conflicts;
  ▹ Recognizing that these violent threats are strongly associated with poverty, lack of state capacity and other forms of inequities;
  ▹ Emergency assistance, conflict prevention and resolution, peace-building are the main concerns of this approach.

▸ **Freedom from Want:**
  ▹ The threat agenda should be broadened to include hunger, disease and natural disasters because they are inseparable concepts in addressing the root of human insecurity.

➔ **complimentary, NOT contradictory!**

Source: http://www.slideshare.net/triwidodowutomo/public-administration-and-human-security accessed 0n June 16,2016.

Human Security and the Responsibility to Protect (R2P)

In the post-Cold War era, the importance given to people's security has grown in salience. One reason for this is the rising incidence of civil wars and intra-state conflicts involving ethnic cleansing and displacement of people. Traditional national security approaches have not been sufficiently sensitive towards conflicts that arise over cultural, ethnic and religious differences. Each state has a responsibility to protect its citizens from mass killings. If that state is unable or unwilling to exercise that responsibility, or is itself a perpetrator of atrocities, its sovereignty is abrogated while the responsibility to protect devolves to the international community of states. Following the 1994 genocide in Rwanda and ethnic cleansing in the Balkans and Kosovo in 1995 and 1999, the international community began to seriously debate, as to how to protect such human rights violations. R2P was endorsed by the 2005 World Summit, and has since shaped international responses to such mass atrocities. R2P embraces three specific responsibilities:

- Responsibility to Prevent, by addressing both the root and immediate causes of conflict,
- Responsibility to React, by reacting to situations of human rights violations, e.g. by imposing sanctions,
- Responsibility to Rebuild, by providing full assistance with recovery and reconstruction.

Source: Kumar, Chanchal and Sanju Gupta, *United Nations and Global Conflicts* (New Delhi: Regal, 2013). p. 565.

While all the advocates of human security agree that people are the referent object, they seem to be divided over the type of threat that should be prioritised or securitised. The dispute over prioritising threats has divided advocates of human security into the narrow and the broad school. From the narrow perspective, human security is the protection of individuals and communities from war and other forms of violence. This narrow definition has been simplified as 'freedom from fear' of the threat or use of political violence. On the other hand, the broad school argues that human security means more than a concern with the threat of violence. Human security in this analysis is not only 'freedom from fear', but also 'freedom from want', which is the focus of human development today. Protagonists of the broad school maintain that human security is concerned with the protection of people from critical life-threatening dangers, regardless of whether the threats are rooted in anthropogenic activities or natural events, whether they lie within or outside states, and whether they are direct or structural. Members of the 2003 Commission on Human Security argue that the objective of human security is to protect the vital core of all human lives in ways that advocate human freedoms and human fulfilment.

Though there is a dramatic growth of international efforts at preventive diplomacy, peace-making and peace-building, there are still some horrible costs associated with violent conflicts today. The share of civilian casualties in armed conflicts has greatly increased since the Second World War, with many of these victims being women, children and the elderly. Some of the more serious issues of human security in armed conflict still need to be highlighted and overcome. These relate to the child soldiers as well as landmines. According to the human security report 2005, 75 percent of the armed conflicts today involve child soldiers and landmines and unexploded ordinance cause around 20,000 casualties each year. Analysts have identified links between poverty and terrorism, pointing out that terrorists often exploit poverty and exclusion in order to tap into popular discontent. Fragile states and their vulnerable populations for example, in Somalia or in Afghanistan, become easy victims for such violence. Places like Darfur are witnessing traditional inter-communal conflicts over scarcity of resources While concerns related to people and their security is greatly concentrating to the analysis of civil wars and armed conflicts today, the relationship between gender and human security is also emerging as a serious ongoing debate.

Holding firmly to the central idea that women and girls experience human 'insecurity' differently from men, the emerging feminist literature on international security researches emphasised in three significant areas. (i) Impact of armed conflict on women, gender relations and gender roles (ii) The ways in which international peacekeeping operations and humanitarian interventions widen or diminish exploitation (iii) Women's absence from decision making positions that are crucial to peace-building. When rape and ethnic cleansing are used as instruments of war, then it is not sufficient to think of security in terms of national/territorial security alone. Feminists looking at global politics share a normative and empirical concern that the international system is gender hierarchical. They argue that factoring gender into security studies is imperative for transforming knowledge about the multi-dimensional threats to human security today.

Human Security and Women: Prospects for Peace

Like most violence that occurs in the course of armed conflict, violence against women is not accidental. It is a weapon of war, a tool to achieve objectives such as ethnic cleansing, spreading political terror, breaking the resistance of a community etc. This is what happened in Sierra Leone, where 64,000 women were victims of war related sexual violence, or in Croatia and Bosnia-Herzegovina, or even in Rwanda where up to half a million women were raped during the 1994 genocide. Though international institutions have done considerable work regarding women and armed conflict, they tend to ignore the wider aspects of the problem. Numerous reports and studies on the impact of conflict include women in the general category of civilians. Hence, they tend to disregard the fact that experiences of men and women civilians are glaringly different during conflicts. Despite the voluminous literature on post-conflict reconstruction strategies, there seem to be a significant reluctance to take cognisance of women specific experiences as also their orientations, capacities and skills. Human security when understood as durable peace will relate to moving towards a transformative agenda that includes broader concerns of social justice, participatory rights and gender. Bringing women and their concerns centre-stage can thus initiate a process which will enhance the prospects for peace.

Source: Gupta, Sanju, 'Human Security, Women and Conflict: Rwanda in Retrospect, *Interdisciplinary Journal of Social Sciences.*

The widening and broadening of security, specially, the broad definitions of human security have received great amounts of criticism, at times to the extent of the critics claiming to dismiss the entire concept. Critical perspectives highlight that human security encompasses everything from substance abuse to genocide. From this perspective, the number of causal hypothesis from human insecurity becomes so vast that any frameworks for research and policy become difficult to formulate. The debates between the narrow and broad schools of definitions relating to human security have brought in the question of the means for enhancing human security. The issue is further complicated by arguments over the role of the states.[16] Is the state the guarantor or is it merely the facilitator or an agent of human security? In many situations where state is the perpetrator of violence, is human security impossible? Some states wilfully behave badly, but will it qualify all states to be dismissed as actors and all state-centric positions as working against human security? How to explain the international quest for states participants in major global institutions oriented towards the betterment of humanity. Apart from the state, is it not necessary to involve a variety of other actors i.e. institutions of global governance, non-state actors and civil society in addressing the broad and narrow agendas.

It is true that addressing human insecurity as violence will involve a plethora of measures and a multiplicity of actors. Regardless of concerns about the role of states, it is true that properly functioning states will be indispensable actors, and more than the states themselves, the state-based aid programs, global institutions, local and international NGOs and civil society groups will be at the helm. Understandably, human security is a wide-ranging concept that demonstrates the weaknesses and vulnerabilities of human beings as well as their potential. Opportunities for growth and development are increasingly linked, yet can become sources of insecurity. Reducing risk therefore implies greater coordination of national and global policies. To the extent that vulnerabilities and threats to international security increase, pressure will be put on states to take action in a context in which the state itself has less resources of real power. Hence, it is essential to foster effective multilateralism.

Human Security: Opportunities, Weaknesses and Vulnerabilities

Variables	Ecology (life) Environmental capital	Economy (wealth) Economic capital	Society (support) Social capital	Politics (power) Political capital	Culture (knowledge) Cultural capital
Effects	Sustainability Disaster	Prosperity Poverty	Equality Inequality	Peace Violence	Wisdom Ignorance
Globalization	A world of associated effect, such as the 'greenhouse effect'	Dark side of globalization and competition, more inequality	Refugees Migrations Hyper-urbanization	Governance Global regimes Cooperation/ Conflict	Identities Values
Use of force	Bio-terrorism	Financial crisis Cyberterrorism Money laundering	Polarization Ungovernability Rebellion Citizen security	Landmines Child soldiers Small arms Traditional disarmament	Intolerance and religious wars Local identities clashing with national and global ones

Source: Rojas Aravena, Francisco, 'Human Security: Emerging Concept of Security in the 21st Century', http://www.peacepalacelibrary.nl/ebooks/files/UNIDIR_pdf-art1442.pdf

As can be seen from the table above, human security maybe analysed and understood from five different dimensions or variables: ecology, economy, society, politics and culture. It is interesting to note that each of these variables has come to be informed by globalisation as well as the use of force in the contemporary context. Globalisation has been tantamount to increasing differences and having adverse effect on cultural practices and national and local identities. This has also been accompanied by economic and social polarisation in different areas of the world. However, the entire concern with human security has also visualised a new global order based on global humanism. The core issue is to solve the population's basic needs within the framework of globalisation and interdependence. This vulnerable balance requires respect for universal values as well as tolerance towards multicultural diversity.

Notes

1. Gupta, Chanchal Kumar and et.al.*Contemporary Issues in Global Politics: An Asian Perspective,* (New Delhi: Regal Publications, 2013),p.23.
2. Booth, Ken and J. Wheeler,*The Security Dilemma,*(New York: PagraveMcmillan, 2008), p.268.
3. Rosenau, James and Ersel, "Globalisation, Security and the Nation-State", URL: http://www. sunypress.edu/p-4095-globalization-security-and-the-.aspx., accessed on June 30,2016.
4. McSweeney, Bill, *Security, Identity and Interests,* (Cambridge: Cambridge University Press, 1999), p.13.
5. Ibid.
6. Baylis, John and Steve Smith,*The Globalization of World Politics* (Oxford: Oxford University Press,2013).
7. Dannreuther, Roland,*International Security: The Contemporary Agenda* ,(UK: Polity Press,2007),pp.14-29.
8. Buzan, Barry and Lene Hansen,*The Evolution of International Security Studies* (Cambridge: Cambridge University Press,2009), pp.158-162.
9. Buzan, Barry and Lene Hansen,*International Security: Volume III, Widening Security,* (London and New Delhi: Sage Publications,2007),p.2.
10. Aravena, Francisco Rojas, "Human Security", URL: http://mercury.ethz.ch/serviceengine/ Files/ISN/48442/ichaptersection_singledocument/964b7943-9e3f-4bbf-bbb2-c83011664865/ en/03_Human+Security.pdf., accessed on June 30,2016.
11. Ibid.
12. Ibid.
13. See, "Human Development Report, 1994" URL,http://hdr.undp.org/en/content/human-development-report-1994, accessed on May 6, 2016.
14. See, "Work for Human Development, Human Development Report 2015", URL: http://hdr. undp.org/sites/default/files/2015_human_development_report.pdf,accessed on July 8, 2015.
15. McSweeney, Bill *Security, Identity and Interests,* Cambridge: Cambridge University Press,1999) p.14.
16. Collins, Alan, *Contemporary Security Studies* (New York: Oxford University Press,2010), p.125.

www.ingramcontent.com/pod-product-compliance
Lightning Source LLC
Chambersburg PA
CBHW080243030426
42334CB00023BA/2681